European Yearbook of International Economic Law

EYIEL Monographs - Studies in European and International Economic Law

Volume 4

EYIEL Monographs is a subseries of the European Yearbook of International Economic Law (EYIEL). It contains scholarly works in the fields of European and international economic law, in particular WTO law, international investment law, international monetary law, law of regional economic integration, external trade law of the EU and EU internal market law. The series does not include edited volumes. EYIEL Monographs are peer-reviewed by the series editors and external reviewers.

More information about this series at http://www.springer.com/series/15744

Sophia Müller

The Use of Alternative Benchmarks in Anti-Subsidy Law

A Study on the WTO, the EU and China

Springer

Sophia Müller
Frankfurt, Germany

ISSN 2364-8392 ISSN 2364-8406 (electronic)
European Yearbook of International Economic Law
EYIEL Monographs - Studies in European and International Economic Law
ISBN 978-3-030-08494-3 ISBN 978-3-319-77613-2 (eBook)
https://doi.org/10.1007/978-3-319-77613-2

Printed on acid-free paper

This Springer imprint is published by the registered company Springer International Publishing AG part of Springer Nature.
The registered company address is: Gewerbestrasse 11, 6330 Cham, Switzerland

Preface

This study is a truly global product of research. Its completion has sent me well around the world—from Passau to Beijing, Shanghai, and finally Brussels. Each stay has left its traces on both work and authoress and has shaped the study's content in its very unique way. The months and years spent on the completion of my thesis have been challenging academically and personally—but at the same time so diverse and enriching that I would not like to have missed one single moment.

I would like to deeply thank my supervisor Professor Christoph Herrmann, who already in the year 2014, when China's WTO accession provisions had not yet been that heavily discussed in the scientific community, showed immediate curiosity concerning my somewhat "exotic" research topic and with his constant support and encouragement enabled me to conclude this study in a way I could never have imagined.

I also would like to give my thanks to Professor Marc Bungenberg for his second assessment of my dissertation and, especially, his vivid interest in my research from very early on.

My time in China would never have been possible without Dean Meng Wan and Professor Yanxia Yao from Beijing Foreign Studies University, whom I would like to thank again for their warm welcome and hospitality during my time in Beijing.

I would also like to thank Professor Zhijie Yuan of Beijing Normal University and the students of his German Law class, whom I had the pleasure to teach and whose dedication in learning was both deeply impressive and inspiring.

The teams of law firms GvW Graf von Westphalen in Shanghai around Mr. Patrick Heid and of Cleary Gottlieb Steen & Hamilton in Brussels around Dr. Till Müller-Ibold also deserve my thanks for providing me with exciting insights in trade remedies law and China-related legal practice.

Some special thanks go to Dr. Xueping Liu and Ms. Fanglei Wang for making me increasingly familiar with the charms of Chinese language—and the culinary trials of Chinese cuisine.

Last, I would like to deeply thank my family and friends, who shared both worries and joys of the working process—and the final smile when everything was done.

Frankfurt, Germany
January 2018

Sophia Müller

Contents

Abbreviations

ADA	Anti-Dumping Agreement
ASCM	Agreement of Subsidies and Countervailing Measures
BASR	Basic Anti-Subsidy Regulation
CAP	Protocol of Accession of the People's Republic of China
CIRR	Commercial Interest Reference Rate
CRS	Cold-rolled steel
DSR	Dispute Settlement Reports
DSU	Dispute Settlement Understanding
EC	European Community
ECJ	European Court of Justice
e.g.	*exempli gratia* (for example)
EU	European Union
F.2d.	Federal Reporter, second series
Fed. Reg.	Federal Register
FIT	Feed-in tariff
GA	General Assembly
GATT	General Agreement on Tariffs and Trade
GC	General Court
GDP	Gross domestic product
HRS	Hot-rolled steel
i.e.	*id est* (that is to say)
ICITO	International Committee for the International Trade Organization
IMF	International Monetary Fund
ITO	International Trade Organization
LUR	Land-use right
MES	Market economy situation
MFN	Most-favoured nation
NME	Non-market economy
NMES	Non-market economy situation
No.	Number
OECD	Organisation for Economic Development and Cooperation

OJ	Official Journal of the EU
p.	Page
para.	Paragraph
Pub. L.	Public Law
RSC	Revised Statutes of Canada
SCM Agreement	Agreement of Subsidies and Countervailing Measures
SIMA	Special Import Measures Act
SLI	Select Legislative Instrument
SOCB	State-owned commercial bank
SOE	State-owned enterprise
Stat.	United States Statutes at Large
TBT	Technical Barriers to Trade
TEU	Treaty of the European Union
TiSA	Trade in Services Agreement
TPP	Trans-Pacific Partnership
TTIP	Transatlantic Trade and Investment Partnership
UN	United Nations
UNTS	United Nations Treaty Series
USC	United States Code
VCLT	Vienna Convention on the Law of Treaties
WTO	World Trade Organization

Chapter 1
Introduction

"Silence is a source of great strength."[1] In principle, this is also true for the area of law. But the way this strength unfolds itself is a double-edged sword. On the one hand, silence in legal provisions ensures flexibility, so that the provisions readily adapt to new developments and circumstances. On the other hand, the ampler the amount of silence in a provision, the easier it can be subject to arbitrariness and misuse. This dilemma is particularly acute in anti-subsidy law. Here, an imprecise legal framework, additionally afflicted with lacunae, makes the anti-subsidy remedy an easy means for WTO members to implement protectionist interests.[2]

Especially Article 14 ASCM,[3] the provision that regulates the calculation of the amount of benefit conferred to a producer through the subsidy, which ultimately determines the final amount of countervailing duty, is deemed *"one of the most important"*,[4] but also one of the *"least developed provisions"*[5] of the ASCM.

Basically, the amount of benefit is determined by assessing the financial contribution received by the producer in comparison to the market conditions otherwise prevailing in the respective country of origin. Put differently, the prices or costs for the producer, which are affected through the subsidy, are compared to respective in-country market prices. As long as the existing in-country market prices that are used for the benefit calculation are undistorted, the resulting margin reflects the actual benefit conferred.

---

[1]Laozi, Daodejing, at chapter 26, for the original Chinese text (静为躁君, *jing wei zao jun*, literally translating as "the still is the ruler of the temperamental") see http://ctext.org/dao-de-jing/ens (last visited 1 January 2018).

[2]Zhao/Wang, Policy Research Working Paper No. 4560 (2008), 1, at 36.

[3]Agreement on Subsidies and Countervailing Measures, LT/UR/A-1A/9, 15 April 1994, 1869 UNTS 14.

[4]Durling in Wolfrum et al. (eds.), at para. 24.

[5]Durling in Wolfrum et al. (eds.), at para. 24.

S. Müller, *The Use of Alternative Benchmarks in Anti-Subsidy Law*,
European Yearbook of International Economic Law 4,
https://doi.org/10.1007/978-3-319-77613-2_1

But how to proceed with the calculation in cases where there is no or no reliable in-country market price turns out problematic. Which are the circumstances that render an existing in-country price unreliable? What type of market is the base that is actually being referred to for assessing unreliability? May surrogates be used instead? As indicated, dealing with NMES in the course of benefit calculation poses numerous questions.

Answers are scarce as yet. The Appellate Body has addressed the use of alternative benchmarks in the course of benefit calculation in NMES majorly in *US – Softwood Lumber IV*[6] and *US – Anti-Dumping and Countervailing Duties (China).*[7]

Based on Article 14 ASCM, the tribunal has derived prerequisites which have to be fulfilled in order to reject an existing in-country price and to resort to an alternative benchmark methodology to create a surrogate market price for the purpose of benefit calculation. The prerequisites have, however, remained fragmentary and imprecise to date. The existing legal framework only provides little guidance for the process of reasoning. Consequently, it equips investigating authorities with a large amount of discretion in the use of alternative benchmark methodologies, i.e. in the determination of a surrogate market price that resembles the market price that would prevail in the country under investigation to the closest possible extent if not for the distortive government influence.

In NMES, benefit calculation in anti-subsidy investigations enters the grey area, where the discretion of the investigating authority ends and protectionism begins. As the alternative price tends to be higher than the price that actually exists or would exist on the in-country market, the amount of the benefit conferred and, ultimately, the amount of countervailing duty, is inflated.[8] This can result in excess duties, e.g. an amount of countervailing duty of over 600%, which was the case for several producers in US investigation *Circular Welded Carbon Quality Steel Pipe (China).*[9] Anti-subsidy, the supposed *"less-evil brother to anti-dumping"*,[10] is apparently catching up.

The high degree of flexibility in the use of alternative benchmark methodologies becomes particularly virulent in the case of China. Being the most prominent country

---

[6]Appellate Body Report, *United States – Final Countervailing Duty Determination with Respect to Certain Softwood Lumber from Canada*, WT/DS257/AB/R, adopted 17 February 2004, DSR 2004: II, 571.

[7]Appellate Body Report, *United States – Definitive Anti-Dumping and Countervailing Duties on Certain Products from China*, WT/DS379/AB/R, adopted 25 March 2011, DSR 2011:V, 2869.

[8]Zheng, 19 *Minnesota Journal of International Law* (2010), 1, at 33 et seq.; Ahn/Lee, 14 *Journal of International Economic Law* (2011), 329, at 349; Detlof/Fridh, 63 *Global Trade and Customs Journal* (2007), 265, at 280. The effect can also be stated for anti-dumping law, see MacLean in Herrmann/Terhechte (eds.), 189, at 199.

[9]For Tianjin Shuangjie Steel Pipe Co., Ltd., Shuangjie Steel Pipe Group Co., Ltd., Tianjin Wa Song Imp. & Exp. Co., Ltd,. and Tianjin Shuanglian Galvanizing Products Co., Ltd. a net subsidy rate in the amount of 615.92 % was determined, see *Circular Welded Carbon Quality Steel Pipe from the People's Republic of China*, Case C-570-911, Final Affirmative Countervailing Duty and Final Affirmative Determination of Critical Circumstances, 73 Fed. Reg. 31966, 5 June 2008, at 31969.

[10]Zhao/Wang, Policy Research Working Paper No. 4560 (2008), 1, at 36.

investigated in anti-subsidy proceedings,[11] the singular character of China's economy is deemed to generally render the employment of existing in-country prices impossible. On the legal side, its Protocol of Accession[12] confers to China a special role by stipulating a written country-specific alternative benchmark regime for anti-subsidy law in Section 15(b) CAP—a complete novelty in the WTO legal hemisphere. Thus, anti-subsidy investigations against China usually resort to alternative prices for the benefit calculation. Countervailing duties in the amount similar to the above mentioned 600% and higher are looming constantly.

Concurrently, the number of countries launching anti-subsidy investigations against China is on the rise. After Canada and the US have started applying anti-subsidy law towards China in 2004 and 2006 respectively,[13] the EU followed the North-American lead in 2010, initiating the *Coated Fine Paper (China)* case.[14] Although the EU has only started twelve anti-subsidy investigations in total against China to date,[15] there are indications that let assume EU anti-subsidy practice will gain in importance in the near future.[16] The expiry of the permission to use alternative benchmark methodologies in anti-dumping proceedings against China on 11 December 2016,[17] presently still the *"cornerstone of EU trade defense policy and practice as a whole"*,[18] furthers the quest for new strategies in EU trade defence. Although the recent reform of EU anti-dumping law indicates that the EU relies on continuation of its well-established trade remedy policy, the increasingly active role of China in front of the WTO judiciary, in particular with regard to matters of

---

[11]Of the total number of 445 anti-subsidy investigations initiated from 1 January 1995 to 31 December 2016, 119 have been conducted against China (27%). Data from WTO statistics available at http://www.wto.org/english/tratop_e/scm_e/CV_InitiationsByExpCty.pdf (last visited 1 January 2018).

[12]Protocol on the Accession of the People's Republic of China, WT/L/432, 23 November 2001.

[13]Ahn/Lee, 14 *Journal of International Economic Law* (2011), 329, at 339 and 350.

[14]OJ C 99/13, 17 April 2010.

[15]As of 1 January 2018, see http://trade.ec.europa.eu/tdi/completed.cfm (last visited 1 January 2018).

[16]Vermulst/Gatta, 11 *World Trade Review* (2012), 527, at 529.

[17]Section 15(a)(ii) CAP, which permitted the use of alternative methodologies in anti-dumping investigations against China, was set to expire "[i]n any event [...]15 years after the date of accession" (Section 15(d), second sentence CAP). Uncontroversially accepted upon conclusion of the CAP in 2001, the question whether the use of alternative benchmark methodologies in anti-dumping proceedings against China could be continued beyond this deadline has been disputed and discussed intensely in recent years, see Kleimann, EUI Working Paper RSCAS No. 37 (2016); Zang, 14 *Journal of International Economic Law* (2012), 869, at 877; Gatta, 9 *Global Trade and Customs Journal* (2014), 165; Miranda, 9 *Global Trade and Customs Journal* (2014), 94; Tietje/Nowrot, Policy Papers on Transnational Economic Law No. 34 (2011), 2, at 10 et seq.; Ahn/Lee, 14 *Journal of International Economic Law* (2011), 329, at 343; Cornelis, 1 *Global Trade and Customs Journal* (2007), 105, at 109; O'Connor (2011), available at http://www.voxeu.org/article/chinamarketeconomy (last visited 1 January 2018).

[18]Vermulst/Gatta, 11 *World Trade Review* (2012), 527, at 531.

anti-dumping law,[19] however, clearly shows that this quest is not to be conducted at the expense of China.

In the light of these developments, the use of alternative benchmarks in anti-subsidy investigations calls for close scrutiny.

1.1 Research Objective

It is the objective of this study to contribute to the scientific discussion by ultimately suggesting a viable future concept for the use of alternative benchmarks in NMES in anti-subsidy investigations in WTO law.

Studying anti-subsidy law between the poles of the WTO, the EU and China lets four aspects in particular come to the fore:

- With the overall legal relationship between the WTO acquis and the new generation of accession protocols still unclear, the emergence and manifestation of an alternative benchmark regime for NMES in general WTO anti-subsidy law through Appellate Body jurisprudence and the parallel existence of a China-specific framework raise the question to the exact relationship between the two legal regimes. Which is China's applicable WTO anti-subsidy law?
- In creating its own anti-subsidy legal framework, the EU has closely adhered to the WTO role model. But some of the EU-genuine features in law and case practice, which have evolved especially in investigations against China since the EU started applying anti-subsidy law in NMES in 2010, make one wonder whether they truly find themselves in accordance with WTO law prerequisites. Are EU anti-subsidy law and practice in conformity with WTO anti-subsidy law as such and as applied?
- The adoption of China-specific rules in the CAP upon accession has shattered the once uniform applicability of the framework of WTO rules towards all members without exception and without differentiation. In the light of the WTO having been deliberately designed as opposed to the "GATT à la carte" of its predecessor, splitting the rules framework presents itself as highly dubious approach. Is the introduction of country-specific accession commitments into the WTO legal anti-subsidy framework legal and legitimate, i.e. justified?
- Apart from structural dissonance, the extension of the applicability of anti-subsidy law to NMES has substantively upset WTO law. Although economically mystifying in its conception, the law has allowed for the applicability of anti-subsidy law in NMES nevertheless. But not only economic inconsistencies spread uncertainty regarding the validity of this approach. Does general WTO

[19] Request for Consultations by China, *US – Measures Related to Price Comparison Methodologies*, WT/DS515/1, 15 December 2016 and the correspondent Request for Consultations by China, *EU – Measures Related to Price Comparison Methodologies*, WT/DS516/1, 15 December 2016.

anti-subsidy law permit the introduction of an alternative benchmark regime for NMES through Appellate Body reports in terms of legality and legitimacy?

After disclosing existing deficiencies of the current concept and establishing the need for reform, the thesis discusses various ideas to eliminate the deficits of the present alternative benchmark regime. Circuiting economic Scylla and legal Charybdis, this study develops a reform proposal for a new alternative benchmark regime that has the ability to effect the direly necessary enhancements with regard to legal certainty and transparency.

1.2 Object and Scope of the Study

The thesis focuses on the use of alternative benchmark methodologies for NMES in anti-subsidy law in the process of benefit calculation, i.e. on the determination of a comparable in-country price as substitute for altogether non-existing or distorted and consequently discarded existing in-country prices. The legal prerequisites that have to be observed and the methodologies that may be employed to generate price substitutes form the object of the study.

The final determination of the amount of benefit, i.e. the overall process of price comparison that brings together the in-country price with the export price, is excluded from the scope of this study. Furthermore, a general solution regarding the integration of the new generation of accession protocols like the CAP into the present WTO framework is not within the scope of this study.

1.3 Methodical Approach and Course of the Study

This study unites issues prevalent to anti-subsidy investigations in general and generalizable issues emerging from the example of EU anti-subsidy investigations against China in order to reach its aim of suggesting a viable concept for an alternative benchmark regime for NMES in anti-subsidy law. More precisely, it conducts a five-step approach.

First, the WTO as legal environment and subsidisation as factual environment of the study are presented briefly. Then, the general mechanisms of benefit calculation for both MES and NMES are introduced. In this connection, the paramount influence of the use of alternative benchmarks on calculating the amount of countervailing duty is demonstrated.

Second, the legal prerequisites at WTO level for the use of alternative benchmark methodologies in anti-subsidy law against China are examined. This analysis covers the general WTO prerequisites for the use of alternative benchmarks in anti-subsidy proceedings as derived from Article 14 ASCM by the interpretation of the Appellate Body in *US – Softwood Lumber IV* and *US – Anti-Dumping and Countervailing*

Duties (China) as well as the China-specific provision of Section 15(b) CAP. Thus, the complete existing regulatory framework for the determination of a comparable in-country price substitute in NMES as "legal backbone" of China's applicable WTO law is shown. Its lack of clarity and lacunae are uncovered, which demonstrates the abusive and discriminatory potential of these provisions. Because these once solely China-specific provisions have been adopted in accession protocols of other acceding countries, the significance of such provisions now extends beyond a mere China-specific context. Therefore, the scrutiny of China's alternative benchmark regime exemplary offers the possibility to examine the most comprehensive existing legal framework at WTO level in this regard. Ultimately assisting in clarifying the interdependency between general and country-specific alternative benchmark regime forms a major long-term objective of this study, for which a foundation is built in its course.

Third, the example of EU anti-subsidy investigations against China is employed to scrutinise the use of alternative benchmark methodologies in case practice. After introducing the respective legal framework on EU level, this study conducts an analysis of EU anti-subsidy cases against China, hereby identifying evolving patterns of reasoning in connection with the use of alternative benchmarks regarding the different types of subsidies. Subsequently, the EU alternative benchmark regime is scrutinised with respect to conformity with WTO law as such and as applied. After examining the present EU approach against China, further latitude granted to the EU by the WTO framework is fathomed, thus depicting the utmost legally possible approach for the EU to adopt. All in all, the analysis of EU cases against China visualises the effect of the fragmentary and imprecise prerequisites for the use of alternative benchmarks at WTO level: once an investigating authority has developed a feasible approach for alleging distortion of existing in-country prices and consequently applying price substitutes, it keeps reapplying it—however arbitrary the reasoning might seem. Countries investigated are almost entirely at the discretion of the investigating authorities. Actual breaches of WTO law are hardly provable. These effects obtrude the notion of reform.

Therefore, in a fourth step, the need to reform the current alternative benchmark regime for NMES in WTO anti-subsidy law, which is easily prone to protectionism on the one hand and subject to the inclination of the members to fully take advantage of this latitude on the other, is ascertained by taking the global perspective. Recollecting the rationales of both anti-subsidy law and the WTO itself, the thesis distinguishes between the mere legality and the legitimacy of the exercise of political authority to show that the very position of the WTO as leading organisation in international trade will be undermined if the developments in NMES anti-subsidy law on alternative benchmarks are allowed to continue as before.

Fifthly and lastly, the study develops a reform proposal that tackles the deficits that have been identified. After discussing various substantive options for improvement, it considers the available legal means of implementation at WTO level and concludes with stipulating a concrete reform proposal for a future alternative benchmark regime for NMES in WTO anti-subsidy law.

Chapter 2
The Significance of the Use of Alternative Benchmark Methodologies in the Process of WTO Anti-Subsidy Investigations

The use of alternative benchmarks in anti-subsidy investigations is embedded in the context of the WTO regulation of subsidies. This chapter hence sets a common basic understanding by presenting the factual and legal environment of the issues under scrutiny. It presents the WTO as major institution for international trade regulation (Sect. 2.1) and lays down the case for the regulation of subsidies (Sect. 2.2) as well as the respective legal framework in WTO law (Sect. 2.3). The particularities of the benefit calculation conclude the chapter (Sect. 2.4).

2.1 The WTO as Institution of International Trade Regulation

When it comes to international trade regulation, no way skirts the major organisation in this area—the WTO.

For decades, the WTO and its predecessor, the GATT 1947,[1] have shaped the area of global trade by a multitude of agreements. As Article XVI:1 WTO Agreement explicitly states that the WTO shall be guided by the decisions, procedures and customary practices that have developed under the GATT 1947, even today the destiny of the WTO is still largely influenced by its predecessor.

[1]General Agreement on Tariffs and Trade, LT/UR/A-1A/1/GATT/2, 30 October 1947, 55 UNTS 194.

S. Müller, *The Use of Alternative Benchmarks in Anti-Subsidy Law*,
European Yearbook of International Economic Law 4,
https://doi.org/10.1007/978-3-319-77613-2_2

2.1.1 The GATT 1947 as Predecessor of the WTO

The origins of GATT 1947 lie in the Bretton Woods Conference of 1944.[2] To avoid the interwar experience of global economic seclusion—where in particular US trade policy had been overly restrictive[3]—the US and the United Kingdom sought to reduce trade barriers and discriminatory trade policies to open up markets.[4] Apart from the IMF and the World Bank, the ITO has been envisioned as third pillar in a new economic global order.[5] At the Geneva meeting of 1947 the 23 negotiating parties discussed the ITO charter, but also already agreed on tariff reductions and "general clauses" that were to preserve the commitments on tariff reductions,[6] in particular the three principles which still serve as the cornerstones of the WTO today: the most-favoured nation principle, reciprocity and economic liberalism.[7] These agreements formed the GATT 1947.[8] While the draft ITO charter was completed only one year later at the Havana meeting, the negotiating parties enacted the Protocol of Provisional Application for the GATT 1947, so that it already came into effect on 1 January 1948.[9] The contracting parties committed themselves only *"to the fullest extent not inconsistent with existing legislation"*.[10] This "grandfather clause" made it possible to provisionally apply the GATT 1947 without prior ratification of the treaty through the negotiating parties' national legislatures.[11] The ITO itself, however, then never came into existence.[12] Instead, the GATT 1947 as *"bargaining vehicle"*[13] with only narrow regulatory scope and almost entire

---

[2]Winham in Bethlehem et al. (eds.), 5, at 14.

[3]One particularly infamous example for the United States' protectionist trade policy is the Smoot-Hawley Tariff Act of 1930, Pub. L. 71-361, 46 Stat. 59019, 17 June 1930, imposing on imports the highest tariffs ever in US history, see Barton et al., Evolution of the trade regime, at 33; Mavroidis in Horn/Mavroidis (eds.), 1, at 2; Bagwell/Staiger/Sykes in Horn/Mavroidis (eds.), 68, at 94.

[4]Irwin, 85 AEA Papers and Proceedings (1995), 323, at 324.

[5]Winham in Bethlehem et al. (eds.), 5, at 14; Jackson in Bethlehem et al. (eds.), 30, at 33; Jackson, The World Trading System, at 32.

[6]Jackson, The World Trading System, at 37; Irwin, 85 AEA Papers and Proceedings (1995), 323, at 325.

[7]Barton et al., Evolution of the trade regime, at 39.

[8]Jackson, The World Trading System, at 37.

[9]Barton et al., Evolution of the trade regime, at 42; Jackson, The World Trading System, at 39; Jackson in Bethlehem et al. (eds.), 30, at 34.

[10]Kock, International Trade and Policy, at 65.

[11]Ratification was to happen later jointly with the completed draft ITO charter, see Jackson, The World Trading System, at 40.

[12]The US officially gave up all attempts to ratify the draft ITO charter in 1951, which practically buried the idea of creating an international organisation for the regulation of global trade, see Jackson in Bethlehem et al. (eds.), 30, at 34; Barton et al., Evolution of the trade regime, at 42; Irwin, 85 AEA Papers and Proceedings (1995), 323, at 325.

[13]Barton et al., Evolution of the trade regime, at 38.

lack of organisational structure[14] had to fill the void.[15] Advancing economic integration and liberalisation, it gradually evolved into a *de facto* international organisation in the area of global trade regulation.[16]

While further tariff reductions formed the agenda of the first five negotiation rounds, the focus of the contracting parties tentatively shifted from tariff to non-tariff barriers in the Kennedy Round (1963–1967) and in particular in the following Tokyo Round (1973–1979).[17] But two oil crises, the rising number of developing countries amongst the contracting parties with only few rights and obligations under the GATT 1947 and the weakened role of the United States as the "motor of GATT" clearly showed that the GATT 1947 in its present state no longer provided an adequate means for trade regulation.[18] To remove existent deficiencies and to build the future of international trade regulation on solid ground, the contracting parties of the GATT 1947 entered into the eighth and last negotiation round, the Uruguay Round (1986–1994).

2.1.2 The Foundation of the WTO

In 1994, the final agreement of the Uruguay Round, the Final Act,[19] was signed.[20] It *inter alia* comprised the Agreement of Marrakech establishing the World Trade Organization.[21] What had failed 50 years before, now came into existence: with the concluded agreements taking effect on 1 January 1995, the WTO as a new *"legal and institutional foundation of the multilateral trading system"*[22] was created to finally take its place next to the IMF and the World Bank.[23] The "provisional

[14]The constituted body of the GATT 1947 was the ICITO, which had been created as interim organisational structure for the preparation of the ITO. During the time of provisional application of the GATT 1947, it served as the *de facto* GATT Secretariat, see Jackson in Bethlehem et al. (eds.), 30, at 35.

[15]Jackson, The World Trading System, at 59; Irwin, 85 AEA Papers and Proceedings (1995), 323, at 325; Barton et al., Evolution of the trade regime, at 43 et seq.

[16]Jackson, The World Trading System, at 59.

[17]Winham in Bethlehem et al. (eds.), 5, at 16; Barton et al., Evolution of the trade regime, at 45; Jackson, The World Trading System, at 73.

[18]Barton et al., Evolution of the trade regime, at 45 et seq.

[19]Final Act Embodying the Results of the Uruguay Round of Multilateral Trade Negotiations, LT/UR/A/1, 15 April 1994, 1867 UNTS 14.

[20]Jackson, The World Trading System, at 46.

[21]Marrakech Agreement Establishing the World Trade Organization, LT/UR/A/2, 15 April 1994, 1867 UNTS 154.

[22]Blackhurst in Krueger (ed.), 31, at 32.

[23]Winham in Bethlehem et al. (eds.), 5, at 24.

application" of the GATT 1947 ended by withdrawal of all contracting parties on 30 August 1995.[24]

Unlike its predecessor, the WTO is *"not a 'best endeavors' organization"*.[25] It was designed as formal international body empowered to set binding rules for its members in the area of global trade.[26] The "single undertaking" approach made the newly agreed commitments binding on all members (Article II:2 WTO Agreement), ending previous grandfathering and the "GATT à la carte".[27] Furthermore, the competences of the WTO were expanded to include more non-tariff barrier issues to trade, e.g. intellectual property (TRIPs) and trade in services (GATS).[28] Unlike the GATT 1947, the WTO was endowed with a proper institutional framework comprising the Ministerial Conference as highest decision-making organ,[29] the General Council as its permanent representative[30] as well as the Secretariat in Geneva as supporting administrative body.[31]

The WTO is a *"member-driven, consensus-based organisation"*.[32] Power still lays in the hands of the members, i.e. of the Ministerial Conference and the General Council, as the WTO Agreement does not delegate power.[33]

Decisions are generally made by negotiation and consensus (Article IX:1 WTO Agreement) . To arrive at a consensus, informal meetings and discussions play a vital role—otherwise, consensus is almost impossible.[34] Transparency and processing information are key features to keep decision-making fair and balanced. Only if consensus cannot be reached and other stipulations do not exist, the issue may be decided by majority voting (Article IX:1 WTO Agreement).

2.1.3 The WTO in 2018

Over 20 years after its foundation, the WTO has arrived at crossroads. The accession of new members, especially from Eastern Europe and Asia, has provoked an internal crisis questioning the WTO's self-conception as well as the

---

[24]Jackson, The World Trading System, at 64; Jackson in Bethlehem et al. (eds.), 30, at 38 et seq.

[25]Blackhurst in Krueger (ed.), 31, at 32.

[26]Article II:2 WTO Agreement; Article 3.2 DSU in connection with Annex 1; Article VIII:1 WTO Agreement.

[27]Barton et al., Evolution of the trade regime, at 65 et seq.; Jackson, The World Trading System, at 47; Winham in Bethlehem et al. (eds.), 5, at 20.

[28]Barton et al., Evolution of the trade regime, at 47; Jackson in Bethlehem et al. (eds.), 30, at 38.

[29]Jackson in Bethlehem et al. (eds.), 30, at 39.

[30]Jackson in Bethlehem et al. (eds.), 30, at 43.

[31]Jackson in Bethlehem et al. (eds.), 30, at 43.

[32]Bansal, The World Trade Organisation, at vi.

[33]Bansal, The World Trade Organisation, at vi.

[34]Jackson in Bethlehem et al. (eds.), 30, at 44.

validity of the institution's basic principles.[35] Whereas the WTO had been designed as a *"menu du jour"*,[36] accession procedures have created country-specific rules within a supposedly equality-based binding legal regime that let presume a reversal towards a *"WTO à la carte"*.[37]

Externally, the recent global economic and financial crisis has led members to reconsider whether further enhancement of globalisation is truly beneficial for their economic interests.[38] Moreover, issues like human rights or environmental protection, genuinely alien to trade, are now seen as being deeply connected and thus part of trade regulation.[39]

The WTO has so far not been able to provide a satisfactory and convincing solution for these challenges. Attempts to trade policy reform are constantly overshadowed by the impasse of the Doha Round that started in 2001.[40] The small-scale reforms of the Bali Package of 2013[41] and the Nairobi Package of 2015[42] do only insufficiently address the needs of the WTO members, so that they increasingly seek to realise their economic policy goals at regional level—mega-regionals like TTIP, TPP or TiSA are examples of what this *"new regionalism"*[43] might grow into.[44] How the shift to bi- and plurilateral cooperation will affect the role of the WTO as major forum for the regulation of global trade in the future remains to be seen.[45]

---

[35]Meunier (2009), available at https://www.princeton.edu/~pcglobal/conferences/wtoreform/Meunier_memo.pdf, 1, at 3 et seq.

[36]Hoekman/Mavroidis, 26 *European Journal of International Law* (2015), 319, at 321.

[37]Hoekman/Mavroidis, 26 *European Journal of International Law* (2015), 319, at 319.

[38]Meunier (2009), available at https://www.princeton.edu/~pcglobal/conferences/wtoreform/Meunier_memo.pdf, 1, at 1.

[39]Meunier (2009), available at https://www.princeton.edu/~pcglobal/conferences/wtoreform/Meunier_memo.pdf, 1, at 2.

[40]Koul, Guide to the WTO & GATT, at 30 et seq.

[41]Bali Ministerial Declaration, WT/MIN(13)/DEC, 11 December 2013.

[42]Nairobi Ministerial Declaration, WT/MIN(15)/DEC, 21 December 2015.

[43]Francois, 15 CESifo Forum (2014), 14, at 14.

[44]Francois, 15 CESifo Forum (2014), 14, at 14; Hoekman, Supply Chains, Mega-Regionals and Multilateralism, at 8 et seq. and 30 et seq.

[45]The effect of the recent surge of regional trade agreements on the WTO is yet assessed very differently, see e.g. Meléndez-Ortiz, in WEF (ed.), at 6 and 13 et seq.; Baldwin, in WEF (ed.), at 8 and 26 et seq.; Bhagwati (2014), available at http://www.notenstein-laroche.ch/sites/nlr_ch/files/attachments/white_paper_series_jagdish_bhagwati.pdf, at 5 et seq.; Stoler (2013), at 1 and seq. and 6, available at http://e15initiative.org/wp-content/uploads/2015/09/E15-Regional-Trade-Agreements-Stoler-FINAL.pdf.

2.2 The Case for the Regulation of Subsidisation in International Trade Law

Subsidisation by governments is regulated by a large array of rules in international trade law. The reason why regulation is deemed necessary is not immediately obvious, though. It roots in the prevalence of economic models postulating free trade on private markets as basis for global welfare.

2.2.1 *Free Trade as Guarantor of Maximum National Welfare*

All countries ultimately aim at maximising their national welfare.[46] This includes the optimum supply of the population with goods.[47] Instead of pursuing the goal of optimising national welfare autonomously, a country concentrates on the selective production of only those goods it can provide for more efficiently than other countries, so that consequently, they engage in trade.[48] But views differ on how maximum national welfare can be realised. Several economic models exist.

The most prevalent is the so-called theory of comparative advantages.[49] Developed by David Ricardo and John Stuart Mill,[50] maximum efficiency and national welfare are achieved if each country focuses on producing the goods it can manufacture at lower opportunity costs than other countries.[51] Opportunity costs are the amounts of one good that need to be given up in order to produce one additional unit of another good.[52] Using opportunity costs instead of mere production costs like the

---

46 Bagwell/Staiger, 89 *American Economic Review* (1999), 215, at 215.

47 Winham in Bethlehem et al. (eds.), 5, at 6 et seq.

48 Schwartz/Harper, 70 *Michigan Law Review* (1972), 831, at 840; Hoekmann/Kostecki, Political Economy of the World Trading System, at 7 and 32 et seq.; Winham in Bethlehem et al. (eds.), 5, at 8.

49 The theory has been developed based on trade in goods, so that other areas of trade, e.g. services, will not be mentioned separately in the following. The validity of the theory, however, extends to these areas as well.

50 Whereas the original idea of the concept of comparative advantages goes back to *Robert Torrens'* 'Essay on the External Corn Trade' (1815), it was made popular in economics through *David Ricardo* in *On the Principles of Political Economy and Taxation* (1817) and *James Mill* in *Elements of Political Economy* (1821), see Suranovic, International Trade, at 40-0.

51 Schwartz/Harper, 70 *Michigan Law Review* (1972), 831, at 840; Winham in Macrory et al. (eds.), 3, at 5; Hoekmann/Kostecki, Political Economy of the World Trading System, at 33; extensively on the notion of comparative advantage Sykes, 1 *Journal of International Economic Law* (1998), 49, at 49 et seq.

52 Suranovic, International Trade, at 40-0.

ideological predecessor, Adam Smith's theory of absolute advantages,[53] constitutes the major advancement of Ricardo's and Mill's model. According to Smith, *"if a foreign country can supply us with a commodity cheaper than we ourselves can make it, better buy it of them with some part of the produce of our own industry, employed in a way in which we have some advantage"*.[54] Each country concentrates on producing the goods it can manufacture at lower costs than other countries—and this specialisation consequently requires countries to trade.[55] But if a country is able to produce all of its goods at lower cost than other countries, the theory of absolute advantages cannot explain why it engages in trade nevertheless. According to the theory of comparative advantages, if one country is e.g. three times as productive in making a certain good and only two times as productive in producing another in comparison to another country, it should nevertheless only produce the former, the good it manufactures "most best".[56] To the contrary, the other country ought to focus on producing the latter good. From the point of view of global trade, the production of both goods will rise, enhancing global welfare.[57] The theory of comparative advantages still forms the *"basis for the case of free trade"*[58] and is reiterated in all conventional free trade models today.[59]

---

[53]Suranovic, International Trade, at 40-0; Coppens, WTO Disciplines on Subsidies and Countervailing Measures, at 8.

[54]Smith, A., Wealth of Nations, at 457.

[55]Schwartz/Harper, 70 *Michigan Law Review* (1972), 831, at 840; Winham in Macrory et al. (eds.), 3, at 5; Hoekmann/Kostecki, Political Economy of the World Trading System, at 33.

[56]Suranovic, International Trade, at 40-0.

[57]The effect is illustrated by the following example: if a lawyer needs one hour to type a document and her secretary needs two hours for the same task, then the lawyer possesses both the absolute advantage for rendering legal advice and typing a document. Considering that the lawyer's hourly rate is at EUR 200 and the secretary's at EUR 20, however, it still proves advantageous to both parties if the lawyer employs the secretary. The lawyer has to pay to the secretary 40 EUR – but she can employ the then free time at hand for client work which earns her 200 EUR. Thus, both lawyer and secretary benefit from this arrangement. See Winham, in Macrory et al. (eds.), 3, at 4 et seq.; Trebilcock/Fishbein in Guzmán/Sykes (eds.), 1, at 1 et seq.; Winham in Bethlehem et al. (eds.), 5, at 8 et seq.

[58]Winham in Bethlehem et al. (eds.), 5, at 9.

[59]Trebilcock et al., The Regulation of International Trade, at 4. The theory of comparative advantages is, however, not without alternatives. *Heckscher* and *Ohlin*, for instance, developed the so-called factor proportions model. Their theory takes into account economies of scale – i.e. that employing one "won" capacity of labour from producing one good does not necessarily effect the same increase in productivity with regard to the manufacture of another good. The country would therefore enjoy a comparative advantage in manufacturing the good most intensively making use of its most abundantly available resources, see Winham in Bethlehem et al. (eds.), 5, at 9. The model of *List* focuses solely on national development, see Winham in Bethlehem et al. (eds.), 5, at 9; for miscellaneous other approaches see Kreinin/Plummer in Macrory et al. (eds.), 1602, at 1602 et seq.

2.2.2 Subsidisation as Trade Distortion

According to the theory of comparative advantages, or most other economic efficiency models, the type of market that forms the foundation of free trade is a perfect market. The most efficient allocation of goods, or "Pareto efficiency", is achieved *"when no possible reorganization of production can make anyone better off without making someone else worse off"*[60,61] only through the market forces of supply and demand.[62] Generally, only transactions by private individuals are regarded as permitting truly free trade.[63] Externalities[64] like government subsidisation or other practices that irritate in any way the free operation of supply and demand—i.e. all "unfair" practices—are deemed to diminish the allocative efficiency of the market.[65] The *"hypothetical market equilibrium without the presence of government"*[66] forms the ideal benchmark.[67]

The problem that quickly becomes apparent is that a perfect market is *"impossible to find"*[68] in reality. Market prices on existing markets always reflect externalities.[69] The "market-as-is" fundamentally differs from a perfect market.

Some market actors also deliberately pursue strategies that conflict with the overall ideal of effecting maximum efficiency in the allocation of goods in a perfectly competitive market.[70] For example, in order to not only having to rely on their natural competitive advantages but to influence the allocative powers of the market in their favour, companies offer their goods on a foreign market at a price far

---

[60]Samuelson/Nordhaus, Economics, at 158.

[61]Further research, however, demonstrated that the conclusions, which are drawn from the simple economic model presuming a perfectly competitive market, are also valid for distorted markets (e.g. considering the economics of scale), see Grossmann/Horn in Horn/Mavroidis (eds.), 9, at 42.

[62]Samuelson/Nordhaus, Economics, at 26; Zheng, 19 *Minnesota Journal of International Law* (2010), 1, at 35.

[63]Schwartz/Harper, 70 *Michigan Law Review* (1972), 831, at 839 et seq.; Coppens, WTO Disciplines on Subsidies and Countervailing Measures, at 6 et seq.

[64]Externalities are defined as benefits or costs that are associated with the operation of market that are not reflected in the prices charged for a good or a service or in the prices that purchasers are willing to pay for them, see Sykes, 1 *Journal of International Economic Law* (1998), 49, at 73.

[65]Coppens, WTO Disciplines on Subsidies and Countervailing Measures, at 7.

[66]Sykes, University of Chicago Law & Economics Olin Working Paper No. 186 (2003), 1, at 3.

[67]Rubini, The Definition of Subsidy and State Aid, at 204.

[68]Rubini, The Definition of Subsidy and State Aid, at 204.

[69]Zheng, 19 *Minnesota Journal of International Law* (2010), 1, at 22; Rubini, The Definition of Subsidy and State Aid, at 204. As will be demonstrated at a later stage, the discrepancy between the ideal of a perfect market and the reality of a "market-as-is" has great impact on the benefit calculation in anti-subsidy law, see Sects. 2.4.2.4 and 6.1.4.1.1.

[70]One of the most objectionable amongst such strategies is the so-called *"beggar-thy-neighbour approach"*, where a country uses its superseding economic power to further enlarge it on the expense of its neighbour states, see Jackson, 1 *Journal of International Economic Law* (1998), 1, at 2; Sykes, 89 *Columbia Law Review* (1989), 199, at 246; Hoekmann/Kostecki, Political Economy of the World Trading System, at 217.

lower than on their domestic market and also far lower than their competitors. Although this leads to the company suffering severe losses, the company condones them, because if its *"predatory pricing"*[71] succeeds, it will ultimately obtain the monopoly position on the targeted market.[72] The losses suffered previously can then be regained.

This *"beggar-thy-neighbour"*[73] approach to rule out foreign competitors through enhancing the competitive position of domestic industries by granting financial support or assistance in kind forms an important objective on a state's political agenda.[74]

2.2.3 The Necessity of Regulating Subsidisation

Undue advantages bestowed upon companies by the state are particularly dangerous to free trade because of the sheer unlimited capacity of governmental means. The case for the regulation of subsides seems to be made.

The problem with the regulation—and thus restriction—of the use of subsidies, however, is that they cannot be attributed undesirable welfare-decreasing effects on global trade across-the-board. Rather, the respective motivation behind the bestowal of subsidies makes them either "good" or "bad" subsidies.[75]

Governments often use subsidies to offset regional structural discrepancies.[76] They might wish to absorb positive externalities that derive from consumer comportment into the *"socially-optimal price"*[77] of a good or service on the market—and lastly promote national welfare.[78] Even the "beggar-thy-neighbour" approach can be attributed positive effects for the consumers on foreign markets, who profit from low prices that result from the governmental support, and should rather send a

[71]According to *Sykes*, a predatory price is defined as a *"price that entails a sacrifice of profit in the short run for the purpose of driving competitors from the market, with the anticipation that the exit of those competitors will enable the predator firms to raise prices and earn monopoly or 'supracompetitive' profits thereafter"*, see Sykes, 89 *Columbia Law Review* (1989), 199, at 241.

[72]Sykes, 89 *Columbia Law Review* (1989), 199, at 241. *Viner* considers this form of dumping the *"most objectionable form of dumping from the point of view of the country dumped on"*, see Viner, Dumping, at 26. Also see Viner, Dumping, at 23 et seq., for an extensive classification of dumping.

[73]Smith, A., Wealth of Nations, at 493; Jackson, 1 *Journal of International Economic Law* (1998), 1, at 2.

[74]Lincicome, Policy Analysis No. 710 (2012), 1, at 4; Smith, A., Wealth of Nations, at 493; Jackson, 1 *Journal of International Economic Law* (1998), 1, at 2.

[75]Mavroidis, The Regulation of International Trade, at 191; Sykes, Stanford Law and Economics Olin Working Paper No. 380 (2009), 1, at 2 et seq.; Lester, 12 *Melbourne Journal of International Law* (2011), 1, at 3 et seq.

[76]Coppens, WTO Disciplines on Subsidies and Countervailing Measures, at 12 et seq.

[77]Coppens, WTO Disciplines on Subsidies and Countervailing Measures, at 8.

[78]Coppens, WTO Disciplines on Subsidies and Countervailing Measures, at 8.

"thank-you note".[79] Besides, the immediately apparent effect of subsidies also makes them an attractive means of embellishing political achievements[80] or secure the ties to lobbyists.[81] Economics is global, but politics is local[82]—and subsidies are also granted to support individual political aspirations rather than truly intending economic advancement.

But apart from the question of actually contributing to the advancement or the decline of free trade and maximisation of welfare, the many different motives behind subsidisation clearly demonstrate the great influence that can be exerted through their bestowal. Unrestricted employment of financial contributions by governments would very quickly result in protectionism and misuse of state power and assets to enhance the economic positions of national companies on the market. The harmful potential makes subsidies subject to regulation in order to control their use if they cause adverse effects.[83] With regard to trade agreements, subsidies are able to undermine negotiated tariff commitments and ought thus to be subject to restrictions.[84]

2.3 WTO Regulation of Subsidies

Departing from its understanding of subsidisation, WTO law has adopted its own distinct regulatory approach towards subsidisation as unfair trading practice.

2.3.1 The Theoretical Concept of Subsidisation in WTO Law

The idea of subsidisation that underlies WTO trade regulation is the understanding of transfer of economic value by a government to the advantage of a private recipient.[85]

Dependent on the recipient, two broad categories of subsidies are distinguished: consumer subsidies and producer subsidies.[86] The latter category is divided further

---

[79] Sykes, University of Chicago Law & Economics Olin Working Paper No. 186 (2003), 1, at 11.

[80] Coppens, WTO Disciplines on Subsidies and Countervailing Measures, at 13; Baylis in Kerr/Gaisford (eds.), 347, at 351 et seq.

[81] Lincicome, Policy Analysis No. 710 (2012), 1, at 4.

[82] Jackson, 1 *Journal of International Economic Law* (1998), 1, at 2.

[83] Consentient Mavroidis, The Regulation of International Trade, at 193.

[84] Mavroidis, The Regulation of International Trade, at 191.

[85] Appellate Body Report, *US – Softwood Lumber IV*, at para. 51; see Coppens, WTO Disciplines on Subsidies and Countervailing Measures, at 5.

[86] Coppens, WTO Disciplines on Subsidies and Countervailing Measures, at 5 et seq; Strand in Strand (ed.), at 5.

into export subsidies, which are granted exclusively to merchandise that is destined for out-of-country use, and domestic subsidies, which are bestowed to promote goods or services no matter their intended place of consumption.[87] Domestic subsidies can take miscellaneous forms. Taking reference to the conditions they are granted under, they can be set apart into production subsidies, research and development subsidies, labour subsidies, local content subsidies, which require the use of in-country factors of production, and many other types.[88]

2.3.2 The WTO Legal Framework for Subsidies Regulation

Trade regulation in the WTO is characterised by numerous different agreements that interact with each other according to predetermined rules of conflict.

The agreements are all organised under the roof of the WTO Agreement. The multilateral agreements in Annex 1 A of the WTO Agreement comprise the WTO agreements with regard to the different areas of trade the WTO encompasses: goods, services and intellectual property.[89] The area of trade in goods is where the GATT 1947 is encountered again: together with other agreements, it forms the GATT 1994,[90] which constitutes the main product of the Uruguay Round negotiations concerning trade in goods.[91] Besides the GATT 1994, there are other agreements dealing with specific issues of trade in goods. In particular, the ADA[92] and the ASCM shall be mentioned here—they will play major roles in the study later on.

All the multilateral agreements on trade regulation in Annex 1 A, e.g. the GATT 1994, the ADA and the ASCM, are integral parts of the WTO Agreement, and are binding on all Members (Article II:2 WTO Agreement). The Appellate Body interpreted this "single undertaking" approach to result in the multilateral agreements all being applicable equally, so that no distinction according to their legal ranking is permitted.[93] *"The WTO Agreement is thus a single treaty"*.[94] As,

[87]Mavroidis, The Regulation of International Trade, at 186; Stanbrook/Bentley, Dumping and Subsidies, at 8.

[88]Coppens, WTO Disciplines on Subsidies and Countervailing Measures, at 6.

[89]Jackson, The World Trading System, at 47.

[90]General Agreement on Tariffs and Trade, LT/UR/A-1A/1/GATT/1, 15 April 1994, 1867 UNTS 187.

[91]Jackson, The World Trading System, at 47.

[92]Agreement on the Implementation of Article VI of the General Agreement on Tariffs and Trade 1994 (Anti-dumping Agreement), LT/UR/A-1A/3, 15 April 1994, 1868 UNTS 201.

[93]Appellate Body Report, *Brazil – Measures Affecting Desiccated Coconut*, WT/DS22/AB/R, adopted 20 March 1997, DSR 1997:I, 167, at 12.

[94]Van den Bossche/Zdouc, The Law and Policy of the World Trade Organization, at 41.

however, the WTO agreements were negotiated in a somewhat incoherent manner, the legal texts contain several inconsistencies and differences in wording.[95]

Concerning the WTO Agreement and the agreements in Annex 1, Article XVI:3 WTO Agreement states that in the event of a conflict between a provision of the WTO Agreement and a provision of any of the multilateral trade agreements, the provision of the WTO Agreement shall prevail to the extent of the conflict. Hence, the WTO Agreement has been conferred a higher legal rank than the multilateral agreements and is the ultimate legal resort to be consulted.

WTO law comprises two instruments to regulate unfair trading: anti-dumping law and anti-subsidy law, also called countervailing law.[96] Besides, safeguard law provides the possibility to impose measures in the form of temporary trade restrictions, e.g. tariffs or quotas, in cases of sudden economic distortion through a raise in imports.[97]

Anti-dumping law sanctions competition-distorting actions of private individuals by allowing *inter alia* the imposition of anti-dumping duties.[98] While most trade-distortive practices are addressed by the anti-dumping remedy, there has been a slight surge of anti-subsidy investigations during the past couple of years. Frequently investigated countries are India and China—major instigator of the anti-subsidy remedy is the USA.[99]

Two WTO agreements regulate subsidisation. Since the creation of the GATT in 1947, it contains rules on countervailing duties. Besides, the Uruguay Round negotiations resulted in the enactment of the ASCM, an agreement which deals exclusively with anti-subsidy law. Article VI GATT covers both the imposition of anti-dumping and countervailing duties. It sets down the essential features of a countervailing duty. Besides, Article XVI GATT also addresses subsidisation by requiring e.g. the notification of subsidies. But the provisions only set a comparatively loose regulating framework.[100] The ASCM addresses substantive and procedural issues of subsidy regulation. Apart from the necessary prerequisites to be

[95]Van den Bossche/Zdouc, The Law and Policy of the World Trade Organization, at 41; Jackson, in Bethlehem et al. (eds.), 30, at 41 et seq.

[96]Sykes in Guzmán/Sykes (eds.), 62, at 62.

[97]Sykes in Guzmán/Sykes (eds.), 62, at 62.

[98]Tarullo, 100 *Harvard Law Review* (1987), 546, at 549.

[99]From 1 January 1995 to 31 December 2016, of 445 anti-subsidy proceedings initiated altogether, India faced 74, China 119, see https://www.wto.org/english/tratop_e/scm_e/CV_InitiationsByExpCty.pdf (last visited 1 January 2018). In the same period of time, the US initiated 195 of the 445 anti-subsidy investigations, constituting 44% of the total amount of investigations, see https://www.wto.org/english/tratop_e/scm_e/CV_InitiationsByRepMem.pdf (last visited 1 January 2018).

[100]Trebilcock et al., The Regulation of International Trade, at 365 et seq; Sykes, Stanford Law and Economics Olin Working Paper No. 380 (2009), 1, at 7. Arguing for the loose GATT regime having a more beneficial effect on the WTO and the multilateral trading system than the more legalised regulatory concept that has been developed in the Uruguay Round Bagwell/Staiger, 96 *American Economic Review* (2006), 877, at 879 et seq.

fulfilled for imposing a countervailing duty, it contains the basic framework for conducting anti-subsidy investigations.

GATT and ASCM both constitute multilateral agreements of Annex 1 A WTO Agreement. According to the general interpretative note to Annex 1 A, the special agreements officially prevail over the GATT in cases of conflict. Article 10 ASCM, however, states that a countervailing duty shall only be imposed in accordance with GATT provisions. Thus, reflecting the Appellate Body's *"principle of harmonious interpretation"*,[101] the conditions of both agreements have to be taken into account.

2.3.3 The Substantive Prerequisites for Imposing a Countervailing Duty

Three substantive prerequisites must be met to impose a countervailing duty. First, the investigation must yield the existence of a countervailable subsidy. Second, the domestic industry must suffer material injury or must be exposed the threat thereof. Third and last, the injury must be caused by the subsidy.

2.3.3.1 Countervailable Subsidy

A crucial question of an anti-subsidy investigation is thus what kind of contribution constitutes a subsidy according to the ASCM. For decades, this essential requirement had been lacking a clear and precise definition under the GATT.[102] Only the Uruguay Round filled the void by enacting Article 1.1 ASCM, which for the first time in history of GATT and WTO anti-subsidy law comprised a definition of subsidy.[103] To ascertain the existence of a subsidy, three prerequisites have to be met.

First, a financial contribution or any other form of income or price support in the sense of Article XVI GATT must have been provided. Secondly, the financial contribution must have been bestowed upon the producer by a government or any public body within the territory of a WTO member. Thirdly, it is necessary that the governmental contribution confers a benefit to the producer.

Apart from the definition in Article 1.1 ASCM, the existence of a subsidy can also be determined through reference to the Illustrative List of Subsidies.[104] The

[101] Appellate Body Reports, *European Communities – Measures Prohibiting the Importation and Marketing of Seal Products*, WT/DS400/AB/R / WT/DS401/AB/R, adopted 18 June 2014, DSR 2014:1, 7, at para. 5.123.

[102] Adamantopoulos in Wolfrum et al. (eds.), Article 1 SCMA, at para. 4.

[103] Adamantopoulos in Wolfrum et al. (eds.), Article 1 SCMA, at para. 5; Trebilcock et al., The Regulation of International Trade, at 368.

[104] Sykes in Macrory et al. (eds.), at 94.

Illustrative List of Subsidies contains miscellaneous practices that would likely be deemed to constitute subsidies. It was originally compiled by a GATT working party in 1960 and was included as annex into the Tokyo Round Subsidies Code[105] in 1979. The Illustrative List was, however, not signed by all GATT contracting parties.

A subsidy is only countervailable in cases where it is specific, i.e. the contribution is granted exclusively to producers singled out by certain criteria.[106] If the state support is generally available, it may not be countervailed under the ASCM.

Furthermore, not all specific subsidies are countervailable. The ASCM groups subsidies in prohibited (Articles 3 and 4 ASCM), actionable (Articles 5–7 ASCM.) and non-actionable subsidies (Articles 8 and 9 ASCM), commonly referred to as red light, yellow or amber light and green light subsidies.[107]

Of these three categories, the latter comprises subsidies which are never subject to anti-subsidy investigations. Although possibly constituting specific financial contributions on part of a government causing adverse effects, in some situations, the support of producers is regarded more beneficial than harmful to the economy as a whole.[108] Areas like research and development, grave regional structural differences or environmental protection are deemed to be worthy of receiving state benefits improving the situation of respective producers, serving other than mere economic policy considerations. But the rules on green light subsidies have only been temporary and have not been renewed upon their expiry in 2000.[109]

Prohibited subsidies comprise all export subsidies[110] and local content subsidies (Article 3 ASCM). Due to their obvious intention to promote domestic industries, regardless of any proven negative economic effect, members can always take action against such kind of subsidies.[111] Prohibited subsidies are also *de jure* deemed specific and thus, countervailable (Article 2.3 ASCM).

Lastly, actionable subsidies are all subsidies which are specific and cause adverse effects to the interests of other members. The ASCM lists three situations of adverse effects: injury to the domestic industry of another member, nullification or impairment of benefits accruing directly or indirectly to other members under the GATT and serious prejudice to the interests of another member (Article 5 ASCM).

---

[105] Agreement on Interpretation and Application of Articles VI, XVI and XXIII of the General Agreement on Tariffs and Trade, MTN/NTM/W/236, 12 April 1979, 1186 UNTS 204.

[106] Articles 1.2 and 2 ASCM.

[107] Sykes, Stanford Law and Economics Olin Working Paper No. 380 (2009), 1, at 8.

[108] Sykes, Stanford Law and Economics Olin Working Paper No. 380 (2009), 1, at 9 et seq. and 33; see Article 8.2 ASCM for an enlistment of non-actionable subsidies.

[109] Sykes, Stanford Law and Economics Olin Working Paper No. 380 (2009), 1, at 10.

[110] Regarding the historic discussions whether and to what extent production subsidies were to be included amongst export subsidies see Lester, 12 *Melbourne Journal of International Law* (2011), 1, at 7 et seq.

[111] Trebilcock et al. The Regulation of International Trade, at 376; Lester, 12 *Melbourne Journal of International Law* (2011), 1, at 9.

2.3.3.2 Injury

As second requirement, material injury to the domestic industry, or threat thereof, must exist. For this prerequisite, however, the ASCM does still not provide a definition. The only indicator regarding the determination of its scope is a reference in Article 15.1 ASCM to Article VI GATT.[112] At least Articles 15.1 and 15.2 ASCM provide some guidelines how to assess the materiality of injury. First, the volume and the price effect of the subsidised imports shall be established. In a second step, the impact of these imports on the state of the domestic market for the like product must be evaluated. This analysis always requires a case-specific assessment of the facts.[113]

In cases where there is yet only a threat of injury to the national industry, the threat must be clearly foreseeable and imminent (Article 15.7 ASCM). In such situations, the imposition of a countervailing duty is to be considered with special care (Article 15.8 ASCM).

2.3.3.3 Causation

Thirdly and lastly, the subsidised imports have to cause the injury to the domestic economy (Article 15.5 ASCM). To detect this causal link, it needs to be ascertained at first that further subsidised imports would aggravate the injury.[114] Then, the investigating authority has to exclude any known factors concurrently adding to the injurious potential. This analysis includes the listing of the factors and, subsequently, a separate examination of each factor as regards its respective injurious effect in contrast to the subsidised imports.[115]

What is to be noted here in particular is that no causal link needs to be shown between the subsidies themselves and the injury to the domestic producers. As the wording of Article 15.5 ASCM explicitly states, it is sufficient to demonstrate the injurious effect of the subsidised imports. Thus, only a "two-tier", not a "three-tier" causation test applies.

---

[112]Coppens, WTO Disciplines on Subsidies and Countervailing Measures, at 228.

[113]Panel Report, *European Communities and Certain Member States – Measures Affecting Trade in Large Civil Aircraft*, WT/DS316/R, adopted 1 June 2011, as modified by Appellate Body Report, WT/DS316/AB/R, DSR 2011:II, 685. at para. 7.2083.

[114]Appellate Body Report, *US – Softwood Lumber IV*, at para. 132.

[115]Panel Report, *Mexico – Definitive Countervailing Measures on Olive Oil from the European Communities*, WT/DS341/R, adopted 21 October 2008, DSR 2008:IX, 3179, at para. 7.305.

2.3.4 *The Course of Procedure of an Anti-Subsidy Investigation*

In cases where a countervailable subsidy causes injury to a state's domestic industries, the state has various options to respond and offer protection to its industries. The WTO provides for a multilateral and a unilateral approach to thwart price discrimination practices effected through subsidisation.[116]

WTO members can choose the multilateral track and file a complaint regarding the allegedly unfair price discrimination of foreign companies against the companies' respective home state in front of the WTO DSB.[117] Only a minority of subsidies, however, is addressed this way.[118]

Members can also respond to countervailable subsidisation endangering the economic success of their national companies unilaterally.[119] Adhering to the principles set down in WTO law, members are allowed to conduct trade defence investigations and impose remedies to offset the unfair advantage of the foreign producers.[120]

Anti-subsidy investigations constitute a unilateral means of response to countervailable subsidisation. In principle, anti-subsidy proceedings are to be concluded within one year after their commencement (Article 11.1 ASCM). Only under special circumstances they may last up to 18 months. According to WTO case law, this constitutes the maximum time limit and may not be prolonged for any reason.[121]

2.3.4.1 Initiation

In principle, an anti-subsidy investigation can be initiated via written application by or on behalf of the domestic industry of a WTO member (Article 11.1 ASCM). Only special circumstances award the possibility to the investigating authority to directly commence an investigation, i.e. without having received a prior application (Article 11.6 ASCM). This procedure is permitted in cases where sufficient evidence of the substantive requirements for the imposition of a countervailing duty has been acquired. Because anyway, if there is not enough supporting evidence, the investigation shall be terminated (Article 11.9 ASCM).

As the involvement of states makes anti-subsidy investigations extremely precarious,[122] the WTO members being about to be subjected to an anti-subsidy

[116]Sykes in Guzmán/Sykes (eds.), 62, at 101 et seq.

[117]Coppens, WTO Disciplines on Subsidies and Countervailing Measures, at 197 et seq.

[118]Lincicome, Policy Analysis No. 710 (2012), 1, at 6.

[119]Coppens, WTO Disciplines on Subsidies and Countervailing Measures, at 197.

[120]Coppens, WTO Disciplines on Subsidies and Countervailing Measures, at 220.

[121]Panel Report, *Mexico – Olive Oil*, at para. 7.120 et seq.

[122]Coppens, WTO Disciplines on Subsidies and Countervailing Measures, at 222.

investigation—i.e. during the period of time after the application has been filed but before the actual investigation starts—are entitled to partake in consultations with the member having received the complaint.

2.3.4.2 Investigation

Because of the highly sensitive nature of the information required during anti-subsidy proceedings, the rules regarding the collection of evidence are of particular importance.

Every interested member, and every interested party (Article 12.9 ASCM),[123] is first given the chance to present all the evidence they consider relevant for the ongoing investigation voluntarily (Articles 12.1 and 12.2 ASCM). This information must be verified by the investigating authority during the course of the investigation (Article 12.5 ASCM).

In order to reappraise the information that has been provided or to discover necessary information that has not been provided for, investigating authorities are entitled to conduct investigations in the territory of the charged member (Article 12.6 ASCM).

If necessary information is deliberately withheld or the information that has been provided turns out to be false, all determinations as regards the setting of countervailing duties may be made on the basis of facts available (Article 12.7 ASCM). Before missing information may be replaced by reasonable information from secondary sources, however, all the substantiated facts the party provided have to be duly considered.[124]

Before the final duty is set, the investigating authority must present all the evidence the final countervailing duty is based on to the parties involved (Article 12.8 ASCM).

2.3.4.3 Imposition of the Countervailing Duty

If the findings of the investigation are positive, the investigating authority may impose a final countervailing duty (Articles 19.1 and 19.2 ASCM). The kind of duty imposed on the imports is an *ad valorem* countervailing duty to offset the unfair

[123]According to the Appellate Body in *Japan – DRAMs (Korea)*, it is sufficient if the investigating authority deems it advantageous if another actor were to join as a party. Besides the investigating authority being "mindful of the burden that such designation may entail for other interested parties", no other substantive requirements have to be fulfilled, see Appellate Body Report, *Japan – Countervailing Duties on Dynamic Random Access Memories from Korea*, WT/DS336/AB/R and Corr.1, adopted 17 December 2007, DSR 2007:VII, 2703, at para. 150 et seq.

[124]Appellate Body Report, *Mexico – Definitive Anti-Dumping Measures on Beef and Rice*, Complaint with Respect to Rice, WT/DS295/AB/R, adopted 20 December 2005, DSR 2005:XXII, 10853, at para. 192 et seq.

price advantage. The amount of countervailing duty may be less than the subsidisation actually found if the lesser amount suffices to offset the injury of the national industry (Article 19.2 ASCM), but it must never exceed the established amount of subsidy (Article 19.4 ASCM). As a result, a level playing field of competitive conditions in the affected market is re-established.

2.4 The Calculation of the Amount of Benefit

What finds itself at the heart of the determination of the existence of a subsidy is the amount of benefit conferred to the producer through the subsidy. The process and the methodologies employed to calculate the amount of benefit are therefore of particular interest and importance. They depend on the nature of the market conditions present in the country under investigation. The basic procedure in cases of MES has to be distinguished from the one in NMES, which employs the alternative benchmark methodologies forming the object of the study.

2.4.1 The Benefit as Countervailable Part of the Governmental Financial Contribution

The financial contribution bestowed upon a private recipient by a government does not to its full extent constitute the countervailable subsidy. Instead, as Article 1.1(b)(1) ASCM states, only the part of the contribution that actually confers a benefit to the private actor results in a positive finding of subsidy under the ASCM and may subsequently be offset by a countervailing duty. Determining the amount of financial contribution does not inhere much significance in the process of an anti-subsidy investigation. Rather, it is the determination of the benefit the whole investigation hinges at.

The term "financial contribution" is used to describe a government practice that provides assistance for domestic industries.[125] What the ASCM envisions to be within the scope of such a contribution can be seen in Article 1.1(a)(1) ASCM, which lists several state actions that are deemed to promote in some way the country's economy, e.g. government practices involving a direct transfer of funds (Article 1.1. (a)(1)(i) ASCM), but also the provision or the purchase of goods or services other than general infrastructure by the government (Article 1.1. (a)(1)(iii) ASCM). What constitutes a financial contribution under the ASCM, is to be determined in close connection with this enlistment because otherwise, the accuracy of the ASCM's subsidy definition would be blurred.[126]

[125] Adamantopoulos in Wolfrum et al. (eds.), Article 1 SCMA, at para. 9.

[126] Adamantopoulos in Wolfrum et al. (eds.), Article 1 SCMA, at para. 11.

A financial contribution is *per se* measured in terms of economic value. As the WTO Appellate Body put it, a financial contribution is a *"transfer of economic value from the government to the recipient either in the form of a monetary transfer or a transfer in kind"*.[127] As economic value is, however, generally an abstract concept[128] and hence unsuitable for a concise calculation process, the market price as "translation" of this economic value is employed.[129]

According to Article 1.1(b) ASCM, to constitute a subsidy, the financial contribution of the government must confer a benefit on the recipient. The ASCM lacks a clear definition of benefit.[130] Only the provision of Article 14 ASCM exemplarily stipulates some guidelines for the calculation of the subsidy in terms of benefit to the recipient for four types of subsidies: the government provision of equity capital (Article 14(a) ASCM), loans (Article 14(b) ASCM), loan guarantees (Article 14 (c) ASCM) and goods or services or the purchase of goods or services (Article 14 (d) ASCM).[131] As these guidelines are rather vague, the term has been subject to extensive interpretation by the WTO judiciary. It defined a benefit as *"an advantage, if it is provided on terms more advantageous than those that would have been available to the recipient on the market"*.[132] The recipient of the financial contribution is made *"better off [. . .] than [. . .] absent the financial contribution"*.[133]

In economic terms, the benefit constitutes the *"difference in economic value between what the recipient has actually obtained as a result of the government's financial contribution and what the recipient would otherwise have obtained [. . .] in the absence of the governmental action in question"*.[134] "The market benchmark" as such is, however, an abstract notion, just like economic value.[135] Instead, what is employable for the process of benefit calculation, is the result of such a translation: the market price.[136] The benefit calculation in MES thus refers to market prices in

---

[127]Appellate Body Report, *US – Softwood Lumber IV*, at para. 52; Adamantopoulos in Wolfrum et al. (eds.), Article 1 SCMA, at para. 12.

[128]Chichilniski in Koellner (ed.), 204, at 212. In economics, there is not only one single notion of economic value, see Zheng, 19 *Minnesota Journal of International Law* (2010), 1, at 2. Instead, several concepts exist. Basically, value "in use" and value "in exchange" are distinguished, see Smith, A., Wealth of Nations, at 44. According to the concept of value in use, each commodity inheres economic value. The idea of economic value in exchange, however, grounds on the preferences of sellers and buyers attributing to a good a certain economic value, see Stuart, 4 *Journal of Political Economy* (1896), 208, at 210.

[129]Reich, National Accounts and Economic Value, at 12.

[130]Adamantopoulos in Wolfrum et al. (eds.), Article 1 SCMA, at para. 92.

[131]Zheng, 19 *Minnesota Journal of International Law* (2010), 1, at 16.

[132]Panel Report, *Canada – Measures Affecting the Export of Civilian Aircraft*, WT/DS70/R, adopted 20 August 1999, upheld by Appellate Body Report, WT/DS70/AB/R, DSR 1999:IV, 1443, at para. 9.112.

[133]Appellate Body Report, *Canada – Measures Affecting the Export of Civilian Aircraft*, WT/DS70/AB/R, adopted 20 August 1999, DSR 1999:III, 1377, at para. 157.

[134]Adamantopoulos in Wolfrum et al. (eds.), Article 1 SCMA, at para. 92.

[135]Chichilniski in Koellner (ed.), 204, at 212.

[136]Reich, National Accounts and Economic Value, at 12.

order to establish the amount of the financial contribution of the government that may eventually be offset through countervailing duties.

WTO jurisprudence makes clear that the existence of a benefit always requires the existence of a recipient, as it is the perspective of the recipient that has to be relied upon when assessing the amount of benefit.[137] Though contrary to the wording of Annex IV para. 1 ASCM, explicitly stating that *"[a]ny calculation of the amount of a subsidy for the purpose of paragraph 1(a) of Article 6 shall be done in terms of the cost to the granting government"*, the recipient perspective is applied constantly in the determination process.[138]

In addition, the financial contribution has to be transferred to the recipient. According to the interpretation of *"conferred"* by the Appellate Body in *Canada – Aircraft*, *"the past participle in its passive form ("is conferred") [footnote omitted] implied the accomplished result of the recipient having received an advantage."*[139] The recipient, however, does not have to make actual use of the benefit.[140]

With the benefit as the pivotal element in the determination of the amount of countervailable subsidy, the final amount of countervailing duty imposed is entirely dependent on the findings made with respect to the benefit.[141]

2.4.2 *Benefit Calculation in MES*

Despite its paramount significance, no provision in WTO law lays down an exact methodology for the benefit calculation. The detailed process of how it is calculated remains in the discretion of each WTO member.

2.4.2.1 Article 14 ASCM as Framework for the Benefit Calculation

WTO law only sets a—very basic—framework marking the boundaries members' investigating authorities have to observe when determining the amount of benefit conferred. Article 14 ASCM lays down the general WTO rules for conducting anti-subsidy investigations in MES:

> For the purpose of Part V, any method used by the investigating authority to calculate the benefit to the recipient conferred pursuant to paragraph 1 of Article 1 shall be provided for in the national legislation or implementing regulations of the Member concerned and its

---

[137] Appellate Body Report, *Canada – Aircraft*, at para. 154 et seq.

[138] Adamantopoulos in Wolfrum et al. (eds.), Article 1 SCMA, at para. 93 and footnote 84; Trebilcock et al., The Regulation of International Trade, at 371.

[139] Appellate Body Report, *Canada – Aircraft*, at para. 154.

[140] Adamantopoulos in Wolfrum et al. (eds.), Article 1 SCMA, at para. 103.

[141] Durling in Wolfrum et al. (eds.), at para. 3.

application to each particular case shall be transparent and adequately explained. Furthermore, any such method shall be consistent with the following guidelines:

(a) government provision of equity capital shall not be considered as conferring a benefit, unless the investment decision can be regarded as inconsistent with the usual investment practice (including for the provision of risk capital) of private investors in the territory of that Member;

(b) a loan by a government shall not be considered as conferring a benefit, unless there is a difference between the amount that the firm receiving the loan pays on the government loan and the amount the firm would pay on a comparable commercial loan which the firm could actually obtain on the market. In this case the benefit shall be the difference between these two amounts;

(c) a loan guarantee by a government shall not be considered as conferring a benefit, unless there is a difference between the amount that the firm receiving the guarantee pays on a loan guaranteed by the government and the amount that the firm would pay on a comparable commercial loan absent the government guarantee. In this case the benefit shall be the difference between these two amounts adjusted for any differences in fees;

(d) the provision of goods or services or purchase of goods by a government shall not be considered as conferring a benefit unless the provision is made for less than adequate remuneration, or the purchase is made for more than adequate remuneration. The adequacy of remuneration shall be determined in relation to prevailing market conditions for the good or service in question in the country of provision or purchase (including price, quality, availability, marketability, transportation and other conditions of purchase or sale).

The chapeau of Article 14 ASCM requires WTO members to lay down any method used by the investigating authorities to calculate the benefit to the recipient in national legislation or implementing regulations. Furthermore, the application shall be transparent and adequately explained. Article 14 ASCM exemplarily lists four different types of subsidies and provides methodologies to calculate the benefit conferred through the financial contribution of the government.

Article 14(a) ASCM deals with the government provision of equity capital. This kind of contribution shall not be considered a benefit as long as the investment decision can be regarded as consistent with the usual investment practice (including the provision of risk capital) of private investors in the territory of that WTO member.

Article 14(b) ASCM concerns the provision of loans. A loan by a government shall not be considered as conferring a benefit, unless there is a difference between the amount that the firm receiving the loan pays on the government loan and the amount the firm would pay on a comparable commercial loan which the firm could actually obtain on the market. In this case the benefit shall be the difference between these two amounts.

Article 14(c) ASCM, addressing loan guarantees by a government, largely resembles the previous Article 14(b) ASCM. These contributions shall not be considered as conferring a benefit unless there is a difference between the amount that the firm receiving the guarantee pays on a loan guaranteed by the government and the amount that the firm would pay on a comparable commercial loan absent the government guarantee. In this case, the benefit shall be the difference between these two amounts adjusted for any differences in fees.

The provision of goods or services or the purchase of goods by a government is covered by Article 14(d) ASCM. Such provision or purchase shall not be considered as conferring a benefit unless the provision is made for less than adequate remuneration, or the purchase is made for more than adequate remuneration. The adequacy of remuneration shall be determined in relation to prevailing market conditions for the good or service in question in the country of provision or purchase (including price, quality, availability, marketability, transportation and other conditions of purchase or sale).

2.4.2.2 The Market Benchmark as Foundation of the Benefit Calculation

That WTO law has adopted the market benchmark as point of reference for the benefit calculation has not always been a choice without alternative. During the negotiations of the Uruguay Round alternatives to the market benchmark have been discussed.

Originally, the draft of the ASCM comprised an additional guideline for a fifth type of subsidy.[142] For cases where the government was the sole provider or purchaser of a good or service, draft Article 14(e) ASCM stated that no benefit was conferred *"unless the government discriminates among users or providers of the good or service"*. This presents a different benchmark concept. The point of reference is not the market, but the peer group of other users or providers of a particular product. A benefit is conferred if the government differentiates between respective buyers or users without a justifiable reason, i.e. discriminatorily.[143] The market is not completely ruled out as benchmark in that conception, though. Differences in treatment *"due to normal commercial considerations"* are labelled non-discriminatory. The overall focus of draft Article 14(e) ASCM remains, of course, on preferentiality. For reasons unknown, draft Article 14(e) ASCM did, however, not find its way into the final version of the ASCM that was adopted by the Uruguay Round negotiating parties.[144]

By today, *"the market"* has, however, established itself as benchmark in the benefit calculation. In the much-cited case *Canada – Aircraft*, the panel stated that *"an advantage, if it is provided on terms more advantageous than those that would have been available to the recipient on the market"*[145] constituted a benefit. This *"private market test"*[146] manifested itself in later decisions. In miscellaneous

[142]MTN.GNG/NG10/23, 7 November 1990, at 15; Zheng, 19 *Minnesota Journal of International Law* (2010), 1, at 18.

[143]Zheng, 19 *Minnesota Journal of International Law* (2010), 1, at 14, footnote 76.

[144]Zheng, 19 *Minnesota Journal of International Law* (2010), 1, at 14, footnote 76.

[145]Panel Report, *Canada – Aircraft*, at para. 9.112.

[146]Coppens, WTO Disciplines on Subsidies and Countervailing Measures, at 60.

subsequent cases the WTO judiciary constantly referred to *"the market",*[147] *"the marketplace",*[148] a *"proper market"*[149] or like terms[150] to describe the benchmark against which the suitability of existing prices was to be measured in order to examine whether or not in-country prices were distorted.

Measuring the benefit against the market is therefore now applicable general practice under WTO law.[151] The market itself is characterised as *"the area of economic activity in which buyers and sellers come together and the forces of supply and demand affect prices"*[152] or *"[g]enerally, any context in which the sale and purchase of goods and services takes place"*[153] and *"[a] collection of homogenous transactions. A market is created whenever potential sellers of a product are brought into contact with potential buyers and a means of exchange."*[154]

2.4.2.3 The Determination of the Relevant Market

Recent Appellate Body jurisprudence has introduced a methodology for the determination of the relevant market in WTO anti-subsidy law. In *Canada – Renewable Energy* and *Canada – FIT Program*, the WTO Appellate Body embarked on a competition law-like market determination procedure before performing the benefit analysis. It held that *"[t]he definition of the relevant market is central to, and a prerequisite for"*[155] the correct calculation of the benefit. An *"analysis of*

---

[147]Panel Report, *Canada – Aircraft*, at para. 9.112.

[148]Appellate Body Report, *Canada – Aircraft*, at para. 157; Appellate Body Reports, *Canada – Certain Measures Affecting the Renewable Energy Generation Sector / Canada – Measures Relating to the Feed-in Tariff Program*, WT/DS412/AB/R / WT/DS426/AB/R, adopted 24 May 2013, at 5.208; Panel Reports, Canada – Certain Measures Affecting the Renewable Energy Generation Sector / Canada – Measures Relating to the Feed-in Tariff Program, WT/DS412/R and Add.1 / WT/DS426/R and Add.1, adopted 24 May 2013, as modified by Appellate Body Reports WT/DS412/AB/R / WT/DS426/AB/R, DSR 2013:II, 471, at para. 7.271.

[149]Appellate Body Report, *US – Carbon Steel (India)*, at para. 4.151 (quoting Appellate Body Report, *EC and certain Member States – Large Civil Aircraft*, at para. 975.).

[150]The "market standard" was referred to by the Appellate Body in *Japan – DRAMs (Korea)*, see Appellate Body Report, *Japan – DRAMs (Korea)*, at para. 172.

[151]Sykes in Guzmán/Sykes (eds.), 62, at 104.

[152]Appellate Body Report, *United States – Countervailing Measures on Certain Hot- Rolled Carbon Steel Flat Products from India*, WT/DS436/AB/R, adopted 19 December 2014, DSR 2014:V, 1727, at para. 4.150 (quoting Appellate Body Report, *United States – Subsidies on Upland Cotton*, WT/DS267/AB/R, adopted 21 March 2005, DSR 2005:I, 3, at para. 4.04).

[153]Appellate Body Report, *European Communities and Certain Member States – Measures Affecting Trade in Large Civil Aircraft*, WT/DS316/AB/R, adopted 1 June 2011, DSR 2011:I, 7, at para. 1120, footnote 2467.

[154]Appellate Body Report, *EC and certain Member States – Large Civil Aircraft*, at para. 1120, footnote 2467.

[155]Appellate Body Reports, *Canada – Renewable Energy* and *Canada – FIT Program*, at para. 5.169.

demand-side and supply-side factors"[156] was to be performed to establish the relevant market for the benefit calculation. Both factors were essential parts of the reasoning and had to be addressed. *"Demand-side substitutability – that is, when two products are considered substitutable by consumers – is an indispensable, but not the only relevant, criterion to consider when assessing whether two products are in a single market. Rather, a consideration of substitutability on the supply-side may also be required. For example, evidence on whether a supplier can switch its production at limited or prohibitive cost from one product to another in a short period of time may also inform the question of whether two products are in a single market."*[157]

Only after the relevant market had been found, the determination of the amount of benefit could proceed in a meaningful way.[158]

2.4.2.4 The Market Conception in WTO Anti-Subsidy Law

The exact character of the market benchmark WTO anti-subsidy law envisions—a market-as-is, a perfect market, or something different altogether—is, however, not directly revealed in WTO law. As the market conception forms the pivot of the entire benefit analysis, the answer to this question is essential. But indications in both written WTO law and panel and WTO Appellate Body jurisprudence are scarce.

2.4.2.4.1 Indications in the Wording of Article 14 ASCM

Article 14 ASCM has been identified as the only provision explicitly addressing benefit calculation. Does it contain any hints which type of market it envisions to underlie WTO anti-subsidy law?

2.4.2.4.1.1 The Chapeau of Article 14 ASCM

The chapeau allows the use of *"any method [...] to calculate the benefit"*. Interpreted in a wide sense, this wording could mean that not only existing in-country prices may be used for the benefit calculation—but a definite answer remains out of reach. Equally, it may be argued that *"method [...] to calculate"* is to be understood in a narrow sense, referring directly to the process of calculation itself and not containing any statement regarding the values employed for this purpose.

---

[156] Appellate Body Reports, *Canada – Renewable Energy* and *Canada – FIT Program*, at para. 5.172; Coppens, WTO Disciplines on Subsidies and Countervailing Measures, at 79 et seq.

[157] Appellate Body Reports, *Canada – Renewable Energy* and *Canada – FIT Program*, at para. 5.171 (quoting Appellate Body Report, *EC and certain Member States – Large Civil Aircraft*, at para. 1121).

[158] Appellate Body Reports, *Canada – Renewable Energy* and *Canada – FIT Program*, at para. 5.169.

2.4.2.4.1.2 Article 14(a) ASCM

For the first type of subsidy in Article 14(a) ASCM, the government provision of equity capital, *"the usual investment practice [...] of private investors in the territory of that Member"* constitutes the point of reference for the comparison.

The reference to the *"territory of that Member"* expressly disallows deviation from in-country prices. The wording seems to demand the use of the conditions of the market-as-is.

But in fact, the mere requirement to use in-country conditions does not yet in any way positively describe these conditions. This is left to *"the usual investment practice [...] of private investors"*. The *"practice [...] of private investors"* does not provide for an unequivocally clear answer. It could either be read as market-as-is stipulation (emphasis on practice) or a perfect market requirement (emphasis on private investors).[159] Requiring, however, relation to the *"usual [...] practice"* could turn the balance in favour of a market-as-is approach. *"Usual"* means *"habitually or typically occurring or done; customary"*.[160] But then, the conditions which are customarily found on a market depend on the very model the conception of market is based on. The reference to *"usual"* remains circular.

All in all, Article 14(a) ASCM could be interpreted as either purporting a market-as-is or a perfect market approach.[161]

2.4.2.4.1.3 Article 14(b) ASCM

Article 14(b) ASCM requires a *"comparable commercial loan which the firm could actually obtain on the market"*.

The loan having to be *"comparable"* does not offer any further clarity, as its comparability is exactly what stands to be discovered by searching for the underlying market conception. Relying on it for guidance in the benefit analysis would constitute circular reasoning.[162]

A *"commercial loan"* appears to refer to the perfect market. *"Commercial"* means *"concerned with or engaged in commerce"*,[163] i.e. trade[164] or *"making or*

[159] Also, the reference to a "private" investor could be seen as circular. How "private" the market has to be, i.e. whether it has to be a perfectly private market or whether the existence of externalities may also be regarded as a feature of a still sufficiently private market, is just the question under scrutiny.

[160] http://www.oxforddictionaries.com/definition/english/usual (last visited 1 January 2018).

[161] Different Zheng, 19 *Minnesota Journal of International Law* (2010), 1, at 22, who concludes on a market-as-is approach.

[162] Different Zheng, 19 *Minnesota Journal of International Law* (2010), 1, at 22 et seq., who rather interprets "comparable" as indicating the employment of the perfect market approach.

[163] http://www.oxforddictionaries.com/definition/english/commercial?searchDictCode=all (last visited 1 January 2018).

[164] http://www.oxforddictionaries.com/definition/english/commerce (last visited 1 January 2018).

intended to make a profit".[165] Thus, a commercial loan has to be a profitable loan. But how profitable does it have to be? Is an amount of profit based on the conditions of a market-as-is or of a perfect market deemed sufficient? The question of market conception in WTO anti-subsidy law only seems to pose itself in a different guise. One could assume that by reference to *"commercial"* only the "real", i.e. existing market conditions, are included, as *"commercial"* is usually employed to describe actual courses of trade. But this assumption remains unsubstantiated. The requirement of a *"commercial loan"* could ultimately be understood both-ways.[166]

That the firm *"could actually obtain"* the loan on the market is equally ambiguous. Understanding *"could actually obtain"* in a past tense meaning of "was actually able to obtain on the market at the time it received the government loan instead", this supports a market-as-is comparison at the time of the provision of the loan. On the other hand, by interpreting *"could obtain"* in a conditional sense, it would refer to the hypothetical conditions for a loan on the market, i.e. envision a perfect market. This conclusion is weakened, however, by the word *"actually"*—it rather refers to the existing market conditions than mere fictitious ones.[167]

Conclusively, Article 14(b) ASCM remains ambiguous.

2.4.2.4.1.4 Article 14(c) ASCM

For loan guarantees under Article 14(c) ASCM, the *"amount that the firm would pay on a comparable commercial loan absent the government guarantee"* is stipulated as point of reference for the comparison.

The use of the conditional mode, i.e. the amount the firm *"would pay"*, rather hints at the hypothetical amount on the undistorted market and thus seems to envision a perfect market.

The same is true for the requirement of a *"commercial"* loan and a *"comparable"* loan, which is circular here as well.[168]

That the amount of interest is to be identified *"absent the government guarantee"* can be interpreted twofold: on the one hand, it could mean that the amount of interest is to be established by simply referring to existing market terms instead of government conditions. On the other hand, however, this phrase could be given a more amplified meaning and require that the government influence is to be banned completely from the market benchmark. Subsequently, existing market terms for

---

[165] http://www.oxforddictionaries.com/definition/english/commercial?searchDictCode=all (last visited 1 January 2018).

[166] Again, Zheng, 19 *Minnesota Journal of International Law* (2010), 1, at 22 et seq., rather concludes on a perfect market approach.

[167] Ending with the same conclusion Zheng, 19 *Minnesota Journal of International Law* (2010), 1, at 22.

[168] Regarding the circularity of a "comparable" loan see Sect. 2.4.2.4.1.3.

loan guarantees could not be resorted to as they are, too, influenced by the government action and therefore unsuitable for comparison. Hence, only a perfect market price would fulfil the criteria for the price comparison.

Consequently, Article 14(c) ASCM could be understood to refer to both the market-as-is and the perfect market model.

2.4.2.4.1.5 Article 14(d) ASCM

Lastly, Article 14(d) ASCM states that the provision of goods or services or the purchase of goods by a government shall not be considered a benefit, if it is made for *"less"* respectively *"more than adequate remuneration"*. Whether the remuneration is adequate, is to be measured *"in relation to prevailing market conditions for the good or service in question in the country of provision or purchase"*.

The adequacy of remuneration could be understood either way, as the term itself leaves unclear by what standard adequacy is to be assessed.[169]

The instruction in sentence 2 to employ *"prevailing market conditions"* does, however, appear to indicate the use of a market-as-is as benchmark. *"Prevailing"* means *"[e]xisting at a particular time; current"*.[170] On the other hand, it could be argued that a government-distorted market does not possess any *"market conditions"* and can therefore not be qualified as market at all.

Although the adoption of the market-as-is benchmark appears more likely, it cannot be concluded on beyond any doubt.

2.4.2.4.2 Indications in WTO Jurisprudence

Absent a direct answer from the wording of Article 14 ASCM or another provision of WTO anti-subsidy law, the question of the underlying market benchmark has merited WTO Appellate Body and panel examination in various cases.

2.4.2.4.2.1 Canada – Aircraft

Canada – Aircraft has been the first case in which the WTO judiciary referred to the market as point of reference for the benefit calculation. Concerning the interpretation of the term *"benefit"* as in Article 1.1(b) ASCM, the reports of both the panel and the WTO Appellate Body let shine through a ray of the market conception in WTO anti-subsidy law.

Interpreting the term *"benefit"* in Article 1.1(b) ASCM, the panel stated that in order to assess whether an advantage has been conferred to the recipient by the government's financial contribution, *"the only logical basis for determining the*

---

[169]See Zheng, 19 *Minnesota Journal of International Law* (2010), 1, at 23.

[170]http://www.oxforddictionaries.com/definition/english/prevailing (last visited 1 January 2018).

position the recipient would have been in absent the financial contribution is the market".[171] Unfortunately, this general description does not aid the present cause in any way. It merely assures that one type of market is to be adopted as point of reference for the comparison.

The panel then referred to the guidelines for the calculation of the benefit in Article 14 ASCM and concluded that all of them "*employ a commercial benchmark*".[172] Hence, it was the "*commercial market*"[173] that the government terms were to be measured against. With "*commercial*" meaning "*concerned with or engaged in commerce*",[174] i.e. trade,[175] or "*making or intended to make a profit*",[176] the term expressed efforts to obtain an economically advantageous position. But clarification faltered, because what was deemed "truly profitable" was mentioned nowhere.

On appeal, the question of the underlying market conception itself was not raised. The Appellate Body merely stated that "*[...] the marketplace provides an appropriate basis for comparison in determining whether a 'benefit' has been conferred, because the trade distorting potential of a 'financial contribution' can be identified by determining if the recipient has received a 'financial contribution' on terms more favourable than those available to the recipient in the market.*"[177]

Thus, the reference to a "*commercial market*" did ultimately not shed further light on the conception of market in WTO anti-subsidy law.

2.4.2.4.2.2 Brazil – Aircraft

The panel in *Brazil – Aircraft* was *inter alia* dealing with the question whether particular governmental export credit practices for the regional aircraft industry constituted a "*material advantage*" in the meaning of item (k) of the Illustrative List of Export Subsidies that is annexed to the ASCM.[178]

---

[171] Panel Report, *Canada – Aircraft*, at para. 9.112.

[172] Panel Report, *Canada – Aircraft*, at para. 9.113.

[173] Panel Report, *Canada – Aircraft*, at para. 9.113.

[174] http://www.oxforddictionaries.com/definition/english/commercial?searchDictCode=all (last visited 1 January 2018).

[175] http://www.oxforddictionaries.com/definition/english/commerce (last visited 1 January 2018).

[176] http://www.oxforddictionaries.com/definition/english/commercial?searchDictCode=all (last visited 1 January 2018).

[177] Appellate Body Report, *Canada – Aircraft*, at para. 157; see Zheng, 19 *Minnesota Journal of International Law* (2010), 1, at 21.

[178] Panel Report, *Brazil – Export Financing Programme for Aircraft*, WT/DS46/R, adopted 20 August 1999, as modified by Appellate Body Report WT/DS46/AB/R, DSR 1999:III, 1221, at para. 7.15 et seq.

In this connection, Brazil argued that it was permitted to use a credit rate below CIRR,[179] if it was able to demonstrate that *"the marketplace"* actually offered such a rate.[180]

Hence, the question was raised whether the market indeed included only *"purely commercial transactions, i.e. transactions not benefitting from official support"*[181] or government-supported transactions as well.[182] As the context was clearly on the discussion of the argumentative position of appellant Canada, and there were no indications that the panel wanted to make a general statement by adopting this definition, it is more convincing that the panel did not provide its own definition of *"commercial"* here.

In the following, the panel conceded that resorting to a benchmark other than CIRR was allowed if it could be ascertained that such a commercial benchmark really existed.[183] Confronted with the argument that as regards the commercial marketplace, export credits secured by government guarantees could not be taken into account, the panel considered it quite significant that the guarantee was a *"government guarantee"*,[184] whereas the interest rate in question had to result from the *"commercial marketplace"*.[185] This may let assume that the panel did not support the idea of government actions being part of a commercial market at all, so that any involvement of the government rendered market conditions meaningless—and endorsed the overall model of a perfect market.

The panel, however, merely continued stating that Brazil failed to prove that the government-supported interest rate could be regarded as commercial in the present case.[186] This does not allow the conclusion that government influenced terms were always excluded from being part of the commercial marketplace. Indeed, the statement only bears significance with regard to not satisfying the requirements of prove. Ultimately, the panel itself declared the question whether Brazil had managed to satisfy the necessary burden of proof requirements, and not whether *"any below-CIRR commercial interest rates"* transferred a material advantage in the sense of item (k), the issue at heart in the present case.[187] The tribunal slightly and implicitly broached the question of underlying market conception but, lastly, did not offer any significant contribution.

---

[179]CIRR is the Commercial Interest Reference Rate provided by the OECD setting the minimum interest rates for governmental supported export credits, see http://www.oecd.org/tad/xcred/cirrs.pdf also for the latest rates (last visited 1 January 2018).

[180]Panel Report, *Brazil – Aircraft*, at para. 6.79.

[181]Panel Report, *Brazil – Aircraft*, at para. 6.88; This definition is reiterated by the Panel at para. 6.91. As the context is clearly on the discussion of the argumentative position of Canada, the reiteration bears no significance in terms of the Panel providing an own definition of "commercial".

[182]Panel Report, *Brazil – Aircraft*, at para. 6.90.

[183]Panel Report, *Brazil – Aircraft*, at para. 6.92.

[184]Panel Report, *Brazil – Aircraft*, at para. 6.95 [emphasis in original].

[185]Panel Report, *Brazil – Aircraft*, at para. 6.95 [emphasis in original].

[186]Panel Report, *Brazil – Aircraft*, at para. 6.95.

[187]Panel Report, *Brazil – Aircraft*, at para. 6.104.

2.4.2.4.2.3 US – Softwood Lumber III

When interpreting Article 14(d) ASCM with regard to the question of adequacy of remuneration, the panel in *US – Softwood Lumber III* rather fervently countered the argument of the United States that in-country prices merely constituted a reference point and not necessarily an end-point for the comparison.[188] It concluded that *"[t]he prevailing market conditions in the country of provision are the benchmark and operate as reference point or the point of comparison for the adequacy of remuneration".*[189] The market conditions yielding the market price for the comparison did not need *"to be those of a hypothetical undistorted or perfectly competitive market".*[190] The investigating authority had no choice *"but to use as benchmark the market [. . .] as it exists in the country of provision".*[191]

Unquestionably, the panel adopted a market-as-is approach.

2.4.2.4.2.4 US – Softwood Lumber IV

In the consecutive Softwood Lumber dispute, the issue of underlying market conception was again subject of both panel and WTO Appellate Body discussion.

The panel was confronted with the argument of the United States that *"it is well established that a benefit from a governmental financial contribution is to be determined in comparison to the commercial market."*[192] According to the United States' understanding of the ASCM, the commercial market *"must, necessarily, be undistorted by the government's intervention",*[193] hence had to be a perfect market.

The panel did not endorse this opinion. It concluded that *"Article 14(d) SCM Agreement does not qualify in any way the 'market' conditions which are to be used as the benchmark."*[194] It argued that it could not be determined with absolute certainty that Article 14(d) ASCM understood the market as *"'pure' market",*[195] as a *"market 'undistorted by government intervention'"*[196] or as generating *"a 'fair market value'".*[197] In contrast, because the conditions of the market were described as *"prevailing"* in Article 14(d) ASCM, i.e. *"'as they exist' or 'which are*

---

[188]Panel Report, *United States – Preliminary Determinations with Respect to Certain Softwood Lumber from Canada*, WT/DS236/R, adopted 1 November 2002, DSR 2002:IX, 3597, at para. 4.83.

[189]Panel Report, *US – Softwood Lumber III*, at para. 7.44.

[190]Panel Report, *US – Softwood Lumber III*, at para. 7.50.

[191]Panel Report, *US – Softwood Lumber III*, at para. 7.53.

[192]Panel Report, *United States – Final Countervailing Duty Determination with Respect to Certain Softwood Lumber from Canada*, WT/DS257/R and Corr.1, adopted 17 February 2004, as modified by Appellate Body Report WT/DS257/AB/R, DSR 2004:II, 641, at para. 7.38.

[193]Panel Report, *US – Softwood Lumber IV*, at para. 7.38.

[194]Panel Report, *US – Softwood Lumber IV*, at para. 7.51.

[195]Panel Report, *US – Softwood Lumber IV*, at para. 7.51.

[196]Panel Report, *US – Softwood Lumber IV*, at para. 7.51.

[197]Panel Report, *US – Softwood Lumber IV*, at para. 7.51.

predominant' [footnote omitted] in the country of provision".[198] This could only mean *"the market conditions 'as can be found'".*[199] *"[A]s long as there are prices determined through independent operators following the principle of supply and demand, even if supply or demand are affected by the government's presence in the market, there is a 'market' in the sense of Article 14(d) SCM Agreement."*[200]

Confronted with the argument that the panels in both *Canada – Aircraft* and *Brazil – Aircraft* had concluded on a perfect market, the panel emphasised that both panels had in fact addressed completely different issues in their reasoning, so that their conclusions were not transferable to the question presently under scrutiny.[201] All in all, the panel adopted a market-as-is approach.

The Appellate Body agreed with the panel insofar as Article 14(d) ASCM *"does not qualify in any way the 'market' conditions which are to be used as the benchmark".*[202] It added that the other authentic Spanish and French versions of the ASCM[203] were supporting this view.[204] Both the Spanish phrase *"condiciones reinantes en el mercado"* and the French counterpart *"aux conditions du marché existantes"* did not permit a different interpretation. According to the WTO Appellate Body, Article 14(d) ASCM contained no indications as to the type of market benchmark in WTO anti-subsidy law.[205]

2.4.2.4.2.5 US – Carbon Steel (India)

The Appellate Body in *US – Carbon Steel (India)* elaborated on the term *"prevailing market conditions"*, which formed the benchmark for the assessment of the adequacy of remuneration. The term *"conditions"* meant *"characteristics or qualities".*[206] The scope of its meaning was influenced by the term *"market"* on the one hand and the term *"prevailing"* on the other. Whereas the former was *"'a place [. . .] with a demand for a commodity or service'; 'a geographical area of demand for commodities or services'; 'the area of economic activity in which buyers and sellers come together and the forces of supply and demand affect prices'",*[207] the latter

[198]Panel Report, *US – Softwood Lumber IV*, at para. 7.50.

[199]Panel Report, *US – Softwood Lumber IV*, at para. 7.51.

[200]Panel Report, *US – Softwood Lumber IV*, at para. 7.60.

[201]Panel Report, *US – Softwood Lumber IV*, at para. 7.52 et seq.

[202]Appellate Body Report, *US – Softwood Lumber IV*, at para. 87.

[203]See Article XVI WTO Agreement for a reference to English, French and Spanish being the authentic languages of the WTO Agreement.

[204]Appellate Body Report, *US – Softwood Lumber IV*, at para. 87.

[205]Different again Zheng, 19 *Minnesota Journal of International Law* (2010), 1, at 27, who concludes on a perfect market approach adopted by the Appellate Body.

[206]Appellate Body Report, *US – Carbon Steel (India)*, WT/DS436/AB/R, adopted 19 December 2014, DSR 2014:V, 1727, at para. 4.150 (quoting Appellate Body Report, *United States – Subsidies on Upland Cotton*, WT/DS267/AB/R, adopted 21 March 2005, DSR 2005:I, 3, at para. 4.04).

[207]Appellate Body Report, *US – Carbon Steel (India)*, at para. 4.150 (quoting Appellate Body Report, *United States – Subsidies on Upland Cotton*, at para. 4.04).

meant *"'predominant', or 'generally accepted'"*.[208] *"Prevailing market conditions"* in Article 14(d) ASCM were thus to be understood as *"generally accepted characteristics of an area of economic activity in which the forces of supply and demand interact to determine market prices"*.[209] Whereas *"generally accepted criteria"* let assume a market-as-is approach, the determination of market prices through supply and demand rather induced to conclude on a perfect market benchmark. But in the end, also the elaboration of the Appellate Body in *US – Carbon Steel (India)* did not add clarity to the underlying market conception of WTO anti-subsidy law.

2.4.2.4.2.6 Canada – Renewable Energy *and* Canada – FIT Program

In *Canada – Renewable Energy* and *Canada – FIT Program*, on the other hand, the WTO Appellate Body made very plain which type of market benchmark it considered to underlie the benefit determination in the present case. The case concerned a feed-in tariff programme for the promotion of wind and solar energy launched by the government of the Canadian province of Ontario.[210] Affirming that government intervention alone did not unduly influence the conditions on the market in the country investigated,[211] especially if it resulted in the creation of otherwise non-existent markets,[212] the Appellate Body decided that in such situations, the suitable benchmark for the benefit calculation was to be found *"in the markets for wind- and solar PV-generated electricity, which are defined by the Government of Ontario's choice of the energy supply-mix."*[213] It was of the opinion *"that all the other in-province and out-of-province blended electricity benchmarks [...] are not appropriate benefit benchmarks."*[214] Therefore, it clearly referred to the market-as-is as relevant type of market benchmark.

As the determinations of the tribunal were very much tailored to the circumstances of the present case, however, it cannot be concluded that the Appellate Body generally embraced a market-as-is approach.[215] Rather, the decision on the type of

---

[208] Appellate Body Report, *US – Carbon Steel (India)*, at para. 4.150.

[209] Appellate Body Report, *US – Carbon Steel (India)*, at para. 4.150.

[210] Appellate Body Reports, *Canada – Renewable Energy* and *Canada – FIT Program*, at para. 4.6 et seq.

[211] Appellate Body Reports, *Canada – Renewable Energy* and *Canada – FIT Program*, at para. 5.190.

[212] Appellate Body Reports, *Canada – Renewable Energy* and *Canada – FIT Program*, at para. 5.185.

[213] Appellate Body Reports, *Canada – Renewable Energy* and *Canada – FIT Program*, at para. 5.199.

[214] Appellate Body Reports, *Canada – Renewable Energy* and *Canada – FIT Program*, at para. 5.204.

[215] Appellate Body Reports, *Canada – Renewable Energy* and *Canada – FIT Program*, at para. 5.225.

market, just as in previous investigations, seemed to emanate *ad hoc* from the circumstances of the case.

2.4.3 Benefit Calculation in NMES

Referring to existing in-country market prices does, however, not always prove feasible. Certain state practices, like the provision of subsidies, impair the allocative efficiency of the market. In such situations, the market price as product of the interplay between supply and demand does no longer adequately reflect the economic value of the traded good or service. Instead, misallocation resulting from governmental subsidisation artificially lowers the market price in comparison to the price of the traded good or service in cases where there is no government influence. In NMES, market price and market value of a good or service do not equate any more.

So far, a universally accepted definition of a NMES does not exist.[216] In general, two different kinds of NMES are distinguished: either a market price is completely non-existent or it exists, but is so heavily distorted by government influence that the existing domestic "market" price does not render meaningful results in the benefit calculation.[217]

2.4.3.1 The Necessity of a Meaningful Market Benchmark

For the purpose of conducting a proper benefit calculation, it is, however, essential to employ meaningful market prices. If market prices do no longer truthfully depict economic value, but are distorted, and these distorted prices are then compared to the government prices to establish the benefit conferred, this ultimately results in comparing apples with apples: in cases where market distortion from state influence becomes overbearing, the government price is virtually compared to itself.[218] The comparison becomes circular.

For this reason, it is often argued that in NMES, subsidisation cannot exist.[219] The central notion or rationale of WTO anti-subsidy law is offsetting the benefit conferred upon the producer through the financial contribution of the government. The amount of benefit is determined by comparing the value of the governmental input to the value of the like input on the market. WTO trade remedy law thus underlies the

---

[216]Zang, 14 *Journal of International Economic Law* (2012), 869, at 885 et seq. As a result, one important element of the benefit calculation is missing: a meaningful market price for the comparison with the price of the governmental financial contribution.

[217]Sykes in Guzmán/Sykes (eds.), 62, at 105.

[218]Van Bael/Bellis, EU Anti-Dumping and Other Trade Instruments, at 140.

[219]This discussion has been particularly prevalent in the US in the aftermath of the *Georgetown Steel Corp. v. United States* case. See Sect. 5.1.2.1; Hoyt, 136 *University of Pennsylvania Law Review* (1988), 1647, at 1665 et seq.

assumption that the prices employed for calculation purposes have been determined by reliable market forces.[220] In NMES, however, there is no market. This means that a subsidy cannot exist in terms of difference to market-based economic conditions because the market as core element needed for the identification of a subsidy is lacking.[221] Exemplarily, this effect shows with regard to socialist WTO members like Cuba. It has no reliable in-country market for price building—and is thus often said not to have any enforceable obligations under the ASCM.[222]

To avoid a circular comparison and to be able to apply anti-subsidy law in NMES, investigating authorities therefore resort to alternative benchmark methodologies to create hypothetical prices, which are comparable to the undistorted in-country market prices in a meaningful way. As the Appellate Body in *Canada – Renewable Energy* and *Canada – FIT Program* put it, *"[t]he very purpose of resorting to an [alternative] benchmark is to replicate competitive market conditions that are absent in the country of purchase".*[223]

2.4.3.2 The Alternative Benchmark Methodologies

To build hypothetical prices that closely resemble undistorted prices in the country under investigation, miscellaneous methodologies are employed. In principle, three different approaches are used: price construction and two out-of-country methodologies, the third-country methodology and the world market price.

2.4.3.2.1 Price Construction

The methodology of price construction creates market prices from scratch. Different components that usually render a market-based price are valuated and summed up. Usually, the costs of production form the basis of the price construction and a reasonable amount is added for profits as well as administrative and selling costs.[224]

2.4.3.2.2 Out-of-Country Methodologies

Out-of-country methodologies allow to use existing prices of countries other than the country investigated for the benefit calculation.

---

[220]Feldman/Burke, 62 *American University Law Review* (2008), 787, at 804; Qin, 7 *Journal of International Economic Law* (2004), 863, at 870.

[221]Feldman/Burke, 62 *American University Law Review* (2008), 787, at 804 et seq.

[222]Qin, 7 *Journal of International Economic Law* (2004), 863, at 870.

[223]Appellate Body Reports, *Canada – Renewable Energy* and *Canada – FIT Program*, at para. 5.184.

[224]Adamantopoulos in Wolfrum et al. (eds.), Article VI GATT, at para. 19.

2.4.3.2.2.1 The Rationale of Out-of-Country Benchmarks

Depending on the kind of asset in question, the economic justification for employing out-of-country benchmarks differs. Using alternative prices for tangible assets grounds on the "law of one price", while intangible assets are considered suitable due to the notion of comparability of prices sharing common characteristics.

The "law of one price" assumes that in maximum efficient markets, identical goods are necessarily traded at identical prices.[225] This notion roots in the effects of market arbitrage.[226] Without factors such as transportation costs or different knowledge levels, the prices for goods in countries across the border are all supposed to be of the same amount. Any price differences in markets of tangible goods are hence invariably caused by government subsidies, so that the higher—and correct—price of another country can be used for the calculation of the benefit conferred to a producer in the country under investigation.

Shared common characteristics of economic environments are deemed to guarantee conditions that render comparable market prices.[227] A condition generally regarded to produce reliable comparable prices is the GDP *per capita*.[228] If the GDP *per capita* in two countries is of the same amount, the prices of intangible assets such as land will also be the same and be suitable as surrogate prices for the purpose of benefit calculation.

2.4.3.2.2.2 The Different Kinds of Out-of-Country Benchmarks

Two different kinds of out-of-country benchmarks have emerged in investigation practice and are frequently resorted to. First, the price of a good in one single third country serves as point of reference for the surrogate price. Second, the world market price forms the benchmark. The world market price is usually built using data from the biggest supplier countries or regions from each continent or the biggest suppliers worldwide in general.

2.5 Chapter Summary

Although economically controversial in its expediency, the WTO as major institution for the regulation of global trade has opted for a legal control regime on subsidisation. It bases on the understanding that a true market equilibrium that guarantees free trade is created only by transactions of private individuals. Due to their trade-distortive effect, the use of subsidies is restricted.

---

[225]Zheng, 19 *Minnesota Journal of International Law* (2010), 1, at 41; Lamont/Thaler, 17 *Journal of Economic Perspectives* (2003), 191.

[226]Zheng, 19 *Minnesota Journal of International Law* (2010), 1, at 41.

[227]Zheng, 19 *Minnesota Journal of International Law* (2010), 1, at 42.

[228]Zheng, 19 *Minnesota Journal of International Law* (2010), 1, at 43.

In the event of illegal subsidisation, importing WTO members may impose countervailing duties to offset undue advantages of foreign exporters that emanate from financial governmental support.

The countervailing duty calculation is not based on the full amount of financial contribution, but focuses only on the benefit conferred to the recipient.

In MES, the amount of benefit is easily ascertainable by referring to the in-country market prices of the country under investigation as benchmarks for assessing the advantage that has been transferred to the recipient of the financial contribution.

In NMES, however, this procedure is not feasible. Non-existent or distorted market prices make it impossible to adhere to the general procedure and employ in-country market prices. In order to receive a meaningful result in the benefit calculation, alternative benchmarks have to be resorted to. Investigating authorities enjoy a large amount of discretion in their determination. With the establishment of the amount of benefit constituting the pivot of the entire process of countervailing duty calculation, the way alternative benchmark methodologies are used in NMES to render comparable substitute prices as benchmarks for the purpose of benefit calculation is decisive and predetermines the outcome of the whole investigation.

Neither written WTO law nor the WTO judiciary, however, do so far positively provide for a definite answer on the market conception that underlies WTO anti-subsidy law. This leads to complications in the distinction between MES and NMES and opens the door for potential arbitrariness on part of the investigating authorities.

Chapter 3
The WTO Framework for the Use of Alternative Benchmark Methodologies in Anti-Subsidy Investigations Against China

After having created a profound understanding of both the background and the fundamental parameters for the use of alternative benchmark methodologies, this study now turns its focus to the legal framework at WTO level. Since the adoption of the original framework in the GATT 1947 and the subsequent changes and innovations in connection with the foundation of the WTO, the legal rules in this area have undergone several significant developments.

To date, there exists not only the alternative benchmark regime in general WTO law, which is based on Article 14 ASCM (Sect. 3.1). Accession proceedings of new WTO members have added country-specific provisions for the benefit calculation in NMES. The first and also the most significant accession process encompassing the introduction of respective country-specific rules was the accession of the People's Republic of China on 11 December 2001. Until today, the legal framework, which has been created for China in Section 15(b) CAP, remains unsurpassed in its extensiveness (Sect. 3.2).

3.1 The General Alternative Benchmark Regime in WTO Anti-Subsidy Law

The main general legal provision in WTO law containing prerequisites for the use of alternative benchmark methodologies in anti-subsidy investigations is Article 14 ASCM. Despite its textual ambiguities, which render it rather imprecise,[1] Article 14 ASCM until today still remains the only general stipulation offering any guidance on the use of alternative benchmarks in the WTO legal hemisphere. Although since

---

[1]On the lack of stipulating a precise market conception for WTO anti-subsidy law see Sects. 2.4.2.4 and 6.1.1.1.

S. Müller, *The Use of Alternative Benchmarks in Anti-Subsidy Law*,
European Yearbook of International Economic Law 4,
https://doi.org/10.1007/978-3-319-77613-2_3

the foundation of the WTO in 1995 its agreements have been moderately added to,[2] no attempt of enhancing clarity by introducing more detailed rules on the use of alternative benchmarks has ever been made with respect to Article 14 ASCM.

3.1.1 Excursus: Alternative Benchmark Regimes Outside the ASCM

In contrast, WTO anti-dumping law does contain—with Article VI GATT, *Ad* Note 2 Article VI:1 GATT and Articles 2.2, 2.3 and 2.7 ADA albeit few—provisions on alternative benchmarks for the determination of normal value in proceedings against NME countries, i.e. when the prices on the domestic market of the country investigated are deemed unfit for the price comparison conducted to calculate the dumping margin. Besides, the predecessor of the ASCM, the Tokyo Round Subsidies Code of 1979, contained in Article 15 a provision dealing with *"special situations"* created by state economies that explicitly laid down alternative methodologies for the benchmark calculation. These regimes are essential to comprehensively understand the current developments under the ASCM.

3.1.1.1 The Alternative Benchmark Regime in Article VI:1 GATT 1947

Article VI GATT, which has already formed part of the GATT 1947, contains methodologies that may be resorted to in cases where a meaningful in-country price for the purpose of price comparison is unavailable.

3.1.1.1.1 The Range of Alternative Methodologies

According to Article VI:1 GATT, if existing, the *"comparable price, in the ordinary course of trade, for the like product when destined for consumption in the exporting country"* shall be employed to assess whether a product is imported into another country at less than its normal value.[3] In cases where there is no comparable domestic price, Article VI:1(b) GATT lays down two alternative methodologies that may be used to yield a comparable in-country price as substitute. Either *"the highest comparable price for the like product for export to any third country in the*

[2]The only additions as far as multilateral agreements are concerned are the insertion of Article 31*bis* TRIPS in 2005 and the adoption of the new Trade Facilitation Agreement in 2013. Both additions have not yet reached the necessary quorum of ratifications and thus still lack legal effect. See Hughes in Dadush/Osakwe, 309, at 329 et seq.; Koul, Guide to the WTO & GATT, at 34.

[3]Adamantopoulos in Wolfrum et al. (eds.), Article VI GATT, at para. 17 et seq.

ordinary course of trade" or *"the cost of production of the product in the country of origin plus a reasonable addition for selling cost and profit"* may be employed.[4]

3.1.1.1.2 The Applicability of Article VI:1 GATT in Anti-Subsidy Investigations

Article VI GATT in its entirety deals with the imposition of both anti-dumping and countervailing duties. It therefore needs to be ascertained that the alternative methodologies set down in paragraph 1 can indeed be applied in anti-subsidy proceedings and not only in anti-dumping proceedings.

Considering the wording of Article VI:1 GATT, applicability does seem rather doubtful. Paragraph 1 exclusively covers dumping, in particular the determination of normal value for the purpose calculating the dumping margin, which constitutes the starting point for the calculation of the amount of anti-dumping duty. An explicit reference to countervailing duties is found only as early as in paragraph 3.

On the other hand, it could be argued that paragraphs 1 and 2 only nominally deal with dumping, but substantively include anti-subsidy law. As dumping is substantively defined in Article VI:1 GATT as conduct *"by which products of one country are introduced into the commerce of another country at less than the normal value of the products"*, the reason for the underpricing is not explicitly stated. Thus, price-lowering governmental contributions would not *per se* be excluded from the GATT definition of dumping. The alternative methodologies could therefore be deemed applicable also in anti-subsidy proceedings.

Article VI:2 GATT, however, expressly stipulates that dumping shall be offset by an anti-dumping duty. The alternative methodologies of paragraph 1 are explicitly referred to as providing means for the determination of the dumping margin, which constitutes the pivotal element in the calculation of the amount of an anti-dumping duty. Since in the following paragraphs 4–6, both anti-dumping and countervailing duties are referred to side by side as two different terms, it can rather be concluded that the GATT systematically and expressly distinguishes between anti-dumping regulations on the one hand and anti-subsidy regulations on the other hand.

Moreover, in paragraph 3, a countervailing duty is defined as a special duty levied to offset any bounty or subsidy bestowed upon the manufacture, production or export of any merchandise. This kind of phenomenon would already be comprised in the wider term of dumping. If anti-subsidy law had therefore already been

[4]WTO law today does not impose any rule of priority with regard to either methodology, so that the two methodologies may be applied interchangeably at the complete discretion of the respective national investigating authorities. The 1959 Report, WT/L/978, 21 December 2015, at para. 10, however, expressed concern that the use of third-country export prices may yield imprecise results, see Adamantopoulos in Wolfrum et al. (eds.), Article VI GATT para. 17, footnote 45.

addressed in paragraphs 1 and 2, the special definition of a countervailing duty in paragraph 3 would be rendered superfluous.

Altogether, it is more convincing to deny the applicability of Article VI:1 and 2 GATT to anti-subsidy investigations.[5] The stipulated alternative methodology regime can thus not be resorted to for the benefit calculation via direct reference to the provision.

3.1.1.2 The Alternative Benchmark Regime in Article 15 Subsidies Code

Besides Article VI GATT, anti-subsidy law prior to the foundation of the WTO in 1995 comprised another set of rules. After over 30 years, during which Article VI GATT constituted the sole provision with respect to the use of alternative benchmark methodologies in WTO law, it was only in 1979 that the Tokyo Round enacted the Subsidies Code, which provided for a more detailed legal framework.

3.1.1.2.1 The Range of Alternative Methodologies

Just like Article VI:1 GATT, Article 15.2 Subsidies Code lists alternative methodologies for *"special situations"*. But Article 15.2 Subsidies Code expressly applies to the benefit calculation in anti-subsidy law.

3.1.1.2.1.1 Third-Country Benchmark and Constructed Price

For calculating the amount of benefit, Article 15 Subsidies Code on the one hand allowed to resort to third-country prices of a like product (Article 15.2(a) Subsidies Code). Furthermore, it permitted the use of a *"constructed value of a like product"* (Article 15.2(b) Subsidies Code).

One major prerequisite that needs to be fulfilled for the applicability of the alternative methodologies is the particular character of the exporting country. Existing domestic prices were allowed to be disregarded only if found in a *"country described in NOTES AND SUPPLEMENTARY PROVISIONS to the General Agreement (Annex I, Article VI, paragraph 1, point 2)"* (Article 15.1 Subsidies Code). As defined there, such a country had to meet two prerequisites in order to be classified accordingly. The country had to be *"a country which has a complete or substantially complete monopoly of its trade and where all domestic prices are fixed by the State"*. Such a kind of country therefore had to possess an economy that, firstly, was to at least a large preponderant extent dominated by the government, and where, secondly, the government was ultimately responsible for the price setting. Such a type of economy is variably referred to in GATT and WTO terminology as either

[5] Consenting Lynam, 42 *Case Western Reserve Journal of International Law* (2010), 739, at 752.

"state-trading economy",[6] *"centrally-planned economy"*[7] or, in particular of late, *"non-market economy"*.[8] When Article 15 Subsidies Code talks of *"special situations"*, it can be concluded that the speciality of a situation occurs wherever such a kind of economy exists. Before alternative benchmarks may be resorted to for the benefit calculation, it has to be duly scrutinised whether the country under investigation is indeed a country of such an economic nature.

3.1.1.2.1.2 Adjustment of the Existing In-Country Price in the Country Investigated

Article 15.3 Subsidies Code introduced a novel benchmark for the determination of a comparable price for the benefit calculation. If the employment of the alternative methodologies listed in Article 15.2 Subsidies Code did not yield a workable result for the process of benefit calculation, *"the price in the importing signatory, if necessary duly adjusted to reflect reasonable profits, may be used"*. The existing in-country price of the country leading the investigation functions as last resort in cases where the other alternative benchmark methodologies relating to third countries fail.

The gradual alternative benchmark regime of Article 15 Subsidies Code may be explained from the perspective of fairness—employing in-country prices of the investigating country instead of the country investigated reeks of arbitrariness. In this scenario, using prices relating to an unconnected third country introduces an element of neutrality into the calculation process.

Despite the presumably good intentions, the two-tier alternative-country regime remains unconvincing from both an economic and a legal point of view. The goal of the alternative benchmark regime is to find prices that are comparable to the price of the product in the country investigated if not for the governmental distortion. Taking this aim into account, why prices of an unconnected third country are deemed to be necessarily more accurate than prices of the investigating country lacks reason. A methodology that might lead to the most exact result in certain cases is debarred by an artificial legal barrier.

3.1.1.2.2 The Legal Force of the Subsidies Code

As with all agreements negotiated after the enactment of the GATT 1947, their scope of application has to be assessed individually. In particular, the foundation of the WTO in 1995 may have affected the validity of the agreement, if it has not been included in one of the annexes to the WTO Agreement.

---

[6]E.g. Article XVII GATT; see also Hoogmartens, EC Trade Law, at xviii.

[7]E.g. Article 29.1 ASCM; see also Matsushita et al., The World Trade Organization: Law, Practice, and Policy, at 244.

[8]E.g. Section 15(d), third sentence CAP.

When the Subsidies Code was concluded at the end of the Tokyo Round negotiations in 1979, it was signed by 24 contracting parties only.[9] It constituted a plurilateral agreement, exercising binding force merely on the respective signatory countries.[10] All other countries, though perhaps signatories to the GATT 1947, remained unaffected by its legal force. Despite the USA and the EU being Subsidies Code signatories, the agreement remained of little influence, as it did not prove able to effectively solve arising subsidy disputes during the GATT era.[11]

In any case, after the foundation of the WTO, the Subsidies Code would only still be applicable today if it had been incorporated into the WTO Agreement. According to Article II:1 WTO Agreement, only *"agreements [...] included into the Annexes of this Agreement"* still form part of the WTO legal regime. The Subsidies Code as plurilateral agreement would have to be listed as part of Annex 4 (Article II:3 WTO Agreement). It is, however, not listed and was also not accepted by all members during negotiations as a multilateral agreement, and has therefore not been transferred into the WTO legal hemisphere. Instead, the ASCM as multilateral agreement has taken the place of the Subsidies Code and has been incorporated into Annex 1 A.

3.1.1.3 The Alternative Benchmark Regime in the ADA

Anti-dumping regulations can be found in two different WTO agreements.[12] On the one hand, Article VI GATT lays down basic guidelines for the determination of normal value, i.e. the in-country price, for the purpose of calculating the dumping margin.[13] In addition, since the Uruguay Round, dumping has been subjected to the regulations of the ADA. It constitutes a multilateral agreement of Annex 1 A of the WTO Agreement and sets down a binding legal framework for the area of anti-dumping regulation which all WTO members have to conform with. The ADA embellishes basic Article VI GATT and provides for more detailed anti-dumping rules.[14]

For the determination of normal value, Article 2.2 ADA states that generally, the price of the like product in the ordinary course of trade in the domestic market of the exporting country shall be used.[15] Wherever there are no sales of a like product or these sales do not permit proper comparison, i.e. in NMES, alternative methodologies shall be employed for the determination of normal value. The provision permits to resort to either representative export prices of the like product to third countries or

---

[9]Coppens, WTO Disciplines on Subsidies and Countervailing Measures, at 27.

[10]Trebilcock et al., The Regulation of International Trade, at 366.

[11]Trebilcock et al., The Regulation of International Trade, at 367.

[12]Bentley/Silberston, Anti-Dumping and Countervailing Action, at 10.

[13]See Sect. 3.1.1.1.

[14]Wu (2015), available at http://papers.ssrn.com/sol3/papers.cfm?abstract_id=2306345 (last visited 1 January 2018), 1, at 4.

[15]Zang, 14 *Journal of International Economic Law* (2012), 869, at 879.

to the cost of production in the country of origin plus a reasonable amount for administrative, selling and general costs and for profits.

Hence, Article 2.2 ADA more or less repeats the two alternative methodologies laid down in Article VI:1 GATT. In contrast to Article VI:1 GATT, the export price of a like product to a third country is not required to be the *"highest comparable price"* (Article VI:1 GATT), but merely needs to be *"representative"* (Article 2.2 ADA). Moreover, Article VI:1 GATT allows to employ the export price to *"any third country"*, whereas Article 2.2 ADA stipulates that the third country has to be *"appropriate"*.[16] With respect to the second cost-based alternative methodology, Article 2.2 ADA also lists administrative and general costs to calculate the surrogate export price.

What constitutes a situation in which existing normal values may be disregarded for the reason of not being in the ordinary course of trade is regulated in Article 2.2.1 ADA. *"[O]nly if the authorities determine that such sales are made within an extended period of time in substantial quantities and are at prices which do not provide for the recovery of all costs within a reasonable period of time"*, deviation is permitted. However, to be noted here in particular is Article 2.7 ADA. It refers to Note 2 *Ad* Article VI:1 GATT. The *ad* note acknowledges that with regard to state-trading countries, the determination of normal value may be burdened with *"special difficulties"* that endow investigating authorities with more discretion in determining normal value, because a *"strict comparison with domestic prices in such a country may not always be appropriate"*.[17] This *ad* note will be discussed in more detail below.[18] What shall be held for now is the fact that Article 2.2.1 ADA does not by itself comprehensively set down all situations in which the existing normal value may be substituted, but points to Note 2 *Ad* Article VI:1 GATT by reference in Article 2.7 ADA.

With regard to the production cost alternative, Article 2.2.1.1 ADA lays down that the costs should generally be based on the records of the respective producer or exporter. Article 2.2.2 ADA sets down guidelines for the establishment of additional cost elements and profits.

3.1.1.4 Conclusion

WTO anti-dumping law as well as GATT era anti-subsidy law have already recognised the possibility of deviating from existing in-country prices for the

---

[16] The requirement of appropriateness does, however, not preclude that EU anti-dumping investigations render bizarre results at times. In Regulation (EC) No. 1355/2008, OJ 2008 L 350/35, the EU Commission used Spanish market prices for preserved mandarins, the product concerned, as substitutes for distorted Chinese prices. The Spanish National Federation of Associations of Processed Fruit and Vegetables had previously initiated the EU anti-dumping proceedings itself. See MacLean in Herrmann/Terhechte (eds.), 189, at 191.

[17] Cornelis, 2 *Global Trade and Customs Journal* (2007), 105, at 106.

[18] See Sect. 3.2.2.2.1.4.

purpose of duty calculation. Basically, the regimes provide for two different alternative methodologies to yield a comparable surrogate price: the sales price of a like product to a third country and production costs plus additions for profits. Moreover, adjustment of the existing in-country price and approximation to the price in the investigating country instead of a third country have been included amongst the alternative methodologies. Each of the regulatory regimes, however, ultimately lacks clear and precise rules under what circumstances exactly existing prices may be disregarded and how the alternative price is then to be determined.

3.1.2 The Alternative Benchmark Regime of Article 14 ASCM

With explicit rules missing, the alternative benchmark regime in general anti-subsidy law as of today derives from the Appellate Body's interpretation of Article 14 ASCM. For two of its four paragraphs, Articles 14(b) and (d) ASCM, the WTO Appellate Body has so far permitted investigating authorities to employ alternative benchmark methodologies in the process of benefit calculation. In its reasoning in *US – Softwood Lumber IV* and *US – Anti-Dumping and Countervailing Duties (China)*, the tribunal has granted the possibility to use alternative benchmarks in cases of non-existence of in-country market prices and governmental market distortion. In the recent cases *Canada – Renewable Energy* and *Canada – FIT Program*, the use of alternative benchmarks has also been permitted in situations of government creation of a market.

3.1.2.1 The Alternative Benchmark Regime of Article 14(d) ASCM

The first time the permissibility of deviation from existing in-country prices presented itself as relevant issue in front of the WTO judiciary was in the *US – Softwood Lumber IV*case, which was initiated in 2002.[19]

In the long-abiding conflict between the USA and Canada, the matter in dispute was how Canada set stumpage fees for timber.[20] Most of the timberland in Canada was owned by the Canadian provincial governments, which granted to certain timber producers the right to harvest standing timber. The US alleged that the administratively determined fees for harvesting timber did not constitute adequate remuneration as required by Article 14(d) ASCM and therefore conferred a benefit on respective timber producers. The US argued that according to the ASCM, only

[19]Request for Consultations by Canada, *US – Softwood Lumber IV,* WT/DS257/1, 13 May 2002.

[20]Zheng, 19 *Minnesota Journal of International Law* (2010), 1, at 23 et seq. For detailed reports of *US – Softwood Lumber IV* see e.g. Lysons, 32 *Seattle University Law Review* (2009), 407; Carmody, 100 *The American Journal of International Law* (2006), 664; on the Softwood Lumber dispute saga as a whole see e.g. Zhang, The Softwood Lumber War.

perfect market prices were acceptable for the calculation of benefit, hence rejected Canadian in-country prices as distorted and instead used fees for harvesting timber in the US states adjacent to the Canadian border. Canada, on the other hand, contended the approach of the USA and persisted that Article 14(d) ASCM only allowed for the use of prices as they existed in the country of investigation.

3.1.2.1.1 The Permissibility of Using Alternative Benchmarks

The line of reasoning that has been embarked upon by the WTO judiciary in *US – Softwood Lumber IV* regarding the question whether and under which circumstances Article 14(d) ASCM permits the substitution of distorted existing in-country prices for the process of benefit calculation forms the starting point of the entire alternative benchmark regime for NMES in general WTO anti-subsidy law.

3.1.2.1.1.1 US – Softwood Lumber IV

The argumentation of the panel and the Appellate Body regarding the permissibility of using alternative benchmarks differed significantly.

3.1.2.1.1.1.1 The Reasoning of the Panel

The pivot of the panel's argumentation was the term *"in relation to"* in the second sentence of Article 14(d) ASCM. According to the tribunal, this term, as its French counterpart *"par rapport aux"*, was to be understood in the meaning of *"in comparison with"*.[21] The point of comparison that Article 14(d) ASCM set were the prevailing market conditions in the country of provision or purchase, which were *"the market conditions 'as can be found'"*.[22] The compulsoriness of the exclusive use of existing in-country prices was supported by the term *"shall"*, which emphasised the *"mandatory manner"*[23] in which Article 14(d) ASCM stipulated the framework for the use of alternative benchmark methodologies.[24] Indeed, the panel concluded that there was *"nothing in the text of Article 14(d) that would justify disregarding those prices on grounds that they were 'distorted' or did not reflect the 'fair market value' of the goods provided."*[25]

Continuing, however, the panel seemed to quickly abandon its newly found reasoning. It recognised that *"certain situations"*[26] might occur, in which the existing in-country price was not employable for the benefit calculation. Wherever

[21]Panel Report, *US – Softwood Lumber IV*, at para. 7.48.
[22]Panel Report, *US – Softwood Lumber IV*, at para. 7.51.
[23]Panel Report, *US – Softwood Lumber IV*, at para. 7.51.
[24]Panel Report, *US – Softwood Lumber IV*, at para. 7.49.
[25]Panel Report, *US – Softwood Lumber IV*, at para. 7.51.
[26]Panel Report, *US – Softwood Lumber IV*, at para. 7.57.

the government was either the monopoly supplier of the good in question or administratively controlled all the prices for the good, the purely governmental determined price could not be used for the calculation in a meaningful way.[27] To conclude the investigation, the investigating authority would have to resort to *"the construction of some sort of proxy".*[28] This statement is diametrically opposed to the absolute negation of the possibility to disregard existing in-country prices under Article 14(d) ASCM only a few paragraphs before. The rigorous way the panel made clear that no feature of Article 14(d) ASCM granted the permission to deviate poses the question why *"certain situations"* were now to be treated in a different manner. As the panel itself stated that no reason could justify deviation, the only "reason" left seemed to be considerations of expedience and practicability.

Before further elaborating on this approach, the panel relented and reiterated its initial finding of non-permissibility. Although it acknowledged that the comparison of government prices with themselves was ultimately circular,[29] it refused to *"substitute its economic judgement for that of the drafters"*,[30] as it regarded the economic irrationality *"inherent"*[31] to Article 14(d) ASCM.

As a result, although causing irritations by recognising certain situations in which deviation from existing in-country prices could be permitted, the panel refrained from opening Article 14(d) ASCM to an alternative benchmark regime by denying the permissibility to disregard domestic prices.

3.1.2.1.1.1.2 The Reasoning of the Appellate Body

On appeal, the Appellate Body took a different stance.

It argued that the meaning of *"in relation to"* in Article 14(d) ASCM was not, as the panel had concluded, *"in comparison with"*, but rather *"as regards"* or *"with respect to"*.[32] Thus, Article 14(d) ASCM did not mandate the kind of strict comparison advocated for by the panel, but was to be interpreted in a broader sense. Contrary to the panel's findings, the drafters had not intended to exclude the possibility of deviation. Although existing in-country prices constituted the primary benchmark for the benefit calculation,[33] Article 14(d) ASCM allowed for the employment of alternative prices as long as the surrogate price *"relates or refers to, or is connected with, the conditions prevailing in the market of the country of provision."*[34]

[27] Panel Report, *US – Softwood Lumber IV*, at para. 7.57.
[28] Panel Report, *US – Softwood Lumber IV*, at para. 7.57.
[29] Panel Report, *US – Softwood Lumber IV*, at para. 7.58.
[30] Panel Report, *US – Softwood Lumber IV*, at para. 7.59.
[31] Panel Report, *US – Softwood Lumber IV*, at para. 7.59.
[32] Appellate Body Report, *US – Softwood Lumber IV*, at para. 89.
[33] Appellate Body Report, *US – Softwood Lumber IV*, at para. 90.
[34] Appellate Body Report, *US – Softwood Lumber IV*, at para. 89.

By unjustifiably narrowing down the possibilities of comparison, the panel had also not sufficiently observed the chapeau of Article 14 ASCM, which allowed to use *"any method"* in the benefit calculation and hence did not refer exclusively to existing in-country prices.[35]

Moreover, the Appellate Body agreed with the panel that the use of *"shall"* in the chapeau indicated that the framework in Article 14 ASCM set mandatory parameters for the benefit calculation, but did not postulate the use of only one single methodology.[36] Rather, the objective of Article 14 ASCM, which ultimately required a positive finding of benefit, demanded disregarding existing prices if they were not useable to effectively determine the amount of benefit conferred to avoid the comparison from becoming circular.[37] In addition, the objective of the ASCM as a whole was endangered if deviation from existing in-country prices was not permitted.[38] The ASCM served to discipline the use of subsidies and countervailing measures, while on the other hand granting WTO members the right to use remedies whenever their economies were injured by subsidised imports. If the benefit calculation did not yield a correct result, fully offsetting the disadvantage to the respective WTO member's national economy would not be possible, leaving the imposition of a countervailing duty a useless tool.

All in all, the Appellate Body argued that Article 14(d) ASCM permitted deviation from existing in-country prices for the purpose of benefit calculation.[39]

3.1.2.1.1.2 Further WTO Jurisprudence

In further WTO cases, the question of permissibility of using alternative benchmark methodologies no longer constituted a real point of interest but quickly became well-established practice in anti-subsidy investigations. Explicitly justifying the permissibility of deviation was no longer considered a necessity. In the next dispute adding to the alternative benchmark regime under Article 14(d) ASCM, *US – Anti-Dumping and Countervailing Duties (China)*, parties, third parties and tribunals alike had already accepted the Appellate Body's conclusion that Article 14(d) ASCM permitted the use of alternative benchmarks under certain prerequisites and simply referred to the Appellate Body's findings in *US – Softwood Lumber IV* .[40] In addition, the

[35] Appellate Body Report, *US – Softwood Lumber IV*, at para. 91.

[36] Appellate Body Report, *US – Softwood Lumber IV*, at para. 92.

[37] Appellate Body Report, *US – Softwood Lumber IV*, at para. 93.

[38] Appellate Body Report, *US – Softwood Lumber IV*, at para. 95.

[39] Appellate Body Report, *US – Softwood Lumber IV*, at para. 96.

[40] See Panel Report, *United States – Definitive Anti-Dumping and Countervailing Duties on Certain Products from China*, WT/DS379/R, adopted 25 March 2011, as modified by Appellate Body Report WT/DS379/AB/R, DSR 2011:VI, 3143, at para. 10.24 et seq.; Appellate Body Report, *US – Anti-Dumping and Countervailing Duties (China)*, at para. 427, where China appealed only the finding that rejecting existing in-country prices solely based on the evidence of the government being the predominant supplier of the respective good was in breach of Article 14(d) ASCM, not the question of permissibility of deviation as a whole.

recent panel decision in *US – Countervailing Measures (China)* once more expressly brought to mind that the use of alternative benchmarks was not limited to situations of government market distortion, but that they only constituted one amongst many NMES in which price surrogates could be applied for the benefit calculation.[41]

3.1.2.1.2 The Prerequisites for Using Alternative Benchmarks

An issue even more challenging than the mere yes-or-no question of deviation proved to be which prerequisites exactly needed to be fulfilled in order to legally deviate from existing in-country prices. The WTO judiciary has so far addressed this question in three cases altogether: the already familiar *US – Softwood Lumber IV* dispute, then in *US – Anti-Dumping and Countervailing Duties (China)* of 2011 and in *US – Countervailing Measures (China)* of 2014.

3.1.2.1.2.1 US – Softwood Lumber IV

In its reasoning regarding the prerequisites for the use of alternative benchmark methodologies for the benefit calculation, the Appellate Body in *US – Softwood Lumber IV* largely referred to the panel report. Apart from the two situations, in which even the principally negating panel had recognised the possibility to disregard existing domestic prices, i.e. the government being the sole supplier of a good and the government administratively setting all the prices for the good in one country,[42] upon the claim made by the United States, the Appellate Body acknowledged that there existed a third situation, in which deviation from existing prices was permitted. It also limited its analysis to this third situation due to the scope of the appeal.[43] Wherever prices were *"substantially influenced"* or *"effectively determined"* by the state, i.e. where the government acted with such a degree of predominance on the market that the other participants were to adapt their prices in order to remain competitive, the use of an alternative benchmark was also permitted.[44] The factual circumstances that allowed for deviation were thus *"market distortion"* and the *"effect on prices"* of the government's conduct.[45] The benefit calculation required the use of undistorted prices to fully serve the objective of the ASCM as a whole.[46]

But not any distortion found on the in-country market *per se* allowed for the employment of alternative benchmark methodologies. The tribunal reasoned that in

[41]Panel Report, *United States – Countervailing Duty Measures on Certain Products from China*, WT/DS437/R and Add.1, adopted 16 January 2015, as modified by Appellate Body Report WT/DS437/AB/R, at para. 7.190, 7.192 and 7.195.

[42]Panel Report, *US – Softwood Lumber IV*, at para. 7.57.

[43]Appellate Body Report, *US – Softwood Lumber IV*, at para. 98 et seq.

[44]Appellate Body Report, *US – Softwood Lumber IV*, at para. 99.

[45]Appellate Body Report, *US – Softwood Lumber IV*, at para. 100.

[46]Appellate Body Report, *US – Softwood Lumber IV*, at para. 101.

situations the government proved to be *"a significant supplier of goods"*, the fact of distortion itself was not substantiated by this finding alone.[47] Rather, the determination of the *"government's predominant role in the market, as a provider of certain goods, would have to be made on a case-by-case basis, according to the particular facts underlying each countervailing duty investigation"*.[48]

3.1.2.1.2.2 US – Anti-Dumping and Countervailing Duties (China)

Further elaboration was given by the WTO judiciary in its subsequent reports in *US – Anti-Dumping and Countervailing Duties (China)*, having been initiated in 2008.[49]

3.1.2.1.2.2.1 The Reasoning of the Panel

After the decision in *US – Softwood Lumber IV*, it was unclear whether the government being a significant supplier and being a predominant supplier were to be regarded as separate concepts or merely two different designations of the same concept.

In its analysis, the panel clearly distinguished between the three different levels of government significance, government predominance and government monopoly, ascending according to the amount of influence the government exercises on the price building of the respective market.[50] It regarded the *"concept of predominance [...] in relation to the domestic market as a whole for the good in question in the country, including imports"*.[51] With regard to real substantive requirements defining the concept of predominance, however, the panel report added little.

The other question raised was whether government predominance *per se* constituted sufficient evidence of market distortion or whether other additional evidence was required, in particular, if the investigating authority had to conduct a market analysis to prove that the distortion resulted from government action.[52] The panel concluded that Article 14(d) ASCM did not contain a *"'per se' rule, whereby in every case and regardless of other evidence, the fact that the government was the predominant supplier of a particular good would be a sufficient basis for rejecting private in-country prices as benchmark."*[53]

Though not the only evidence required, the finding of government predominance constituted the *"principal evidence"*.[54] The prevention of a circular price

[47]Appellate Body Report, *US – Softwood Lumber IV*, at para. 102.

[48]Appellate Body Report, *US – Softwood Lumber IV*, at para. 102.

[49]Request for Consultations by China, *US – Anti-Dumping and Countervailing Duties (China)*, WT/DS379/1, 22 September 2008.

[50]Panel Report, *US – Anti-Dumping and Countervailing Duties (China)*, at para. 10.46.

[51]Panel Report, *US – Anti-Dumping and Countervailing Duties (China)*, at para. 10.46.

[52]Panel Report, *US – Anti-Dumping and Countervailing Duties (China)*, at para. 10.38 et seq.

[53]Panel Report, *US – Anti-Dumping and Countervailing Duties (China)*, at para. 10.40.

[54]Panel Report, *US – Anti-Dumping and Countervailing Duties (China)*, at para. 10.41.

comparison and thereby the maintenance of the objectives of both Article 14 ASCM and the ASCM as a whole were the essential aims to be achieved.[55] Government predominance served as *sine qua non* piece of evidence, and could prove to be the only evidence, but the reference to other evidence was neither prohibited nor required if none was available.[56]

Rather, a case-by-case analysis was called for. Whether, however, this case-by-case analysis had to be conducted as a specific market distortion analysis, as argued by China, was an issue the panel neglected to address.[57]

Thus, government predominance constituted a piece of *sine qua non* evidence. As the investigation had to discover and weigh all evidence comprehensively and carefully, government predominance could prove the only evidence being sufficient for a finding of distortion at the end of the investigation, but not *per se* once it had been established. The threefold concept of government significance, government predominance and government monopoly signified that the more extensive the governmental influence, the less other evidence was required to prove a price distortion through government actions.

3.1.2.1.2.2.2 The Reasoning of the Appellate Body

With respect to the issues regarding the interpretation of Article 14(d) ASCM raised on appeal, the Appellate Body upheld the panel's findings in their core, although rendering several corrections and clarifications.

According to the tribunal, the concept of government predominance did not solely comprise the establishment of price distortion on the basis of the government's market shares.[58] Instead, besides the mere formal indicator of market shares, the concept also included market power as substantive parameter for the assessment of government predominance. Because investigating authorities ultimately needed to show price distortion in order to disregard existing in-country prices,[59] which also manifested itself in the ability to effectively determine prices,[60] the concept also required a substantive standard.[61]

The Appellate Body, like the panel, regarded the concepts of government predominance and government significance as two distinct concepts, the latter featuring a weaker degree of state influence.[62] The near lack of difference between government predominance and a state monopoly[63] justified the conclusion that in the event

[55]Panel Report, *US – Anti-Dumping and Countervailing Duties (China)*, at para. 10.42 et seq.
[56]Panel Report, *US – Anti-Dumping and Countervailing Duties (China)*, at para. 10.45.
[57]Panel Report, *US – Anti-Dumping and Countervailing Duties (China)*, at para. 10.47.
[58]Appellate Body Report, *US – Anti-Dumping and Countervailing Duties (China)*, at para. 444.
[59]Appellate Body Report, *US – Anti-Dumping and Countervailing Duties (China)*, at para. 446 and 453.
[60]Appellate Body Report, *US – Softwood Lumber IV*, at para. 93.
[61]Appellate Body Report, *US – Anti-Dumping and Countervailing Duties (China)*, at para. 444.
[62]Appellate Body Report, *US – Anti-Dumping and Countervailing Duties (China)*, at para. 441.
[63]Appellate Body Report, *US – Anti-Dumping and Countervailing Duties (China)*, at para. 442.

of predominance, market distortion proved to be more likely than in cases of mere government significance.[64] In consequence, the amount of alternative evidence for the establishment of market distortion became less the greater the amount of government influence.[65]

The Appellate Body confirmed that Article 14(d) ASCM did not allow for a *per se* rule for concluding on price distortion in cases of government predominance.[66] The concept of predominance was not fixable upon a particular threshold which, once crossed, implied price distortion.[67] By not requiring to consider alternative evidence besides the high degree of government presence on the market with the same diligence, the Appellate Body did, however, effect a kind of "*per se* devaluation" of alternative evidence.

3.1.2.1.2.3 US – Countervailing Measures (China)

Finally, in *US – Countervailing Measures (China)* the WTO judiciary further elaborated on the standard of evidence regarding the use of alternative benchmarks under Article 14(d) ASCM. It dealt with the question whether the presence of SOEs on the market may *per se* be used as evidence to conclude on government predominance on this market and, ultimately, on a degree of price distortion that allowed for the use of alternative benchmarks.[68] In particular in connection with China, establishment of major SOE presence on a market would facilitate extremely the determination of market distortion for investigating authorities. If SOEs formed part of the notion of "*government*" as in Article 14(d) ASCM, their presence on the market could be used not only as constituent but as the only piece of evidence for government market distortion. As the definition of "*government or public body*" in Article 1.1(a)(1) ASCM had already been subject to Appellate Body interpretation stating that neither the concept of "*government*" nor the concept of "*public body*" automatically included SOEs,[69] the answer depended on whether or not the standards for the notion of government under Article 1.1(a)(1) ASCM and Article 14(d) ASCM corresponded.[70]

But neither panel nor Appellate Body adopted this formalistic approach.[71] Instead, they stressed that with regard to Article 14(d) ASCM, the essential requirement for deviation from existing in-country prices under the alternative benchmark

[64] Appellate Body Report, *US – Anti-Dumping and Countervailing Duties (China)*, at para. 441.

[65] Appellate Body Report, *US – Anti-Dumping and Countervailing Duties (China)*, at para. 443.

[66] Appellate Body Report, *US – Anti-Dumping and Countervailing Duties (China)*, at para. 445.

[67] Appellate Body Report, *US – Anti-Dumping and Countervailing Duties (China)*, at para. 444.

[68] Panel Report, *US – Countervailing Measures (China)*, at para. 7.162.

[69] Appellate Body Report, *US – Anti-Dumping and Countervailing Duties (China)*, at para. 320 and 346.

[70] Panel Report, *US – Countervailing Measures (China)*, at para. 7.162.

[71] Appellate Body Report, *United States – Countervailing Duty Measures on Certain Products from China*, WT/DS437/AB/R, adopted 16 January 2015*)*, at para. 4.61; Panel Report, *US – Countervailing Measures (China)*, at para. 7.194.

regime was the government's ability to affect the prices on the domestic market.[72] The amount of SOE presence on a market would therefore be useful in assessing the governmental influence on domestic prices,[73] but it was unsuitable as exclusive *"per se piece of evidence"* in the determination of distorting government influence on a market.[74]

3.1.2.1.3 The Selection of the Alternative Benchmark

After the WTO Appellate Body had concluded that resorting to alternative methodologies was permitted under Article 14(d) ASCM and that, amongst other situations, government predominance in particular allowed for the deviation from existing in-country prices, it stood to be discovered which alternative benchmark methodologies were allowed to be used for yielding an employable surrogate price.

So far, only one WTO case, *US – Softwood Lumber IV*, explicitly referred to requirements alternative benchmark prices have to fulfil. According to the Appellate Body in *US – Softwood Lumber IV*, the benchmarks finally used in the benefit calculation *"could include proxies that take into account prices for similar goods quoted on world markets, or proxies constructed on the basis of production costs"*.[75] Although, ultimately, the tribunal declined to decide on the matter, as it considered it to be outside the scope of the subjects appealed, it did stress that an alternative methodology had to result in a surrogate price that *"relates or refers to, or is connected with, prevailing market conditions in the country of provision, and must reflect price, quality, availability, marketability, transportation and other conditions of purchase or sale, as required by Article 14(d)"*.[76]

Thus, as long as the general requirements in Article 14(d) ASCM are observed, no restrictions have so far been placed on the range of methodologies for the selection of the alternative benchmarks. Investigating authorities are equipped with a large amount of discretion when it comes to determine the exact price substitute for the benefit calculation.

3.1.2.1.4 Derogation from the Alternative Benchmark Regime of Article 14 (d) ASCM

In the year 2013, the WTO Appellate Body held that under certain exceptional circumstances, the alternative benchmark regime of Article 14(d) ASCM did not

[72] Appellate Body Report, *US – Countervailing Measures (China)*, at para. 4.60.

[73] Appellate Body Report, *US – Countervailing Measures (China)*, at para. 4.62.

[74] Panel Report, *US – Countervailing Measures (China)*, at para. 7.194 et seq.

[75] Appellate Body Report, *US – Softwood Lumber IV*, at para. 106.

[76] Appellate Body Report, *US – Softwood Lumber IV*, at para. 106.

apply. In *Canada – Renewable Energy* and *Canada – FIT Program* the tribunal concluded that cases in which a market was created through government intervention did not constitute market distortion and were thus exempt from the *"now well-established"*[77] alternative benchmark regime of Article 14(d) ASCM. The exact systemic integration of the *Canada – Renewable Energy* and *Canada – FIT Program* jurisprudence into the entirety of the alternative benchmark regime of Article 14(d) ASCM is, however, not yet unequivocally clear. While the majority in academic literature as well as the Appellate Body itself tend to treat it as derogation from the alternative benchmark regime of Article 14(d) ASCM,[78] *Coppens* rather seems to conclude on the Appellate Body setting up an altogether separate alternative benchmark regime for market creation under Article 14(d) ASCM.[79] Furthermore, the Appellate Body report in *Canada – Renewable Energy* and *Canada – FIT Program* could be regarded in the light of the reasoning of the panel in *US – Softwood Lumber IV* and its exception classified as subcategory of government price setting, which the panel then had identified as one of two exceptional circumstances warranting recourse to alternative benchmarks.[80] Seeing the *Canada – Renewable Energy* and *Canada – FIT Program* decision in connection with the WTO Appellate Body's argumentation in *US – Carbon Steel (India)* depicts the former as fitting the category of non-verifiable information about the quality of existing market prices, which the tribunal indicated as further situation that allowed the application of alternative benchmark methodologies under Article 14(d) ASCM in the latter case, but which has not yet made its way into the NMES canon.[81] In order to clarify the significance of *Canada – Renewable Energy* and *Canada – FIT Program* for the purpose of the thesis, the findings of panel and Appellate Body need to be discussed.

3.1.2.1.4.1 The Facts of the Cases

The cases concerned the renewable energy policy of the Canadian province of Ontario, which had set up several schemes to promote generation and support generators of renewable energy, e.g. a FIT programme for solar and wind energy. A province authority bought all the renewable energy that was produced at fixed prices, which were higher than the prices on Ontario's wholesale energy market, and thus ensured constant sustainable supply in line with the province's energy policy.

---

[77] Appellate Body Report, *Japan – DRAMs (Korea)*, at para. 7.275; Coppens, WTO Disciplines on Subsidies and Countervailing Measures, at 63.

[78] See e.g. Rubini, EUI Working Paper RSCAS No. 5 (2014), 1; Genest, 10 *International Journal of Sustainable Development Law and Policy* (2014), 239; Nedumpara, 9 *Indian Journal of Law & Technology* (2013), 1; Charnovitz/Fischer, FEEM Working Paper No. 94 (2014), 1.

[79] Coppens, WTO Disciplines on Subsidies and Countervailing Measures, at 81 et seq.

[80] Panel Report, *US – Softwood Lumber IV*, at para. 7.59.

[81] See Appellate Body Report, *US – Carbon Steel (India)*, at para. 4.189.

3.1.2.1.4.2 The Reasoning of the Panel

The panel reasoned that government purchases of goods at government-set prices that lay above the market level *per se* conferred a benefit as they constituted *"subsidies par excellence"*.[82,83] In the benefit analysis, it regarded the identified market benchmark for the calculation of the amount of benefit—the wholesale energy market in Ontario—as distorted due to the FITs.[84] In searching the alternative benchmark, the panel rejected the alternative benchmark options suggested by the contending parties EU and Japan as insufficient and concluded that no benefit could be determined in the present case.[85]

The bone of contention constituted the delineation of the relevant market for the benefit calculation. In *obiter dicta*, the panel recognised that the wholesale market for energy in Ontario was not the suitable benchmark, but that the benefit had to be assessed with regard to the individual markets for solar and wind energy respectively. Nevertheless, it adhered to the prevailing understanding of the alternative benchmark regime of Article 14(d) ASCM.

3.1.2.1.4.3 The Reasoning of the WTO Appellate Body

The reasoning of the WTO Appellate Body, however, constituted a major departure from the hitherto established alternative benchmark regime.

The Appellate Body in the end also concluded that no benefit was conferred through the renewable energy and FIT programmes. But its argumentation in the benefit analysis followed a fundamentally different course. While the finding of subsidisation should have been made *"with little difficulty"*[86] in the eyes of most, the Appellate Body emphasised that government intervention did not always result in a NMES that consequently permitted the use of alternative benchmark methodologies—but that certain circumstances warranted derogation from the usual approach.

3.1.2.1.4.3.1 The Limited Permissibility to Use Alternative Benchmarks

In particular, the *"creation of markets by a government does not in and of itself give rise to subsidies [. . .]"*.[87] This kind of government intervention was to be distinguished from market distortion. *"Where a government creates a market, it cannot be said that the government intervention distorts the market, as there would not be a*

[82]Coppens, WTO Disciplines on Subsidies and Countervailing Measures, at 466 [emphasis in original].

[83]Panel Reports, *Canada – Renewable Energy* and *Canada – FIT Program*, at para. 7.274.

[84]Panel Reports, *Canada – Renewable Energy* and *Canada – FIT Program*, at para. 7.308.

[85]Panel Reports, *Canada – Renewable Energy* and *Canada – FIT Program*, at para. 7.320.

[86]Other appellant submission by the European Union, *Canada – FIT Program*, AB-2013-1 / DS426, 11 February 2013, at para. 162.

[87]Appellate Body Reports, *Canada – Renewable Energy* and *Canada – FIT Program*, at para. 5.188.

market if the government had not created it."[88] Wherever the government only set the basic framework, within these *"broad parameters of the market, 'significant scope will remain for private actors to operate within those parameters on the basis of commercial considerations' [footnote omitted]."*[89]

Regarding the benefit calculation, it followed that government-set prices on newly created markets could be suitable for the benefit analysis, if they indeed accommodated commercial considerations. *"Government-administered prices such as FIT may or may not reflect what a hypothetical market would yield."*[90] If they did, the benefit benchmark was to be found within the government-created market.[91] The alternative benchmark regime of Article 14(d) ASCM did not apply. Whether the derogation will remain limited in scope to the renewable energy sector, policy considerations in general or ultimately include all situations of market creation has yet to manifest itself.

3.1.2.1.4.3.2 The Prerequisites for Using Alternative Benchmarks

According to the Appellate Body, only limited recourse was to be taken to alternative benchmark methodologies. If the market determination of the government-set prices could not be established because *"no information [exists] about the methodology that was used or the methodology used does not assist in determining whether the administered price is or is not reflective of what a market would yield"*,[92] alternative benchmarks were to be employed for the purpose of benefit calculation.

3.1.2.1.4.3.3 The Selection of the Alternative Benchmark

The range of potential alternative benchmarks recommended by the Appellate Body comprised *"administered prices for the same product (in the country of purchase or in other countries, subject to adjustments), provided that it was determined based on a price-setting mechanism that ensures a market outcome. Alternatively, such benchmarks were also to be found in price-discovery mechanisms such as competitive bidding or negotiated prices, which ensure that the price paid by the government is the lowest possible price offered by a willing supply contractor."*[93] Thus, in-country or adjusted out-of-country administrative prices for the same products or

---

[88] Appellate Body Reports, *Canada – Renewable Energy* and *Canada – FIT Program*, at para. 5.188.

[89] Appellate Body Reports, *Canada – Renewable Energy* and *Canada – FIT Program*, at para. 5.189.

[90] Appellate Body Reports, *Canada – Renewable Energy* and *Canada – FIT Program*, at para. 5.228.

[91] Appellate Body Reports, *Canada – Renewable Energy* and *Canada – FIT Program*, at para. 5.190.

[92] Appellate Body Reports, *Canada – Renewable Energy* and *Canada – FIT Program*, at para. 5.228.

[93] Appellate Body Reports, *Canada – Renewable Energy* and *Canada – FIT Program*, at para. 5.228.

prices resulting from price-discovery mechanisms could be referred to instead of the government-set prices.

3.1.2.1.5 Conclusion

Article 14(d) ASCM has been interpreted by the WTO judiciary to allow for the use of alternative methodologies in cases of NMES.

If in-country prices for a certain product do not exist at all or if the prices are distorted by government action, mostly becoming apparent in the situation of government predominance, which constitutes the only situation the WTO judiciary has explicitly elaborated on so far, the provision permits investigating authorities to disregard existing in-country prices and use surrogate prices for the benefit calculation instead.

Government predominance is understood as the ability to substantially influence or effectively determine the price building on the respective market. Government predominance ought to be evidenced both formally and substantively. Both market shares and market power serve as indicators to establish the government's predominant role. The presence of SOEs on the market may serve as indicator of government influence in this process. The amount of additional evidence for proving distortion varies depending on the level of government influence found to be present on the market. The higher the level of government influence, the less other evidence is required.

As regards the exact methodology for the establishment of the surrogate price, written WTO law itself only offers the general stipulation in Article 14(d), sentence 2 ASCM, that requires the relation to prevailing market conditions. To accommodate this stipulation, existing in-country prices principally have to be adjusted as far as possible before being rejectable altogether. Due to the lack of concise legal guidance, however, investigating authorities of WTO members enjoy a large amount of discretion in the determination process.

Explicitly exempt from the alternative benchmark regime of Article 14(d) ASCM, because having been deemed not to constitute market distortion, is the government creation of markets that would otherwise not exist. In such situations, the alternative benchmark regime of Article 14(d) ASCM only applies if it cannot be ascertained whether or not the government-set prices indeed reflect "true" market conditions.

3.1.2.2 The Alternative Benchmark Regime of Article 14(b) ASCM

The interpretation of Article 14(d) ASCM allowing for the use of alternative benchmark prices for the benefit calculation in NMES raised the question whether alternative benchmark regimes also existed for the other types of subsidies listed in Article 14 ASCM. Apart from Article 14(d) ASCM, this question has been subject to WTO jurisprudence with regard to Article 14(b) ASCM, which regulates government loans.

3.1.2.2.1 The Permissibility of Using Alternative Benchmarks

The permissibility to use alternative benchmark methodologies for the calculation of benefit under Article 14(b) ASCM was addressed in *US – Anti-Dumping and Countervailing Duties (China)*. Initiated by China in 2008, the dispute concerned various anti-dumping and countervailing measures of the United States on Chinese imported products, e.g. steel pipes, woven sacks and tyres.[94]

3.1.2.2.1.1 The Reasoning of the Panel

For the panel, the *"central legal question"* in the interpretation of Article 14 (b) ASCM was *"whether, and if so under what circumstances, Article 14(b) of the SCM Agreement permitted the rejection of in-country interest rates as benchmarks for government-provided loans"*.[95] The tribunal eventually answered this question in the affirmative.[96]

According to the panel, the chapeau of Article 14 ASCM set guidelines which contained flexibility with regard to the methodology to establish the benefit conferred.[97]

Moreover, it was a general principle of Article 14 ASCM to employ only *"commercial market terms"* for the comparison.[98] Hence, if market conditions were distorted, deviation from existing in-country prices had to be allowed to adhere to this general principle and to yield acceptable results for the calculation.

In addition, the use of the conditional mode (*"would pay"* and *"could [. . .] obtain"*) in Article 14(b) ASCM illustrated that real interest rates had not to be used under all circumstances but that *"some degree of approximation is inevitable"*.[99] Rather, the panel considered the *"identification of a loan benchmark pursuant to Article 14(b) [to be] a series of concentric circles"*[100] that permitted deviation from existing in-country prices as ideal benchmarks.

3.1.2.2.1.2 The Reasoning of the Appellate Body

On appeal, the Appellate Body upheld the panel's main substantive findings—despite first rephrasing the question of the panel, in that the central issue of scrutiny was not whether Article 14(b) ASCM, correspondent to Article 14(d) ASCM, also permitted out-of-country benchmarks instead of being limited to in-country

[94]https://www.wto.org/english/tratop_e/dispu_e/cases_e/ds379_e.htm (last visited 1 January 2018).

[95]Panel Report, *US – Anti-Dumping and Countervailing Duties (China)*, at para. 10.105.

[96]Panel Report, *US – Anti-Dumping and Countervailing Duties (China)*, at para. 10.130.

[97]Panel Report, *US – Anti-Dumping and Countervailing Duties (China)*, at para. 10.107.

[98]Panel Report, *US – Anti-Dumping and Countervailing Duties (China)*, at para. 10.110.

[99]Panel Report, *US – Anti-Dumping and Countervailing Duties (China)*, at para. 10.117.

[100]Panel Report, *US – Anti-Dumping and Countervailing Duties (China)*, at para. 10.118.

benchmarks because the wording of the provision contained no restriction in this regard.[101] Rather, the issue in dispute was whether Article 14(b) ASCM contained a requirement of *"strict and formalistic compliance with all the conditions specified therein"*[102]—i.e. whether it allowed for disregarding existing benchmarks under certain conditions.[103]

In the following analysis, the Appellate Body examined if *"considering the constituent elements of a benchmark loan under Article 14(b), that is 'comparable', 'commercial', and a 'loan which the firm could actually obtain on the market'"*,[104] deviation was permitted in cases where no meaningful result would be rendered by the use of existing market conditions.

"Comparable" was understood to require *"sufficient similarities for a meaningful comparison"*.[105] As the ideal loan was rarely discoverable, the wording permitted loans which did not exact the benchmark.[106]

The term *"commercial"* was seen as the key element ensuring a meaningful comparison.[107] In contrast to the panel, however, the Appellate Body did not consider a loan made by a government *ipso facto* constituting a non-commercial loan.[108] Rather, the term *"commercial"* did not comprise any presumption regarding the quality of the loan dependent on its provider.[109]

Also, the employment of the conditional mode, in that a loan which the firm could actually obtain on the market was to be used for the calculation (*"would"*; *"could"*), indicated the possibility to use fictional benchmark interest rates.[110] It ought to be oriented to the borrower's risk profile, thus also permitting to use loans not actually obtained by the firm.[111]

Rather, the Appellate Body concluded that a *"formalistic interpretation"* prevented the ASCM from serving its purpose so that the employment of an approximated loan was allowed by Article 14(b) ASCM.[112]

The benchmark loan did not have to be *"comparable in every respect"*[113]; rather, performing adjustments was inherent to the provision: Article 14(b) ASCM contained *"no inherent limitations in Article 14(b) that would prevent an investigating authority*

[101] Appellate Body Report, *US – Anti-Dumping and Countervailing Duties (China)*, at para. 472.

[102] Appellate Body Report, *US – Anti-Dumping and Countervailing Duties (China)*, at para. 482.

[103] Appellate Body Report, *US – Anti-Dumping and Countervailing Duties (China)*, at para. 472.

[104] Appellate Body Report, *US – Anti-Dumping and Countervailing Duties (China)*, at para. 475.

[105] Appellate Body Report, *US – Anti-Dumping and Countervailing Duties (China)*, at para. 476.

[106] Appellate Body Report, *US – Anti-Dumping and Countervailing Duties (China)*, at para. 476.

[107] Appellate Body Report, *US – Anti-Dumping and Countervailing Duties (China)*, at para. 478.

[108] Appellate Body Report, *US – Anti-Dumping and Countervailing Duties (China)*, at para. 479.

[109] Appellate Body Report, *US – Anti-Dumping and Countervailing Duties (China)*, at para. 478.

[110] Appellate Body Report, *US – Anti-Dumping and Countervailing Duties (China)*, at para. 480, 487.

[111] Appellate Body Report, *US – Anti-Dumping and Countervailing Duties (China)*, at para. 480.

[112] Appellate Body Report, *US – Anti-Dumping and Countervailing Duties (China)*, at para. 484.

[113] Appellate Body Report, *US – Anti-Dumping and Countervailing Duties (China)*, at para. 485.

from using as benchmarks interest rates on loans denominated in currencies other than the currency of the investigated loan, or from using proxies instead of observed interest rates, in situations where the interest rates on loans in the currency of the investigated loan are distorted and thus cannot be used as benchmarks".[114]

3.1.2.2.2 The Prerequisites for Using Alternative Benchmarks

It was then necessary to establish under which circumstances alternative interest rates may be used in the benefit calculation. Panel and Appellate Body in *US – Anti-Dumping and Countervailing Duties (China)* also addressed this question.

3.1.2.2.2.1 The Reasoning of the Panel

Correspondent to the interpretation of Article 14(d) ASCM by the Appellate Body in *US – Softwood Lumber IV*, the panel held that *"a situation in which the interest rates to commercial borrowers do not reflect the operation of market forces, but instead are distorted in the sense that they are effectively established by the government"*[115] constituted the prerequisite for deviation.

In its reasoning, the panel listed several situations it considered to be of a distortive nature. Thereby, it provided a certain degree of guidance for investigating authorities as to which specific situations were to be viewed as distortive and which were not. Wherever the differences between commercial loans and government loans of a borrower were so great that adjustments could not remedy the distortion of the government provided loan,[116] wherever the government loan proved to be the only loan of the borrower or if all its other loans were also from the government (so that no comparison to the borrower's actually received market terms is possible),[117] wherever the government acted not as implementer of general monetary policy but effectively fixed the lending rates itself,[118] or wherever the government assumed a dual role as main lender on the commercial market on the one hand and exercising control over the interest rates on the other hand,[119] the market interest rate was to prove distorted enough for investigating authorities to legally reject it.

[114]Appellate Body Report, *US – Anti-Dumping and Countervailing Duties (China)*, at para. 487.
[115]Panel Report, *US – Anti-Dumping and Countervailing Duties (China)*, at para. 10.130.
[116]Panel Report, *US – Anti-Dumping and Countervailing Duties (China)*, at para. 10.119.
[117]Panel Report, *US – Anti-Dumping and Countervailing Duties (China)*, at para. 10.119.
[118]Panel Report, *US – Anti-Dumping and Countervailing Duties (China)*, at para. 10.128 et seq.
[119]Panel Report, *US – Anti-Dumping and Countervailing Duties (China)*, at para. 10.130.

3.1.2.2.2.2 The Reasoning of the Appellate Body

The Appellate Body agreed with the interpretation of the panel.

In order to deviate from existing in-country interest rates, investigating authorities had to prove a distortion of the lending market by government actions and were subsequently permitted to employ alternative interest rates for the benefit calculation.[120]

The Appellate Body also elaborated upon *"certain circumstances"*,[121] which rendered a positive finding of distortion. It considered the actual differences between market and government loan conditions being too great for adjustment[122] and the government as effectively setting interest rates and not simply implementing general monetary policy[123] as reasons for deviation. How exactly distortion of interest rates was to be established, however, was not specified.

In opposition to the panel,[124] the Appellate Body fully rejected the option that the term *"commercial"* implied that the mere fact the loan had been provided by a government served as viable reason permitting deviation from existing interest rates.[125]

Moreover, it held that in order to rightfully employ alternative interest rates, investigating authorities did not have to establish that the government conditions of the loan were artificially low and how exactly this was caused.[126]

3.1.2.2.3 The Selection of the Alternative Benchmark

What remained to be decided on were rules or guidelines for the selection of the alternative benchmark in accordance with Article 14(b) ASCM.

3.1.2.2.3.1 The Reasoning of the Panel

The panel described the process of establishing a loan benchmark according to Article 14(b) ASCM as *"series of concentric circles"*.[127] Before an altogether constructed proxy could be resorted to, the existing in-country interest rate had to be adjusted as far as possible.

The panel did, however, provide its understanding of some fundamental elements of the perfect benchmark loan. The loan was to have to be granted around the same

---

[120] Appellate Body Report, *US – Anti-Dumping and Countervailing Duties (China)*, at para. 479, 484.

[121] Appellate Body Report, *US – Anti-Dumping and Countervailing Duties (China)*, at para. 484.

[122] Appellate Body Report, *US – Anti-Dumping and Countervailing Duties (China)*, at para. 485.

[123] Appellate Body Report, *US – Anti-Dumping and Countervailing Duties (China)*, at para. 494, 498.

[124] Panel Report, *US – Anti-Dumping and Countervailing Duties (China)*, at para. 10.111.

[125] Appellate Body Report, *US – Anti-Dumping and Countervailing Duties (China)*, at para. 479.

[126] Appellate Body Report, *US – Anti-Dumping and Countervailing Duties (China)*, at para. 506.

[127] Panel Report, *US – Anti-Dumping and Countervailing Duties (China)*, at para. 10.118.

time, possess the same structure and similar maturity as the government loan, be about the same size and be denominated in the same currency.[128] Furthermore, the risk profile of the borrower gave indications as to the commercial lending rate.[129] Thus, any constructed benchmark loan was to approximate to this kind of standard. A constructed proxy could include a *"similar commercial loan granted to another borrower with a similar credit risk profile of the investigated borrower"*,[130] if identifiable. Otherwise, a benchmark loan proxy could be constructed by the investigating authorities although the panel admitted that Article 14(b) ASCM provided *"no specific guidance as to how this would need to be done"*.[131] Either way, whether adjustments or entire proxies were employed as alternative benchmarks, *"the resulting benchmarks must be appropriate"*.[132]

Conclusively, the panel gave its definition of an ideal benchmark loan for the purpose of benchmark approximation and enclosed several suggestions for proxies. Alas, it did not provide any general instructions on the selection of the alternative benchmark.

3.1.2.2.3.2 The Reasoning of the Appellate Body

The Appellate Body agreed with the findings of the panel and all in all embarked on an approach for selecting the alternative benchmark under Article 14(b) ASCM that closely resembled the approach taken with respect to Article 14(d) ASCM.

The benchmark chosen was to approximate a commercial loan.[133] Pursuing the "concentric circle approach" in finding the appropriate benchmark interest rate, investigating authorities had to perform the necessary adjustments to ensure comparability to the investigated government loan.[134] The Appellate Body also acknowledged that in this process, the benchmark loan would not have to be in the same currency as the government loan, as this was likely to contravene the objective of Article 14 ASCM because ultimately no meaningful benchmark was yielded.[135]

But in the main points, the Appellate Body confirmed the panel's approach. It did, however, not add any more precise instructions how to select the actual alternative benchmark.

---

[128] Panel Report, *US – Anti-Dumping and Countervailing Duties (China)*, at para. 10.112.

[129] Panel Report, *US – Anti-Dumping and Countervailing Duties (China)*, at para. 10.113.

[130] Panel Report, *US – Anti-Dumping and Countervailing Duties (China)*, at para. 10.119.

[131] Panel Report, *US – Anti-Dumping and Countervailing Duties (China)*, at para. 10.119.

[132] Panel Report, *US – Anti-Dumping and Countervailing Duties (China)*, at para. 10.117.

[133] Appellate Body Report, *US – Anti-Dumping and Countervailing Duties (China)*, at para. 484.

[134] Appellate Body Report, *US – Anti-Dumping and Countervailing Duties (China)*, at para. 485 et seq.

[135] Appellate Body Report, *US – Anti-Dumping and Countervailing Duties (China)*, at para. 484, 487.

3.1.2.2.4 Conclusion

Article 14(b) ASCM was interpreted by the WTO panel and Appellate Body in *US – Anti-Dumping and Countervailing Duties (China)* to contain sufficient flexibility to allow for the deviation from existing in-country interest rates. Article 14(b) ASCM was not limited in its wording to in-country benchmarks.

The prerequisite for deviation from existing in-country interest rates was held to be a distortion of the interest rate through government actions. Both panel and Appellate Body in *US – Anti-Dumping and Countervailing Duties (China)* provided certain exemplary situations constituting distortion, thus offering at least a little guidance for investigating authorities and thus excluding some possible interpretations or approaches in connection with the prerequisites for deviation and the selection of alternative benchmark interest rates.

Neither tribunal, however, gave detailed instructions as to how the alternative benchmark interest rate for the benefit calculation was to be found. A comprehensive overall concept is still lacking. Therefore, as with Article 14(d) ASCM, the fragmentary alternative benchmark regime under Article 14(b) ASCM also equipped investigating authorities with a large amount of discretion and created legal insecurity for the countries subject to anti-subsidy investigations.

3.1.2.3 The Alternative Benchmark Regimes Under Article 14 (a) and (c) ASCM

Whether Article 14(a) and (c) ASCM allow for resorting to alternative benchmark methodologies to calculate the benefit conferred by a financial contribution of a government has not yet been subject before the WTO judiciary.

The panel in *US – Anti-Dumping and Countervailing Duties (China)* did, however, acknowledge that the concepts for alternative benchmark regimes developed for Article 14(b) and (d) ASCM were *"equally applicable [...] to Article 14 in its entirety"*.[136]

Thus, it is likely that wherever a panel or the Appellate Body gets confronted with the question whether or not Article 14(a) or (c) ASCM permitted deviation from existing in-country benchmarks in NMES, it would decide this question in the affirmative and consequently widen the scope of the alternative benchmark regimes in WTO anti-subsidy law.[137]

---

[136] Panel Report, *US – Anti-Dumping and Countervailing Duties (China)*, at para. 10.122.

[137] For an analysis of Article 14(a) and (c) ASCM regarding the permissibility of using alternative benchmarks see Sects. 2.4.2.4.1.2 and 2.4.2.4.1.4.

3.1.2.4 The Legal Impact of the Appellate Body's Alternative Benchmark Regime on Article 14 ASCM

Appellate Body jurisprudence in *US – Softwood Lumber IV* and *US – Anti-Dumping and Countervailing Duties (China)* added alternative benchmark regimes to Article 14(b) and (d) ASCM. From a legal point of view, it stands to be clarified what impact the extensive interpretation has in the WTO legal hemisphere.

3.1.2.4.1 The Legal Impact of WTO Jurisprudence

The legal boundaries within which the Appellate Body and panels are permitted to operate are set by Articles 3.2 and 19.2 DSU[138] on the one hand and Articles IX:2 and X WTO Agreement on the other.

According to Articles 3.2 and 19.2 DSU, tribunals must not *"add to or diminish the rights and obligations provided in the covered agreements"*. *Per se*, Appellate Body and panel reports are legally binding only upon the parties of the dispute. The main function of the WTO judiciary is to provide clarification regarding the existing WTO framework. It *"serves to preserve the rights and obligations of Members under the covered agreements, and to clarify the existing provisions of those agreements in accordance with customary rules of interpretation of public international law."* Such customary rules of interpretation are contained in Articles 31 and 32 VCLT.[139,140] Accordingly, wording, context as well as purpose and objective of a provision have to be examined first in order to lessen ambiguity. If the meaning of the provision then still lacks clarity, the negotiating history and the *traveaux préparatoires* may additionally be consulted.

Despite these strict legal boundaries, the Appellate Body has developed quite a taste for extensive treaty interpretation since its foundation.[141] Creating a permanent

---

[138] Understanding on Rules and Procedures governing the Settlement of Disputes, LT/UR/A-2/DS/U/1, 15 April 1994, 1869 UNTS 401.

[139] Vienna Convention on the Law of Treaties, 23 May 1969, 1155 UNTS 331.

[140] Appellate Body Report, *United States – Standards for Reformulated and Conventional Gasoline*, WT/DS2/AB/R, adopted 20 May 1996, DSR 1996:I, 3, at para. 16 et seq.; Appellate Body Report, *Japan – Taxes on Alcoholic Beverages*, WT/DS8/AB/R, WT/DS10/AB/R, WT/DS11/AB/R, adopted 1 November 1996, DSR 1996:I, 97, at para. 104; Panel Reports, *China – Measures Related to the Exportation of Various Raw Materials*, WT/DS394/R, Add.1 and Corr.1 / WT/DS395/R, Add.1 and Corr.1 / WT/DS398/R, Add.1 and Corr.1, adopted 22 February 2012, as modified by Appellate Body Reports WT/DS394/AB/R / WT/DS395/AB/R / WT/DS398/AB/R, DSR 2012:VII, 3501, at para. 7.114 et seq.; Tyagi, 15 *Journal of International Economic Law* (2012), 391, at 399; Palmeter/Mavroidis, 92 *The American Journal of International Law* (1998), 398, at 409; for details of the principles of treaty interpretation by the Appellate Body see Miranda, 9 *Global Trade and Customs Journal* (2014), 94, at 101 et seq.

[141] Steinberg, 98 *The American Journal of International Law* (2004), 247, at 255 et seq.; on the implications of a "too effective" WTO judiciary for the organisation's basic framework see Broncker s, 2 *Journal of International Economic Law* (1999), 547, at 553 et seq.

judicial body that could fill gaps and clarify ambiguities in the organisation's underlying legal framework raised the probability that such a body would tend to actually produce new law by setting legal precedent.[142] Indeed, the WTO has embarked on a process of *"judicialization"*.[143] WTO panels and the Appellate Bodies almost without exception follow their own precedent and slowly but steadily keep developing new legal rules by following a *"de facto stare decisis"*[144] approach.[145]

There are few explicit legal boundaries to these law-making tendencies.[146] The most definite is Article X WTO Agreement, assuring the WTO members' exclusive right to amend any WTO agreement. In addition, binding authoritative interpretations may only be rendered by the Ministerial Conference or the General Council (Article IX:2 WTO Agreement).

Set against this framework, the WTO judiciary is empowered to mere interpretation of the existing agreements. In interpreting it shall observe the principles of *in dubio mitius* and *non liquet*.[147] Thus, a cautious interpretative approach is warranted. The WTO judiciary may render interpretations which are binding to the parties of the respective dispute,[148] but not generally on all members.

3.1.2.4.2 The Legal Status of the Alternative Benchmark Regimes in Article 14 ASCM

The alternative benchmark regimes for Article 14(b) and (d) ASCM are therefore no formal amendments or official judicial modifications of Article 14 ASCM. The content of the provision *per se* remains unaffected by the Appellate Body's extensive interpretation.

Due to the *"de facto stare decisis"*[149] approach, however, the regimes obtained wider recognisance than formally provided for. The WTO judiciary itself tended to

[142]Steinberg, 98 *The American Journal of International Law* (2004), 247, at 252 and 257. On the reasons for the development of a powerful judiciary in times of political and legislative impotence see Ferejohn, 65 *Law and Contemporary Problems* (2002), 41, at 55 et seq.

[143]Ferejohn, 65 *Law and Contemporary Problems* (2002), 41, at 41.

[144]Steinberg, 98 *The American Journal of International Law* (2004), 247, at 254.

[145]Luo, Anti-dumping in the WTO, the EU, and China, at 98; van Damme, 21 *European Journal of International Law* (2010), 605, at 611.

[146]On the inutility of the WTO's procedural mechanisms for the clarification of rules through authoritative interpretation and amendment see Broncker s, 2 *Journal of International Economic Law* (1999), 547, at 551 et seq.

[147]Steinberg, 98 *The American Journal of International Law* (2004), 247, at 258; Qin, Wayne State University Law School Legal Studies Research Paper Series No. 09-18 (2009), 1, at 17 and 48 et seq.

[148]McNelis, 37 *Journal of World Trade* (2003), 647, at 652; Palmeter/Mavroidis, 92 *The American Journal of International Law* (1998), 398, at 404.

[149]Steinberg, 98 *The American Journal of International Law* (2004), 247, at 254.

refer to its own interpretation and apply it to subsequent disputes. This induced WTO members to consider this jurisprudence in their respective investigation practice or even in their national legislation.

3.1.3 Conclusion

Article 14 ASCM is the general WTO law provision that deals with the calculation of benefit. Of the four different types of subsidies, which are exemplarily listed in Article 14 ASCM, two types, Article 14(b) ASCM regulating government loans and Article 14(d) ASCM regulating the government provision or purchase of goods, have been interpreted by the WTO judiciary to contain an alternative benchmark regime for NMES.

In cases of non-existence or distortion of the market due to government action, existing in-country interest rates or prices may be replaced by alternative benchmarks for the purpose of benefit calculation. The causation of market distortion by a government presents itself mainly as substantive concept, asking for the government's ability to exercise influence on price building on the domestic market. Certain formal aspects like market shares constitute important indicators in the process of establishing distortion, but they are not the only evidence to be evaluated. Detailed general guidelines how the prerequisite for deviation, i.e. market distortion by the government, is to be discovered, have not yet been provided for by WTO jurisprudence.

The alternative benchmark regimes under Article 14(b) and (d) ASCM also lack precise and detailed regulations for the selection of the actual benchmark value. Thus, investigating authorities are endowed with a large amount of discretion for this determination. This raises doubts with respect to impartiality and fairness on part of the investigating authorities as well as with respect to justiciability of the findings of the investigations.

Regarding Article 14(a) and (c) ASCM, no alternative benchmark concepts have yet been developed, as the question of permissibility has not yet presented itself in front of the WTO judiciary. If that was the case, it seems very likely that Article 14 (a) and (c) ASCM will be interpreted in correspondence with their sibling provisions.

The development of alternative benchmark regimes presents itself as a process highly in motion with the WTO judiciary at its driving force—but on a weak textual basis.[150]

[150] Whether judicial interpretation by WTO Panels and the Appellate Body suffices to render legally sound alternative benchmark regimes will be addressed further below, see Sect. 5.2.3.1.6.

3.2 The China-Specific Alternative Benchmark Regime for Anti-Subsidy Investigations

Besides the general WTO framework for the use of alternative benchmark methodologies in anti-subsidy investigations in cases of NMES, which has been derived from the interpretation of Article 14 ASCM by the WTO judiciary, a China-specific WTO regime exists. It is stipulated in Section 15(b) CAP. As the rules for China constitute the most extensive set of rules existing at WTO level in this area, they merit examination to complete the picture of NMES anti-subsidy regulation.

3.2.1 The Background of the Adoption of China-Specific WTO Rules

China has presented the WTO with a large number of challenges during its process of accession. Addressing these challenges eventually led to the CAP and the Working Party Report on the Accession of China[151] containing a special set of rules that added to the general commitments China took on as a new WTO member.

3.2.1.1 The WTO Accession Process of China

Overall, the process of the accession of China to the WTO was slow and cumbersome. After applying for accession in 1986, it took 15 years of lengthy negotiations until another *"long march"*[152] in China's history was completed. Finally, China became the 143th member of the WTO on 11 December 2001.[153]

Originally, China had already been a member of the GATT 1947.[154] After the Revolution in 1949 and the flight of the *guomindang* party-led government to Taiwan, the very government declared China's withdrawal from the GATT 1947.[155] Although the newly-established communist regime in Beijing never recognised this declaration, the influential Western countries accepted this announcement at the time and continued to acknowledge the Taiwan-based government as the official government of China until 1971.[156]

[151] Report of the Working Party on the Accession of China, WT/ACC/CHN/49, 1 October 2001.

[152] Yu, 8 *Asian Journal of WTO and International Health Law* (2013), 77, at 87.

[153] Wu, 10 *Chinese Journal of International Law* (2011), 227, at 237; Gertler in Bhattasali et al. (eds.), 21, at 24.

[154] Gertler in Bhattasali et al. (eds.), at 21.

[155] Gertler in Bhattasali et al. (eds.), at 21.

[156] United Nations General Assembly Resolution 2758, A/RES/2758(XXVI), 25 October 1971; see Wu, 10 *Chinese Journal of International Law* (2011), 227, at 230; Rhodes/Jackson, 2 *Journal of International Economic Law* (1999), 497, at 499.

After starting to slowly open up its economy under Deng Xiaoping from 1978, China requested GATT observer status, which it was granted in 1984.[157] Subsequently, in 1986, it applied to revive its status as GATT contracting party.[158] In the beginning, negotiations went speedy, but were then heavily detained for several reasons.[159] Throughout the accession process of first to the GATT and after 1995 to the WTO, China promised to open up its market and conducted several reforms in this regard. Western countries, however, resented the way China tried to preserve certain elements of its centrally planned economy, pursuing a *"dual-track approach"*[160] of economic reform. Furthermore, the lack of transparency and rule of law in China's political and legal system raised fears of non-compliance with WTO obligations.[161] In addition, the foundation of the WTO raised the hurdles regarding the commitments to be undertaken on part of China.[162] Political tensions also slowed down the negotiations.[163] Throughout the whole process of accession, the fear of the incumbent WTO members of the enormous economic power China was beginning to unfold was looming constantly.[164] All in all, the climate of the negotiations can justly be described as a *"cauldron of anxiety"*,[165] preventing a timelier conclusion of the accession process, which had been the hope on both parts at the start.[166]

3.2.1.2 The Legal Basis for the Integration of a Country-Specific Legal Regime into WTO Law

Upon reflection of the WTO's founding principle of non-discrimination, the introduction of country-specific rules into its legal framework makes one wonder on what legal basis such an approach would be permitted, though, and not simply be discarded as blatant contravention against the single undertaking approach. Surprisingly, WTO law does *per se* indeed provide for this possibility.

---

[157] Hoogmartens, EC Trade Law, at 51; Wu, 10 *Chinese Journal of International Law* (2011), 227, at 230 et seq.; Gertler in Bhattasali et al. (eds.), at 21; Rhodes/Jackson, 2 *Journal of International Economic Law* (1999), 497, at 500.

[158] Hoogmartens, EC Trade Law, at 51 et seq.; Wu, 10 *Chinese Journal of International Law* (2011), 227, at 231; Gertler in Bhattasali et al. (eds.), at 21.

[159] Wu, 10 *Chinese Journal of International Law* (2011), 227, at 231 et seq.

[160] Wu, 10 *Chinese Journal of International Law* (2011), 227, at 233.

[161] Barfield/Groombridge in Ostry et al. (eds.), 30, at 31 and 36 et seq.; Wu, 10 *Chinese Journal of International Law* (2011), 227, at 233 et seq.

[162] Grynberg et al., Paying the Price for Joining the WTO, at 5; Wu, 10 *Chinese Journal of International Law* (2011), 227, at 234 et seq.

[163] Gertler in Bhattasali et al. (eds.), 21, at 22; Wu, 10 *Chinese Journal of International Law* (2011), 227, at 235.

[164] Thorstensen et al., 1 *Latin American Journal of International Trade Law* (2013), 765, at 782.

[165] Wu, 10 *Chinese Journal of International Law* (2011), 227, at 236.

[166] Wu, 10 *Chinese Journal of International Law* (2011), 227, at 232.

According to Article XII:1 WTO Agreement, if a state or separate customs territory wishes to accede to the WTO, the terms of accession are to be negotiated individually between the candidate and the WTO. Besides, there are no detailed regulations on the process of accession,[167] so that here much discretion is bestowed on the WTO Ministerial Conference, which ultimately must accept the candidate country by a two-third majority of its members (Article XII:2 WTO Agreement). In the context of accession negotiations, Article XII:1 WTO Agreement served as *"loophole in the system"*[168] that enabled the individual treatment of acceding countries, including specific regulations.

During the accession process, WTO accession candidates and the WTO membership negotiate rule-based commitments on the one hand and market access commitments on the other.[169] While rule-based commitments usually comprise the obligation of the prospective member to fully comply with existing WTO law as laid down in the WTO Agreement and its annexes, the amount of market access commitments depends on the state of openness of the candidate's national economy for imports of WTO members. Thus, the latter type of obligations is always country-specific, balancing the interests of WTO members and applicant country.[170]

Rule-based commitments, though, reflect the principle of non-discrimination and secure the binding force of the existing WTO legal acquis towards all members. This kind of commitments is usually adopted uniformly for every acceding member.[171] Exceptions have so far only occurred to a very limited extent in the case of least-developed countries. In order to facilitate their compliance with the WTO legal acquis and to accommodate their special needs, certain rights and obligations of general WTO law have sometimes been deviated from.[172] Deviations are made either way—both WTO-plus commitments and WTO-minus commitments may be agreed upon.[173] Whereas the former impose upon the acceding country additional obligations that stretch beyond those of the uniform WTO framework, WTO-minus

[167]Cattaneo/Primo Braga, Policy Research Working Paper No. 5116 (2009), 1, at 12 et seq.; Michalopoulos in Hoekman et al. (eds.), 61, at 61 et seq.; Nguyen, 22 *Temple International & Comparative Law Journal* (2008), 243, at 246 et seq; Gertler in Bhattasali et al. (eds.), at 21; Grynberg et al., Paying the Price for Joining the WTO, at 4.

[168]Qin, 55 *Virginia Journal of International Law* (2015), 369, at 389.

[169]Qin, Wayne State University Law School Legal Studies Research Paper Series No. 07-31 (2008), 1, at 5; Qin, 37 *Journal of World Trade* (2003), 483, at 484.

[170]Grynberg et al., Paying the Price for Joining the WTO, at 5; Qin, 37 *Journal of World Trade* (2003), 483, at 485.

[171]Qin, 37 *Journal of World Trade* (2003), 483, at 485.

[172]Nguyen, 22 *Temple International & Comparative Law Journal* (2008), 243, at 258.

[173]Qin, 37 *Journal of World Trade* (2003), 483, at 488 et seq.; Nguyen, 22 *Temple International & Comparative Law Journal* (2008), 243, at 257; Grynberg et al., Paying the Price for Joining the WTO, at 5 et seq. Exact definitions of the terms "WTO-plus" and "WTO-minus" are, however, still in a state of controversial academic discussion, see only Nguyen, 22 *Temple International & Comparative Law Journal* (2008), 243, at 257.

commitments preclude the application of the uniform WTO legal rules in certain areas.[174]

3.2.1.3 The Rationale of the China-Specific Provisions

In the case of the accession of China, however, the general principle that deviations from the WTO rules regime are absolutely exceptional was departed from. Besides individual market access commitments,[175] as to be expected, China also was confronted with the WTO members' efforts to agree on a massive amount of country-specific WTO legal rules of conduct.[176] After having remained unrelenting during the multilateral negotiations, China eventually consented to the special set of rules during the bilateral negotiations with the United States in order to complete the already long and cumbersome accession process.[177] The CAP, integrating miscellaneous provisions from the Working Party Report by reference, was then made an *"integral part"* of the WTO agreements (Section 1.2 CAP).[178]

Amongst these special rules was the alternative benchmark regime of Section 15 CAP. This provision has its origin in the Sino-US bilateral negotiations, with the Sino-US Agreement on the Accession of China containing the exact wording of *inter alia* Section 15(b) CAP.[179]

Considering the comparatively unusual terms of accession, one would assume that this approach has been pursued for good reason. When enquiring after the rationale of the China-specific WTO regime, however, the accession documents yield very little. More often than not the sole reason for the adoption of a special regime for China is perceived to be the wish of the other WTO members to protect their domestic producers from the *"China threat"*.[180,181] In particular with regard to WTO-minus provisions, it is hard to perceive what benefit they confer to China in

[174]Qin, 37 *Journal of World Trade* (2003), 483, at 488 and 490.

[175]For an overview and assessment of China's market accession commitments and the underlying Open Door policy (门户开放, *menhu kaifang*) see Kong, China and the World Trade Organization, at 18 et seq.

[176]Qin, Wayne State University Law School Legal Studies Research Paper Series No. 07-31 (2008), 1, at 5; on the amendments of China's foreign trade-related laws in adoption of the WTO legal acquis see He/Sappideen, 43 *Journal of World Trade* (2009), 847, at 851 et seq.

[177]Qin, 7 *Journal of International Economic Law* (2004), 863, at 913.

[178]The Working Party Report on the Accession of China was also integrated into the CAP to a large extent, see Section 342 Working Party Report of China; Qin, 7 *Journal of International Economic Law* (2004), 863, at 913; On the impact of the CAP during the first 15 years of China's membership in the WTO see Mueller, 27 *Europäische Zeitschrift für Wirtschaftsrecht* (2016), 291 et seq.

[179]Qin, 7 *Journal of International Economic Law* (2004), 863, at 913; Barry, International Economic Review (February/March 2000), at 7; Barfield/Groombridge in Ostry et al. (eds.), 30, at 32.

[180]Wu, 10 *Chinese Journal of International Law* (2011), 227, at 236.

[181]Qin, 7 *Journal of International Economic Law* (2004), 863, at 912.

the process of bringing its national law in compliance with the WTO agreements. Besides hopes of entering an emerging high potential market on improved terms and conditions, the very size of China's economy stirred fears of the impact its accession would have on the existing WTO system.[182] Thus, WTO members took full advantage of the discretion Article XII:1 WTO Agreement granted and negotiated China-specific terms of accession.[183]

Instead of concluding the *"the most one-sided trade deal in history"*[184] an approach effectively aiding China to advance its transformation into a market economy by permitting certain categories of subsidies that promote and support necessary reforms would by far have been preferable.[185] For example, it could have been distinguished between temporarily permitted subsidies to SOEs which are essential to change them into privately-owned companies and prohibited subsidies to SOEs that unjustifiably preserve or even enhance their existing prevalent market positions. This approach was, however, not embarked upon.

3.2.2 The China-Specific Alternative Benchmark Regime for NMES in Section 15(b) CAP

Altogether, Section 15 CAP deals with price comparability in anti-dumping and anti-subsidy proceedings. Section 15(a) and (d) CAP address anti-dumping law, while Section 15(b) CAP contains specific anti-subsidy rules. Section 15(c) CAP eventually addresses both types of remedies, stipulating the obligation of WTO members to notify all methodologies adopted under Section 15(a) and (b) CAP to the Committee on Anti-Dumping Practices or the Committee on Subsidies and Countervailing Measures respectively.

The relevant substantive parts of Section 15 CAP regarding the alternative benchmark regime in anti-subsidy law comprise the chapeau and Section 15 (b) CAP:

> "Article VI of the GATT 1994, the Agreement on Implementation of Article VI of the General Agreement on Tariffs and Trade 1994 ("Anti-Dumping Agreement") and the SCM Agreement shall apply in proceedings involving imports of Chinese origin into a WTO Member consistent with the following:
>
> [...]

182Thorstensen et al., 1 *Latin American Journal of International Trade Law* (2013), 765, at 782.

183Hoogmartens, EC Trade Law, at 57; Qin, 7 *Journal of International Economic Law* (2004), 863, at 913. Regarding the question whether the adoption of country-specific WTO rules commitments through accession protocols constitutes a legal and legitimate approach see Sect. 5.2.2.

184Wu, 10 *Chinese Journal of International Law* (2011), 227, at 244 (words originally used by US President Clinton).

185Qin, 7 *Journal of International Economic Law* (2004), 863, at 912.

(b) In proceedings under Parts II, III and V of the SCM Agreement, when addressing subsidies described in Articles 14(a), 14(b), 14(c) and 14(d), relevant provisions of the SCM Agreement shall apply; however, if there are special difficulties in that application, the importing WTO Member may then use methodologies for identifying and measuring the subsidy benefit which take into account the possibility that prevailing terms and conditions in China may not always be available as appropriate benchmarks. In applying such methodologies, where practicable, the importing WTO Member should adjust such prevailing terms and conditions before considering the use of terms and conditions prevailing outside China."

3.2.2.1 The Permissibility of Using Alternative Benchmarks

In contrast to Article 14 ASCM, the permissibility of deviation is explicitly stipulated in Section 15(b) CAP. When conducting unilateral anti-subsidy remedies against Chinese imports influenced by types of subsidies listed in Article 14 ASCM in accordance with Part V of the ASCM, Section 15(b) CAP orders investigating authorities to primarily apply the *"relevant provisions of the SCM Agreement"*, i.e. Article 14 ASCM, for the calculation of the amount of benefit conferred. Despite having been provided for with a separate set of rules, the general standard WTO anti-subsidy regime shall also be applied in investigations against China. The permissibility of deviation from existing Chinese market benchmarks is, *"however"*, acknowledged almost immediately afterwards in the text of Section 15(b) CAP.

3.2.2.2 The Prerequisites for the Use of Alternative Benchmarks

Investigating authorities are permitted to use alternative benchmark methodologies in cases where *"special difficulties"* in the application of the general WTO rules occur. If *"prevailing market terms and conditions in China"* no longer constitute *"appropriate benchmarks"* for the calculation, they may be rejected. Although seemingly setting clear requirements, the open nature of the terms renders it difficult to perceive their meaning.[186]

3.2.2.2.1 "Special Difficulties"

Unfortunately, the CAP itself does not contain a precise definition of the term *"special difficulties"*.

---

[186] Consentient Du, 63 *International & Comparative Law Quarterly* (2014), 409, at 433; Ahn/Lee, 14 *Journal of International Economic Law* (2011), 329, at 343; especially for the prerequisite of "special difficulties" He, The WTO and Infant Industry Promotion in Developing Countries, at 205.

3.2.2.2.1.1 The Meaning of "Special Difficulties"

A *"difficulty"* exists if *"a thing [. . .] is hard to accomplish, deal with or understand"*.[187] Thus, the application of Article 14 ASCM to China must confront investigating authorities with impediments. *"Hard"* implies that the impediment must possess a certain degree of severity. From the standard of diligence and consideration that is usually expected from investigating authorities, it is to be presumed that the degree of severity must be rather high. How high exactly, however, cannot be derived.

"Special" can denote either something *"better, greater or otherwise different from what is usual"*[188] but also something *"designed or organized for a particular person, purpose or occasion"*.[189] Although close in meaning, the precise connotations differ. In the present context of alternative benchmark regimes in anti-subsidy law, being *"different from what is usual"* merely refers to the fact that with Article 14 ASCM and Section 15(b) CAP, two different alternative benchmark regimes exist of which the latter constitutes the "unusual", i.e. the deviation from the general standard. On the other hand, perceiving the concept in Section 15(b) CAP as having been *"designed [. . .] for a particular [. . .] purpose or occasion"*, would attach it more closely to China. The *"purpose"* would refer to the rationale of the Protocol provisions, the *"occasion"* to China's accession to the WTO. Such an understanding would emphasise not so much the mere difference in regulatory content between Article 14 ASCM and Section 15(b) CAP, but rather stress the exclusiveness of the alternative benchmark regime in Section 15(b) CAP and do so without regard to the general WTO regime, it simply adheres to special legal rules for China.

But these findings do not offer much substantial guidance for practical application. The term *"special difficulties"* remains unwieldy and hardly justiciable.

3.2.2.2.1.2 The Context of "Special Difficulties"

From a systematic point of view, Section 15(b) CAP constitutes an exception from the general anti-subsidy regime of Article 14 ASCM. Thus, all difficulties also encounterable under the regular alternative benchmark regime of the ASCM could be perceived not to fall within the scope of the China Protocol, as its regime is only applicable in cases of *"special difficulties"*. The provisions would only be used whenever the difficulty of application arises in a uniquely China-specific context.[190]

---

[187] http://www.oxforddictionaries.com/definition/english/difficulty (last visited 1 January 2018).

[188] http://www.oxforddictionaries.com/definition/english/special (last visited 1 January 2018).

[189] http://www.oxforddictionaries.com/definition/english/special (last visited 1 January 2018).

[190] Gao in Deere-Birkbeck (ed.), 153, at 171, who also raises concerns that following such an interpretation, Section 15(b) CAP would be rendered virtually inapplicable.

This line of argumentation has initially been pursued by China in *US – Anti-Dumping and Countervailing Duties (China).*[191] China argued that the US authorities had rejected existing Chinese prices for the benefit calculation without having scrutinised the existence of *"special difficulties"* in the application of the general regime that justified the deviation.[192] The view of the panel remained in the dark, as both parties agreed not to pursue their arguments under Section 15(b) CAP and the panel—obviously relieved in the face of lacking distinct prerequisites and any guidance on its interpretation—consequently limited its analysis to Article 14 ASCM.[193]

3.2.2.2.1.3 "Special Difficulties" in the Light of the Rationale of the CAP

Another way to shed some light on the meaning of *"special difficulties"* could be taking into consideration the rationale of the CAP. Besides the protectionist tendency,[194] the clear intention of the drafters was to address concerns specifically attached to economy, political framework and demographic structure of China. Taking this into account, *"special difficulties"* could refer to problems arising in the application of anti-subsidy law that are genuinely China-specific.

China-specific difficulties in a wider sense could include all problems that somehow arise in connection with China, but could possibly also create an impediment in the course of investigations against other countries. China-specific problems in a narrow sense would, on the other hand, only cover problems that exclusively exist with regard to China. Any general legal applicability problems would not be addressed, but only difficulties deriving from the special nature of China.

Hence, Section 15(b) CAP would be applicable in cases where legal problems arise in resorting to the general anti-subsidy regime and these problems are to a certain extent—either remotely or exclusively—connected to China.

3.2.2.2.1.4 The Genesis of "Special Difficulties"

The term *"special difficulties"* has a history dating back to the early days of the GATT. For the first time, the term *"special difficulties"* appeared in the *ad* note to Article VI:1 GATT 1947. As already laid down above, Article VI:1(b) GATT 1947 lays down an alternative benchmark regime for the dumping margin calculation.[195] In number 2, the *ad* note recognises that *"in the case of imports from a country which has a complete or substantially complete monopoly of its trade and where all*

[191] Request for Consultations by China, *US – Anti-Dumping and Countervailing Duties (China)*, WT/DS379/1, 22 September 2008, at p. 4.

[192] Panel Report, *US – Anti-Dumping and Countervailing Duties (China)*, at para. 10.10, footnote 460.

[193] Panel Report, *US – Anti-Dumping and Countervailing Duties (China)*, at para. 10.12.

[194] See Sect. 3.2.1.3.

[195] See Sect. 3.1.1.1.

domestic prices are fixed by the state, special difficulties may exist in determining price comparability [...] and in such cases importing contracting parties may find it necessary to take into account the possibility that a strict comparison with domestic prices in such a country may not always be appropriate". Putting it briefly, *"special difficulties"* justify the application of alternative benchmarks in the calculation of the dumping margin because domestic normal values are *"not [...] appropriate"*.

The *ad* note itself does, however, not provide any guidance with regard to how *"special difficulties"* are defined and no such attempt has ever been made by the contracting parties.[196] For more insight, one has to look at the genesis of the *ad* note.

3.2.2.2.1.4.1 The Origin of "Special Difficulties"

The term *"special difficulties"* has its roots in the GATT review session of 1954–55.[197] During this review session, Czechoslovakia proposed an amendment of Article VI:1 GATT 1947. It expressed concern that Article VI:1 GATT 1947 did not satisfactorily address the establishment of price comparability in state-trading countries, one of which Czechoslovakia had just turned into.[198] The government feared this kind of countries would be disadvantaged by the use of existing in-country prices for the calculation of the dumping margin. Article VI:1 GATT 1947 only addressed the question of alternative methodologies in cases of absence of an in-country price. In a state trading economy, however, domestic prices were not absent, but set centrally and independently by the state. Export prices thus tended to be lower, which consequently resulted in a finding of dumping by other countries.

Czechoslovakia therefore suggested to amend Article VI:1(b) GATT 1947 to preferentially allow for the resort to alternative methodologies in each case the price of products from such countries was calculated.[199] In detail, it proposed that *"to remove difficulties caused by the application of certain standards relating to the definition of normal value in paragraph 1 of Article VI – which difficulties are due to the fact that no comparison of export prices with prices in the domestic market of the exporting country is possible when such domestic prices are not established as a result of fair competition in that market but are fixed by the state"*.

Thus, the term *"difficulties"* was used to circumscribe the situation of mismatched price comparison in the calculation of the dumping margin in cases of government-fixed prices in a state economy.

This strikes as remarkable. It signifies that the use of alternative methodologies for establishing surrogate prices was intended to result in a fairer and less arbitrary

---

[196]Hu in Hu et al. (eds.), 137, at 151.

[197]Van Bael/Bellis, EU Anti-Dumping and Other Trade Instruments, at 140.

[198]Thorstensen et al., 1 *Latin American Journal of International Trade Law* (2013), 765, at 778.

[199]Proposals by the Czechoslovak Delegation, W.9/86, 9 December 1954.

treatment of state-trading countries, as the employment of existing in-country prices would almost invariably result in a positive finding of dumping.[200]

Instead of pursuing the proposed amendment of Article VI:1 GATT 1947, the GATT 1947 CONTRACTING PARTIES issued an interpretative note.[201] In this note, the GATT 1947 Contracting Parties recognised that regarding countries, which have *"a complete or substantially complete monopoly of their trade and where all domestic prices are fixed by the state, special difficulties may exist in determining price comparability for the purposes of paragraph 1, and in such cases importing contracting parties may find it necessary to take into account the possibility that a strict comparison with domestic prices in such a country may not always be appropriate"*.

Although not plainly perceivable, the GATT contracting parties principally adopted the Czechoslovak proposal, albeit in somewhat mysterious language. As implied by the proposal, the alternative benchmark regime in Article VI:1(2) GATT 1947 was deemed applicable only to market economy countries.[202] Otherwise, it would not have been considered necessary to amend or clarify anything with regard to NME countries. Besides lowering the values of the alternative benchmarks, e.g. by not choosing the highest comparable third-country price, but only the average price, it was the aim of the Czechoslovak proposal to amplify the scope of the types of economies covered by the alternative benchmark regime of Article VI:1 GATT 1947. By acknowledging that *"special difficulties"* in the application of the general methodologies for the benefit calculation existed also with respect to NME countries as defined in the interpretative note, the CONTRACTING PARTIES abided by the general idea of reform expressed by Czechoslovakia. A *"strict comparison with domestic prices"* from a NME country, which would have been the result under Article VI:1 GATT 1947 as it stood, was considered to be *"not always [...] appropriate"*.

Thus, all the interpretative note was designed for was approving that alternative benchmarks should also be applicable in anti-dumping investigations against state-trading countries to result in their overall fairer treatment.

3.2.2.2.1.4.2 The Evolution of "Special Difficulties"

In the course of time, however, the comportment of the WTO members' investigating authorities fundamentally changed the impact of the interpretative note.[203] Instead of protecting NME countries from unfair findings of dumping, the alternative benchmark regime was used to deliberately substitute existing in-country prices by

[200]Polouektov, 36 *Journal of World Trade* (2002), 1, at 7; Thorstensen et al., 1 *Latin American Journal of International Trade Law* (2013), 765, at 778.

[201]Polouektov, 36 *Journal of World Trade* (2002), 1, at 6 et seq.; Thorstensen et al., 1 *Latin American Journal of International Trade Law* (2013), 765, at 778.

[202]Lynam, 42 *Case Western Reserve Journal of International Law* (2010), 739, at 754.

[203]Polouektov, 36 *Journal of World Trade* (2002), 1, at 7.

much higher prices from third countries, subsequently resulting in higher dumping margins and higher anti-dumping duties. The term *"special difficulties"* was not regarded in the light of its historic genesis, or even as real legal prerequisite for the deviation from existing in-country prices after thorough establishment of its fulfilment, but rather as a soft term allowing for the rejection of domestic prices at the discretion of the investigating authority.[204] Thereby, instead of improving the protection of NME countries, the content of the interpretative note has been twisted to effect the exact opposite of its intention.[205]

The problems of arbitrariness and misuse that later arose from the interpretative note are due to the fact that the note does not specify which benchmark regime exactly is to be applied to state-trading countries. Whether the benchmark regime for market economies in Article VI:1 GATT 1947 was applicable, a separate benchmark regime for NME countries, or whether the choice of alternative methodologies was placed entirely in the discretion of the investigating authority, i.e. depending on every single case, was completely left open. The first option seems most likely, but the wording of the *ad* note leaves a lot of room for interpretation.

3.2.2.2.1.4.3 The Application of "Special Difficulties" Towards China

The fact that the term *"special difficulties"* is by its origin inherently connected to state-trading economies gives rise to ambiguities in its application to China. Does this connection also automatically transfer to China the status of a state-trading country? Or rather the opposite, does it constitute an additional requirement for the application of the China-specific alternative benchmark regime in the sense that the state-trading character of China must be established by investigating authorities? Or was the term only transferred in an adapted meaning and does no longer include a reference to state-trading countries when applied under the CAP?

Albeit still possessing NME features,[206] China today does no longer qualify as a state-trading country as defined in the *ad* note Article VI:1 GATT 1947, i.e. *"a country which has a complete or substantially complete monopoly of its trade and where all the prices are fixed by the State"*.[207] Rather, market reforms have created a

---

[204]He, The WTO and Infant Industry Promotion in Developing Countries, at 205.

[205]Polouektov, 36 *Journal of World Trade* (2002), 1, at 7; Thorstensen et al., 1 *Latin American Journal of International Trade Law* (2013), 765, at 778.

[206]On the state of internal reform of China's former state economy into a market economy see Du, 63 *International & Comparative Law Quarterly* (2014), 409, at 413 et seq; on the degree of subsidisation that is still present China's steel, glass, paper and auto-parts industries see Haley/Haley, Subsidies to Chinese Industry, at 56 et seq.

[207]Consenting Watson, Free Trade Bulletin No. 65 (2016), 1, at 2; Michalopoulos in Hoekman et al. (eds.), 61, at 68; Du, 63 *International & Comparative Law Quarterly* (2014), 409, at 410; He/Sappideen, 43 *Journal of World Trade* (2009), 847, at 864; Szamosszegi/Kyle, An Analysis of State-owned Enterprises and State Capitalism in China, 1, at 4.

form of state capitalist economy with the state as leading actor on the market.[208] Consequently, the view that *"special difficulties"* in the CAP also transferred to China the status of a state-trading country within the meaning of the ad note is highly problematic. This approach would persevere an anachronistic feature of GATT law without factual grounds.

Instead, as the characterisation as state-trading economy in the understanding of the *ad* note constitutes a prerequisite for the use of the alternative benchmarks, it could be argued that the integration of the term *"special difficulties"* into Section 15 (b) CAP also transferred this requirement as "unwritten annex". Before applying the China-specific regime, investigating authorities would first have to establish the state-trading character of China's economy.[209] As this will hardly be feasible, the application of Section 15(b) CAP will be made nearly impossible.

Because only the term *"special difficulties"* by itself was integrated into the CAP, however, it could also be contended that thereby, its connection to state-trading countries has been cut and it has been integrated into Section 15(b) CAP only in a respectively adapted meaning.[210] Transferring the term into the CAP would have acknowledged that benchmark problems cannot arise only with respect to full state-trading economies, but also "lesser forms" of non-market economies. In its adapted meaning, the term would then signify that the provision was designed to address difficulties in the use of alternative benchmark methodologies in anti-subsidy investigations that arise because of NME features, which are still part of China's economic system today.

Which understanding prevails cannot be established beyond doubt. In addition, with the preparatory work of a treaty and the circumstances of its conclusion serving only as supplementary means of interpretation (Article 32 VCLT),[211] the findings from historical interpretation are not to be attested too much significance, especially in the present case, where not the preparatory work and circumstances of the relevant provision itself but of the "parental" provision with the same wording, but a completely different context in time and occasion is scrutinised. Nevertheless, because the application of *"special difficulties"* within the China-specific context of Section 15(b) CAP yields nothing definite, the historical dimension is not to be

---

[208]Du, 63 *International & Comparative Law Quarterly* (2014), 409, at 410, also for a discussion of the term "state capitalism".

[209]*Cornelis* argues in this way. According to him, the only legally feasible solution to continue the application of the NMES methodologies to China after its WTO accession, is via Note 2 *Ad* Article VI:1 GATT. Thus, investigating authorities would have to prove that China still was a state-trading economy in the sense of the *ad* note. Because this would have turned out impossible, upon accession, the adoption of Section 15(a) CAP for the purpose of securing further applicability of the alternative benchmark regime for NMES in anti-dumping investigation was essential, see Cornelis, 2 *Global Trade and Customs Journal* (2007), 105, at 108 et seq.

[210]The approach corresponds the concept of autonomous meaning, that only takes into account a meaning that can be attributed to a wording as part of a certain treaty and rejects any comparison with or transfer from other treaties. For details see Orakhelashvili, The Interpretation of Acts and Rules in Public International Law, at 335 et seq.

[211]See Sect. 3.1.2.4.1.

completely discarded, in particular as it lets shine through a ray of the often presumed "rationale" behind the China-specific provisions.[212]

3.2.2.2.2 "Appropriateness" of Using Existing Chinese Benchmarks

When an existing benchmark is no longer deemed *"appropriate"* for use is hard to determine.

The term *"appropriate"* can be described as *"suitable or proper in the circumstances"*.[213] This signifies that the in-country price used for the calculation of the benefit is not meaningful, as there are *"circumstances"* which render its use of little value in determining and fully offsetting the actual benefit through a matching amount of duty. By itself, however, the wording does not set any standard against which appropriateness could be measured. Thus, the interpretation of the wording itself does not bring further clarification.

Taking additionally into account the implications of the *ad* note Article VI:1 GATT 1947, the *"circumstances"* rendering the existing price insignificant would account to constitute aforementioned *"special difficulties"* caused by prices being fixed by the state. Thus, each time a price is set by a government, it is considered not to be *"appropriate"* for the calculation of the dumping margin.

It is likely but cannot be taken for granted, however, that Section 15(b) CAP mirrors the understanding of *"appropriate"* in the meaning of the ad note Article VI:1 GATT. Thus, while the term can be filled with some significance in relation to the stipulations of the *ad* note, it remains uncertain whether these results can be transferred to interpret Section 15(b) CAP.

3.2.2.3 The Selection of the Alternative Benchmark

For the selection of the alternative benchmark, other *"methodologies for identifying and measuring the subsidy benefit"* may be employed. The plural *"methodologies"* already implies that both in-country and out-of-country alternative benchmarks may be used.[214] In its sentence 2, Section 15(b) CAP does indeed explicitly allow the resort to *"terms and conditions prevailing outside China"*. Before out-of-country benchmarks may be chosen as surrogates, the investigating authority *"should adjust"* existing Chinese in-country values. An exception of previous adjustment is granted in cases where it is not *"practicable"*. Again, the wording of the CAP leaves much room for interpretation. Neither does it clarify which alternative methodologies exactly may be used nor is in any way indicated when the adjustment

---

[212] See Sect. 3.2.1.3.

[213] http://www.oxforddictionaries.com/definition/english/appropriate (last visited 1 January 2018).

[214] See the correspondent reasoning of the Appellate Body in *US – Softwood Lumber IV* with respect to the term "any method", Appellate Body Report, *US – Softwood Lumber IV*, at para. 91.

of Chinese benchmarks is no longer *"practicable"*, i.e. when immediate resort to out-of-country benchmarks is granted.

3.2.2.3.1 The Meaning of "Practicable"

The term *"practicable"* has not been used as legal prerequisite in WTO law before.

"Practicable" can be circumscribed as *"able to be done or put into practice successfully"*.[215] This could indicate that an adjustment of existing prices must be manageable within due time and measure and yield a result employable for the benefit calculation. Put differently, investigating authorities are to primarily use corrected domestic prices, if this is somehow feasible with a meaningful result within reasonable time. This interpretation would follow the principle of good faith or *bona fide*, which the Appellate Body has recognised as a general principle in international law and WTO law.[216] Wherever a member is granted a right it must not exercise this right in an abusive manner, but reasonably.[217]

But nothing in Section 15(b) CAP or other WTO law indicates the efforts that can be "reasonably" expected to be undertaken by investigating authorities in the adjustment of prices, or whether the efforts actually displayed were "reasonable", and it is hence "impracticable" to adjust the existing in-country price because it is indeed too heavily distorted. The circumscriptive definition as well as the reference to *bona fide* in Appellate Body jurisprudence do eventually not add clarity.

3.2.2.3.2 The Compulsory Nature of the Adjustment Requirement

Section 15(b) CAP states that existing in-country benchmarks *"should be adjusted"* before their rejection and resort to alternative benchmarks is allowed. It is questionable whether this obliges the investigating authority to adjust the existing in-country benchmark or merely offers the choice to adjust it subject to the authority's discretion. This depends on the mandatory character of the word *"should"*.

On the one hand, *"should"* is *"used to indicate obligation, duty or correctness"*.[218] This would imply that investigating authorities are mandatorily required to adjust existing benchmarks in all cases. Only if an adjustment is completely and utterly impossible, the use of alternative benchmarks is permitted.

---

[215] http://www.oxforddictionaries.com/definition/english/practicable (last visited 1 January 2018).

[216] Appellate Body Report, *United States – Import Prohibition of Certain Shrimp Products*, WT/DS58/AB/R, adopted 6 November 1998, at para. 158; Appellate Body Report, *United States – Tax Treatment for "Foreign Sales Corporations"*, WT/DS108/AB/R, adopted 20 March 2000, at para. 166; in particular in connection with trade remedies (anti-dumping) Appellate Body Report, *United States – Anti-Dumping Measures on Certain Hot-Rolled Steel Products from Japan*, WT/DS184/AB/R, adopted 23 August 2001, at para. 101.

[217] Appellate Body Report, *US –Shrimp*, at para. 158.

[218] http://www.oxforddictionaries.com/definition/english/should (last visited 1 January 2018).

On the other hand, *"should"* is also *"indicating a desirable or expected state"*.[219] From this point of view, investigating authorities would not be bound to adjust prices. As being merely desirable, it would fully suffice if they briefly consider the possibility of adjustment and then resort to alternative benchmarks without much deliberation. Being expected to adjust would signify that existing in-country benchmarks do in principle have to be adjusted. Unlike an obligation, however, deviation from existing benchmarks is possible at an earlier stage, i.e. not only when using existing prices or rates is completely impossible, but e.g. already when the adjustment can only be conducted with utmost efforts.

Lastly, the use of the term *"should"* in Section 15(b) CAP leaves open whether it imposes on investigating authorities an obligation to adjust or grants them full discretion whether or not to adjust in-country prices.

3.2.2.3.3 The Range of Potential Alternative Benchmark Methodologies

Unlike, for instance, Article VI:1(2) GATT 1947, Section 15(b) CAP does not contain any indication to the alternative benchmark methodologies that are available for the determination of in-country price or interest rate substitutes. Thus, this determination again falls completely in the discretion of investigating authorities. The lack of a codified alternative benchmark regime as standard of reference or control weakens judicial scrutiny of the investigating authorities' decisions.

3.2.3 The Integration of the China-Specific Alternative Benchmark Regime into General WTO Anti-Subsidy Law

The chapeau of Section 15 CAP connects the China-specific alternative benchmark regime of Section 15(b) CAP with general WTO anti-subsidy law and thus provides China with a comprehensive legal framework in this area.

The chapeau lists the general WTO law provisions that are modified by Section 15 CAP as a whole and contains regulations regarding the relationship between the general and the China-specific anti-subsidy rules. According to the chapeau, the ASCM is to be applied in proceedings against China *"consistent with the following"* regulations laid down in Section 15 CAP. *"Consistent with"* is to be understood as *"compatible or in agreement with something"*.[220] Thus, general WTO law in form of the ASCM only remains applicable as long as it does not contravene the special provisions of the CAP.

[219] http://www.oxforddictionaries.com/definition/english/should (last visited 1 January 2018).

[220] http://www.oxforddictionaries.com/definition/english/consistent (last visited 1 January 2018).

3.2.3.1 The Rank of Accession Protocols in WTO Law

The compatibility of China's special WTO anti-subsidy law with the general provisions depends on the legal relationship of the respective provisions. But the exact legal rank of accession protocols within the WTO legal framework remains unclear to date.[221]

3.2.3.1.1 The Rank of Accession Protocols According to the Protocol Provisions

As commonly stated in the accession protocols themselves, in the case of China in Section 1.2 CAP, the accession commitments form an *"integral part of the WTO Agreement"*. The same phrasing is used in Article II:2 WTO Agreement, which describes the relationship between the WTO Agreement and the annexed multilateral trade agreements, e.g. GATT and ASCM. The actual legal relationship between the WTO Agreement and the multilateral agreements in cases where a conflict of law occurs is, however, addressed separately by Article XVI:3 WTO Agreement, so that the use of the *"integral part"* terminology does *per se* not already indicate which legal rank is conferred to accession protocols.

3.2.3.1.2 The Rank of Accession Protocols According to the WTO Appellate Body

In WTO jurisprudence, the question of legal rank of accession protocols posed itself in *China – Rare Earths*. Here, the Appellate Body considered at length the interaction between the CAP on the one hand and the WTO Agreement and its annexes on the other hand.[222] It held that the accession commitments, *"[j]ust as the Multilateral Trade Agreements"*,[223] formed an *"an integral part of the Marrakesh Agreement"*[224] and thereby of the *"single package of WTO rights and obligations"*.[225] The accession protocols would thus be attributed the same legal rank as the multilateral trade agreements in Annex 1 A of the WTO

[221]Qin, 55 *Virginia Journal of International Law* (2015), 369, at 400; Qin, Wayne State University Law School Legal Studies Research Paper Series No. 09-18 (2009), 1, at 7; Van Damme, Treaty Interpretation by the WTO Appellate Body, at 641; Tyagi, 15 *Journal of International Economic Law* (2012), 391, at 418 et seq.

[222]Appellate Body Reports, *China – Measures Related to the Exportation of Rare Earths, Tungsten, and Molybdenum*, WT/DS431/AB/R / WT/DS432/AB/R / WT/DS433/AB/R, adopted 29 August 2014, DSR 2014:III, 805, at para. 5.52 et seq.; Qin, 55 *Virginia Journal of International Law* (2015), 369, at 426 et seq.

[223]Appellate Body Report, *China – Rare Earths*, at para. 5.57.

[224]Appellate Body Report, *China – Rare Earths*, at para. 5.57.

[225]Appellate Body Report, *China – Rare Earths*, at para. 5.62.

Agreement.[226] The relationship between the agreements, however, could not be determined in the abstract, but had to be ascertained for every kind of obligation on a *"case-by-case basis"*.[227] The relevant pairs of rights and obligations in multilateral agreements and accession protocols were to be discovered by *"an objective link"*[228] between them. A general rule did not exist.

3.2.3.2 The Implications of the Chapeau for China's Alternative Benchmark Regime

For the question of China's applicable WTO anti-subsidy law, the *"objective link"*-jurisprudence of the Appellate Body is of little practical value. Article 14 ASCM is the only general provision in WTO law that addresses the benefit calculation in anti-subsidy investigations and thus is invariably linked to Section 15(b) CAP. The area of alternative benchmark regimes in anti-subsidy law is one of the few areas where the principal relationship between general and country-specific provision is already explicitly legally provided for. But this does not mean that the relationship is also immediately substantially clear.

While Section 15(b) CAP orders the primary application of Article 14 ASCM, the chapeau apparently states vice versa—which makes one wonder whether Section 15 CAP inheres a logical contradiction. From a systemic point of view, the chapeau is the "roof" of Section 15, being applicable to the entire section. One could argue that this bestows on it a legally higher rank than paragraph (b). On the other hand, paragraph (b) could be regarded as *lex specialis* for the regulation of the relationship between CAP and Article 14 ASCM in general WTO law. Considering the objective of the CAP, it would be paradoxical if in cases of conflict the general WTO provisions prevailed. Rather, the tailored rules of the CAP should be applicable.

Taking into consideration the legal situation at the time of enactment of the CAP in 2001 adds to the confusion on the applicable legal anti-subsidy regime. When the drafters of the CAP included a reference to the general provisions of the ASCM, the general WTO anti-subsidy framework had not yet been interpreted to include the use of alternative benchmarks in cases of NMES. Thus, the alternative benchmark methodologies in Section 15(b) CAP had been a real novelty in the area of anti-

[226]Qin, 55 *Virginia Journal of International Law* (2015), 369, at 426.

[227]Appellate Body Report, *China – Rare Earths*, at para. 5.55 and 5.57.

[228]Appellate Body Report, *China – Rare Earths*, at para. 5.57. and 5.61. By its reasoning, the Appellate Body dismissed a promising rule of conflict, Article 30(3) VCLT, as being *"not [..] apposite"*, Appellate Body Report, *China – Rare Earths*, at para. 5.70. This is heavily criticised by Qin, 55 *Virginia Journal of International Law* (2015), 369, at 428 et seq., who subsequently offers proposals for the necessary missing WTO provisions to solve the legal conflict. In particular, *Qin* rejects the "objective link" approach and suggests "systemic coherence" as guiding principle for the interpretation of the relationship between a general WTO provision and an accession protocol provision, see Qin, Wayne State University Law School Legal Studies Research Paper Series No. 2016-05 (2016), 1, at 20 et seq.

subsidy law, and genuinely China-specific law. The development of an alternative benchmark regime in general WTO anti-subsidy was not foreseeable at that time. No conflict existed that Section 15(b) CAP could possibly have been designed to address.[229]

The progressing extensive interpretation of Article 14 ASCM by the Appellate Body in *US – Softwood Lumber IV* and *US – Anti-Dumping and Countervailing Duties (China)* lets one wonder how this affected the legal framework of China's WTO anti-subsidy law. Put differently, what does still remain "specific" about the China-specific provisions? It has to be asked whether the general regime has by now even superseded the China-specific in its rigour, so that it would actually be more advantageous for China to invoke Section 15(b) CAP in front of the WTO judiciary instead of the general regime.[230] In fact, by today several options regarding the applicable legal provisions exist.

3.2.3.2.1 The Alternative Benchmark Regime of China at the Time of Conclusion

The alternative benchmark regime for China at the time of conclusion of the CAP was rather straightforward. As Article 14 ASCM did not yet provide for the possibility of using alternative benchmarks, *"special difficulties"* were the only way to disregard Chinese prices and to employ a surrogate price for the calculation of benefit. Thus, the rules for China, though ultimately tainted by ambiguous wordings, were at least clear as regards their applicable legal framework. Whenever market conditions were deemed deficient in China, resort to the alternative benchmark regime was granted. All in all, China's applicable alternative benchmark regime at WTO level comprised one single model: the general MES regime of Article 14 ASCM and the China-specific NMES regime of Section 15(b) CAP (basic model).

3.2.3.2.2 The Impact of *US – Softwood Lumber IV*

By interpreting Article 14(d) ASCM to allow for the use of alternative benchmarks in NMES, the decision of the Appellate Body in *US – Softwood Lumber IV* in 2004 blurred the line of strict separation between general and China-specific NMES

[229] Mueller, 50 *Journal of World Trade* (2016), 867, at 872 et seq.

[230] China initially alleged contraventions of the US authorities against Section 15(b) CAP in its Request for Consultations in *US – Anti-Dumping and Countervailing Duties (China)* but dropped its claims later, see Panel Report, *US – Anti-Dumping and Countervailing Duties (China)*, at para. 10.10, footnote 460. In *US – Countervailing Measures (China)* China opened its Request for Consultations with an allegation that the US had violated Section 15 CAP, but did not raise any precise claims in this regard, see Request for Consultations by China, *US – Countervailing Measures (China)*, WT/DS437/1, 30 May 2012, at p. 1.

regime. It became uncertain whether the reference in Section 15(b) CAP, ordering the application of Article 14 ASCM before resorting to the China-specific rules, included the newly-derived NME rules, or if for China, Section 15(b) CAP still constituted the only possibility to disregard existing Chinese conditions. Put differently, it was to be questioned whether the reference in the CAP to Article 14 ASCM was of a static or a dynamic character.[231] Formerly, the WTO Appellate Body exercised a narrow "*textualist approach*"[232] and would very likely have answered this question in favour of the former alternative. But in the last years, the reasoning of the Appellate Body has become more holistic, and more often than not its findings relied on subsequent evolution of WTO law,[233] so that the latter alternative would seem its option of choice of today. In any case, following *US – Softwood Lumber IV*, the variety of options regarding the interdependency of Article 14 ASCM and Section 15(b) CAP broadened.

Now, according to model 1 deeming the reference in Section 15(b) CAP static in nature, *US – Softwood Lumber IV* is not applicable towards China. With the interpretation of Article 14(d) ASCM not being China-specific, it could not derogate the special regime set down in the China Accession Protocol.[234]

Model 2 designates the reference to Article 14 ASCM in Section 15(b) CAP to be of a dynamic nature. The *US – Softwood Lumber IV* ruling is therefore considered applicable towards China.

Here, two alternatives have, however, to be distinguished. On the one hand, it is possible that the prerequisites formulated by the Appellate Body in *US – Softwood Lumber IV* are the only prerequisites applicable to Article 14(d)-type subsidies (Model 2 a). The legality of the provision of goods and services or purchases by the government at less than adequate remuneration is judged only according to general WTO law requirements. The China-specific regime of Section 15(b) CAP is narrowed down in its applicability to Article 14(a)-, (b)- and (c)-type subsidies. On the other hand, the prerequisites of *US – Softwood Lumber IV* and the CAP may be applicable jointly to Article 14(d)-type subsidies (Model 2 b).

---

[231]Regarding concept and evolution of treaty interpretation in general international law see Dawidowicz, 24 *Leiden Journal of International Law* (2011), 201; Inagaki, 22 *Journal of International Cooperation Studies* (2005), 127; van Alstine, 146 *University of Pennsylvania Law Review* (1998), 687; Jackson, 98 *The American Journal of International Law* (2004), 109, at 111 et seq. On how evolutive treaty interpretation can alter the character of an international organisation see Arato, 38 *Yale Journal of International Law* (2013), 289.

[232]Qin, Wayne State University Law School Legal Studies Research Paper Series No. 09-18 (2009), 1, at 13.

[233]Inagaki, 22 *Journal of International Cooperation Studies* (2005), 127, at 136 and 140; Qin, Wayne State University Law School Legal Studies Research Paper Series No. 09-18 (2009), 1, at 16; Torp, 6 *European Journal of Legal Studies* (2013), 127, at 131 et seq.; van Damme, Treaty Interpretation by the WTO Appellate Body, at 646.

[234]Lynam, 42 *Case Western Reserve Journal of International Law* (2010), 739.

Model 2 b can be subcategorised further into three options depending on the prerequisites forming one single or two separate sets of rules (one-tier or two-tier test).

First, the prerequisites applicable to decide whether the use of alternative benchmarks against China is justified are the ones of both Article 14 ASCM and Section 15 (b) CAP, being examined jointly in a two-tier test. The respective determination of the alternative benchmark is hence in accordance with WTO law, if e.g. both the requirements of *"market distortion by government predominance"* and *"special difficulties"* are met (model 2 bi).

Secondly, Article 14 ASCM and Section 15(b) CAP can be merged into one single set of rules (model 2 bii). Here, three options are distinguishable further, depending on the respective understanding of *"consistent with"* in the chapeau of Section 15 CAP.

In the first option, Article 14(d) ASCM predominates. Although the wording of the chapeau appears to rule out possible prevalence of the ASCM by implying preponderance of the special CAP rules, it could likewise be argued that Section 15(b) merely refers to the ASCM regime without further ado, so that a prevalence of e.g. Article 14(d)'s *"market distortion by government predominance"* is in fact possible (model 2 biiα).

According to the second option, Section 15(b) CAP is upheld in cases of conflict, promoting e.g. the *"special difficulties"* regulation (model 2biiβ).

The third option presents itself in two shapes. It is based on an understanding of *"consistent with"* as "not contravening"—i.e. not as demanding strict prevalence of either one or the other set of rules, but allowing for a more flexible approach. More favourable requirements of either Article 14 ASCM (model 2 biiγ(1)) or Section 15 (b) CAP (model 2 biiγ(2)) thus remain applicable as long as they are in accordance with the CAP. Although hardly predictable at present, this option will become a real alternative once the Appellate Body has elaborated on the content of the respective prerequisites. For example, if findings of investigating authorities clearly constitute *"government predominance"*, but on the other hand, it is unsure whether they also fulfil the *"special difficulties"* requirement, the selection of an alternative benchmark will still be justified.

Thirdly, Article 14 ASCM and Section 15(b) CAP could be applied consecutively (model 2 biii). In contrast to the two-tier model 2 bi, this model would in a first step require to examine the prerequisites of Article 14 ASCM. Only if these prerequisites are not met, the China-specific regime of Section 15(b) CAP may be resorted to. The requirements of Article 14 ASCM and Section 15(b) CAP are scrutinised one after another.

3.2.3.2.3 The Impact of *US – Anti-Dumping and Countervailing Duties (China)*

US – Anti-Dumping and Countervailing Duties (China) contributed further to the system set up in *US – Softwood Lumber IV*. In particular, it provided a certain amount of clarification regarding the applicable regime by narrowing down the huge variety of possibilities.

With the transfer of the permissibility to use alternative benchmark methodologies in the benefit calculation of Article 14(b)-type subsidies, all model-2-varieties have to be adapted, so that the general alternative benchmark regime also extends to loans.

Furthermore, with *US – Anti-Dumping and Countervailing Duties (China)* being a genuinely China-related case, the Appellate Body ruled out model 1. By applying *US – Softwood Lumber IV* on China without further ado, the Appellate Body implicitly answered the question of static or dynamic interpretation. The view of the reference to Article 14 ASCM in Section 15(b) CAP being of a static nature is obsolete.

3.2.3.2.4 The Comprehensive WTO Alternative Benchmark Regime for China in Anti-Subsidy Law

Today, each still possible applicability model combines in some way both Article 14 ASCM and Section 15(b) CAP.

3.2.3.2.4.1 The Different Models of Alternative Benchmark Regimes

After the *US – Anti-Dumping and Countervailing Duties (China)* decision in 2011, still constituting the latest major development in the evolution of the general alternative benchmark regime of Article 14 ASCM, the framework for the determination of price comparability in anti-subsidy investigations against China comes down to the following different models, of which the table presents an overview (Table 3.1).

For now, each of the models is compatible with the parole of the Appellate Body that all applicable provisions of the WTO framework have to be given effect in the interpretation of the framework.[235] Only once the Appellate Body will have extended Article 14 ASCM to contain the permissibility of deviation according to the *US – Softwood Lumber IV* principles for all types of subsidies, model 2 a, solely relying on Article 14 ASCM in NMES, will contravene this requirement, because it renders the second part of Section 15(b) CAP virtually inapplicable.

3.2.3.2.4.2 Indications Regarding Prevalence of a Dynamic Applicability Model from WTO Jurisprudence

Although the final model for China's applicable alternative benchmark regime cannot be ascertained at present, WTO jurisprudence might already give some hints to future developments.

[235] Appellate Body Report, *US – Gasoline*, at 23.

Table 3.1 Applicability models

	MES	NMES	
		Article 14 (a)/(c)-type subsidies	Article 14(b)/(d)-type subsidies
Model 2 a	Article 14 ASCM	Section 15(b) CAP	Article 14 ASCM
Model 2 bi	Article 14 ASCM	Section 15(b) CAP	Article 14 ASCM and Section 15(b) CAP jointly
Model 2 biiα	Article 14 ASCM	Section 15(b) CAP	Article 14 ASCM and Section 15(b) CAP merged (*"consistent with"* as strict prevalence of Article 14 ASCM)
Model 2 biiβ	Article 14 ASCM	Section 15(b) CAP	Article 14 ASCM and Section 15(b) CAP merged (*"consistent with"* as strict prevalence of Action 15(b) CAP)
Model 2 biiγ(1)	Article 14 ASCM	Section 15(b) CAP	Article 14 ASCM and Section 15(b) CAP merged (*"consistent with"* as minimum requirement with prevalence of Article 14 ASCM)
Model 2 biiγ(2)	Article 14 ASCM	Section 15(b) CAP	Article 14 ASCM and Section 15(b) CAP merged (*"consistent with"* as minimum requirement with prevalence of Section 15(b) CAP)
Model 2 biii	Article 14 ASCM	Section 15(b) CAP	Article 14 ASCM and Section 15(b) CAP consecutively

In *US – Anti-Dumping and Countervailing Duties (China)*, panel and Appellate Body deemed it feasible to decide the parties' claims solely under Article 14 ASCM, expressly not including Section 15(b) CAP.[236] This approach counts in disfavour of models 2 bi and 2 bii. If a merged understanding of the prerequisites was to prevail, only focussing on Article 14 ASCM and thus separating the two regimes for the determination of the alternative benchmark would not have been possible.

Considering other areas of WTO law, situations comparable to the one of China in anti-subsidy investigations can be identified. In WTO safeguards law, for instance, there are also two different legal regimes setting prerequisites for the imposition of definite measures, notably Article XIX GATT and the WTO Agreement on Safeguards. In *Korea – Dairy*, the Appellate Body held that with respect to the prerequisites to be fulfilled for the imposition of definite safeguard measures, the requirements of both Article XIX GATT and the WTO Agreement on Safeguards would have to be met.[237] The same was decided in *US – Line Pipe*.[238]

[236]Panel Report, *US – Anti-Dumping and Countervailing Duties (China)*, at para. 10.10 et seq.; Appellate Body Report, *US – Anti-Dumping and Countervailing Duties (China)*, at para. 436, footnote 401.

[237]Appellate Body Report, *Korea – Definitive Safeguard Measure on Imports of Certain Dairy Products*, WT/DS98/AB/R, adopted 12 January 2000, DSR 2000:I, 3, at para. 77.

[238]Appellate Body Report, *United States – Definitive Safeguard Measures on Imports of Circular Welded Carbon Quality Line Pipe from Korea*, WT/DS202/AB/R, adopted 8 March 2002, DSR 2002:IV, 1403, at para. 69.

This reasoning favours especially model 2 bi. Model 2 a, only scrutinising the Article 14 ASCM prerequisites, does not find itself in accordance with the Appellate Body's tendency to apply both sets of existing rules comprehensively.

3.2.4 Conclusion

Due to the open-termed design of China's alternative benchmark regulations, it is frequently and often deliberately overseen that Section 15(b) CAP *per se* contains legal provisions with distinct prerequisites. Only if the particular prerequisite of *"special difficulties"* is met and if prevailing terms and conditions in China are not available as *"appropriate"* benchmark, existing Chinese in-country prices may be disregarded for the purpose of benefit calculation. The selection of a surrogate also has to follow a certain procedure, including *"practicable"* prior adjustment of existing in-country benchmarks.

Unfortunately, the prerequisites of the concept all remain elusive and offer little guidance. From a historic point of view, at least the meaning of the term *"special difficulties"* can be explained quite well. What continues to afflict its application with doubts and insecurity is the dimension the transfer to a China-specific context entails, i.e. what function *"special difficulties"* have in the alternative benchmark regime of Section 15(b) CAP. This lamentable status quo of the alternative benchmark regime itself is worsened by its unclear interaction with general WTO anti-subsidy law. WTO jurisprudence has blurred the line set by Section 15(b) CAP in NMES. Instead, a bunch of various concepts has emerged, amongst which a finally applicable model cannot be positively singled out today.

Much discretion is therefore conferred to investigating authorities, which is prone to be misused in the interest of protecting national industries. But in the light of the permanent designation of China as NME country in Section 15(b) CAP for the purpose of anti-subsidy investigations, that investigating authorities observe the standard of due process and diligence is of particular importance. Where due process cannot be definitely established due to a lack of substance of the respective provisions, however, this is a problem ultimately to be solved by the WTO itself by modifying the respective rules.

3.3 Chapter Summary

The WTO framework for the use of alternative benchmark methodologies in anti-subsidy investigations against China comprises two different sets of provisions: general WTO law and the China-specific law of the CAP. While general WTO law does not contain any explicit provisions on the use of alternative benchmark methodologies but their employment rests on panels' and the Appellate Body's interpretation of Article 14 ASCM, the China-specific regime is laid own in Section 15(b) CAP.

Both regimes lack clear-cut and definite legal prerequisites. Neither the WTO judiciary nor the negotiating parties on the accession of China have set down concise rules with an unequivocally clear substantive meaning. The regimes rely on concepts which have not yet gained a meaningful shape. They employ terms which are either new to WTO law or which were previously used in a different connection and which cannot be attached an understanding that makes them fit as legal prerequisites. The combination of obscurity and openness endows investigating authorities with a large amount of discretion, which can only too easily be misused for protective purposes. As of today, the WTO judiciary lacks guidance on the alternative benchmark regimes which is essential to assess the conformity of the investigating authorities' comportment with WTO law.

In the case of China, the deplorable situation is worsened by the unclear relationship between the general and the China-specific WTO provisions, which only upon interaction form the final alternative benchmark regime for anti-subsidy investigations against China. Not only the legal prerequisites presently remain in the dark—but the applicable regime itself.

Chapter 4
The Current EU Approach in the Application of Alternative Benchmarks in Anti-Subsidy Investigations Against China

Bearing the state of the legal WTO framework on the use of alternative benchmark methodologies in NMES in mind, it shall now be scrutinised how the theoretical mechanisms are transposed in the case practice of investigating authorities, using the example of EU anti-subsidy investigations against China. Therefore, this chapter conducts a study of EU anti-subsidy cases against China with focus on the use of alternative benchmark methodologies (Sect. 4.1) and then examines the WTO law conformity of the EU's approach (Sect. 4.2). Finally, it briefly depicts prospective developments on EU level (Sect. 4.3).

4.1 The Use of Alternative Benchmark Methodologies in EU Anti-Subsidy Cases Against China: A Case Study

Before the use of alternative benchmark methodologies in EU anti-subsidy cases against China is analysed, the EU legal framework for such investigations shall be laid down briefly, focussing on the alternative benchmark regime for the benefit calculation in NMES and its deviations from the WTO framework with regard to China.

S. Müller, *The Use of Alternative Benchmarks in Anti-Subsidy Law*,
European Yearbook of International Economic Law 4,
https://doi.org/10.1007/978-3-319-77613-2_4

4.1.1 The Alternative Benchmark Regime of the EU

The alternative benchmark regime for NMES in EU anti-subsidy law comprises two legal acts: Article 6 BASR[1] and Guidelines of the EU Commission on the calculation of the amount of subsidy in countervailing duty investigations.[2]

4.1.1.1 Article 6 BASR

Article 6 BASR deals with the calculation of the benefit to the recipient:

> As regards the calculation of benefit to the recipient, the following rules shall apply:
>
> (a) government provision of equity capital shall not be considered to confer a benefit, unless the investment can be regarded as inconsistent with the usual investment practice, including for the provision of risk capital, of private investors in the territory of the country of origin and/or export;
>
> (b) a loan by a government shall not be considered to confer a benefit, unless there is a difference between the amount that the firm receiving the loan pays on the government loan and the amount that the firm would pay for a comparable commercial loan which the firm could actually obtain on the market. In that event the benefit shall be the difference between those two amounts;
>
> (c) a loan guarantee by a government shall not be considered to confer a benefit, unless there is a difference between the amount that the firm receiving the guarantee pays on a loan guaranteed by the government and the amount that the firm would pay for a comparable commercial loan in the absence of the government guarantee. In that case the benefit shall be the difference between those two amounts, adjusted for any differences in fees;
>
> (d) the provision of goods or services or purchase of goods by a government shall not be considered to confer a benefit, unless the provision is made for less than adequate remuneration or the purchase is made for more than adequate remuneration. The adequacy of remuneration shall be determined in relation to prevailing market conditions for the product or service in question in the country of provision or purchase, including price, quality, availability, marketability, transportation and other conditions of purchase or sale.
>
> If there are no such prevailing market terms and conditions for the product or service in question in the country of provision or purchase which can be used as appropriate benchmarks, the following rules shall apply:
>
> (i) the terms and conditions prevailing in the country concerned shall be adjusted, on the basis of actual costs, prices and other factors available in that country, by an appropriate amount which reflects normal market terms and conditions; or
>
> (ii) when appropriate, the terms and conditions prevailing in the market of another country or on the world market which are available to the recipient shall be used.

[1] Regulation (EU) 2016/1037 of the European Parliament and of the Council of 8 June 2016 on protection against subsidised imports from countries not members of the European Union (Basic Anti-Subsidy Regulation), OJ 2016 L 176/55, 30.6.2016.

[2] Guidelines for the Calculation of the Amount of Subsidy in Countervailing Duty Investigations, 98/C 394/04, OJ 1998 C 394/6, 17.12.1998.

In its conception, Article 6 BASR constitutes more or less a word-by-word transcription of Article 14 ASCM.[3] Hence, Article 6(a) BASR covers the government provision of equity capital, Article 6(b) deals with loans, Article 6(c) with loan guarantees and Article 6(d) finally addresses the provision of goods or services and the purchase of goods by a government.

Until 2002, correspondence in wording between Article 14 ASCM and its counterpart Article 6 in predecessor Regulation (EC) No. 2026/97[4] was nearly complete. Then, an additional subsection was added to Article 6(d) BASR. Article 1 Regulation (EC) No. 1973/2002[5] introduced to Article 6 BASR paragraph (d) subsection 2, which set down rules for the determination of alternative benchmarks in NMES for the purpose of benefit calculation.

4.1.1.1.1 The Regulatory Content of Article 6(d)(ii) BASR

The new subsection guides the Commission as EU investigating authority in how to determine a substitute price employable for the subsidy calculation in cases where the market terms and conditions existing in the country under investigation cannot be used as appropriate benchmark.

According to paragraph 1, the conditions prevailing in the respective country shall be adjusted by an appropriate amount to reflect normal market terms and conditions. Paragraph 2 permits the use of third-country terms and conditions *"when appropriate"*.

Seemingly, the options laid down in the two paragraphs can be applied interchangeably. The connector *"or"* implies coequality of both alternatives—and the prerequisite of paragraph 2, that terms and conditions outside the country investigated may only be used *"when appropriate"*, will not pose much of an obstacle with its indistinctness, just like the correspondent in Section 15(b) CAP.[6] But taking into consideration the recitals of Regulation (EC) No. 1973/2002, notably recital 2, it becomes apparent that the adjustment of in-country terms and conditions was meant to be applied prior to third-country market data. Only if an adjustment is *"not practicable"*, third-country prices and costs may be used. This order of priority is not clearly reflected in the amended text of Article 6 BASR.

---

[3]Vermulst/Gatta, 11 *World Trade Review* (2012), 527, at 540.

[4]Council Regulation (EC) No. 2026/97 of 6 October 1997 on protection against subsidized imports from countries not members of the European Community, OJ 1997 L 288/1, 21.10.1997.

[5]OJ 2002 L 305/4, 7.11.2002.

[6]See Sect. 3.2.2.2.2.

4.1.1.1.2 The Reason for the Enactment of Alternative Benchmark Regime in EU Anti-subsidy Law

The question that poses itself is why this amendment of Article 6 BASR been deemed desirable by the European legislator. At WTO level, no changes had been made to the ASCM in this regard. Consulting once again the recitals, the Council considered a clarification regarding the applicable benchmark for the calculation of the subsidy amount *"prudent [...] in cases where a market benchmark does not exist in the country concerned"* (Recital 1 Regulation (EC) No. 1973/2002). Apart from the Council's sagacity, neither recitals nor the additional history of the regulation give a more detailed explanation of this sudden need for clarification. It may thus be speculated that—given the timing of the amendment in 2002, not even one year after the accession of the People's Republic of China to the WTO, and the strong resemblance in wording of Section 15(b) CAP and Article 6(d)(ii) BASR—the EU transferred the respective China-specific provisions of the CAP into general EU anti-subsidy law. Considering that at WTO level, deviation from existing in-country prices in anti-subsidy law has been permitted by the Appellate Body in *US – Softwood Lumber IV* only in 2004, this fact seems noteworthy. It is also striking that the EU's alternative benchmark regime has been limited in scope to Article 6(d)-type subsidies, as Section 15(b) CAP places no restrictions.

4.1.1.2 Guidelines of the Commission (98/C 394/04)

Apart from Article 6 BASR, the Commission has issued guidelines for the calculation of the amount of subsidy in countervailing duty investigations. Having been enacted in 1998 already to provide clarification for the calculation under the former regime of Regulation (EC) No. 2026/97, they are still legally applicable[7] and relied on today in investigation practice,[8] as the provisions of the predecessor regulations have more or less been transferred into the currently applicable BASR in 2016. The aim of the Guidelines is to offer explanation regarding the application of the provisions on subsidy calculation and to clarify the methodology being used (Section A(1) Guidelines).

4.1.1.2.1 The Regulatory Content of the Guidelines

In Section E, the Guidelines lay down regulations for the calculation of certain types of subsidy. The categorisation of subsidies under the Guidelines differs from the partition under ASCM and BASR, as being more detailed in the Guidelines. Altogether, the Guidelines distinguish seven types of subsidies: grants, loans, loan guarantees, the

[7] Adamantopoulos/Pereyra-Friedrichsen, EU Anti-Subsidy Law, at 5-052.

[8] See e.g. *Gold East Paper and Gold Huasheng Paper v Council*, Case T-444/11, Judgment of the General Court (Third Chamber) of 11 September 2014, ECLI:EU:T:2014:773, at para. 11.

provision of goods and services by the government, purchases of goods by the government, the government provision of equity capital and the forgiveness of a government-held debt. For each type of subsidy, the Guidelines assist the Commission in how to proceed with the calculation of the subsidy in different situations.

The Guidelines also stipulate alternative benchmark methodologies for certain categories to be resorted to in cases where the market price in the country investigated is not reliable. Thus, regarding loans, the provision of goods and services by the government, purchases of goods by a government and the government provision of equity capital, the Guidelines set rules how to select an alternative market price to perform the subsidy calculation. Considering the types of subsidy with alternative benchmark regimes, they correspond to Article 14(b) and (d)-type subsidies or Article 6 (b) and (d)-type subsidies respectively. Remarkably, the Commission's guidelines from 1998 reflect to a large extent the Appellate Body's reasoning in *US – Softwood Lumber IV* from 2004 and *US – Anti-Dumping and Countervailing Duties (China)* from 2011.

4.1.1.2.2 The Legal Nature of the Guidelines

As stated in Section A recital 1, special circumstances may warrant a deviation from the written Guidelines—again entirely in the discretion of the investigating authority. Furthermore, Section A recital 2 expressly stipulates that the Guidelines do *"not bind the Community institutions in any way"*.[9] Hence, although guidelines principally exert some influence on the addressees' behaviour and *de facto* effect compliance,[10] they are not enforceable in front of the ECJ,[11] so that countries investigated cannot rely on the methodologies set down in the Guidelines to be actually applied in their case. Because of their imprecise terminology, their inherent recognisance of using other methodologies and, above all, their lack of legal force, the Guidelines confer only a very limited degree of legal security.

4.1.2 The Use of Alternative Benchmarks in EU Anti-Subsidy Investigations Against China

Within the EU Commission, the competent authority for conducting anti-subsidy investigations is its Directorate-General Trade, more specifically Directorate H "Trade Defence".[12]

---

[9]Regarding the development of the "soft law approach" in EU law see Cini, 8 *Journal of European Public Policy* (2011), 192, at 194 et seq.

[10]Barani, ConWEB No. 2/2006, 1, at 28.

[11]Barani, ConWEB No. 2/2006, 1, at 22.

[12]Adamantopoulos/Pereyra-Friedrichsen, EU Anti-Subsidy Law, at 7-007; Bishop, European Union Law for International Business, at 83.

4.1.2.1 The EU Anti-Subsidy Investigation Procedure

The main parties involved in an anti-subsidy investigation besides the Commission comprise the Union industry, the governments of third countries allegedly subsidising exports, the producers of the investigated product, EU importers, consumer organisations and end-users.[13]

An anti-subsidy proceeding is usually started by the Union industry or a Member State launching a complaint with the EU Commission alleging illegal subsidisation by a foreign government and consequent injury to EU producers of like products.[14] If there is sufficient evidence of the existence of countervailable subsidies, injury and causal link, and no written complaint has been made, the Commission has the right to initiate an investigation *ex officio* (Article 10(8) BASR).

If the Commission deems the complaint being sufficiently founded in substance, it embarks on pre-initiation consultations with the governments of the foreign countries *"with the aim of clarifying the situation and arriving at a mutually agreed solution"* (Article 10(9) BASR). This practice roots in the respect of the sovereignty of the third country as its national legislation is subject of the investigation.[15]

If, however, no solution can be agreed upon, the Commission initiates the actual investigation. To establish whether or not illegal subsidisation on part of the third country exists, respective data is collected by sending out questionnaires, conducting hearings or verification visits.[16] In case of non-cooperation of the producers of the country of investigation and of the government itself, *"facts available"* may be used by the Commission for the purpose of assembling the relevant information for the assessment of the existence of countervailable subsidisation (Article 28 BASR).

Once provisional positive findings have been made—i.e. positive indications of the existence of a countervailable subsidy, injury to the EU industry, a causal link and a Union interest in the imposition of countervailing duties against the third country—the Commission imposes provisional countervailing measures. The provisional measures may be imposed from within 60 days after the initiation of the investigation, but are usually imposed 9 months after this point of time, and stay in force for a maximum of 4 months.[17] If the country or exporter under investigation offers acceptable undertakings, the investigation is terminated despite the provisional findings (Article 13 BASR).[18]

After the Commission has ascertained the existence of countervailable subsidisation by definitive findings, and no acceptable undertakings on part of the

---

[13] Adamantopoulos/Pereyra-Friedrichsen, EU Anti-Subsidy Law, at 7-002.

[14] Avgustidi/Ballschmiede in Wolfrum et al. (eds.), Comparative Overview: Subsidies, at para. 177.

[15] Adamantopoulos/Pereyra-Friedrichsen, EU Anti-Subsidy Law, at 7-017.

[16] Van Bael/Bellis, EU Anti-Dumping and Other Trade Instruments, at 711.

[17] Giannakopoulos, A Concise Guide to the EU Anti-dumping/Anti-subsidies Procedures, at 130; Adamantopoulos/Pereyra-Friedrichsen, EU Anti-Subsidy Law, at 7-024.

[18] Giannakopoulos, A Concise Guide to the EU Anti-dumping/Anti-subsidies Procedures, at 131; Adamantopoulos/Pereyra-Friedrichsen, EU Anti-Subsidy Law, at 8-011.

third state have been offered, definitive countervailing duties are imposed through a Commission regulation or implementing regulation. All in all, the investigation must not exceed the duration of 13 months.[19]

4.1.2.2 An Overview on EU Anti-Subsidy Cases Against China

Until 1 January 2018, the EU has launched twelve anti-subsidy investigations against China.[20]

Compared to 92 anti-subsidy investigations altogether, mostly against India (27 cases, 29%),[21] twelve cases appear to be a moderate number (13%). It starkly contrasts with the large number of anti-dumping investigations that the EU has initiated against China. Of 764 cases in total, 157 were directed against Chinese exporters (21%).[22] This makes China the EU's number one anti-dumping target.

Considering, however, that the EU only started initiating anti-subsidy proceedings against China in 2010, the amount of cases against China already adding up to 13% of the EU's total amount of cases is rather remarkable. It affirms the potential of this type of trade remedy for future EU practice, in particular against the background of the expiry of the alternative methodologies for anti-dumping cases against China in December 2016.[23]

The opening case of EU anti-subsidy investigations against China was *Coated Fine Paper (China).*[24] Following the lead of the United States, which had brought action against subsidies to China's coated paper industry in 2006 already,[25] the Commission initiated correspondent proceedings against China on 17 April 2010,[26]

---

[19]Van Bael/Bellis, EU Anti-Dumping and Other Trade Instruments, at 711; Avgustidi/Ballschmiede in Wolfrum et al. (eds.), Comparative Overview: Subsidies, at para. 201.

[20]As of 1 January 2018, see http://trade.ec.europa.eu/tdi/completed.cfm (last visited 1 January 2018).

[21]As of 1 January2018, see http://trade.ec.europa.eu/doclib/docs/2006/december/tradoc_113191.12.2015.xls, http://trade.ec.europa.eu/doclib/docs/2017/january/tradoc_155243.pdf, http://trade.ec.europa.eu/doclib/docs/2017/december/tradoc_156415.pdf and http://trade.ec.europa.eu/tdi/completed.cfm (last visited 1 January 2018).

[22]As of 1 January 20182017, see http://trade.ec.europa.eu/doclib/docs/2006/december/tradoc_113191.12.2015.xls, http://trade.ec.europa.eu/doclib/docs/2017/january/tradoc_155243.pdf, http://trade.ec.europa.eu/doclib/docs/2017/december/tradoc_156415.pdf and http://trade.ec.europa.eu/tdi/completed.cfm (last visited 1 January 2018).

[23]See Introduction, at 3, in particular footnote 17.; consentient Vermulst/Gatta, 11 *World Trade Review* (2012), 527, at 537 et seq.

[24]Council Implementing Regulation (EU) No 452/2011 of 6 May 2011 imposing a definitive anti-subsidy duty on imports of coated fine paper originating in the People's Republic of China, OJ 2011 L 128/18, 14.5.2011.

[25]*Coated Free Sheet Paper from the People's Republic of China*, Case C-570-907, Notice of Initiation of Countervailing Duty Investigations, 71 Fed. Reg. 68546, 27 November 2006; Qian, 46 *Journal of World Trade* (2012), 961, at 962.

[26]Notice of initiation of an anti-subsidy proceeding concerning imports of coated fine paper originating in the People's Republic of China (2010/C 99/13), OJ 2010 C 99, 30, 17.4.2010.

which resulted in definitive measures on 6 May 2011.[27] Subsequently, the EU started a (so far) moderate number of anti-subsidy proceedings, climaxing in 2012 and 2013 with the initiation of six investigations altogether. Six of the investigations resulted in the imposition of definitive countervailing duties (*Coated Fine Paper (China)*,[28] *Certain Organic Coated Steel Products (China)*,[29] *Solar Panels (China)*,[30] *Solar Glass (China)*,[31] *Certain Filament Glass Fibre Products (China)*,[32] *Certain Hot-rolled Flat Products of Iron, Non-alloy or Other Alloy Steel (China)*[33]), four were terminated without measures (*Wireless Wide Area Networking (WWAN) Modems (China)*,[34] *Bicycles (China)*,[35] *Polyester Staple Fibres (China)*,[36] *Stainless*

[27] *Coated Fine Paper (China)*, Council Implementing Regulation (EU) No. 452/2011 of 6 May 2011 imposing a definitive anti-subsidy duty on imports of coated fine paper originating in the People's Republic of China, OJ 2011 L 128/18, 14.5.2011.

[28] Council Implementing Regulation (EU) No. 452/2011 of 6 May 2011 imposing a definitive anti-subsidy duty on imports of coated fine paper originating in the People's Republic of China, OJ 2011 L 128/18, 14.5.2011.

[29] Council Implementing Regulation (EU) No. 215/2013 of 11 March 2013 imposing a countervailing duty on imports of certain organic coated steel products originating in the People's Republic of China, OJ 2013 L 73/16, 15.3.2013.

[30] Council Implementing Regulation (EU) No. 1239/2013 of 2 December 2013 imposing a definitive countervailing duty on imports of crystalline silicon photovoltaic modules and key components (i.e. cells) originating in or consigned from the People's Republic of China, OJ 2013 L 325/66, 5.12.2013.

[31] Commission Implementing Regulation (EU) No. 470/2014 of 13 May 2014 imposing a definitive anti-dumping duty and collecting definitively the provisional duty imposed on imports of solar glass originating in the People's Republic of China, OJ 2014 L 142/23, 14.5.2014.

[32] Commission Implementing Regulation (EU) No. 1379/2014 of 16 December 2014 imposing a definitive countervailing duty on imports of certain filament glass fibre products originating in the People's Republic of China and amending Council Implementing Regulation (EU) No. 248/2011 imposing a definitive anti-dumping duty on imports of certain continuous filament glass fibre products originating in the People's Republic of China, OJ 2014 L 367/22, 23.12.2014.

[33] Commission Implementing Regulation (EU) 2017/969 of 8 June 2017 imposing definitive countervailing duties on imports of certain hot-rolled flat products of iron, non-alloy or other alloy steel originating in the People's Republic of China and amending Commission Implementing Regulation (EU) 2017/649 imposing a definitive anti-dumping duty on imports of certain hot-rolled flat products of iron, non-alloy or other alloy steel originating in the People's Republic of China, OJ 2017 L 146/17, 9.6.2017.

[34] Commission Regulation (EU) No. 209/2011 of 2 March 2011 terminating the anti-dumping and anti-subsidy proceedings concerning imports of wireless wide area networking (WWAN) modems originating in the People's Republic of China and terminating the registration of such imports imposed by Regulations (EU) No. 570/2010 and (EU) No. 811/2010, OJ 2011 L 58/36, 3.3.2011.

[35] Commission Decision 2013/227/EU of 22 May 2013 terminating the anti-subsidy proceeding concerning imports of bicycles originating in the People's Republic of China, OJ 2013 L 136/15, 23.5.2013.

[36] Commission Implementing Decision 2014/918/EU of 16 December 2014 terminating the anti-subsidy proceeding concerning the imports of polyester staple fibres originating in the People's Republic of China, India and Vietnam, OJ 2014 L 360/65, 17.12.2014.

Steel Cold-rolled Flat Products (China)[37] and two are still on-going (*Tyres for buses or lorries (new and retreaded) (China)*,[38] *Bicycles (electric) (China)*[39]).

4.1.2.3 Case Study on the Use of Alternative Benchmarks in NMES

Although case law of EU investigations against China is still sparse, distinct patterns of reasoning in the application of the alternative benchmark methodologies in NMES may already have recognizably evolved in the Commission's case handling. Therefore, the first 5 years of the Commission's investigation practice against China shall be subjected to close scrutiny, notably the cases leading to the imposition of definitive anti-subsidy measures.

4.1.2.3.1 Coated Fine Paper (China) (2011)

In *Coated Fine Paper (China)*, subsidies of three different categories to the paper-making industry were identified. First, miscellaneous Article 6(a) BASR- type subsidies, i.e. tax, tariff and grant programmes, were found countervailable on the basis of existing in-country prices. Besides, preferential lending to the coated paper industry was discovered, i.e. an Article 6(b)-type subsidy. Furthermore, the Commission concluded that the system of land-use rights practiced in China constituted an undue provision of goods by the government, i.e. an Article(d)-type subsidy. In the course of the benefit calculation of the two latter types of subsidies, the Commission rejected the use of existing Chinese prices and employed alternative benchmarks.

4.1.2.3.1.1 Preferential Lending

As regards the lending market in China, the Commission concluded that due to *"substantial government intervention"*,[40] the Chinese banking sector could not be regarded as a *"functioning market"*.[41] Hence, it did not employ the existing

[37]Commission Implementing Regulation (EU) 2015/1206 of 23 July 2015 terminating the anti-subsidy proceeding concerning imports of stainless steel cold-rolled flat products originating in the People's Republic of China and repealing Implementing Regulation (EU) No. 1331/2014 making imports of stainless steel cold-rolled flat products originating in the People's Republic of China and Taiwan subject to registration, OJ 2015 L 196/4, 24.7.2015.

[38]Notice of initiation of an anti-subsidy proceeding concerning imports of new and retreaded tyres for buses or lorries originating in the People's Republic of China, OJ 2017 C 346/9, 14.10.2017.

[39]Notice of initiation of an anti-subsidy proceeding concerning imports of electric bicycles originating in the People's Republic of China, OJ 2017 C 440/22, 21.12.2017.

[40]Council Implementing Regulation (EU) No. 452/2011, *Coated Fine Paper (China)*, at para. 97.

[41]Council Implementing Regulation (EU) No. 452/2011, *Coated Fine Paper (China)*, at para. 97.

in-country interest rates that had been identified during the investigation, but adjusted them *"to reflect normal market risk"*.[42]

4.1.2.3.1.1.1 The Establishment of Market Distortion

The prerequisites developed by the WTO Appellate Body for deviation in cases of loan subsidies require proof of the distortion of the market interest rate through government action. The Commission made reference to several government actions it considered to exercise distortive effect.

First, it examined governmental plans and policies, i.e. certain legal instruments, notably the 2007 Papermaking Plan and Decision No. 40.[43] It concluded that these instruments were used by the government of China to exert undue state influence on the papermaking industry.[44] Decision No. 40, a binding legal document, listed the papermaking industry as *"encouraged industry"*,[45] a status by which certain privileges, e.g. financial support or VAT and import duty exemptions, were transferred to companies of the respective sector. Article 18 and 19 of the Decision even explicitly ordered authorities to stop financial institutions from supplying loans.[46] As regards the 2007 Papermaking Plan, it was found to set *"specific conditions, orientations and targets"*[47] for the papermaking industry. It also awarded credit ratings for papermaking companies. Furthermore, the plan contained a chapter on "investment and financing" of the papermaking industry, which, inter alia, ordered that no loans ought to be issued to projects not meeting the requirements of the plan. For these reasons, the Commission classified the plan as *"compulsory industrial policy tool"*,[48] which secured the government of China's influence on this section of the lending market.

Although the Chinese government countered that plans in general possessed no binding legal force, the Commission persisted on plans being an element of proof of undue governmental influence, citing a passage from the 2007 Papermaking Plan stating the plan to be the main instrument to secure the prosperity of the papermaking industry.[49] It also expressed astonishment at the existence of a legally binding implementing circular to an allegedly non-binding plan, the eleventh Five Year

---

[42]Council Implementing Regulation (EU) No. 452/2011, *Coated Fine Paper (China)*, at para. 98.
[43]Council Implementing Regulation (EU) No. 452/2011, *Coated Fine Paper (China)*, at para. 75.
[44]Council Implementing Regulation (EU) No. 452/2011, *Coated Fine Paper (China)*, at para. 75.
[45]Council Implementing Regulation (EU) No. 452/2011, *Coated Fine Paper (China)*, at para. 75.
[46]Council Implementing Regulation (EU) No. 452/2011, *Coated Fine Paper (China)*, at para. 76.
[47]Council Implementing Regulation (EU) No. 452/2011, *Coated Fine Paper (China)*, at para. 77.
[48]Council Implementing Regulation (EU) No. 452/2011, *Coated Fine Paper (China)*, at para. 77.
[49]Council Implementing Regulation (EU) No. 452/2011, *Coated Fine Paper (China)*, at para. 78: "The industrial development policy is formulated based on the requirements of perfecting the reform of the socialist market economy and the related laws and regulations, so as to establish a fair market order and good development environment, solve the issues existing in the development of papermaking industry and direct the healthy development of the industry."

Plan.[50] Moreover, Article 34 Commercial Banking Law stated that loans shall be issued *"under the guidance of the State industrial policy"*.[51]

Additionally, the Commission discovered that SOCBs acquired all loans of Chinese companies due to foreign banks in 2008 without properly adjusting the risk premium, which it also counted as evidence for unlawful influence on part of the government of China.[52]

As well, the Commission analysed the structure of the Chinese lending market and found out that the majority of the banks were state-owned.[53] Thus, they constituted the *"predominant players in the financial market"*,[54] which corresponded with their ability to effectively influence the market conditions.

Via the People's Bank of China, one of the SOCBs, the government was able to influence the setting of lending rates.[55] This made the government the effective rate setter and not merely an implementer of monetary policy, and thus corresponded to the example provided for by the Appellate Body in *US – Anti-Dumping and Countervailing Duties (China).*[56]

4.1.2.3.1.1.2 The Selection of the Alternative Benchmark

Upon the positive finding of distortion of the Chinese lending market, the Commission proceeded by adjusting existing in-country lending rates *"to reflect normal market risk"*.[57] To assess the market risk attributed to loans to Chinese companies, it referred to a rating of one of the three big credit rating agencies, Bloomberg. It *"deemed [it] appropriate"*[58] to award to companies of the Chinese papermaking industry grade BB, which constitutes the highest "non-investment grade" available.[59] Besides, it also added an *"appropriate"*[60] risk premium.

Confronted with the objection of one producer, APP, that it had in fact received an A1 rating from Moody's, another of the big three rating agencies, in 2007 and 2008, the EU Commission stuck to its reasoning nevertheless, declaring that the Moody rating had been based on respective advantages gained by APP via illegal subsidisation through the Chinese government. The more favourable credit rating

[50]Council Implementing Regulation (EU) No. 452/2011, *Coated Fine Paper (China)*, at para. 78.
[51]Council Implementing Regulation (EU) No. 452/2011, *Coated Fine Paper (China)*, at para. 79.
[52]Council Implementing Regulation (EU) No. 452/2011, *Coated Fine Paper (China)*, at para. 83.
[53]Council Implementing Regulation (EU) No. 452/2011, *Coated Fine Paper (China)*, at para. 84.
[54]Council Implementing Regulation (EU) No. 452/2011, *Coated Fine Paper (China)*, at para. 85.
[55]Council Implementing Regulation (EU) No. 452/2011, *Coated Fine Paper (China)*, at para. 87.
[56]Appellate Body Report, *US – Anti-Dumping and Countervailing Duties (China)*, at para. 498.
[57]Council Implementing Regulation (EU) No. 452/2011, *Coated Fine Paper (China)*, at para. 98.
[58]Council Implementing Regulation (EU) No. 452/2011, *Coated Fine Paper (China)*, at para. 99.
[59]Council Implementing Regulation (EU) No. 452/2011, *Coated Fine Paper (China)*, at para. 99.
[60]Council Implementing Regulation (EU) No. 452/2011, *Coated Fine Paper (China)*, at para. 99.

was marked *"a circular issue"*[61] and consequently rejected as "fruit of the poisonous tree".[62]

4.1.2.3.1.2 The Provision of Land-Use Rights

The other type of subsidy in *Coated Fine Paper (China)* meriting examination is the governmental provision of LURs, where the WTO Appellate Body had allowed deviation from existing in-country prices and the employment of alternative benchmarks in cases where the market has been distorted through government action.

4.1.2.3.1.2.1 The Establishment of Market Distortion

Upon the evidence collected and, rather to a larger extent, the application of facts available, the Commission concluded that China possessed no market for land-use rights. It stated that *"there appear to be no available private benchmarks at all in China"*.[63] According to Article 2 of the Land Administration Law, all land in China was in the ownership of the state.[64] Only land-use rights could be obtained by private individuals through public bidding, quotation or auction. In addition, the government also controlled the secondary market as all transfers of LURs from one private individual to another depended on governmental approval.[65] Thus, the government held the predominant role as a provider of LURs and the role of a monopolist in the supervision of LUR transfers.

Furthermore, the Commission compared the conditions in China to the conditions in Taiwan, the country chosen as alternative benchmark, and reasoned that the huge price deficit on the Chinese side *"demonstrates that the amount paid for land-use rights by the cooperating exporters is well below the normal market rate"*.[66] Moreover, as the parallel anti-dumping investigation showed, LURs were granted to respective exporters *"in view of their papermaking projects"*.[67]

Hence, the market of LURs in China was not only distorted to a major degree, but actually non-existent.

4.1.2.3.1.2.2 The Selection of the Alternative Benchmark

After establishing distortion, the Commission selected the alternative benchmark. It negated the possibility of adjustment because of the complete non-existence of a

[61] Council Implementing Regulation (EU) No. 452/2011, *Coated Fine Paper (China)*, at para. 326.

[62] Regarding the dubiousness of the Commission's argumentation see Vermulst/Gatta, 11 *World Trade Review* (2012), 527, at 549 et seq.

[63] Council Implementing Regulation (EU) No. 452/2011, *Coated Fine Paper (China)*, at para. 260.

[64] Council Implementing Regulation (EU) No. 452/2011, *Coated Fine Paper (China)*, at para. 249.

[65] Council Implementing Regulation (EU) No. 452/2011, *Coated Fine Paper (China)*, at para. 354.

[66] Council Implementing Regulation (EU) No. 452/2011, *Coated Fine Paper (China)*, at para. 251.

[67] Council Implementing Regulation (EU) No. 452/2011, *Coated Fine Paper (China)*, at para. 257.

private market in China and then chose Taiwan as alternative third-country market. It mainly relied on the difference in GDP *per capita* and population density between the Chinese provinces the exporters were located in and the Taiwanese data not being huge.[68] More precisely, the Commission took nine factors into account. It considered the similar level of economic development and structure of Taiwan and the respective Chinese provinces, physical proximity, the high level of infrastructure on both sides, strong economic cross-border connections, population density, the similarity between type of land and transaction, common demographic, linguistic and cultural features, the fact that both Chinese provinces in question, Jiangsu and Shandong, had been designated top manufacturing provinces and, finally, the similarity of the GDP real growth rates in Taiwan and the two Chinese provinces.[69] In its opinion, these shared characteristics secured that the selected Taiwanese benchmark was *"closely connected"*[70] to prevailing conditions in China.

In particular, upon objection of the producer APP, which considered India more apt a benchmark country, the Commission stressed the comparability of the alternative benchmark concluded on because of the comprehensiveness of the factors that have been taken into account. It reasoned that GDP *per capita* and population density *"cannot be the only decisive factors"*[71] for the choice of analogue country, but that the other factors were necessary as well.

4.1.2.3.2 *Certain Organic Coated Steel Products (2013)*

The next EU anti-subsidy case against China resulting in the imposition of duties was only conducted in 2013, 2 years after *Coated Fine Paper (China)*. In *Certain Organic Coated Steel Products (China)*, alleged subsidisation of another major Chinese industrial sector, the steel industry, was dealt with. Again, several (b)- and (d)-type subsidies were subject of the investigation, the findings resulting in the application of alternative benchmarks in three cases—with regard to preferential lending, the provision of LURs and the provisions of HRS and CRS.

4.1.2.3.2.1 Preferential Loans and Interest Rates

Just as before with respect to the papermaking industry, the financing of the steel industry was scrutinised with particular attention by the Commission. The reasoning regarding preferential lending to the steel industry was highly geared to the pattern of argumentation of *Coated Fine Paper (China)*. Partly, the sections of the Council Implementing Regulations even coincide word-by-word.

---

[68]Council Implementing Regulation (EU) No. 452/2011, *Coated Fine Paper (China)*, at para. 261.
[69]Council Implementing Regulation (EU) No. 452/2011, *Coated Fine Paper (China)*, at para. 356.
[70]Council Implementing Regulation (EU) No. 452/2011, *Coated Fine Paper (China)*, at para. 357.
[71]Council Implementing Regulation (EU) No. 452/2011, *Coated Fine Paper (China)*, at para. 361.

4.1.2.3.2.1.1 The Establishment of Market Distortion

In determining distortion of the market interest rate through governmental interference, the Commission basically relied on two arguments.

First, the investigation yielded that the major part of the large Chinese banks was in the ownership of the state.[72] The government of China was the major shareholder of these banks,[73] which enabled it to exert considerable influence on the market, as state-owned banks constituted more than two-thirds of the Chinese banking sector.[74] According to the facts discovered in the course of the investigation, the five largest Chinese SOCBs represented more than half of the country's banking sector.

In addition to the formal aspect of shareholding, the Commission ascertained that the government of China also secured its predominant role on the lending market by directly and indirectly exerting influence on the steel industry-related lending practice through various laws and policies. The People's Bank of China as largest SOCB set specific limits for interest rates which had to be used by other banks, state and privately- owned, when issuing loans to the steel industry.[75] Besides, the Chinese government secured the state policy-conform conduct of privately-owned commercial banks in China through miscellaneous laws and policies, resulting in the alignment of the lending practice of state-owned and privately-owned commercial banks. Articles 34 and 38 Commercial Banking Law required all commercial banks to perform their business with particular attention to the needs of the national economy and within the spirit of state industrial policies.[76] In this regard, it was noteworthy that Article 17 of Decision No. 40 stated that incentives to the steel industry as *"encouraged industry"* were to be granted, including financial support.[77] Articles 24 and 25 State Council Order No. 35 stipulated that loans may only be granted to companies complying with the respective national policies for the iron and steel industry.[78] Furthermore, there was no credit risk assessment of exporting producers before issuing the loans.[79]

---

[72]Council Implementing Regulation (EU) No. 215/2013, *Certain Organic Coated Steel Products (China)*, at para. 165.

[73]Council Implementing Regulation (EU) No. 215/2013, *Certain Organic Coated Steel Products (China)*, at para. 159.

[74]Council Implementing Regulation (EU) No. 215/2013, *Certain Organic Coated Steel Products (China)*, at para. 166.

[75]Council Implementing Regulation (EU) No. 215/2013, *Certain Organic Coated Steel Products (China)*, at para. 169.

[76]Council Implementing Regulation (EU) No. 215/2013, *Certain Organic Coated Steel Products (China)*, at para. 172.

[77]Council Implementing Regulation (EU) No. 215/2013, *Certain Organic Coated Steel Products (China)*, at para. 182.

[78]Council Implementing Regulation (EU) No. 215/2013, *Certain Organic Coated Steel Products (China)*, at para. 173, 183.

[79]Council Implementing Regulation (EU) No. 215/2013, *Certain Organic Coated Steel Products (China)*, at para. 177.

4.1.2.3.2.1.2 The Selection of the Alternative Benchmark

Rejecting the existence of market-driven structures on the Chinese lending market, the Commission constructed and applied an alternative benchmark on the basis of Chinese lending rates, taking into consideration an appropriate credit risk assessment of respective exporters.[80] The Commission awarded to the Chinese producers the lowest non-investment grade rating, BB at Bloomberg, and calculated the duties accordingly.[81]

4.1.2.3.2.2 The Provision of Hot-Rolled and Cold-Rolled Steel

Amongst the government provision of goods at allegedly less than adequate remuneration was the provision of both HRS and CRS.

4.1.2.3.2.2.1 The Establishment of Market Distortion

Regarding HRS, the *"very conservative analysis"*[82] of the market by the Commission yielded that 63% of all HRS were provided for by SOEs. Due to the predominance of SOEs in this sector, other private producers aligned their prices to the low government level to remain competitive.[83] With respect to CRS, only 18% of the market amount were reported to be provided for by SOEs. The estimated number, however, was supposed to be much higher—according to the World Steel Capacity Book cited as evidence, more than 70% of CRS were produced by SOEs.[84] Moreover, much of the steel was put on the market via trading companies and was thus not directly attributable to the government of China. Overall, the findings disclosed a strong involvement of the state in this sector of industry. Because of the predominant influence of the government, the prices for HRS and CRS were regarded as distorted.[85]

---

[80]Council Implementing Regulation (EU) No. 215/2013, *Certain Organic Coated Steel Products (China)*, at para. 191.

[81]Council Implementing Regulation (EU) No. 215/2013, *Certain Organic Coated Steel Products (China)*, at para. 192 et seq.

[82]Council Implementing Regulation (EU) No. 215/2013, *Certain Organic Coated Steel Products (China)*, at para. 76.

[83]Council Implementing Regulation (EU) No. 215/2013, *Certain Organic Coated Steel Products (China)*, at para. 77.

[84]Council Implementing Regulation (EU) No. 215/2013, *Certain Organic Coated Steel Products (China)*, at para. 78.

[85]Council Implementing Regulation (EU) No. 215/2013, *Certain Organic Coated Steel Products (China)*, at para. 81.

4.1.2.3.2.2.2 *The Selection of the Alternative Benchmark*

For the then necessary choice of an alternative benchmark, an adjustment of Chinese prices was not deemed feasible, as the distortion spread across the whole market.[86] The benchmark adopted by the Commission was constructed based on world market prices for HRS and CRS instead.[87] In doing so, it consulted several steel journals and chose the country or region which was the biggest market on each continent—i.e. Europe, the USA, Turkey, Japan and Brazil.[88] The Commission justified its selection by stressing that none of the countries or regions chosen had the highest prices on the world market, they were all WTO members, all were amongst the ten biggest steel producers worldwide and located in different continents.

4.1.2.3.2.3 *The Provision of Land-Use Rights*

Allegedly, the steel industry also profited from the provision of land-use rights at less than adequate remuneration by the government.

4.1.2.3.2.3.1 *The Establishment of Market Distortion*

Basically, the reasoning regarding the determination of market distortion corresponds to the reasoning of *Coated Fine Paper (China)*, where the provision of land-use rights to companies of the respective industry also constituted a major issue.

As stated by Article 2 Land Administration Law and Article 137 Real Right Law, all land in China belonged to the people and is distributed by the government through public bidding, quotation or auction.[89] As however, the examples of the sampled producers demonstrated, the acquisition of land-use rights did not always follow this procedure, but could apparently also be effected through mere government action.[90] Accordingly, it was concluded that the situation regarding the provision and acquisition of land in China was *"unclear and non-transparent"*.[91] Upon these findings, the Commission stated that China possessed no functioning market.[92]

---

[86] Council Implementing Regulation (EU) No. 215/2013, *Certain Organic Coated Steel Products (China)*, at para. 81.

[87] Council Implementing Regulation (EU) No. 215/2013, *Certain Organic Coated Steel Products (China)*, at para. 82.

[88] Council Implementing Regulation (EU) No. 215/2013, *Certain Organic Coated Steel Products (China)*, at para. 103.

[89] Council Implementing Regulation (EU) No. 215/2013, *Certain Organic Coated Steel Products (China)*, at para. 111, 113.

[90] Council Implementing Regulation (EU) No. 215/2013, *Certain Organic Coated Steel Products (China)*, at para. 114 for Panhua Group Co. Ltd. and at para. 115 for Zhejiang Huadong Light Steel Building Material Co. Ltd.

[91] Council Implementing Regulation (EU) No. 215/2013, *Certain Organic Coated Steel Products (China)*, at para. 116.

[92] Council Implementing Regulation (EU) No. 215/2013, *Certain Organic Coated Steel Products (China)*, at para. 118.

In addition, the comparison between the alternative benchmark chosen and actual prices in China vividly demonstrated that the price level in China was *"well below the normal market rate"*.[93]

4.1.2.3.2.3.2 The Selection of the Alternative Benchmark

An adjustment of existing in-country prices was not deemed possible due to the complete lack of private benchmarks.[94] In correspondence with the reasoning in *Coated Fine Paper (China)*, Taiwanese prices were chosen as appropriate third-country benchmark, once more with particular reference to the comparable GDP *per capita* level and population density.[95]

4.1.2.3.3 *Solar Panels (2013)*

The investigation in *Solar Panels (China)* resulted in definitive findings of countervailable subsidies under rejection of in-country prices for the calculation of the amount of benefit with respect to three different kinds of governmental contributions: once more regarding preferential lending and the provision of land-use rights and, for the first time, the provision of credit lines.

4.1.2.3.3.1 Preferential Lending

Like the papermaking and the steel industry, the photovoltaic industry allegedly benefitted from lending terms and conditions more favourable than could be obtained under regular market conditions.

4.1.2.3.3.1.1 The Establishment of Market Distortion

In accordance with its previous reasoning in *Coated Fine Paper (China)* and *Certain Organic Coated Steel Products (China)*, the Commission argued that the Chinese government both directly and indirectly exerted undue influence on the lending market. For a start, SOCBs, constituting the largest part of the Chinese banking sector, issued loans at preferential conditions.[96] In addition, by several laws and policies, e.g. Articles 34 and 38 Commercial Banking Law, privately owned banks

---

[93]Council Implementing Regulation (EU) No. 215/2013, *Certain Organic Coated Steel Products (China)*, at para. 118.

[94]Council Implementing Regulation (EU) No. 215/2013, *Certain Organic Coated Steel Products (China)*, at para. 120.

[95]Council Implementing Regulation (EU) No. 215/2013, *Certain Organic Coated Steel Products (China)*, at para. 120 et seq.

[96]Council Implementing Regulation (EU) No. 1239/2013, *Solar Panels (China)*, at para. 53, 170.

were obliged to act according to state policy goals.[97] With the photovoltaic industry having been classified as *"encouraged"*, additional financial support was conferred to respective companies.[98] Moreover, the setting of the interest rate range by the People's Bank of China required all commercial banks to align their interest rate policies to the low People's Bank of China allowance.[99] Hence, as also the comparison with the alternative benchmark rates clearly showed the NME conditions in China, the Commission regarded the Chinese lending market as distorted.[100]

4.1.2.3.3.1.2 The Selection of the Alternative Benchmark

In line with its previous reasoning in *Coated Fine Paper (China)* and *Certain Organic Coated Steel Products (China)*, Chinese rates adjusted for normal market risk were constructed as alternative benchmarks,[101] choosing Bloomberg's BB rating as reference for the assessment of the normal market risk.[102]

4.1.2.3.3.2 The Provision of Credit Lines

For the first time, the complaint of subsidisation included the provision of credit lines.

Regarding the nature of the subsidy under investigation, the Commission adopted a twisted approach. First classifying credit lines as *"essential part"*[103] of preferential lending and considering them as possible direct transfer of funds under Article 3(1) (i) BASR,[104] the Commission finally applied Article 6(d) BASR and regarded the provision of credit lines as governmental provision of financial services at less than adequate remuneration.[105] It condescended, however, that credit lines *"could also be considered a potential transfer of funds"*.[106]

4.1.2.3.3.2.1 The Establishment of Market Distortion

In determining market distortion, the Commission basically referred to the fact that the same banks providing the preferential loans were also responsible for providing credit lines and that this sector had already been demonstrated to be distorted by

97 Council Implementing Regulation (EU) No. 1239/2013, *Solar Panels (China)*, at para. 171.

98 Council Implementing Regulation (EU) No. 1239/2013, *Solar Panels (China)*, at para. 172.

99 Council Implementing Regulation (EU) No. 1239/2013, *Solar Panels (China)*, at para. 173, 182.

100 Council Implementing Regulation (EU) No. 1239/2013, *Solar Panels (China)*, at para. 190.

101 Council Implementing Regulation (EU) No. 1239/2013, *Solar Panels (China)*, at para. 198.

102 Council Implementing Regulation (EU) No. 1239/2013, *Solar Panels (China)*, at para. 199.

103 Council Implementing Regulation (EU) No. 1239/2013, *Solar Panels (China)*, at para. 208.

104 Council Implementing Regulation (EU) No. 1239/2013, *Solar Panels (China)*, at para. 203.

105 Council Implementing Regulation (EU) No. 1239/2013, *Solar Panels (China)*, at para. 213.

106 Council Implementing Regulation (EU) No. 1239/2013, *Solar Panels (China)*, at para. 213.

government predominance.[107] Normally, the provision of credit lines would include a substantial commitment and the payment of administration fees.[108] In the present investigation, Chinese exporters were found not having had to pay any charge at all or only a very moderate fee. Hence, the market for credit lines was distorted.

4.1.2.3.3.2.2 The Selection of the Alternative Benchmark

As regards the selection of the alternative benchmark, adjustment of Chinese values was not deemed possible. The Commission also stated that the *"adequacy of the remuneration for the financial services could not be determined in relation to prevailing market conditions in the PRC"*.[109] The Commission selected a credit line of one Chinese producer obtained by a foreign bank at market terms, i.e. including commitment and administration fees, as alternative benchmark.[110] Quite unlike its usual practice of taking alternative benchmarks from third countries or relying on price construction, in *Solar Panels (China)* the Commission chose the only representative market rate actually discovered in the investigation as proxy.

4.1.2.3.3.3 The Provision of Land-Use Rights

Regarding the provision of land-use rights, however, the Commission followed the already familiar pattern.

4.1.2.3.3.3.1 The Establishment of Market Distortion

Under reference to Article 2 Land Administration Law and Article 137 Real Right Law, it stated that all land in China collectively belonged to the people of China and was issued to private individuals through bidding, auction and competition.[111] The investigation, however, yielded that the system was flawed by the limitation of potential buyers, price setting, non-competitive auctions and funds granted by local authorities to offset LUR prices.[112] As the situation on the Chinese market was *"unclear and non-transparent"*[113] and *"prices are often set arbitrarily by the*

[107]Council Implementing Regulation (EU) No. 1239/2013, *Solar Panels (China)*, at para. 204 et seq.

[108]Council Implementing Regulation (EU) No. 1239/2013, *Solar Panels (China)*, at para. 205.

[109]Council Implementing Regulation (EU) No. 1239/2013, *Solar Panels (China)*, at para. 213.

[110]Council Implementing Regulation (EU) No. 1239/2013, *Solar Panels (China)*, at para. 213.

[111]Council Implementing Regulation (EU) No. 1239/2013, *Solar Panels (China)*, at para. 361 et seq.

[112]Council Implementing Regulation (EU) No. 1239/2013, *Solar Panels (China)*, at para. 364 et seq.

[113]Council Implementing Regulation (EU) No. 1239/2013, *Solar Panels (China)*, at para. 367.

authorities",[114] the market was deemed distorted, as again the alternative benchmark vividly showed the lack of market conditions.[115]

4.1.2.3.3.3.2 The Selection of the Alternative Benchmark

By now rather unsurprising, the Commission repeated its reasoning regarding the provision of land-use rights from *Coated Fine Paper (China)* and used Taiwanese prices as proxies for the benefit calculation as an adjustment of existing in-country prices was not thought feasible.[116] For its determination, the Commission mainly relied upon the high GDP and the high population density, which both made Taiwan and the areas the Chinese producers were located comparable.[117]

4.1.2.3.4 *Solar Glass (2014)*

In *Solar Glass (China)*, alternative benchmarks were resorted to in two cases, regarding preferential loans on the one hand and the provision of land-use rights on the other.

4.1.2.3.4.1 Preferential Lending

To establish market distortion in the lending sector, the Commission basically referred to the results of the investigation in *Solar Panels (China)*.[118] As the banking sector was dominated by SOCBs[119] and the state extended its influence via statutory law and other legal regulations to privately owned banks,[120] the loans constituted a financial contribution to the respective producer.[121] Moreover, comparison to the alternative benchmark showed clearly the lack of market conditions in China.[122]

The selection of the alternative benchmark resulted again in the adjustment of the People's Bank of China's interest rates including the application a market-based credit risk, the BB at Bloomberg rating.[123]

---

[114]Council Implementing Regulation (EU) No. 1239/2013, *Solar Panels (China)*, at para. 367.
[115]Council Implementing Regulation (EU) No. 1239/2013, *Solar Panels (China)*, at para. 369.
[116]Council Implementing Regulation (EU) No. 1239/2013, *Solar Panels (China)*, at para. 371.
[117]Council Implementing Regulation (EU) No. 1239/2013, *Solar Panels (China)*, at para. 372.
[118]Commission Implementing Regulation (EU) No. 470/2014, *Solar Glass (China)*, at para. 71.
[119]Commission Implementing Regulation (EU) No. 470/2014, *Solar Glass (China)*, at para. 71.
[120]Commission Implementing Regulation (EU) No. 470/2014, *Solar Glass (China)*, at para. 83.
[121]Commission Implementing Regulation (EU) No. 470/2014, *Solar Glass (China)*, at para. 95.
[122]Commission Implementing Regulation (EU) No. 470/2014, *Solar Glass (China)*, at para. 105.
[123]Commission Implementing Regulation (EU) No. 470/2014, *Solar Glass (China)*, at para. 103.

4.1.2.3.4.2 The Provision of Land-Use Rights

With respect to the provision of land-use rights, market distortion was established by reference to the proxy market benchmark, which demonstrated the absence of market-driven structures in China.[124]

As alternative benchmark, Taiwan was chosen.[125] In particular the high GDP *per capita* and the high population density as common features of the provinces the producers were located in and Taiwan constituted the foundation of this decision.[126] The idea of selecting a country with corresponding economic level, e.g. Egypt, Armenia, Guatemala, Mongolia or Indonesia, which had been suggested by one of the producers, was rejected by the Commission, because the comprehensive list of criteria compared with respect to the selection of Taiwan was important to render a truly meaningful result.[127] Fully adhering to previous EU case law, the EU Commission's reasoning in *Solar Glass (China)* did not bring forward any new patterns of argumentation.

4.1.2.3.5 *Certain Filament Glass Fibre Products (2014)*

Certain Filament Glass Fibre Products (China), the last case within the 5-year period of examination, also resulted in the imposition of countervailing duties.

4.1.2.3.5.1 Preferential Lending

Once again, preferential lending schemes to the glass industry under investigation were subject to the investigation.

Citing the already familiar legal environment—the banking law, the General Rules on Loans by the People's Bank of China and Decision No. 40[128]—the fact of the government being the major shareholder in the banking sector[129] and the setting of lending rates by the People's Bank of China[130] with subsequent alignment on part of private banks[131] the Commission arrived at the conclusion that the Chinese lending market was distorted by predominant influence of the government.

[124] Commission Implementing Regulation (EU) No. 470/2014, *Solar Glass (China)*, at para. 182.

[125] Commission Implementing Regulation (EU) No. 470/2014, *Solar Glass (China)*, at para. 189.

[126] Commission Implementing Regulation (EU) No. 470/2014, *Solar Glass (China)*, at para. 190.

[127] Commission Implementing Regulation (EU) No. 470/2014, *Solar Glass (China)*, at para. 192.

[128] Commission Implementing Regulation (EU) No. 1379/2014, *Certain Filament Glass Fibre Products (China)*, at para. 106.

[129] Commission Implementing Regulation (EU) No. 1379/2014, *Certain Filament Glass Fibre Products (China)*, at para. 107.

[130] Commission Implementing Regulation (EU) No. 1379/2014, *Certain Filament Glass Fibre Products (China)*, at para. 109.

[131] Commission Implementing Regulation (EU) No. 1379/2014, *Certain Filament Glass Fibre Products (China)*, at para. 117.

The Commission also referred to the results of the investigations in *Solar Panels (China)* and *Solar Glass (China)* to substantiate its reasoning.[132]

Again, the Commission used its already familiar pattern to conclude on a NMES on the lending market that warranted the selection of alternative benchmarks. In the selection of the alternative benchmark, the BB rating from Bloomberg was chosen as suitable credit rating for the loans of the Chinese exporters. Existing Chinese interest rates were adjusted accordingly by adding the calculated risk premium to the applied lending rates.[133]

4.1.2.3.5.2 Provision of Land-Use Rights

Having become a regular in anti-subsidy investigations against China, the provision of land-use rights was also investigated in *Certain Filament Glass Fibre Products (China)*. Here, the Commission employed its "classical" argumentation.

As the acquisition of LURs in China was only possible by bidding, quotation or auction within a system also containing floor prices beyond the agreed price is forbidden to drop,[134] the market for LURs was *"unclear and non-transparent"*[135] and thus distorted by arbitrary price setting.[136]

The Commission once more chose Taiwan as appropriate benchmark, relying on previous well-established criteria.[137]

4.1.3 Conclusion

The EU's alternative benchmark regime largely mirrors the WTO framework of Article 14 ASCM. Particularities on EU level include the alternative benchmark methodologies for Article 6(d)-type subsidies, which are explicitly laid down in the BASR, and elaborating non-binding guidelines on subsidy calculation that provide a limited degree of legal certainty to countries under investigation.

Although not longstanding, the EU has developed a small but very effective anti-subsidy practice against China. Due to the establishment of certain patterns of reasoning and the likeness of the schemes through which the Chinese government

---

[132]Commission Implementing Regulation (EU) No. 1379/2014, *Certain Filament Glass Fibre Products (China)*, at para. 111.

[133]Commission Implementing Regulation (EU) No. 1379/2014, *Certain Filament Glass Fibre Products (China)*, at para. 129 et seq.

[134]Commission Implementing Regulation (EU) No. 1379/2014, *Certain Filament Glass Fibre Products (China)*, at para. 189.

[135]Commission Implementing Regulation (EU) No. 1379/2014, *Certain Filament Glass Fibre Products (China)*, at para. 193.

[136]Commission Implementing Regulation (EU) No. 1379/2014, *Certain Filament Glass Fibre Products (China)*, at para. 193.

[137]Commission Implementing Regulation (EU) No. 1379/2014, *Certain Filament Glass Fibre Products (China)*, at para. 200.

grants subsidies to the different sectors of industries, proving subsidisation of Chinese producers is nowadays not really a difficult task for investigating authorities. Once a certain line of reasoning has proved successful, it is employed again, mostly word-by-word, if the same type of subsidy is allegedly granted to another industry sector. The approach of the Commission has thus become very predictable.

But this finding also permits the conclusion that the reasoning of the Commission remains rather general and superficial and is thus easily adaptable to subsequent investigations. The reasons the Commission states are not irrational, but neither are they necessarily coercive or without alternative. Thus, the interchangeable applicability in different investigations raises suspicions with regard to arbitrariness and random choice. Paired with the request of numerous documents within the rather short investigation deadline (Article 11(2) BASR) and the resulting frequent use of *"facts available"* (Article 28(5) BASR),[138] this comportment provides the Commission with a—from Chinese perspective—dangerous tool.

4.2 WTO Law Conformity of the EU's Alternative Benchmark Approach in Anti-Subsidy Investigations Against China

As a WTO member, the EU is bound to comply with the obligations created in the anti-subsidy-related WTO agreements (Article XVI:4 WTO Agreement and Article 32.5 ASCM).[139]

4.2.1 Conformity with Article 14 ASCM

The EU approach on the use of alternative benchmarks in investigations against China must be in conformity as such and as applied with general WTO law prerequisites that have been developed by the WTO judiciary through interpretation of the Article 14 ASCM.

4.2.1.1 Conformity As Such

WTO law conformity as such can be concluded on if the EU's legal anti-subsidy framework on the use of alternative benchmarks, the BASR, is consistent with WTO prerequisites.

[138]Critical regarding scope and nature of the documents requested by the EU Commission in anti-subsidy investigations against China and the subsequent use of "facts available" Qian, 46 *Journal of World Trade* (2012), 961, at 962.

[139]McNelis, 37 *Journal of World Trade* (2003), 647, at 656.

4.2.1.1.1 The Transposed Parts of the BASR

Of the parts of the BASR that have been transposed from the ASCM, i.e. Article 6 (a), (b), (c) and (d)(i) BASR, the finding of WTO consistency presents no further difficulty with regard to Article 14(a) and (c) ASCM. These Articles have not yet been interpreted by the Appellate Body to contain any particular methodology for NMES.

Article 14(b) and (d) ASCM, on the other hand, have been interpreted to include rules for the application of alternative benchmarks in NMES by the Appellate Body. But the wording of the provisions itself does not reflect this and does therefore not impact BASR provisions because WTO Appellate Body reports *de facto* create a precedent for the practice, but do not *de jure* limit existing legislation (Articles 3.2 and 19.2 DSU).[140]

Altogether, the transposed parts of the BASR do not contravene WTO law.

4.2.1.1.2 The EU Genuine Part of the BASR

The EU genuine part of the BASR, Article 6(d)(ii) BASR, largely mirrors the Appellate Body's *US – Softwood Lumber IV* jurisprudence. It states the adjustment of in-country conditions *"by an appropriate amount"* or the use of conditions *"prevailing in the market of another country or on the world market"* in NMES after existing in-country prices have been disregarded due to distortion.

According to the wording of the provision, the methodologies set down in Article 6(d)(ii) BASR may be resorted to interchangeably.[141] The connector *"or"* implies coequality of all options. The Appellate Body, however, held that the adjustment of in-country prices was to be conducted before employing altogether new prices for the subsidy calculation. Taking into consideration the recitals of Regulation (EC) No. 1973/2002, notably recital 2, it becomes apparent that the adjustment of in-country terms and conditions was indeed meant to be applied prior to the employment of third-country or world market prices. Only if an adjustment is *"not practicable, because, inter alia, such prices or costs do not exist or are unreliable"*, as Recital 2 Regulation (EC) No. 1973/2002 states, third-country prices or costs may be used. Article 6(d)(ii) BASR as enacted does not adequately reflect this order of priority. *"If appropriate"*, third-country or world market prices may be used. This prerequisite is too diffuse to set precise guidance in line with the order of application of the methodologies required by the WTO Appellate Body.

Thus, Article 6(d)(ii) BASR does not infringe WTO law *per se*, but contravenes Appellate Body jurisprudence.[142] If contested in WTO dispute settlement, the EU

[140] On the influence of decisions of the WTO judiciary see Sect. 3.1.2.4.1.

[141] See Sect. 4.1.1.1.1.

[142] On the relationship between WTO law and Appellate Body jurisprudence see Sect. 3.1.2.4.1.

approach may very well be held to be violating Article 14(d) ASCM as the Appellate Body will probably adhere to its own prior decisions.[143]

4.2.1.2 Conformity As Applied

EU investigation practice against China can be divided into two parts. One part, of course, comprises the specific case law of anti-subsidy investigations. The EU Commission Guidelines constitute the other part. Although non-binding, they offer guidance to the Commission how to proceed in certain situations[144] and thus manifest a kind of written general practice approach of the EU that can be scrutinised regarding WTO law consistency with Article 14 ASCM.

4.2.1.2.1 The "General Application" in the Guidelines

For grants and the provision of loan guarantees, no provisions regarding the use of alternative benchmark methodologies exist in WTO law. Provisions like Section E(f)(v) and (vii) Guidelines that offer instructions to the Commission how to proceed in NMES in cases of grants are thus in accordance with WTO regulations.

Regarding loans, the non-existence of commercial benchmarks ought to be met with an *"estimation with reference to indicators at the economic situation prevailing at the time"* (Section E(b)(iv) Guidelines). This suggestion corresponds to the adjustment of in-country rates as required by WTO law after *US – Anti-Dumping and Countervailing Duties (China)*.

If goods or services are provided at less than adequate remuneration and competitive private suppliers actually exist on the market, the difference in pricing of the government terms to the lowest private supplier's price forms the subsidy amount (Section E(d)(ii) Guidelines). The wording implies that a lower governmental price of a production input is always the result of subsidisation, i.e. it creates an irrefutable presumption of government inputs never reflecting the market conditions of their manufacture. But if the government could indeed offer the product at the lowest market-based price, an irrefutable presumption in such a situation would contravene the burden of proof requirements under WTO law according to which the investigating authority has to positively show market distortion on behalf of the government.[145] What "saves" WTO law compatibility of the Guidelines, is the word *"normally"*. Whenever low government prices are economically justified, deviation from the suggested practice remains possible for the Commission.

---

[143]On the WTO Appellate Body's *de facto stare decisis* approach see Sect. 3.1.2.4.1.

[144]On regulatory content and legal nature of the Guidelines see Sect. 4.1.1.2.

[145]Regarding the required standard of evidence for the rejection of in-country benchmarks as distorted see Appellate Body Report, *US – Anti-Dumping and Countervailing Duties (China)*, at para. 443 et seq.

With respect to government monopoly suppliers, the amount of benefit is the full amount of preferential price unless the preferential conditions are justified by economic reasons (Section E(d)(iii) Guidelines).

All in all, the EU Guidelines are in accordance with WTO law prerequisites.

4.2.1.2.2 The EU Approach Regarding Preferential Lending

The conditions in the banking sector have enormous influence on the whole economy. The reasoning of the EU regarding preferential lending thus rewards particular scrutiny.

4.2.1.2.2.1 The Establishment of Market Distortion

The EU referred to several legal and factual findings of the Chinese lending sector to conclude on market distortion.

To provide evidence for a NMES on the Chinese lending market, the Commission first cited various Chinese legal regulations, e.g. laws, policy plans and guidelines like Decision No. 40 or Article 34 and 38 Commercial Banking Law.[146] This approach convinces, if the documents referred to actually serve as means of proof for the exercise of governmental influence. Usually, this is the case with legally binding documents. It is certainly true for the enlisted laws.

Regarding policy plans, however, the Commission's argumentation turns out problematic. Officially, policy plans do not possess legally binding character in China. This is expressed by their current Chinese labelling. Instead of 计划 (*jihua*), plans are now officially named 计规 (*jigui*)—a more fitting translation would thus be *"guideline"* instead of *"plan"*.[147]

Nevertheless, although lacking an official imperative guise, policy guidelines do serve as instrument to effectively secure governmental influence. In combination with binding legislation, e.g. Article 34 and 38 Commercial Banking Law, stating that private banks have to issue loans in accordance with state policy goals laid down in plans and guidelines, *per se* non-binding legal documents like plans substantially exercise the same degree of legal force as formal legislation. Considering their actual effect, guidelines do secure the influence of the government on the lending market. As long as this influence can be traced back to the legal instrument—notwithstanding officially legally binding character—it serves as means of evidence

[146]Council Implementing Regulation (EU) No. 452/2011, *Coated Fine Paper (China)*, at para. 75 et seq.; Council Implementing Regulation (EU) No. 215/2013, *Certain Organic Coated Steel Products (China)*, at para. 172; Council Implementing Regulation (EU) No. 1239/2013, *Solar Panels (China)*, at para. 171; Commission Implementing Regulation (EU) No. 470/2014, *Solar Glass (China)*, at para. 93; Commission Implementing Regulation (EU) No. 1379/2014, *Certain Filament Glass Fibre Products (China)*, at para 112.

[147]Qian, 46 *Journal of World Trade* (2012), 961, at 962.

demonstrating a link from the state to a change of conditions on the respective market and may thus justly be considered in the investigation.

Loan purchases without the usual adjustment of the risk premium sufficiently demonstrate a NMES and constitute a convincing means of proof.

The government acting as major shareholder and owning more than two-thirds of the banks does, however, by itself not signify that the government does not comport itself in accordance with market economy principles. The ability to affect lending rates cannot be equalised with actual influence. In parallel to the Appellate Body stressing that the mere fact of state origin of a contribution to the market does not suffice to prove distortive influence,[148] the mere fact of the government being major shareholder is not enough to conclude on predominance on the market. In addition to the government's position on the market under investigation, positive proof of distortive influence is required to satisfy the prerequisites of the Appellate Body set down in *US – Anti-Dumping and Countervailing Duties (China)*. Therefore, this argument does by itself not meet WTO prerequisites.

In contrast, the SOCB's influence on lending rates was supported by positive proof besides government ownership. This argument of the Commission proves valid.

Finally, the lack of credit risk assessment before the issue of a loan does not correspond to market economy conditions and therefore shows distortive comportment on part of the government.

4.2.1.2.2.2 The Selection of the Alternative Benchmark

For the selection of the alternative benchmark, the EU investigating authority proceeded to adjust existing Chinese interest rates *"to reflect normal market risk"*.[149] In doing so, it chose Bloomberg's BB rating attributed to Chinese companies, added an *"appropriate"*[150] risk premium and accordingly corrected the rates discovered in the investigation. This approach appears solid.

Having to justify its choice, however, the Commission failed to give truly convincing reasons. Upon objections raised by one Chinese producer, APP, which had been granted a more preferential A1 rating by Moody's, another of the "big three" credit rating agencies, the EU declined revising its calculation on the grounds that the Moody rating could only have been received due to the benefits conferred by the governmental contribution which had unduly bettered the economic situation of the company.[151] The Chinese exporter was denied the "fruit of the poisonous tree", i.e. a more favourable treatment.

The same argument, however, could also be applied to the BB rating the Commission finally relied on. Maybe, if not for the "fruit of the poisonous tree",

[148]Appellate Body Report, *US – Anti-Dumping and Countervailing Duties (China)*, at para. 443.

[149]Council Implementing Regulation (EU) No. 452/2011, *Coated Fine Paper (China)*, at para. 98.

[150]Council Implementing Regulation (EU) No. 452/2011, *Coated Fine Paper (China)*, at para. 99.

[151]Council Implementing Regulation (EU) No. 452/2011, *Coated Fine Paper (China)*, at para. 326.

an even worse Bloomberg rating would have been appropriate? The lack of proper justification for the choices made shows their deliberateness. Although not being illegal, the selection of the alternative benchmark could easily have ended with very different results—if EU investigating authorities had decided accordingly. Although not contravening WTO law, this reasoning makes one see how problematic the conferral of a large amount of discretion and lack of efficient means of its control can prove with regard to transparency, legal security and the rule of law.

4.2.1.2.3 The EU Approach Regarding the Provision of Credit Lines

Regarding the provision of credit lines, the Commission basically adopted the same approach as with respect to preferential lending.

4.2.1.2.3.1 The Establishment of Market Distortion

To prove the NMES, the Commission alleged that the same banks in the evidentially distorted banking sector are also responsible for issuing credit lines.[152] The first main line of argumentation thus raises all the objections discussed above.[153]

Secondly, the payment of no or only a moderate fee instead of a substantial commitment and administration fees as usually required on the credit line market clearly demonstrate the gap to market conditions and have justly been enclosed in the reasoning.

Apart from the one argument of the government as major shareholder, whose WTO inconsistency has already been concluded upon,[154] the establishment of market distortion meets the required prerequisites.

4.2.1.2.3.2 The Selection of the Alternative Benchmark

Again, the adjustment of existing in-country prices was deemed impossible. But in the light of the recognised existence of Chinese prices, which could principally be used as basis for an adjustment, simply referring to governmental price distortion as the reason adjustment of existing in-country prices is deemed impossible does not suffice. Government predominance is the necessary prerequisite to proceed to the use of alternative benchmarks at all. Therein, the employment of alternative prices is not the only possible "way out" in cases of NMES. Rather, additional reasons besides the mere fact of market distortion by governmental predominance are required to be allowed to disregard existing in-country prices. Letting governmental distortion alone suffice as evidence for the employment of alternative benchmarks

---

[152] Council Implementing Regulation (EU) No. 1239/2013, *Solar Panels (China)*, at para. 204 et seq.

[153] See Sect. 4.2.1.2.2.1.

[154] See Sect. 4.2.1.2.2.1.

does not adequately take into account price adjustment as part of the legal regime and would obliterate it as necessary requirement.

The Commission, however, did not cite additional evidence but merely referred to the distortion found on the lending market. This sets the process of selecting the alternative benchmark contrary to WTO law.

The final selection of the alternative benchmark, a market-based credit line obtained by one producer, then, however, matches the prerequisites.

This can be held even though the Commission itself seemed to come to a different conclusion. Searching for the alternative benchmark, the EU Commission astonished by considering that the *"adequacy of the remuneration for the financial services could not be determined in relation to prevailing market conditions in the PRC"*.[155] As appropriateness is a major prerequisite in the selection process according to the Appellate Body,[156] not observing it would constitute a blatant contravention against WTO law. The benchmark actually selected, though, is in fact a market-based benchmark including substantial commitment and administration fee. It corresponds to what would have been the outcome of taking a Chinese credit line adjusted to represent market conditions. Contrary to its self-assessment, the EU lastly does respect WTO law prerequisites here.

Whatever the reason behind the irritating phrase in paragraph 213 of the *Solar Panels (China)* investigation report—it has no effect on the positive finding of WTO law consistency of the reasoning as a whole.

4.2.1.2.4 The EU Approach Regarding the Provision of Land-Use Rights

Having already become one of the "classics" in investigation practice, the reasoning of the Commission when dealing with the provision of LURs at less than adequate remuneration has so far always ended with Chinese in-country prices being disregarded and Taiwan being selected as alternative benchmark. With regard to the reasoning itself, it appears diligent and well-founded. But under closer scrutiny, the arguments lose their coerciveness.

4.2.1.2.4.1 The Establishment of Market Distortion

As regards market distortion due to government predominance, by demonstrating the distribution of state-owned land to private individuals never being possible without governmental approval, the Commission appropriately laid down the non-existence of private prices on both the primary and the secondary market for LURs.

Referring to Taiwan, the later alternative benchmark, to argue for disregarding existing Chinese prices, is, however, beside the point. Using the alternative

155 Council Implementing Regulation (EU) No. 1239/2013, *Solar Panels (China)*, at para. 213.

156 Appellate Body Report, *US – Anti-Dumping and Countervailing Duties (China)*, at para. 489.

benchmark to argue for a deviation from the existing benchmark is taking B to argue for the fulfilment of the conditions of A. It constitutes circular reasoning.

4.2.1.2.4.2 The Selection of the Alternative Benchmark

In priorly considering adjustment of existing Chinese LUR prices, the Commission principally complied with the first requirement set down by the Appellate Body in *US – Softwood Lumber IV*. But as with credit lines,[157] merely alleging that Chinese prices were not fully reflecting market-based prices would be too weak an argument to justify complete disregard of existing in-country prices. With regard to LURs, the Commission argued that no private prices have been found on the LUR market at all, but that government presence was ubiquitous. The non-existence of private prices justifies the complete disregard of in-country benchmarks.

The Commission then in all cases chose Taiwanese land prices as alternative benchmark and applied a range of criteria to assure the necessary relation between the Taiwanese land prices and the Chinese land prices without the governmental distortion. The range of factors applied certainly expresses thorough reasoning on part of the Commission. But not all of the altogether nine factors convince.

The similar level of economic development and structure, the high level of infrastructure on both sides and the similarity between the type of land and transaction assure correspondent economic environments and thus effectively serve the purpose of ensuring correspondent conditions to adequately choose the alternative benchmark.

But physical proximity by itself conveys no significance. It is the similarity of the type of land and transaction ascertaining comparability.

Considering strong economic cross-border connections, the fact that the two Chinese provinces the respective producers are designated as *"top manufacturing provinces"* as well as common demographic, linguistic and cultural features to ensure the selection of an appropriate, i.e. comparable benchmark, does not convince. The mere strength of economic relations stands in no connection to respective domestic economic conditions. More often than not, countries with very different economic backgrounds engage in mutual trade.

The fact of *"top manufacturing provinces"* speaks for the economic potency of the two provinces. But in no way does this create a strong link to Taiwan.

Finally, cultural closeness between China and Taiwan does not in any way refer to comparable economic conditions in the land sector. If the cultural link between China and Taiwan would indeed constitute a valid argument, the singularity of the Chinese culture would basically at all times require investigations against China to resort to Taiwan for the selection of the alternative benchmark.

Furthermore, by applying criteria to ensure the general comparability of Chinese and Taiwanese economies as a whole, the Commission misjudges the objective of the alternative benchmark methodologies. In its choice of alternative benchmark, the

---

[157] See Sect. 4.2.1.2.3.2.

Commission should aim at establishing conditions matching the economic situation in China without the governmental distortion in the sector under investigation, not the situation market economy conditions would prevail in the entire Chinese economy.[158] By pursuing the "greater aim", the Commission sets itself at odds with Appellate Body requirements.

Not all the criteria applied conform with WTO prerequisites. But successful challenge in front of the WTO judiciary will rather depend on the process of reasoning and not so much on the actual result.[159] The approach of the EU Commission in selecting an alternative benchmark for Chinese LUR prices might thus well be held incompatible with WTO law—and it might well be not.

4.2.1.2.5 The EU Approach Regarding the Provision of Hot-Rolled and Cold-Rolled Steel

Dealing with the provision of HRS and CRS, the Commission also presented an outwardly solid argumentation.

4.2.1.2.5.1 The Establishment of Market Distortion

Presenting a market analysis revealing that 63% of all HRS were provided by SOEs, the Commission proved government predominance, because other private suppliers tended to align their prices to remain competitive. With regard to CRS, a correspondent market analysis showed only an amount of 18% of all CRS being put on the market by SOEs—not enough to prove predominant influence by the government. The Commission additionally cited the World Steel Capacity Book, stating a SOE share of over 70%, and stressed the intermediary role of trade companies, which made direct attribution to the government of China impossible. Thus, of course, market distortion was also proven for CRS.

But the Commission's approach irritates nevertheless. Why the figure for HRS was readily accepted, while the figure for CRS was rejected, remains in the dark. Maybe the percentage for HRS would even have been higher, if an approach similar to CRS would have been embarked on.[160] Like this, the approach of the Commission creates highly conspicuous circumstances. With no convincing explanation for the Commission's contradictory procedure, it appears as if the original figures for CRS have been rejected simply for the reason of being "too low".

But once more, the reasons the Commission states are *per se* coherent. No matter how dubious their selection—as long as the reasoning is not totally unreasonable or

[158] Vermulst/Gatta, 11 *World Trade Review* (2012), 527, at 573 et seq.

[159] Vermulst/Gatta, 11 *World Trade Review* (2012), 527, at 547.

[160] Regarding the required standard of evidence for the rejection of in-country benchmarks see Appellate Body Report, *US – Anti-Dumping and Countervailing Duties (China)*, at para. 443 et seq.

at fault, which it is not, successfully arguing for a breach of WTO law will prove hard work for China.

4.2.1.2.5.2 The Selection of the Alternative Benchmark

Upon rejection of existing in-country prices as non-adjustable, the Commission embarked on the construction of a world market price for the benefit calculation. Again, it is doubtful whether the Commission was indeed entitled to proceed without prior adjustment of the existing but distorted in-country prices as required under Article 14(d) ASCM. Looking once again closely at the reasoning of the Commission, no reason besides government predominance spreading over the entire market is given to justify deviation.[161] This poses the question where to draw the line with regard to adjustable distortion and non-adjustable distortion. Unlike in the case of LURs, however, private prices, though distorted, have been discovered on the market. This makes it necessary to cite evidence besides the mere fact of government distortion that explains why an adjustment of these prices was impossible, e.g. why essential price components for an adjustment procedure could not be discovered. The reasoning of the Commission as it stands is not enough to satisfy the requirements of the Appellate Body's *US – Softwood Lumber IV* regime but remains too undiversified.

After rejecting existing in-country prices, the Commission proceeded to constructing the world market prices for HRS and CRS as alternative benchmarks. Seemingly, again, the criteria of the Commission make sense. Closer scrutiny, however, uncovers deficits.

Choosing the biggest market on each continent (Europe, the USA, Turkey, Japan and Brazil) certainly renders a price actually representing the economic conditions all around the world. Stressing that the regions and countries of choice are amongst the biggest steel producers worldwide only backs up this argument. The assertion that none of the countries or regions selected had the highest prices on the world market, as if this fact was something desirable in the process of reasoning, bewilders in this context. In establishing a truly representative price, disregarding markets because they also have the highest prices on their continents lacks convincing reason and is contrary to the representativeness that is aspired. Rather, the height of the price by itself bears no significance—despite mitigating the circumstances of investigating a fellow WTO member by seemingly conceding a lenient approach for the selection of the alternative benchmark. As well, when constructing world market prices, stressing that only WTO members have been selected seems somewhat beside the point. Though far-reaching, the WTO member market is not comprehensive—and thus, not entirely a world market. In addition, the feature of WTO membership can confer no guarantee that the selected prices actually constitute market-based prices. Neither can it assure any other meaningful characteristic.

---

[161]Council Implementing Regulation (EU) No. 215/2013, *Certain Organic Coated Steel Products (China)*, at para. 81.

Unconvincing as some of the criteria applied may be—neither is actually unlawful. Whether non-convincibility is enough to induce a panel or the Appellate Body into a finding of WTO-inconsistency, is something only time will show.

All in all, the selection of the alternative benchmarks for HRS and CRS suffers from the too unrefined rejection of the possibility of in-country price adjustment and is for this reason in breach of WTO law.

4.2.2 Conformity with Section 15(b) CAP

The EU approach on the use of alternative benchmarks in investigations against China must also be in conformity with the China-specific WTO regime. According to Section 15(b) CAP, to legally deviate from existing Chinese prices, special difficulties in the application of Article 14 ASCM must occur. Regarding the selection of the alternative benchmark, prior adjustment is mandatory in case of practicability.

4.2.2.1 Conformity As Such

Articles 6(a)–(d)(i) BASR, the transposed parts of the BASR, contain no special provisions for situations dealing in any way with NME conditions. Although Section 15(b) CAP applies to all kinds of subsidies, their content does not contravene the CAP requirements as setting up an alternative benchmark regime is not mandatory.

The EU genuine parts of the BASR, i.e. the alternative benchmark regime of Article 6(d)(ii) BASR is applicable in cases where market economy terms and conditions are not prevailing in the country under investigation.

Recalling the different possibilities to interpret the term *"special difficulties"* in Section 15(b) CAP, the EU provision would be in accordance with the option letting a general unusualness be sufficient to fill the meaning. In cases where China-specific distortions are required, a mere NME environment is not a Chinese particular, but can be found elsewhere. Thus, understanding *"special difficulties"* in a narrow China-exclusive sense, Art. 6(d)(ii) BASR infringes the WTO law prerequisites in the CAP.

Like the CAP, Article 6(d)(ii) BASR stipulates the adjustment of existing in-country prices. According to the BASR, adjustment *"shall be"* conducted—other methodologies remain applicable *"when appropriate"*. As pointed out, this wording does not adequately reflect the order of priority which is *per se* required by WTO law.[162]

What could "save" the BASR rule, however, is the practicability exception in Section 15(b) CAP. If non-practicability of an adjustment matches the freedom to

[162] See Sect. 4.2.1.1.2.

select an out-of-country benchmark if appropriate, is, however, a question hardly fit to be judged at present. Eventual WTO law conformity hinges on panel or Appellate Body assessment. Findings either way are equally probable.

4.2.2.2 Conformity As Applied

After the EU approach has been discovered to be partly contrary to WTO law as such, it appears likely that this finding will be reiterated with regard to conformity as applied.

4.2.2.2.1 The "General Application" in the Guidelines

Unlike Article 14 ASCM, Section 15(b) CAP includes all types of subsidies in its NMES regime. All Guideline provisions must thus find themselves in accordance with the CAP. As all Guideline rules in Section E dealing with NMES refer to general forms of market distortion, in the narrow understanding of *"special difficulties"* they would contravene WTO law. In all other interpretations, they do not constitute violations.

In addition, not all Guideline provisions include references to prior adjustment. This cannot be remedied even by the practicability exception.

The Commission Guidelines might therefore be found in violation of WTO law.

4.2.2.2.2 The EU Approach Regarding Preferential Lending

The citation of miscellaneous Chinese legislative regulations and the references to conditions found on the Chinese market during the investigation can be assessed twofold. On the one hand, they can be regarded as specific examination of Chinese particularities and constitute China-exclusive reasoning in the narrow sense of *"special difficulties"*. On the other hand, the evidence gathered on the Chinese banking sector can be viewed to express a distortion of economic conditions, which can be found also in other countries—supported by different kinds of proof. Again, a definite answer to the question of WTO conformity remains elusive.

The selection process for the alternative benchmark is in line with the requirements of Section 15(b) CAP, because the Commission choses to adjust existing rates for the new benchmark.

4.2.2.2.3 The EU Approach Regarding the Provision of Credit Lines

Correspondent to the approach taken towards preferential lending, the reasoning regarding the provision of credit lines is only in accordance with *"special difficulties"* in a narrow sense, if the evidence of distortion of the Chinese banking sector is considered as China-exclusive and not only as expression of a kind of generally possible market distortion.

Rejecting existing in-country prices as distorted, the Commission only referred to government predominance. As the obligation to adjust is limited by the practicability exception of Section 15(b) CAP, one could argue that in contrast to the general WTO regime mere government predominance would suffice to justify a complete disregard of Chinese prices. But this broad understanding of the practicability exception would in fact invariably lead to a rejection of prior adjustment and *de facto* obliterate a legal prerequisite of any meaningful content. This contravenes the maxim of *"harmonious interpretation"* developed by the Appellate Body, i.e. nothing in a clause must be left to inutility of redundancy.[163] Thus, also under Section 15(b) CAP, more than mere government predominance has to be shown to legally reject the possibility of adjusting in-country prices. The argumentation of the Commission does therefore not meet the required standard of proof.

4.2.2.2.4 The EU Approach Regarding the Provision of Land-Use Rights

Citing governmental control of both primary and secondary LUR market as evidence for distortion, the Commission definitely meets the requirements for *"special difficulties"* in its broader general market distortion meaning. If the narrow meaning is also fulfilled can once more not be determined entirely for sure—either view is possible. The reference to Taiwanese prices, on the other hand, does also not constitute a valid argument under Section 15(b) CAP.

Considering the omnipresent position of the Chinese government on the LUR market, effectively not enabling the development of private prices by market forces at all, adjustment of in-country prices was justly rejected. Regarding the criteria for the selection of Taiwan, the same critique elaborated on above equally applies here.[164]

The EU approach for LURs thus partially violates Section 15(b) CAP.

4.2.2.2.5 The EU Approach Regarding the Provision of Hot-Rolled and Cold-Rolled Steel

The evidence collected for government predominance on the market for HRS and CRS rather reflects general market deficits than China-exclusive features. This would not meet the requirements of the narrow view of *"special difficulties"*. But panel or the Appellate Body might assess this differently when confronted with the issue. Thus, a definite finding as regards WTO law conformity cannot be given.

---

[163] Appellate Body Report, *US – Gasoline*, at 23.

[164] See Sect. 4.2.1.2.4.2.

The rejection to adjust existing prices for HRS and CRS was founded on the grounds of mere governmental distortion of the respective markets and does therefore not accord with the standard of evidence requirements set in Section 15(b) CAP. The reasoning of the Commission contravenes WTO law.

4.2.3 *Overall WTO Law Conformity of the EU Approach on the Use of Alternative Benchmark Methodologies in Anti-Subsidy Investigations Against China*

The final WTO legal framework for China is affected greatly by dubiousness, so that disentangling it completely and setting down concisely the applicable substantive prerequisites is impossible at present.[165] Thus, scrutinising the conformity of the EU legal framework considers all the models elaborated on above.

4.2.3.1 Conformity As Such

Article 6(a)–(d)(i) BASR as transposed parts of the BASR, not containing any explicit NMES methodology, are in conformity with China's WTO anti-subsidy law according to all models.[166]

Article 6(d)(ii) BASR as EU genuine part of the BASR is not in accordance with the *US – Softwood Lumber IV* jurisprudence for Article 14(d) ASCM as the priority of the adjustment of existing in-country prices is not clearly reflected in the wording of the provision.[167] According to models 2 a, 2 bi, 2 biiα and 2 biiγ(1), WTO law conformity has thus to be negated. Pursuant to model 2 biiβ, the lack of clarity regarding the priority of adjustment could be excused by the practicability exception. The wording of Article 6(d)(ii) BASR, however, only referring to general conditions of distortion, contravenes Section 15(b) CAP if understood in a narrow China-specific sense.[168]

As regards models 2 a, bi and biiα, WTO law non-conformity can positively be held. For models 2 biiβ and 2 biiγ(1) and (2), too many unknown factors impede a definite statement.

4.2.3.2 Conformity As Applied

For overall WTO law conformity as applied with regard to China, a similar result stands to expect.

[165] See Sect. 3.2.3.2; Mueller, 50 *Journal of World Trade* (2016), 867, at 872 et seq.

[166] For the applicability models see Sect. 3.2.3.2.4.1.

[167] See Sect. 4.2.1.1.2.

[168] See Sect. 4.2.2.1.

4.2.3.2.1 The "General Application" in the Guidelines

Models 2 a, 2 bi, 2 biiα and 2 biiγ(1), with Article 14 ASCM prevailing, let the Guidelines accord with the overall WTO framework.

Models 2 bi, 2 biiβ and 2biiγ(2), being characterised by Section 15(b) CAP prevalence or decisive influence respectively, do not lead to same result. Because the Guidelines do not stipulate prior adjustment in all cases, they do not meet the Section 15(b) CAP requirements.[169] In addition, a China-exclusive understanding of *"special difficulties"* would also lead to contravention against to the overall WTO framework.

Comprehensively, the Guidelines do not find themselves in full accordance with the overall WTO law prerequisites for the use of alternative benchmarks against China.

4.2.3.2.2 The EU Approach Regarding Preferential Lending

Based on models 2 a, 2 bi, 2 biiα and 2 biiγ(1), the EU approach is partially in violation of overall WTO law because the government being the major shareholder does by itself not constitute a valid argument to prove government predominance. The selection of the alternative benchmark then conforms WTO law.

Models 2 bi, biiβ and 2biiγ(2) find the EU's reasoning for preferential lending at fault if *"special difficulties"* are understood in their narrow sense and if the evidence of distortion in the Chinese banking sector is then not regarded as China-exclusive and but as general form of distortion.

Therefore, the overall conformity of the EU's argumentation with respect to preferential lending cannot be definitely decided on.

4.2.3.2.3 The EU Approach Regarding the Provision of Credit Lines

Regarding the provision of credit lines, models 2 a, 2 bi, 2 biiα and 2 biiγ(1) also render the result of a partial violation with respect to the argument of the government being the major shareholder. As well, the approach is in violation of WTO law because the rejection of adjusting Chinese prices was not adequately supported by evidence beside mere market distortion through government predominance.

For the latter reason, models 2 bi, biiβ and 2biiγ(2) are also violated. In addition, only if the wider understanding of *"special difficulties"* prevails, the evidence presented is in accordance with overall WTO law.

---

[169] See Sect. 4.2.2.2.1.

4.2.3.2.4 The EU Approach Regarding the Provision of Land-Use Rights

Article 14 ASCM prevalence-models 2 a, 2 bi, 2 biiα and 2 biiγ(1) as well as Section 15(b) CAP-determined models 2 bi, biiβ and 2biiγ(2) render a breach of WTO law when looking at the selection process for the alternative benchmark. Some of the criteria chosen to justify resorting to Taiwan as apparently suitable third-country bear no significance for the respective process. Moreover, the indications drawn from the differences between Chinese and Taiwanese conditions do not constitute valid arguments so that the EU approach in the provision of LURs is not in accordance with overall WTO law for China.

4.2.3.2.5 The EU Approach Regarding the Provision of Hot-Rolled and Cold-Rolled Steel

According to models 2a, 2 bi, 2 biiα and 2 biiγ(1), no violation of the EU's reasoning regarding market distortion in the cases of HRS and CRS can be detected. Too unrefined a reasoning when rejecting Chinese in-country prices, however, results in a violation of WTO law.

Pursuant to models 2bi, 2biiβ and 2biiγ(2), the evidence for fulfilling the pre-requisites for deviation is only in accordance if the evidence of distortion of the Chinese HRS and CRS market is regarded as China-exclusive and not only as expression of market irregularities also being possible in other countries. Regarding the selection of the alternative benchmark, more than mere government predominance would have had to be established.

Hence, based on all models, also model 2biii, overall WTO conformity has to be rejected.

4.2.4 Conclusion

The Commission's application of the EU's NMES regime in anti-subsidy investigations against China appears to be legally sound. Cited evidence seems to have been collected carefully, arguments to the point. Upon further examination, however, first-glance coerciveness deteriorates.

The reasoning of the Commission is not fully in conformity with the alternative benchmark regime of Article 14 ASCM as such and as applied. Violations of the EU's approach might be alleged successfully in front of the WTO judiciary. As regards conformity as such, Article 6(d)(ii) BASR might be found to be in breach of the prerequisites set by the WTO Appellate Body for the application of alternative benchmark methodologies in NMES with regard to the provision of goods in its interpretation of Article 14(d) ASCM. With respect to conformity as applied, various arguments of the many the EU Commission has—often repeatedly—contended have been found to contravene Article 14 ASCM, in particular the position that the government acting as major shareholder by itself allowed the conclusion of market distortion. How this affects WTO conformity of the entire reasoning is hard to judge. It will probably depend on how significant a panel or the Appellate Body will regard the reliance of the Commission on the flawed factors in relation to its argumentation as a whole.

Analysing conformity of the Commission's argumentation with Section 15 (b) CAP shows very clearly the diffuseness of the China-specific provisions of the CAP. Definite assessments can only be rendered to a limited extent. Some partial violations of Section 15(b) CAP, spreading over all the examined types of subsidies, have been discovered. But to the far greater extent, the prerequisites of Section 15(b) CAP prove hardly workable. The requirements of *"special difficulties"* or *"practicability"* cannot as of today reasonably be filled with a definite and justiciable meaning. With respect to the argumentation regarding distortion of banking sector and LUR market, it appears more China-exclusive than not and would hence accord with the prerequisites in any way. But their content lastly remains elusive—putting the ultimate decision on conformity with Section 15(b) CAP as such and as applied entirely in the hands of the Appellate Body.

Based upon the different models describing the overall WTO framework of anti-subsidy rules against China, no model eventually renders the result of complete conformity of the Commission's approach. Again, however, if this finding would be mirrored in a report of a panel or the Appellate Body cannot be ascertained. Too many factors remain ultimately open to interpretation and prevent a secure assessment.

Very often, the reasoning of the Commission does not directly and openly violate the requirements for the use of alternative benchmarks in NMES in anti-subsidy investigations, but it shows a very deliberate exercise of discretion that lacks coercive justification. This becomes especially apparent when respective objections are raised by the Chinese government or Chinese exporters. Presented with alternative reasonable evidence which would be more beneficial to respective exporters the EU's argumentation gets into the lurch.

But to successfully put the EU alternative benchmark regime for NMES to challenge in front of the WTO judiciary, China would have to lay down clear breaches of WTO law. Considering the flexible and non-definitive nature of the legal prerequisites of both Article 14 ASCM and Section 15(b) CAP, showing that the final findings of the Commission evidently contravene WTO law will almost be impossible to achieve.[170]

Rather, putting the focus of the defence on the way of reasoning has been deemed more promising.[171] But again, unless plainly violating WTO law, a criterion employed by the EU Commission in its analysis will rarely be proven not to conform with WTO law prerequisites. Just being replaceable by more convincing alternatives

[170]Consentient Vermulst/Gatta, 11 *World Trade Review* (2012), 527, at 553.

[171]Consentient Vermulst/Gatta, 11 *World Trade Review* (2012), 527, at 553.

does not render cited evidence unlawful. Even if China puts all its efforts in countering the EU's way of reasoning in its determinations, however careful and diligent its argumentation—much will remain open to interpretation and ultimately depend on the respective opinion of the WTO Appellate Body.

4.3 Prospective Developments of the EU Approach on the Use of Alternative Benchmark Methodologies in Anti-Subsidy Investigations

The current strategy of the EU Commission in anti-subsidy investigations against China rests on the large amount of discretion investigating authorities possess under the WTO framework. With such a regime already providing ample opportunities—one wonders what prospects for change exist for the EU approach in the use of alternative benchmarks in anti-subsidy investigations. Options for amendments can be found both within the current 2011 state of Appellate Body interpretation of the general WTO law framework and taking into consideration further evolution of the NMES benchmark rules.

4.3.1 Prospects on the Basis of the WTO Framework in the Current 2011 State of Appellate Body Interpretation

On the basis of the WTO framework in the 2011 state of Appellate Body interpretation, both general changes with regard to all countries as well as China-specific amendments are possible.

4.3.1.1 General Changes

In *US – Anti-Dumping and Countervailing Duties (China)* the Appellate Body transferred its *US – Softwood Lumber IV* jurisprudence to loan subsidies and thus set prerequisites for the determination of alternative benchmarks in NMES. These generally applicable prerequisites are—unlike the *US – Softwood Lumber IV* principles in Article 6(d)(ii) BASR—not yet reflected in EU legislation. Although not mandatorily bound by Appellate Body decisions in cases where the EU is no party in,[172] the EU Commission generally keeps in line with WTO jurisprudence.

---

[172]Appellate Body decisions mandatorily legally bind only the respective parties of the dispute, see Sect. 3.1.2.4.1.

For the area of anti-subsidy matters, Article 1(1) Regulation (EU) 2015/476[173] explicitly stipulates that the EU may amend, repeal or adopt any other implementing measure to achieve conformity with regard to Appellate Body decisions in cases where the Union is directly involved as a litigating party. Article 2(1) Regulation (EU) 2015/476 sets down the same framework for cases the EU is not directly involved. Adding the *US – Anti-Dumping and Countervailing Duties (China)* methodology to the wording of the BASR provisions would enhance clarity and legal certainty for countries investigated.

4.3.1.2 China-Specific Changes

Section 15(b) CAP sets rules for the selection of alternative benchmarks in NMES for all types of subsidies. Constituting written legal WTO prerequisites, the EU is formally bound by them. Inserting these stipulations into the BASR would improve legal clarity and certainty, especially for Article 6(a)- and (c)-type subsidies, as the general ASCM regime has not yet been interpreted to contain any restricting requirements in this regard.

Changes in investigation practice with respect to China are also worth a thought. Invoking Section 15(b) CAP instead of the general Article 14 ASCM regime could constitute a valid option even at present, as the prerequisites of either rule have not yet been shaped in a precise manner nor is their relationship fully understood.[174] Thus, if the Article 14 ASCM prerequisites are not supported by sufficient evidence, it might well be argued by investigating authorities that Section 15(b) CAP is applicable and the respective evidence proves *"special difficulties"*—and therefore allows for the application of alternative benchmarks.

4.3.2 Prospects upon Possible Developments at WTO Level

The lack of workable legal prerequisites might, however, well prompt developments at WTO level.

4.3.2.1 General Changes

Considering the propensity of the Appellate Body to transfer the *US – Softwood Lumber IV* principles, further extensive application of Article 14(a) and (c) ASCM is

[173]Regulation (EU) 2015/476 of the European Parliament and of the Council of 11 March 2015 on the measures that the Union may take following a report adopted by the WTO Dispute Settlement Body concerning anti-dumping and anti-subsidy matters, OJ 2015 L 83/6, 27.3.2015.

[174]See Mueller, 50 *Journal of World Trade* (2016), 867, at 872 et seq.

likely.[175] Upon these changes, the EU should consider integrating such jurisprudence in the BASR—irrespective of being a party of the proceedings or not.

As the present legal framework for the alternative benchmarks is afflicted with deficits, amendments at WTO level *per se* constitute a respective remedy. The EU as WTO member would have to comply with such changes (Article XVI:4 WTO Agreement).

4.3.2.2 China-Specific Changes

The China-specific concept in the CAP might be subject to further elaboration on part of the Appellate Body. Once the provisions of Section 15(b) CAP as well as their interdependency to the general Article 14 regime have been clarified, the integration of such explanations into a China-specific BASR section would be advisable. Newly introducing a whole China-specific section into the BASR not only for (a) and (c)-types but for all types of subsidies will contribute to ensure WTO conformity of the EU approach.

Legal changes of the CAP regime are *per se* conceivable although the exactly applicable mechanism for such changes is not fully clear.[176]

4.3.3 Conclusion

That the Appellate Body will extend the general NMES regime of Article 14 CAP seems rather probable—without having effectively tackled the known problems that result from the wide discretion investigating authorities presently enjoy. From the perspective of the EU, there is thus presently and in the foreseeable future neither necessity nor incentive to alter its present anti-subsidy NMES approach against China.

4.4 Chapter Summary

The EU legal framework for the use of alternative benchmarks in anti-subsidy law largely resembles its WTO counterpart. As far as it constitutes EU genuine legislation, WTO law non-conformity might be attested by the WTO judiciary due to the

---

[175] See Sect. 3.1.2.3.

[176] For an extensive discussion of the legal nature of the CAP and the subsequent question of its applicable amendment procedure see Qin, Wayne State University Law School Legal Studies Research Paper Series No. 09-18 (2009), 1, at 9 et seq.

unclear transposition of the order of priority regarding the applicable methodologies in Article 6(d)(ii) BASR, as required by *US – Softwood Lumber IV*.

The example of EU anti-subsidy investigations against China has shown that the use of alternative benchmark methodologies in NMES is handled in a highly arbitrary manner with the intention of protecting the national industries under the guise of legitimately exercised discretion. In their particulars, not all arguments of the Commission convince. Even if they stand the test of WTO law conformity, they are not necessarily coercive. But as the approach serves the EU well, future modifications without previous changes at WTO level are very unlikely.

The examination of EU anti-subsidy investigations against China therefore clearly demonstrates two things: substantial alterations of the current investigation practice appear direly necessary to lessen the deficits resulting from ambiguous legal frameworks and the exercise of discretion—but they are not to be expected on the singular WTO members' own initiative. To introduce a real novel approach for the use of alternative benchmark methodologies in anti-subsidy law, changes directly at WTO level are unavoidable.

Chapter 5
The Need for Reforming the Alternative Benchmark Regime in WTO Anti-Subsidy Law

Alternative benchmark regimes for NMES in WTO anti-subsidy law have proven a large—and still enlarging—area of law. But whether this development is in accord with the WTO's legal framework and with its constitutive core, is doubtful.

The following chapter analyses whether the virulent issues that have been discovered in the course of the study are limited to the EU-China relationship or whether a greater and more global need for reforming the alternative benchmark regimes in WTO anti-subsidy law exists (Sect. 5.1). Then, two major current developments in WTO anti-subsidy law and practice concerning the use of alternative benchmarks are analysed whether or not they are justified under WTO law (Sect. 5.2).

5.1 The Use of Alternative Benchmark Methodologies in NMES: A Global Perspective

Several developments indicate that the use of alternative benchmark methodologies in NMES in anti-subsidy law indeed constitutes a global trend—which compounds the problems which have been uncovered in the previous analysis of EU investigations against China.

5.1.1 The Existence of Country-Specific Anti-Subsidy Rules in the WTO Legal Hemisphere

One indicator is the proceeding integration of country-specific rules on the use of alternative benchmarks into the WTO legal framework. The first country which

S. Müller, *The Use of Alternative Benchmarks in Anti-Subsidy Law*,
European Yearbook of International Economic Law 4,
https://doi.org/10.1007/978-3-319-77613-2_5

accepted such specific rules to accede to the WTO was China.[1] But it has not remained a singular case.

Apart from the CAP, country-specific rules on the application of alternative benchmark methodologies in anti-subsidy proceedings can be found in the accession documents of Viet Nam. Acceding to the WTO on 11 January 2007,[2] the accession negotiations of Viet Nam heavily drew on the approach pursued towards China. Section 255 Working Party Report of Viet Nam,[3] which has become integral part of the WTO agreements through reference in Section 1.2 Protocol of Accession of Viet Nam,[4] mirrors Section 15(b) CAP. Much of the language of the special provisions in the CAP can be rediscovered.[5] One major difference, however, is the non-inclusion of the adjustment requirement into the Vietnamese provision. Apparently, resort to alternative benchmark methodologies is permitted without the intermediary step of having to employ the undistorted existing in-country price first.

A respective framework has obviously also been envisaged for Tajikistan. But while the chapeau of Section 164 of its Working Party Report[6] states that special regulations for the application of the ASCM on Tajik exports were to follow, the following section only contains a special WTO anti-dumping regime, which corresponds to Section 15(a) CAP. Contrary to what is declared in the chapeau, no special anti-subsidy provisions are mentioned.

The introduction of country-specific rules into the WTO framework via accession packages has only been conducted on a small scale. An evolving trend inspired by the CAP cannot be detected so far. But still—WTO members have become well aware of the possibilities country-specific regulations offer to secure their national interests and have found a way to easily bind new WTO members through accession commitments. The door to add country-specific rules to the general WTO framework has been opened and the great achievement of the Uruguay Round, the uniformity of international trade rules, been exposed.

5.1.2 Alternative Benchmark Regimes for NMES in the Anti-Subsidy Law of Other Countries

The EU's provision in the BASR on the use of alternative benchmark methodologies constitutes only one of many transpositions of the WTO role model. Apart from the

[1]On the WTO accession process and respective commitments of China see Sect. 3.2.1.

[2]https://www.wto.org/english/thewto_e/acc_e/completeacc_e.htm (last visited 1 January 2018).

[3]Report of the Working Party on the Accession of Viet Nam, WT/ACC/VNM/48, 27 October 2006.

[4]Protocol on the Accession of the Socialist Republic of Viet Nam, WT/L/662, 15 November 2006.

[5]Gantz, 36 *North Carolina Journal of International Law and Commercial Regulation* (2010), 85, at 94.

[6]Report of the Working Party on the Accession of the Republic of Tajikistan, WT/ACC/TJK/30, 6 November 2012.

EU, the most frequent initiators of anti-subsidy investigations at WTO level—although exact numbers in the two statistics taken reference to differ—are the USA, Canada and Australia.[7] Their respective national anti-subsidy laws also comprise alternative benchmark regimes for NMES.

5.1.2.1 US Anti-Subsidy Law

The anti-subsidy law of the US is contained in the Tariff Act of 1930.[8] § 701 Tariff Act[9] deals with the imposition of countervailing duties. Since an amendment in the year 2012, § 701(f) Tariff Act explicitly stipulates the applicability of general US anti-subsidy legislation in NMES.[10] Previously, the question whether or not countervailing law was applicable in NMES had been subject to controversial debate in the US.[11] In 1986, the US Court of Appeals ruled in the notorious *Georgetown Steel Corp. v. United States* case that governmental contributions in NMES *"do not create the kind of unfair competitive advantage over American firms against which the countervailing duty act was directed"*.[12] As the NMES prevented the finding of a benefit, countervailing law could not be applied.

In 2006, however, the US Department of Commerce decided to initiate an anti-subsidy investigation against China, expressly distinguishing the economic conditions addressed in *Georgetown Steel Corp. v. United States* from the current nature of China's economy.[13] Thus, although on a dubious argumentative foundation,[14] applicability of countervailing law against China was made possible.

---

[7]According to the statistics provided for by the WTO Committee on Subsidies and Countervailing measures, which are based on respective notifications of WTO members, of a total of 431 anti-subsidy investigations between 1 January 1995 and 30 June 2016 the US initiated 191, Canada 53 and Australia 23. The EU is listed with 77 investigations, see https://www.wto.org/english/tratop_e/scm_e/CV_InitiationsByRepMem.pdf (last visited 1 January 2018). According to the Global Countervailing Duty Database by Bown, for the period from 1995 to 2015, the US commenced 187 investigations, Canada 52 and Australia 21. The EU is listed with 76 proceedings, see Bown, Chad P. (2016) "Global Countervailing Duties Database," The World Bank, June, available at http://econ.worldbank.org/ttbd/gcvd/ (last visited 1 January 2018).

[8]Tariff Act of 1930, Pub. L. 71-361, 46 Stat. 59019, 17 June 1930, 19 USC 4 (§§ 1202-1683g), last amended 15 July 2015. §§ 1671-1677h therein refer to anti-subsidy law.

[9]19 USC 4, § 1671.

[10]Pub. L. 112-99.

[11]See Cornelis, 2 *Global Trade and Customs Journal* (2007), 421.

[12]*Georgetown Steel Corp. v. United States*, US Court of Appeals, Judgment of 18 September 1986, 801 F.2d 1308. For a more detailed overview on the history of non-applicability of US countervailing duty law in NMES see Smith, J., U.S. Trade Remedy Laws and Nonmarket Economies, at 5 et seq.

[13]Smith, J., U.S. Trade Remedy Laws and Nonmarket Economies, at 10 et seq.

[14]China sought judicial action against the decision, but its claim was rejected by the US Court of International Trade, see Smith, J., U.S. Trade Remedy Laws and Nonmarket Economies, at 10 et seq.

Today, § 701(f) Tariff Act undisputedly allows for the imposition of countervailing duties against NME countries. A NME country is defined as *"any foreign country that the administering authority determines does not operate on market principles of cost or pricing structures, so that sales of merchandise in such country do not reflect the fair value of the merchandise"*.[15] In order to be able to determine the benefit, the US Department of Commerce as investigating authority may resort to alternative benchmark methodologies.[16]

5.1.2.2 Canadian Anti-Subsidy Law

Canadian anti-subsidy law is regulated in the SIMA.[17] § 15 SIMA stipulates the methodology for the determination of normal value, i.e. in cases of anti-subsidy investigations, the in-country price. If a market price of the goods cannot be determined, because imports come *"from a [...] country where [...] domestic prices are substantially determined by the government of that country and there is sufficient reason to believe that they are not substantially the same as they would be if they were determined in a competitive market, or from any other country where [...] the government of that country has a monopoly or substantial monopoly of its export trade, and domestic prices are substantially determined by the government of that country and there is sufficient reason to believe that they are not substantially the same as they would be if they were determined in a competitive market"*, §§ 19 and 20 SIMA offer the possibility to employ alternative benchmark methodologies. They list out-of-country prices or constructed prices as methodologies of choice.

5.1.2.3 Australian Anti-Subsidy Law

Australia's anti-dumping and countervailing law is contained jointly in one single legal framework, consisting of the Customs Act 1901,[18] the Customs Tariff Act 1975 and the Customs Tariff Regulation 2013.[19] In this framework, the determination of normal value is stipulated in Section 269 Customs Act 1901. In NMES,

[15] 19 USC § 1677(18)(A).

[16] See e.g. *Coated Free Sheet Paper from the People's Republic of China*, Case C-570-907, Amended Preliminary Affirmative Countervailing Duty Determination, 72 Fed. Reg. 17484, 9 April 2007, at 17486 et seq.; Smith, J., U.S. Trade Remedy Laws and Nonmarket Economies, at 16.

[17] Special Import Measures Act, RSC 1985, chapter S-15, last amended on 1 November 2014.

[18] An Act relating to the Customs (Customs Act 1901), C1901A00006 No. 6, 3 October 1901, last amended on 5 May 2016.

[19] Zhou, 49 *Journal of World Trade* (2015), 975, at 978.

Section 269 (2)(a)(ii) allows for the use of alternative benchmarks.[20] Either price construction or export prices to third countries may be resorted to (Section 269(2) (c) and (d) Customs Act 1901).

5.1.3 *The Role of the Use of Alternative Benchmarks in NMES in Anti-Subsidy Law in WTO Dispute Settlement*

That the global advance of alternative benchmark regimes for NMES in anti-subsidy law constitutes an actual significant development and not only a theoretical embellishment of WTO members' national anti-subsidy laws is demonstrated by the number of disputes brought in front of the WTO judiciary involving either Article 14 ASCM, Section 15 CAP, and Section 1.2 of the Protocol of Accession of Viet Nam or Article 255 of its Working Party Report.

From 1 January 1995 to 1 January 2018, 118 disputes in front of the WTO judiciary have concerned the application of provisions of the ASCM.[21] In 24 cases altogether, the Appellate Body had to deal with the interpretation of Article 14 ASCM. Twelve disputes concern the application of alternative benchmark methodologies in NMES.[22] Though small in mere number, the disputes in this

---

[20]Unlike other major economies, Australia does, however, not apply NMES methodologies against China. Rather, Australia has explicitly granted to China market-economy status for trade remedy investigations as part of the China-Australia Free Trade Agreement negotiations in 2005. See Paragraph 2 Memorandum of Understanding between the Department of Foreign Affairs and Trade of Australia and the Ministry of Commerce of the People's Republic of China on the Recognition of China's Full Market Economy Status and the Commencement of Negotiation of a Free Trade Agreement between Australia and the People's Republic of China, 18 April 2005, available at https://dfat.gov.au/trade/agreements/chafta/Documents/mou_aust-china_fta.pdf (last visited 1 January 2018).

[21]For the data see https://www.wto.org/english/tratop_e/dispu_e/dispu_agreements_index_e.htm?id=A20# (last visited 1 January 2018).

[22]Request for Consultations by Canada, *US — Softwood Lumber III*, WT/DS236/1, 27 August 2001; Request for Consultations by Canada, *US — Softwood Lumber IV*, WT/DS257/1, 13 May 2002; Request for Consultations by China, *United States — Preliminary Anti-Dumping and Countervailing Duty Determinations on Coated Free Sheet Paper from China*, WT/DS368/1, 18 September 2007; Request for Consultations by China, *US – Anti-Dumping and Countervailing Duties (China)*, WT/DS379/1, 22 September 2008; Request for Consultations by India, *US – Carbon Steel (India)*, WT/DS436/1, 18 April 2012; Request for Consultations by China, *US – Countervailing Duties (China)*, WT/DS437/1, 30 May 2012; Request for Consultations by Pakistan, *European Union — Countervailing Measures on Certain Polyethylene Terephthalate from Pakistan*, WT/DS486/1, 5 November 2014; Request for Consultations by Canada, *United States — Countervailing Measures on Supercalendered Paper from Canada*, WT/DS505/1, 5 April 2016; Request for Consultations by Brazil, *United States — Countervailing Measures on Cold- and Hot-Rolled Steel Flat Products from Brazil*, WT/DS514/1, 17 November 2016; Request for Consultations by Turkey, *Countervailing Measures on Certain Pipe and Tube Products (Turkey)*,

area constitute 50% of all Article 14 ASCM-related disputes. This indicates that the determination of alternative benchmarks is often perceived as controversial by countries investigated. The NMES disputes have only relatively recently become an issue: ten proceedings have been started from 2007, eight even only from 2012.

The number of disputes involving the CAP is comparatively small. 29 disputes in total are listed to date.[23] In two cases, a violation of Section 15 CAP has initially been alleged (7%).[24] Subsequently, however, the controversies regarding the use of alternative benchmark methodologies have been contended under the ASCM due to the parties' respective disposition.[25]

Although as of 1 January 2018, the Accession Protocol of Viet Nam has indeed been subject to one WTO dispute settlement procedure, the case did not concern the use of the alternative benchmark regime of Viet Nam's accession package.[26]

5.2 Justification of Current Developments in WTO Anti-Subsidy Law and Practice Concerning the Use of Alternative Benchmarks

Since the beginning of the new millennium, WTO anti-subsidy law and practice have undergone significant changes that concern the use of alternative benchmark methodologies. Two major novelties can be accounted for. First, with the accession of China to the WTO in 2001 as starting point, country-specific NMES rules for anti-subsidy investigations have been integrated into the WTO legal framework through accession protocols. Second, general WTO law has been equipped with an alternative benchmark regime for NMES by the Appellate Body.

Substantially, country-specific accession commitments and a general alternative benchmark regime for NMES far exceed the initially enacted legal environment in

WT/DS523/1, 13 March 2017; Request for Consultations by Canada, *United States — Countervailing Measures on Softwood Lumber from Canada*, WT/DS533/1, 28 November 2017; Request for Consultations by Canada, *United States — Certain Systemic Trade Remedies Measures*, WT/DS535/1, 20 December 2017.

[23]For the data see https://www.wto.org/english/tratop_e/dispu_e/dispu_agreements_index_e.htm?id=A30# (last visited 1 January 2018).

[24]Request for Consultations by China, *US – Anti-Dumping and Countervailing Duties (China)*, WT/DS379/1, 22 September 2008; Request for Consultations by China, *US – Countervailing Duties (China)*, WT/DS437/1, 30 May 2012.

[25]In *US – Anti-Dumping and Countervailing Duties (China)*, the US initially also invoked Section 15(b) CAP. In the course of proceedings, however, the US and China agreed on the dispute being entirely solved under the general alternative benchmark regime of the ASCM, see Panel Report, *US – Anti-Dumping and Countervailing Duties (China)*, at para. 10.110; Pauwelyn, 12 *World Trade Review* (2013), 235, at 240.

[26]For the data see https://www.wto.org/english/tratop_e/dispu_e/dispu_agreements_index_e.htm?id=A30# (last visited 1 January 2018).

WTO anti-subsidy law and pose the question whether they are still justified. To accord with framework and conception of the WTO as major organisation for the regulation of global trade, they must not only be legal but also legitimate.

5.2.1 Concepts for the Justification of the Exercise of Authority in the WTO

Legality and legitimacy serve as concepts for the justification of the exercise of authority in the WTO. They both derive from the same Latin term *lex*, meaning *"law"*.[27] For a very long time a distinction between the terms has indeed not been made.[28] The Oxford Dictionary still defines legality and legitimacy alike as *"[t]he quality or state of being in accordance with the law"*[29] or *"[c]onformity to the law or to rules"*.[30] Recently, however, legitimacy has, namely in the area of international law, evolved as a separate distinct concept besides legality that provides for the justification of political authority.

5.2.1.1 The Concepts of Legality and Legitimacy

Legality is used to assess developments of a legal framework or of its practical application with respect to whether the changes are covered by the legal rules of the framework. It is understood as *"lawfulness"*[31] or *"compliance"*.[32] In establishing a justification of authority, it presents itself as a narrow concept that exclusively considers existing structural and substantive rules.

Legitimacy is also employed in international law to explain the acceptance of political authority.[33] But in doing so, legitimacy has attained a wider dimension in providing for justification of authority of legal acts, decisions or institutional proceedings than "mere" legality.[34] Besides accordance with legal prerequisites, legitimacy also considers "the beyond", e.g. fundamental founding principles of an

[27]http://www.oxforddictionaries.com/definition/english/legality (last visited 1 January 2018); http://www.oxforddictionaries.com/definition/english/legitimate (last visited 1 January 2018).

[28]Bodansky, UGA Legal Studies Research Paper No. 07-013 (2007), 1, at 3.

[29]http://www.oxforddictionaries.com/definition/english/legality (last visited 1 January 2018).

[30]http://www.oxforddictionaries.com/definition/english/legitimacy (last visited 1 January 2018).

[31]Qin, 55 *Virginia Journal of International Law* (2015), 369, at 435.

[32]Bodansky, UGA Legal Studies Research Paper No. 07-013 (2007), 1, at 2.

[33]Bodansky, UGA Legal Studies Research Paper No. 07-013 (2007), 1, at 1; Qin, 55 *Virginia Journal of International Law* (2015), 369, at 435; Bronckers, 2 *Journal of International Economic Law* (1999), 547, at 555.

[34]Bodansky, UGA Legal Studies Research Paper No. 07-013 (2007), 1, at 2 et seq.; Qin, 55 *Virginia Journal of International Law* (2015), 369, at 435.

international organisation.[35] It seeks to ensure the *"validity"*[36] of the authority exercised. *"'Legitimacy watches over laws' and 'serves to support, and when necessary, to correct legality'"*.[37] It is understood as a relative concept.[38] Depending on the amount of authority the organisation exercises, the requirements on legitimacy vary. The higher the bindingness of its decisions, the scope of its decision-making authority and the remoteness to its bound subjects, the higher are the requirements to be fulfilled for legitimacy.[39]

Thus, although an act or development might be justified by the rules of a framework, i.e. be legal, it might contravene basic principles and thus be illegitimate.[40] Conversely, legitimacy of an act does not necessarily mean it is also in accordance with its legal prerequisites.

5.2.1.2 The Significance of Legality and Legitimacy for the WTO

In international law, the justification for the exercise of authority is generally derived from state consent alone.[41] Why concepts like legality and legitimacy, i.e. the accordance with rules and principles, should bear relevance for the WTO at all, is thus not immediately obvious.

5.2.1.2.1 The Significance of Legality for the WTO

With the foundation of the WTO, the international trade regime greatly distinguished itself from general international law. The WTO Agreement established a legal framework that took over the function of providing for justification from state consent—by consent of the members.[42] Put differently, the members ceded part of their consensual authority to WTO law and bound themselves by *"a rule-based system"*.[43] The WTO has, however, not been created outside the sphere of international law and constitutes a "self-contained regime" in the sense that the law of the

[35] Qin, 55 *Virginia Journal of International Law* (2015), 369, at 435.

[36] http://www.oxforddictionaries.com/definition/english/legitimacy (last visited 1 January 2018).

[37] Qin, 55 *Virginia Journal of International Law* (2015), 369, at 435.

[38] Bodansky, UGA Legal Studies Research Paper No. 07-013 (2007), 1, at 7.

[39] Bodansky, UGA Legal Studies Research Paper No. 07-013 (2007), 1, at 7.

[40] Qin, 55 *Virginia Journal of International Law* (2015), 369, at 435; Bodansky, UGA Legal Studies Research Paper No. 07-013 (2007), 1, at 3.

[41] Qin, 55 *Virginia Journal of International Law* (2015), 369, at 435; Bodansky, UGA Legal Studies Research Paper No. 07-013 (2007), 1, at 3.

[42] Pauwelyn, Conflict of Norms in Public International Law, at 45; Hilf, 4 *Journal of International Economic Law* (2001), 111, at 116; Shell, 44 *Duke Law Journal* (1995), 829, at 831; Nguyen, 22 *Temple International & Comparative Law Journal* (2008), 243, at 243.

[43] Singapore Ministerial Declaration, WT/MIN(96)/DEC, 18 December 1996, at para. 1.

organisation fully replaced international law and principles.[44] Rather, all the gaps in WTO law are to be filled with general international law, as the WTO only distinguished itself from general international law through the *"single package of rights and obligations"*[45] agreed upon by its members.[46] But then, the original consent of the members to bind themselves by a particular legal framework must not be discarded lightly. With the WTO covering a greater number of subjects than its predecessor, the GATT, the justification for the acceptance of its legal acts dwindles as consensual decisions become more difficult.[47] Adherence to the WTO legal framework, i.e. the legality of an act, is essential in providing for a justification of the exercise of authority in the WTO.

5.2.1.2.2 The Significance of Legitimacy for the WTO

Besides, certain features can be found in the WTO's design that indicate that the foundation of the WTO entailed more than the mere shift from a power-based towards a rule-based system.[48] Looking at the preamble of the WTO Agreement, it becomes apparent that the main goal of its members was *"to develop an integrated, more viable and durable multilateral trading system"* (Recital 4 WTO Agreement). Members were *"determined to preserve the basic principles and to further the objectives underlying this multilateral trading system"* (Recital 5 WTO Agreement). In advancing the transformation of the trade organisation's system from the rule-oriented approach under the GATT[49] the members took care to build an *"embryo world government"*,[50] an organisation with the ability to sustain itself.

This objective manifests itself in the creation of a *"trade 'supercourt'"*[51]—the WTO Appellate Body.[52] The negotiating parties of the Uruguay Round envisioned the tribunal to serve as watchdog of the WTO's founding principles. Thus, in contrast to the GATT panels, the decisions of the Appellate Body are binding upon the parties of the disputes unless all members (including the winning party)

---

[44] Pauwelyn, Conflict of Norms in Public International Law, at 38 et seq; Hilf, 4 *Journal of International Economic Law* (2001), 111, at 121.

[45] Appellate Body Report, *China – Rare Earths*, at para. 5.57.

[46] Appellate Body Report, *EC – Seal Products*, at para. 5.123; Pauwelyn, Conflict of Norms in Public International Law, at 474 et seq.

[47] Qin, 55 *Virginia Journal of International Law* (2015), 369, at 435 et seq.

[48] For a more detailed description of these developments see Hilf, 4 *Journal of International Economic Law* (2001), 111, at 111.

[49] In dependence on *Hilf*, the terms "rule-oriented" and "rule-based" shall be distinguished here, the latter referring to being more fully determined by the rule of law, see Hilf, 4 *Journal of International Economic Law* (2001), 111, at 114.

[50] Bronckers, 2 *Journal of International Economic Law* (1999), 547, at 548.

[51] Shell, 44 *Duke Law Journal* (1995), 829, at 831.

[52] Hilf, 4 *Journal of International Economic Law* (2001), 111, at 116.

unanimously reject a report.[53] This grants the necessary space for rendering decisions which might be uncomfortable for the parties of the dispute itself, but which advance the development of the WTO through recourse to the organisation's general principles.[54]

The adherence to the WTO's core principles does of course not have the power to derogate the law of the WTO agreements—no jurisprudence of the WTO judiciary must add to or diminish the rights and obligations of its members (Articles 3.2 and 19.2 DSU).[55] A finding of illegitimacy of the exercise of authority, e.g. in form of a legal act, does therefore not lead to its immediate and enforceable non-applicability.

But a lack of legitimacy serves as a valid indicator that the existing legal framework has taken a turn of development that conflicts with its intentional initial design and consequently endangers the sustainability and credibility of the WTO as leading organisation in international trade. Over the last 20 years, the WTO has slowly but steadily entered into a legitimacy crisis.[56] Adherence to legitimacy in the exercise of authority is important to eventually prevent the WTO from becoming an *"emperor without clothes"*.[57]

5.2.1.3 The Parameters for the Assessment of Legality and Legitimacy in the WTO

To provide a clear analysis, parameters are needed for assessing legality and legitimacy.

Scrutinising legality presents itself rather straightforward as a check of the relevant legal prerequisites.

In this study, the assessment of legitimacy bases on the concept proposed by *Qin*.[58] In order to sufficiently provide justification for the exercise of authority through the enactment of rules, she argues that they must follow procedural and substantive fairness. This means that first, the reasons for adopting rules or performing actions, i.e. their rationale, must be stated. These reasons must then accord with both the objectives and principles of the WTO and basic principles of international law. In addition to *Qin*, however, the coherence of the underlying rationale shall be examined as an intermediary step. If rules do not actually follow their own rationale, they cannot be justified.

---

[53] Qin, 55 *Virginia Journal of International Law* (2015), 369, at 434; Shell, 44 *Duke Law Journal* (1995), 829, at 833.

[54] Hilf, 4 *Journal of International Economic Law* (2001), 111, at 129 et seq.

[55] Appellate Body Report, *EC Measures Concerning Meat and Meat Products (Hormones)*, WT/DS26/AB/R, WT/DS48/AB/R, adopted 13 February 1998, DSR 1998:I, 135, at para. 124; Hilf, 4 *Journal of International Economic Law* (2001), 111, at 129.

[56] Bronckers, 2 *Journal of International Economic Law* (1999), 547, at 555; Elsig, 41 *Journal of World Trade* (2007), 75; Howse in Coicaud/Heiskanen (eds.), at 355; Armingeon et al. in Cottier/Delimatsis (eds.), 69, at 74; Qin, Wayne State University Law School Legal Studies Research Paper Series No. 2014-11 (2014), 1, at 12 et seq.

[57] Bronckers, 2 *Journal of International Economic Law* (1999), 547, at 556.

[58] Qin, 55 *Virginia Journal of International Law* (2015), 369, at 435 et seq.

The founding principles of the WTO used for assessment shall principally be derived from the preamble of the WTO Agreement. But their elaboration by respective Appellate Body jurisprudence shall also be considered. So far, the Appellate Body has recognised and applied the following principles: trade liberalisation, non-discrimination (comprising both MFN and national treatment), sovereignty and national deference, sustainable development, co-operation and multilateralism, transparency, the rule of law and proportionality.[59]

Apart from the WTO law principles, principles of general international law exist, which are part of either customary international law or constitute general principles according to Article 38(1)(b) or (c) ILC Statute[60] and which provide a minimum standard of protection.

5.2.2 *Justification of the Introduction of Country-Specific Accession Commitments in Anti-Subsidy Law*

In the light of the principal uniformity of rule-based WTO commitments,[61] whether the introduction of country-specific accession commitments in anti-subsidy law is justified under the framework of the WTO raises doubts.

5.2.2.1 Legality of Country-Specific Accession Commitments in Anti-Subsidy Law

The newly created country-specific accession commitments would need to be lawfully integrated into the existing WTO anti-subsidy framework. Their inclusion must be harmonious and not give rise to persistent conflicts of law. If the introduction of country-specific anti-subsidy rules indeed complies with the legal boundaries set by the ASCM, the GATT and the WTO Agreement itself is, however, far from clear.

5.2.2.1.1 Violation of Article XII:1 WTO Agreement

Article XII:1 WTO Agreement is the sole provision in WTO law dealing with accession to the WTO.[62] It stipulates that any state or separate customs union may

[59]Hilf, 4 *Journal of International Economic Law* (2001), 111, at 117 et seq.

[60]Statute of the International Law Commission, UN GA Resolution 174 (II), 21 November 1947.

[61]See Sect. 3.2.1.2.

[62]On particularities of the WTO accession process see Cattaneo/Primo Braga, Policy Research Working Paper No. 5116 (2009), 1, at 12 et seq.; Michalopoulos in Hoekman et al. (eds.), at 61; https://www.wto.org/english/thewto_e/acc_e/acces_e.htm (last visited 1 January 2018).

accede to the WTO Agreement *"on terms to be agreed"* between it and the WTO (Article XII:1 WTO Agreement).

By its wording, Article XII:1 WTO Agreement imposes no explicit requirements on both the procedure to obtain the necessary consent and the character of the accession rules. According to the principles of general international law, state consent serves as foundation of the accession decision. That the consent might not have been given in a fully voluntary manner, but have been the result of pressure at the round table does *per se* not disqualify this *"negotiated consent"*[63]—hardly any consent, especially in the area of international law, is given without compromise.[64] Moreover, the open phraseology is overwhelmingly regarded to put the content of the accession terms entirely in the discretion of the negotiating parties. Consequently, there can be no terms of accession that are *ultra vires*.[65] Country-specific accession commitments would thus be permitted.

5.2.2.1.1.1 The "Terms" of Accession

It is to be asked, though, if the word *"terms"* does not already inherently predefine the nature of the prospective accession commitments. *"Terms"* is used to describe the *"conditions under which an action may be undertaken or agreement reached; stipulated or agreed requirements"*.[66] *Per se*, it possesses a conditional and a factional connotation. In the WTO agreements, *"terms"* is often paired with *"conditions"*, e.g. in Article IX:4 WTO Agreement on waivers, in Article VI:1(b) and (c) GATT on the schedules of concessions. *"Condition"* generally describes *"a situation that must exist before something else is possible or permitted"*.[67] That the *"terms"* are referred to unconnectedly in Article XII:1 WTO Agreements permits the conclusion that the terms are simply to be understood as agreed provisions. This finding is supported by textual evidence from other agreements of both the WTO and general international law, e.g. Articles 10, 19.3, 25.9 ASCM, Article XV:2 GATT and Articles 31(1) and 33 (3) VCLT. The *"terms"* thus need not to be fulfilled by the applicant country before the accession as its precondition but rather focus on the regulation of the relationship between prospective and incumbent members for the time of membership.

5.2.2.1.1.2 Article XII WTO Agreement in Context

According to the Appellate Body's *"principle of harmonious interpretation"*,[68] interpreting the WTO agreements must not give rise to incongruence.

---

[63] Qin, 55 *Virginia Journal of International Law* (2015), 369, at 441.

[64] Qin, 55 *Virginia Journal of International Law* (2015), 369, at 441.

[65] Charnovitz, GWU Law School Public Law Research Paper No. 237 (2013), 1, at 59. For this reason, *Qin* designated the provision as *"loophole in the system"*, see Qin, 55 *Virginia Journal of International Law* (2015), 369, at 389.

[66] https://en.oxforddictionaries.com/definition/term (last visited 1 January 2018).

[67] https://en.oxforddictionaries.com/thesaurus/condition (last visited 1 January 2018).

[68] Appellate Body Report, *EC – Seal Products*, at para. 5.123.

Important context for the understanding of Article XII WTO Agreement is Article XI WTO Agreement, which regulates the prerequisites for original membership in the WTO.[69] The former GATT members had to fulfil two conditions for WTO membership: they had to accept the uniform rules of conduct of the WTO and to agree on schedules of tariff and non-tariff commitments that were to be annexed to the GATT and the GATS. There are no indications that at the time of the conclusion of the Marrakech Agreement, the original members intended a distinction between original and acceded WTO members—to the contrary, the Ministerial Decision on the Acceptance of and Accession to the Agreement Establishing the World Trade Organization[70] expressly stated coequality between incumbent and acceded members.[71]

Furthermore, the WTO lacks the procedural framework for the unlimited integration of country-specific rules. According to Article II GATT and Article XX GATS, the schedules of tariff and non-tariff commitments of the members are to be integrated into the respective agreements as annexes and form integral parts of them (Article II:7 GATT and Article XX:3 GATS). This method of integration confers to the schedules a defined legal rank in the WTO legal hierarchy. It also adheres to the traditional understanding of accession commitments under Article XXXIII GATT.[72] Country-specific rules commitments on accession are not *per se* excluded, though. The WTO agreements leave room for country-specific deviations from the general framework in cases where such exceptions are temporarily necessary for the integration of the acceding countries.[73] Apart from these exceptions, the WTO agreements lack a legal framework for the integration of new country-specific commitments.[74] Article XII:1 WTO Agreement merely states that *"such accession shall apply to this Agreement and the Multilateral Trade Agreements annexed thereto."* Unlike GATT and GATS, the WTO Agreement does not possess an annex for accession commitments.[75] Rather, the accession protocols themselves, like the CAP in Section 1.2 state that they *"shall be an integral part of the WTO Agreement"*. This method of integration leaves doubts. Usually, in international law, and apart from accession agreements in WTO law as well, it is the treaty itself that

[69]Qin, Wayne State University Law School Legal Studies Research Paper Series No. 2016-05 (2016), 1, at 11.

[70]Ministerial Decision, Agreement Establishing the WTO: acceptance of and accession to the agreement, LT/UR/D-6/1, 15 April 1994.

[71]Charnovitz, GWU Law School Public Law Research Paper No. 237 (2013), 1, at 55 et seq.; Qin, Wayne State University Law School Legal Studies Research Paper Series No. 2016-05 (2016), 1, at 12.

[72]Qin, Wayne State University Law School Legal Studies Research Paper Series No. 2016-05 (2016), 1, at 13.

[73]E.g. Articles 27 and 29 ASCM, see Sect. 5.2.2.1.3.1; Qin, Wayne State University Law School Legal Studies Research Paper Series No. 2016-05 (2016), 1, at 12.

[74]Qin, 55 *Virginia Journal of International Law* (2015), 369, at 400 et seq.

[75]Qin proposes the introduction of such an annex to the WTO Agreement to remedy present legal insecurity, see 55 *Virginia Journal of International Law* (2015), 369, at 431.

provides for an integration procedure, not the accession agreement.[76] Moreover, making accession protocols *"integral part of the WTO Agreement"* does not attach a definite legal rank to the rules they contain, without which the respective interaction clause in WTO law cannot be ascertained and their status ultimately remains unclear.

5.2.2.1.1.3 The Rationale of Accession Protocols

From the perspective of legal hierarchy, it appears *"nonsensical"*[77] that accession protocols should have the legal power to modify the original treaty. Accession agreements constitute amendments to the original treaty in the way that they extend its application to the acceding member.[78] Some normative orders widen this scope of amendment by explicitly permitting necessary formal treaty amendments closely relating to the accession, e.g. Article 49 TEU, which allows for *"adjustments to the Treaties on which the Union is founded, which such admission entails"*. Although there is some discussion how far this right to adjustment may go, it is majorly regarded to exclude substantive alterations, which still fall under the formal amendment procedure.[79] This is even more so for accession to the WTO. Article XII WTO Agreement on accession does not stipulate any additional competences of rule-making. Furthermore, the WTO possesses a rigorous regime on treaty amendments in Article X WTO Agreement, which makes apparent that under the conception of the negotiating parties of the Uruguay Round, amendments other than the accession itself fall under Article X and not Article XII.[80] Rather, for the existing WTO obligations, the principle *pacta sunt servanda* applies.[81]

5.2.2.1.1.4 Country-Specific Rule-Making in the GATT Era

The historical dimension of country-specific rule-making upon accession seems to imply that accession commitments on rules that derogate from the general WTO acquis are in fact accepted. When starting in 1967, Poland, Romania and Hungary subsequently entered the WTO, they did so only after agreeing on certain country-specific NMES provisions.[82] The rules included a special safeguards provision and confirmed the use of alternative benchmark methodologies for the calculation of anti-dumping duties. They were deemed necessary because all three countries constituted state economies, so that the standard GATT rules were not always

[76]E.g. the aforementioned Articles II:7 GATT and XX:3 GATS.

[77]Tyagi, 15 *Journal of International Economic Law* (2012), 391, at 414.

[78]Ehlermann/Ehring, 8 *Journal of International Economic Law* (2005), 51, at 57.

[79]De Witte in Biondi et al. (eds.), 107, at 125; Fortunato in Blanke/Mangiameli (eds.), 1357, at 1377; Tatham, Enlargement of the European Union, at 260; Conway, EU Law, at 114.

[80]Charnovitz, GWU Law School Public Law Research Paper No. 237 (2013), 1, at 59.

[81]Pauwelyn, Conflict of Norms in Public International Law, at 38.

[82]Polouektov, 36 *Journal of World Trade* (2002), 1, at 9 et seq; Qin, 55 *Virginia Journal of International Law* (2015), 369, at 383 et seq.

applicable on their economic systems. To take into account the particularities of their respective economic systems, the special provisions were adopted.

As Article XXXIII GATT 1947 corresponds to Article XII WTO Agreement, one could argue that country-specific accession commitments on rules are thus also allowed under the WTO. But this view mistakes the fundamental difference between the GATT and the WTO legal regime. Whereas the former was merely rule-oriented, the latter has been set up as rule-based, so that WTO law inheres a much stronger degree of bindingness.[83] Accession agreements outside the scope of Article XXXIII GATT 1947 were thus possible under the GATT, but no longer under the WTO Agreement. Moreover, the commitments of the three former Soviet countries were much more moderate than the commitments China took on,[84] so that even if they had been correctly adopted under Article XXXIII GATT 1947, this signifies nothing with regard to compliance of the country-specific provisions in the modern accession protocols.

Unless justified, country-specific rule-making upon accession thus contravenes Article XII:1 WTO Agreement.

5.2.2.1.2 Violation of Article I:1 GATT

Article I:1 GATT in particular raises the question why a declaration of non-compliance of the country-specific anti-subsidy accession commitments with WTO law is not immediately rendered. Article I:1 GATT contains the so-called most-favoured-nation principle. It states that *"with respect to customs duties and charges of any kind imposed on or in connection with importation or exportation or imposed on the international transfer of payments for imports or exports [...] any advantage, favour, privilege or immunity granted by any contracting party to any product originating in or destined for any other country shall be accorded immediately and unconditionally to the like product originating in or destined for the territories of all other contracting parties"*. All WTO members must therefore grant every other member the same conditions for the market access of goods. As this obligation also extends to the conduct of trade remedy investigations, country-specific accession commitments that effect differing procedural treatment amongst members or the imposition of different amounts of countervailing duties under the same factual circumstances seem a clear breach of Article I:1 GATT at first glance.

5.2.2.1.2.1 Applicability of Article I:1 GATT on the Pre-accession Phase

As the country-specific provisions are adopted during the accession negotiations, however, it may well be questioned whether Article I:1 GATT already applies. According to the by now notorious *"entry fee"* theory, adopted by the panel in

[83] Hilf, 4 *Journal of International Economic Law* (2001), 111, at 114; see also Sect. 5.2.1.2.1.

[84] Qin, 55 *Virginia Journal of International Law* (2015), 369, at 383 et seq.

China – Raw Materials, Article I:1 GATT would lastly not be applicable to the accession process.[85] The *"terms to be agreed"* between acceding and incumbent members were accepted by consent of all parties as the *"'entry fee' to the WTO system"*.[86] Although having met with much criticism,[87] the opinion of the panel is actually not as ill-founded as it seems. That it does indeed constitute more than a mere *de arguendo* contention roots in the particularities of the accession situation. The accession negotiations still take part outside the circle of the WTO membership. At the beginning of the negotiations, it is uncertain whether they will indeed be completed. All the benefits the WTO ultimately stands for and endows its members with, become effective only once the border of WTO membership has been crossed.

This is also true for Article I:1 GATT. The creation of country-specific rules in the accession negotiations is thus not measurable against the MFN obligation. But once the candidate country accedes to membership, the country-specific rules that have been agreed on during accession take effect in the WTO legal framework, so that conflicts of law with existing WTO law provisions are possible. Article I:1 GATT therefore *per se* constitutes a reference for the assessment of WTO law compliance of the new country-specific rules.

5.2.2.1.2.2 Conflict of Law with the Country-Specific Accession Commitments

To violate Article I:1 GATT, however, the country-specific commitments in the accession protocols must indeed give rise to a conflict of law with the GATT provision. This depends on their rank in the WTO legal hierarchy. The GATT constitutes a multilateral trade agreement of Annex 1 A of the WTO Agreement. With Article XVI:3 WTO Agreement designating the WTO Agreement at the highest level, the GATT ranks on the second level within the WTO legal hierarchy.[88] The legal rank of the country-specific anti-subsidy rules in the accession protocols is not that easy to determine. According to the Appellate Body, the legal rank of accession commitments in relation to the other agreements of Annex 1 A of the WTO Agreement has to be established individually for each provision through finding the *"objective link"* between the respective provisions on a case-by-case basis.[89] A general method of integration does hence not exist.

Applying the *"objective link"*-theory of the Appellate Body connects part of the country-specific accession commitments in anti-subsidy law, both WTO-plus and WTO-minus commitments,[90] with provisions of the ASCM. They thus take the same legal rank in WTO law as the GATT. The WTO-plus commitments, however, that

[85]Panel Reports, *China – Raw Materials*, at para. 7.112.

[86]Panel Reports, *China – Raw Materials*, at para. 7.112; Qin, 55 *Virginia Journal of International Law* (2015), 369, at 439.

[87]Especially by *Qin*, see Qin, 55 *Virginia Journal of International Law* (2015), 369, at 440.

[88]On structure and general hierarchy of the WTO agreements see Sect. 2.3.2.

[89]Appellate Body Report, *China – Rare Earths*, at para. 5.55, 5.57 and 5.61; see Sect. 3.2.3.1.2.

[90]On the different types of accession commitments see Sect. 3.2.1.2.

lack a precise *"objective link"* in WTO anti-subsidy law because they constitute newly designed commitments, would have to be attached to the ASCM in general, or Article VI GATT, as these provisions are at least thematically related, to successfully integrate them into the WTO legal framework. Otherwise, their legal ranking in WTO law and thus the question whether or not they conflict with Article I:1 GATT remains unanswerable at present.

In the light of the scope of the accession commitments, a wide understanding of conflict is due that is not limited to two provisions setting contradictory obligations but includes e.g. the retrenchment of rights.[91] Then, according to the general interpretative note to Annex 1 A, the special agreements officially prevail over the GATT to the extent of the conflict.[92] To the extent of substantive conflicts of law that arise in the aftermath of the integration of the country-specific commitments, the *"objective link"*-theory indeed provides a solution. A substantive conflict of law between the general and the country-specific anti-subsidy provisions is solved exclusively by the application of either a rule of the ASCM or the accession protocol.[93] Lastly, the process would end with the same result if the country-specific commitments concerned Article VI GATT. The existing ASCM provisions legally embellish Article VI GATT. Taking into account the principle of *"harmonious interpretation"*[94] of the WTO agreements, in particular enshrined in Article 10 ASCM, Article VI GATT then also prevails over Article I GATT as otherwise, the legally stipulated regulatory regime of the ASCM would deliberately be rendered ineffective. Any substantive conflict of law will ultimately be solved intrinsically and exclude the application of Article I:1 GATT.

But the *"objective link"*-theory of the Appellate Body leaves the question of the validity of the provisions untouched. The country-specific accession commitments still have to prove themselves according to the exceptions the ASCM and the GATT provide for country-specific rule-making.[95]

5.2.2.1.3 Justification of the WTO Law Violations

Both violations of WTO law could, however, be justified. To a limited extend, WTO law, in its anti-subsidy law and its general framework, as well as general international law permit exceptions to existing binding treaty obligations. They either explicitly allow for country-specific rule-making or offer possibilities for treaty modification.

---

[91]Pauwelyn, Conflict of Norms in Public International Law, at 179 et seq; Qin, 55 *Virginia Journal of International Law* (2015), 369, at 421.

[92]See Sect. 2.3.2.

[93]See Sect. 3.2.3.2 for the China-specific alternative benchmark regime for NMES in Section 15 (b) CAP and the general regime in Article 14 ASCM.

[94]Appellate Body Report, *EC – Seal Products*, at para. 5.123.

[95]See Sects. 5.2.2.1.3.1 and 5.2.2.1.3.2.

5.2.2.1.3.1 Compliance with Articles 27 and 29 ASCM

The notion of country-specific rules is as such not unfamiliar to WTO anti-subsidy law. Articles 27 and 29 ASCM grant developing countries certain exceptions from the general prohibition of export subsidies to aid them in transforming into a market economy (Articles 27.1 and 29.1 ASCM). Article 27 ASCM contains rules on special and differential treatment of developing country members, e.g. with respect to conducting privatisation programmes. Article 29 ASCM allows the application of rules necessary for the transformation into a market economy. The provisions offer a way to legally deviate from the general rule-based regime.[96]

Apart from the fact that both Articles have expired by today (Article 31 ASCM),[97] the character of the adopted rules does mostly not fit the notion of the kind of rules that Articles 27 and 29 ASCM envisioned for developing countries. Many commitments, e.g. the alternative benchmark regimes for NMES, are not merely transitorily supporting but applicable on a permanent basis.

5.2.2.1.3.2 Compliance with Article VI:1 GATT

Article VI:1 GATT allows to set up an alternative benchmark regime for certain NME countries "which may otherwise be inconsistent with other provisions of the GATT 1994, such as Article I:1".[98] Although the provision could arguably also be deemed applicable on anti-subsidy law by interpreting the precondition of dumping in a wide sense, it is lastly more convincing to consider Article VI:1 GATT as exclusively regulating anti-dumping law.[99] It cannot justify the country-specific accession commitments in anti-subsidy law.

5.2.2.1.3.3 Compliance as Reservation

The accession commitments could also be regarded as reservations on part of the acceding country. According to Article 2(1)(d) VCLT, the term reservation is understood as *"a unilateral statement, however phrased or named, made by a State, when signing, ratifying, accepting, approving or acceding to a treaty, whereby it purports to exclude or to modify the legal effect of certain provisions of the treaty in their application to that State"*. Although under the GATT, some of the obligations acceding members agreed to were viewed as reservations,[100] WTO law nowadays expressly and strictly prohibits reservations to the WTO Agreement itself and only allows them with regard to the annexed agreements as far as these agreements provide for this possibility (Article XVI:5 WTO Agreement). No such

[96]Appellate Body Report, *Brazil – Export Financing Programme for Aircraft*, WT/DS46/AB/R, adopted 20 August 1999, DSR 1999:III, 1161, at para. 6.47, footnote 49.

[97]For a more detailed discussion on the reasons for the expiry of the provisions see Sect. 6.1.4.1.1.1.

[98]Appellate Body Report, *EC – Fasteners*, at para. 398.

[99]See Sect. 3.1.1.1.2.

[100]Qin, 55 *Virginia Journal of International Law* (2015), 369, at 401.

permissibility clause exists in anti-subsidy law, so that country-specific accession commitments contravene both existing international law (Article 19(1)(a) and (b) VCLT) and WTO law (Article XVI:5 WTO Agreement)[101] and would thus be null and void.[102]

5.2.2.1.3.4 Compliance as Waiver

WTO accession commitments could be considered as waivers to WTO obligations binding on all members. Principally, Article IX:3 WTO Agreement allows the Ministerial Conference to waive obligations of the WTO Agreement or the multilateral agreements upon request of a member if three quarters of the members agree.

As the recent discussion on the waiver of certain obligations of the TRIPS agreement for the production and export of pharmaceutical products to least-developed countries, which themselves lack respective production facilities, revealed,[103] waivers constitute an important tool in WTO law to allow exceptions from the general acquis in singular cases if these exceptions are deemed necessary to serve a greater good. This conception indeed seems useful for the accession situation, as acceding countries often struggle with the immediate implementation of the entire WTO acquis at the disadvantage of their national economies. Waiving certain obligations would provide necessary breathing space during the period of transition.[104]

But applying the concept of waiver on the WTO-plus and WTO-minus commitments[105] in accession protocols produces rather strange results. As for WTO-plus commitments, the waiver would then not be employed to lessen a burden imposed by a WTO obligation. Instead, in such a constellation the waiver would exempt the acceding country from obligations of the general WTO acquis and impose on it a more stringent obligation. In cases of WTO-minus commitments, the WTO general acquis would not be withheld from the acceding country but from all incumbent WTO members, which would then not be obliged to apply the general regime but the possibly stricter country-specific provisions.

This approach *per se* accords with the wording of Article IX:3 and 4 WTO Agreement. But it conflicts with the objective of a waiver in WTO law. As expressed by the Appellate Body in *EC – Bananas III*, *"the function of a waiver is to relieve a*

---

[101]For a more detailed discussion on designating accession protocols as reservations see Qin, 55 *Virginia Journal of International Law* (2015), 369, at 401 et seq.; Tyagi, 15 *Journal of International Economic Law* (2012), 391, at 418 and 424 et seq.

[102]Consenting Tyagi, 15 *Journal of International Economic Law* (2012), 391, at 418.

[103]Regarding the discussion of the Protocol of Amendment to the TRIPS Agreement introducing the permanent waiver of Article 31*bis* and Annex I to the TRIPS Agreement see Matsushita et al., The World Trade Organization: Law, Practice, and Policy, at 653 et seq.; Kongolo, Unsettled International Intellectual Property Issues, at 22.

[104]On the two initially existing exceptions in anti-subsidy law for developing countries and the transition to a market economy, Articles 27 and 29 ASCM, see Sects. 5.2.2.1.3.1 and 6.1.4.1.1.1.

[105]On the differentiation between WTO-plus and WTO-minus commitments see Sect. 3.2.1.2.

Member, for a specified period of time, from a particular obligation provided for in the covered agreements, subject to the terms, conditions, justifying exceptional circumstances or policy objectives described in the waiver decision. Its purpose is not to modify existing provisions in the agreements, let alone create new law or add to or amend the obligations under a covered agreement or Schedule".[106]

Moreover, waivers are mandatorily temporary (Article IX:4 WTO Agreement). But many of the accession commitments, e.g. the alternative benchmark regime in Section 15(b) CAP, are permanent by design. The country-specific accession commitments are thus not justified as waivers.

5.2.2.1.3.5 Compliance as Amendment

With accession protocols seen as amendments to the WTO Agreement in terms of extending the membership to the acceding country,[107] the additional country-specific accession commitments could be characterised likewise.[108] In general international law, Article 40 VCLT stipulates that for a treaty amendment, unanimity or a certain majority is not required but only consenting members are in turn bound by it. WTO law itself comprises a rigorous regime on amendments. According to Article X:1 WTO Agreement, an amendment to the WTO Agreement or one of the multilateral agreements in Annex 1 shall preferentially be conducted through unanimous consent of the Ministerial Conference and then be accepted by all members, which usually involves ratification. If unanimity is not reached, a two-thirds majority in the Ministerial Conference shall suffice to pass the proposal on to the members for acceptance. The amendment of certain provisions, like Article I:1 GATT, requires acceptance by all members (Article XVI:2 WTO Agreement). Amendments of the WTO Agreement and the multilateral agreements in Annexes 1 A and C, which alter rights and obligations of the members, are binding upon a majority of two-thirds of the members, but only on those members which have actually accepted the respective amendments (Article XVI:3 WTO Agreement). Then, each following accepting member shall be bound immediately upon consent. If rights and obligations are not changed, the two-third majority of the members instantly binds all members (Article XVI:4WTO Agreement).

The main setback in that the accession commitments cannot be regarded as amendments in the sense of Article X WTO Agreement is the lack of procedural equivalence of the accession procedure.[109] With Article XII:2 WTO Agreement

[106]Appellate Body Report, *European Communities — Regime for the Importation, Sale and Distribution of Bananas*, WT/DS27/AB/RW2/ECU, DSR 2001:VIII, 591, at para. 382.

[107]See Sect. 5.2.2.1.1.2.

[108]As regards a discussion of the pros and cons of designating accession protocols as amendments see Qin, 55 *Virginia Journal of International Law* (2015), 369, at 403 et seq.; Tyagi, 15 *Journal of International Economic Law* (2012), 391, at 418 and 424 et seq.; on the requirements for an amendment of WTO provisions in general see Ehlermann/Ehring, 8 *Journal of International Economic Law* (2005), 51, at 57.

[109]Charnovitz, GWU Law School Public Law Research Paper No. 237 (2013), 1, at 47.

permitting the approval of accession terms by the Ministerial Conference upon a two-third majority of all WTO members, this does not suffice to match the respective majority requirements of Article X WTO Agreement because the accession commitments affect rights and obligations of the members. In practice, the issue is likely to not pose much of an obstacle as accession decisions are mostly adopted unanimously.[110] But the fact that the legal prerequisites differ suffices, rather demands to reject coequality of proceedings.[111] Furthermore, accession protocols are not necessarily approved by the Ministerial Conference, as stipulated in Article XII:2 WTO Agreement, but sometimes also by the General Council.[112] In consequence, not all WTO members take part in the decision on accession. In addition, only the parliament of the acceding member is required to ratify the accession package; the parliaments of other WTO members never get to vote on the accession decision.[113] The country-specific accession commitments are thus not justified under Article X WTO Agreement.

5.2.2.1.3.6 Compliance as Authoritative Interpretation

A special feature of WTO law in comparison to previous GATT law is the possibility to issue authoritative interpretations of the WTO Agreement and the multilateral agreements of Annex 1 A (Article IX:2 WTO Agreement).[114] General Council and Ministerial Conference are granted *"exclusive authority"* to issue authoritative interpretations of the said agreements upon a three-quarter majority of the members. Authoritative interpretations are fit to derive mandatory obligations from already existent legal rules.[115] They are legally binding on all WTO members.[116] This is emphasised by Article 3.9 DSU, stating that the provisions of the DSU are *"without prejudice to the rights of Members to seek authoritative interpretation"* according to Article IX:2 WTO Agreement.

But again, a lack of procedural equivalence of Articles IX:2 and XII WTO Agreement prevents compliance of the accession commitments. Furthermore, any authoritative interpretation must not *"undermine the amendment provisions"* of Article X WTO Agreement, as Article IX:2 WTO Agreement expressly states. Although the scope of this requirement is unclear as to whether it includes the organs' right to add to or diminish rights and obligations of the members through

[110]In the case of China, for instance, the accession terms were approved unanimously by all of the then 142 WTO members, see https://www.wto.org/english/news_e/pres01_e/pr252_e.htm (last visited 1 January 2018).

[111]Charnovitz, GWU Law School Public Law Research Paper No. 237 (2013), 1, at 59.

[112]https://www.wto.org/english/thewto_e/acc_e/acces_e.htm (last visited 1 January 2018).

[113]https://www.wto.org/english/thewto_e/acc_e/acces_e.htm (last visited 1 January 2018).

[114]Ehlermann/Ehring, 8 *Journal of International Economic Law* (2005), 51, at 58.

[115]Luo, Anti-dumping in the WTO, the EU, and China, at 99; Ehlermann/Ehring, 8 *Journal of International Economic Law* (2005), 803, at 811.

[116]Luo, Anti-dumping in the WTO, the EU, and China, at 99.

the interpretations,[117] neither Article IX:2 nor Article XII WTO Agreement provide for the possibility of ratification by the national parliaments of the WTO members so that the accession commitments are not justified as authoritative interpretations.

5.2.2.1.3.7 Compliance as Agreement of Non-application

Incumbent members can agree with the candidate country on the non-application of the WTO Agreement and the multilateral trade agreements (Article XIII:3 WTO Agreement). Such exclusions would not necessarily only be temporary, as Article XIII is silent in this regard. The permanent character of some accession commitments would hence not pose an obstacle to regarding them as agreements of non-application.

Depending on whether the meaning of "non-application" is understood in a narrow sense, including merely the barring of existing treaties or treaty provisions,[118] or in a wider sense, so that non-application can also be effected by the imposition of new country-specific rules substantively relating to the respective agreements, the country-specific accession commitments would be justified or not. Only special provisions imposing on the acceding member legal disciplines which have no counterpart in WTO law that is deviated from would not be covered by Article XIII:3 WTO Agreement.

With respect to the wider meaning of non-application, it has to be taken into account that WTO law subjects amendments and any agreement with *de facto* amending effect to a rigorous regime. According to Article X WTO Agreement, every amendment of the WTO agreements has to be ratified by the national parliaments of the WTO members. Article IX:2 WTO Agreement provides that any authoritative interpretation of the WTO agreements must not undermine these amendment requirements. Against this background, non-application of treaty provisions through newly introduced substantive rules would find itself in violation of these distinct legal boundaries. As under international law an illegal act is principally invalid,[119] the same would apply in such a situation to all accession commitments constituting *de facto* amendments.[120]

[117]As argued by *Ehlermann* and *Ehring*, authoritative interpretations may add to or diminish existing rights of WTO members in contrast to Panel and Appellate Body interpretations, which may not. This also accords with the requirement not to undermine Article X WTO Agreement, see Ehlermann/Ehring, 8 *Journal of International Economic Law* (2005), 51, at 58 et seq. *Qin*, on the other hand, distinguishes between mere interpretation of a legal framework as set down in Article 30 (3)(a) VCLT and subsequent agreements with modifying effect, e.g. Article 59 VCLT. Taking a narrow view on Article IX:2 WTO Agreement, she contends authoritative interpretations must not change the existing rules of a legal framework, see Qin, 55 *Virginia Journal of International Law* (2015), 369, at 411 et seq.

[118]The major part of scholarly literature follows this understanding, just see von Bogdany/Wagner in Wolfrum et al., at 6 et seq.; Charnovitz, The Path of World Trade Law in the 21st Century, at 318, footnote 144.

[119]Qin, 55 *Virginia Journal of International Law* (2015), 369, at 412.

[120]Qin, 55 *Virginia Journal of International Law* (2015), 369, at 412.

With regard to non-application in the narrow meaning, just excluding the application of treaty norms and not substituting them by alternative rules would be in line with WTO law. Such an agreement would have to be notified to the Ministerial Conference before the approval of the accession terms. As regards the anti-subsidy commitments, however, the greater part imposes on the acceding country new obligations or grants further rights to the incumbent members, so that only a small part of the commitments would actually be justified as agreement of non-application.

In addition, the practical difficulties that are inevitably to follow the classification of accession protocols as agreements of non-application in the area of anti-subsidy law shall not be concealed. To exactly determine if and to what extent country-specific anti-subsidy rules, e.g. Section 15(b) CAP, deviate from existing general WTO law provisions, the precise scope of each provision would have to be positively identified. But due to the provisions' indefinite wording, answering this question is impossible at present,[121] which makes non-application *de facto* impossible.

5.2.2.1.3.8 Compliance as Subsequent Agreement

General international law provides for the subsequent agreement of a treaty. Article 59 VCLT, for instance, deals with the implicit termination or suspension of a treaty through the conclusion of a subsequent treaty. Article 41 VCLT contains the possibility of "partial" or "relative" treaty modification by an agreement only consented to by some of the original contracting parties.[122]

Generally, the subsequent agreement must be concluded between parties that also formed part of the original treaty. As regards accession commitments, this proves problematic. Accession protocols formally constitute bilateral agreements between the WTO itself and the acceding member, so that in fact neither of these parties is also party of the agreement that is modified by the accession protocol, i.e. the WTO Agreement.[123]

This obstacle is increasingly commonly overcome in international law by piercing the veil of the international organisation and referring to the members behind it acting on its behalf.[124] Discussing the relationship between the Doha Ministerial Declaration and the TBT Agreement, the Appellate Body also adopted this approach and held that the Declaration issued by the Ministerial Conference constituted a subsequent agreement to the TBT Agreement in the sense of Article 31(3)(a) VCLT,

---

[121]See Sect. 3.2.3.2.4.1 for the different models of application; see also Mueller, 50 *Journal of World Trade* (2016), 867, at 872 et seq.

[122]Pauwelyn, Conflict of Norms in Public International Law, at 315 et seq. For a more detailed discussion of the pros and cons of designating accession protocols as amendments see Qin, 55 *Virginia Journal of International Law* (2015), 369, at 403 et seq.; Tyagi, 15 *Journal of International Economic Law* (2012), 391, at 420 et seq.

[123]Pauwelyn, Conflict of Norms in Public International Law, at 44 et seq.; Qin, 55 *Virginia Journal of International Law* (2015), 369, at 405.

[124]Qin, 55 *Virginia Journal of International Law* (2015), 369, at 406.

which had been concluded by the members.[125] Even more openly, this notion has manifested itself with regard to the Council of Trade in Services, which is considered competent to disregard or amend a provision of the WTO agreements without adhering to the formal amendment process of Article X WTO Agreement.[126]

In its strict understanding, however, that the WTO member states acting in their capacity as WTO organs do not act as WTO itself cannot be set aside.[127]

Furthermore, subsequent agreement proves finally unfitting a concept with regard to the acceding country. At the time of conclusion of the agreement, the acceding country is yet neither party of the WTO Agreement nor member of the WTO. Country-specific provisions cannot legally be regarded as subsequent amendment to the WTO Agreement.

5.2.2.1.3.9 Compliance as Subsequent Practice

In contrast to subsequent agreement, subsequent practice offers a more flexible concept that not only considers treaty amendments between the original members, but also includes changes of practice of the international organisation.[128] Subsequent practice can be employed to either establish the original understanding of a treaty provision, i.e. to interpret it, or to change its previously underlying meaning, i.e. to modify it.[129]

At the level of general international law, the method of subsequent practice found itself on the agenda to be integrated into the VCLT, but this idea was not carried through because the parties feared to undermine the formal amendment provisions which usually involved ratification of the new provisions.[130] Subsequent practice was commonly referred to during the GATT era: the whole apparatus of GATT institutions and dispute settlement procedure ultimately goes back hereto.[131] With respect to the WTO itself, the Appellate Body has also recognised this practice, but in principal interpreted it narrowly.[132] The WTO Appellate Body permitted

---

[125] Appellate Body Report, *United States – Measures Affecting the Production and Sale of Clove Cigarettes*, WT/DS406/AB/R, adopted 24 April 2012, DSR 2012:XI, 5751, at para 267; Moloo, 31 *Berkeley Journal of International Law* (2013), 39, at 61; Pauwelyn, Conflict of Norms in Public International Law, at 47.

[126] Pauwelyn, Conflict of Norms in Public International Law, at 45.

[127] Pauwelyn, Conflict of Norms in Public International Law, at 45.

[128] Qin, 55 *Virginia Journal of International Law* (2015), 369, at 411; Arato, 38 *Yale Journal of International Law* (2013), 289, at 307; Arato, 9 *The Law & Practice of International Courts and Tribunals* (2010), 443, at 458 et seq.

[129] Murphy in Nolte (ed.), 82, at 83 et seq.; Arato, 38 *Yale Journal of International Law* (2013), 289, at 307 et seq.

[130] Draft Article 38 VCLT, see Qin, 55 *Virginia Journal of International Law* (2015), 369, at 407; Arato, 38 *Yale Journal of International Law* (2013), 289, at 310.

[131] Qin, Wayne State University Law School Legal Studies Research Paper Series No. 2016-05 (2016), 1, at 14 et seq.; Qin, 55 *Virginia Journal of International Law* (2015), 369, at 407 et seq.

[132] Murphy in Nolte (ed.), 82, at 85.

subsequent practice only for the interpretation, not for the modification of a WTO agreement.[133] In this, the tribunal followed the indications of Article IX:2 WTO Agreement, from which derives that every treaty modification, in contrast to mere interpretation, is illegal because it diminishes the competence of the members to decide on the adoption of new substantive rules.

As mere interpretation of the WTO treaties, country-specific accession commitments could be justified if they already constituted previous GATT practice that was as such simply transferred to the WTO agreements. According to Article XVI:1 WTO Agreement, *"the WTO shall be guided by the decisions, procedures and customary practices followed by the CONTRACTING PARTIES to GATT 1947 and the bodies established in the framework of GATT 1947"*. Arguably, the conclusion of the special accession provisions of Poland, Romania and Hungary could be regarded as such customary practice. But the scope of their accession provisions contrasts drastically with the much more far-reaching provisions of the modern accession protocols like the CAP, so that they cannot serve as foundation of an already existing practice. Furthermore, the reference to GATT practice is only permitted as long as not *"otherwise provided under this Agreement or the Multilateral Trade Agreements"* (Article XVI:1 WTO Agreement). As this presents the question currently under scrutiny, relying on GATT practice lastly proves circular.

In contrast to the previously narrow approach of the WTO Appellate Body, the ICJ has adopted a much wider interpretation and has even recognised subsequent practice of the UN as organisation itself as sufficient for a modification of the UN Charter, which had been concluded by its members.[134] Recent developments in WTO jurisprudence lead to assume that the WTO judiciary has by now also embraced a wider interpretation of subsequent practice. The Panel in *China – Raw Materials* adopted the so-called "entry fee theory". According to the panel, candidate countries have to accept all possible kinds of accession commitments as "price" for joining the WTO.[135] The panel in *China – Publications and Audiovisual Products* explicitly held that *"[t]he preamble to the Accession Protocol refers to the fact that these terms are the result of negotiations between the WTO and China. This being so, we must be mindful of the possibility that the Accession Protocol may impose obligations on China that are not imposed on other Members under the WTO*

[133]Appellate Body Report, *European Communities – Customs Classification of Frozen Boneless Chicken Cuts*, WT/DS269/AB/R, WT/DS286/AB/R, adopted 27 September 2005, and Corr.1, DSR 2005:XIX, 9157, para. 259; Arato, 38 *Yale Journal of International Law* (2013), 289, at 315.

[134]See ICJ cases *Namibia*, Legal Consequences for States of the Continued Presence of South Africa in Namibia (South West Africa) notwithstanding Security Council Resolution 276 (1970), Advisory Opinion, ICJ Reports 1971, 16 and *Wall*, Legal Consequences of the Construction of a Wall in the Occupied Palestinian Territory, Advisory Opinion, ICJ Reports 2004, 136., as well as Appellate Body Report, *India – Patent Protection for Pharmaceutical and Agricultural Chemical Products*, WT/DS50/AB/R, adopted 16 January 1998, DSR 1998:I, 9), at para. 45 et seq.; Qin, 55 *Virginia Journal of International Law* (2015), 369, at 408 et seq.

[135]Panel Report – *China Raw Materials*, at para. 7.112; Qin, 55 *Virginia Journal of International Law* (2015), 369, at 439 et seq.

Agreement, or are stricter than those that are applicable to other Members."[136] The tribunals had no qualms in accepting the evolving new accession practice of country-specific rule-making.[137]

But this assessment of the WTO judiciary is incorrect.

First, the conduct of the WTO members in adopting the country-specific accession commitments does not meet the necessary prerequisites of subsequent practice. According to the Appellate Body, *"in order for 'practice' within the meaning of Article 31(3)(b) [VCLT] to be established: (i) there must be a common, consistent, discernible pattern of acts or pronouncements; and (ii) those acts or pronouncements must imply agreement on the interpretation of the relevant provision".*[138] In this process, *"not each and every party must have engaged in a particular practice for it to qualify as a 'common' and 'concordant' practice. Nevertheless, practice by some, but not all parties is obviously not of the same order as practice by only one, or very few parties".*[139] As regards the introduction of country-specific rules of conduct via accession protocols, the members would have needed to agree to modify the WTO Agreement so that respective amendments would not have to follow the formal procedure of Article X WTO Agreement. The accession negotiations lack such a common understanding. Although e.g. China's accession was approved by consent of all members without exception,[140] this does not constitute the result of a common process of reasoning in the awareness of modifying the formal WTO amendment procedure. Whereas all the members casted votes in favour of China's accession, not all the members took part in the long accession negotiations and actively designed the new country-specific provisions. In fact, the Working Party on the Accession of China counted 58 members of a total of then 119 WTO members upon its establishment in 1996 (49%).[141] This number amounted to 78 of then 142 members shortly before the accession process was finalised in 2001 (55%).[142] Thus, the integration of country-specific rules of conduct was initiated and carried through by only half of the WTO's members, which by all standards is not enough for the positive assumption of *"a common [. . .] pattern"*[143] for such a substantial treaty modification. As there seems to have been no will or awareness of deliberately

[136]Panel Report, *China – Measures Affecting Trading Rights and Distribution Services for Certain Publications and Audiovisual Entertainment Products*, WT/DS363/R and Corr.1, adopted 19 January 2010, as modified by Appellate Body Report WT/DS363/AB/R, DSR 2010:II, 261, para. VII.281.

[137]See Tyagi, 15 *Journal of International Economic Law* (2012), 391, at 415.

[138]Appellate Body Report, *United States – Measures Affecting the Cross-Border Supply of Gambling and Betting Services*, WT/DS285/AB/R, adopted 20 April 2005, DSR 2005:XII, 5663 (and Corr.1, DSR 2006:XII, 5475), at para. 192.

[139]Appellate Body Report, *EC – Chicken Cuts*, para. 259.

[140]https://www.wto.org/english/news_e/pres01_e/pr252_e.htm (last visited 1 January 2018).

[141]Working Party on the Accession of China, WT/ACC/CHN/2, 2 April 1996.

[142]Working Party on the Accession of China, WT/ACC/CHN/2/Rev.11, 7 June 2001, and Corr.1, 22 June 2001.

[143]Appellate Body Report, *US – Gambling*, at para. 192.

amending a written WTO law provision and majorly deviating from the explicit declaration at the time of the foundation of the WTO to never distinguish between original and acceding members,[144] it cannot be concluded that the consent to the accession of China implicitly included approval of derogating the regular amendment process under Article X WTO Agreement.

Second, WTO law offers no room for abdicating the formal amendment procedure by subsequent practice that has emerged in the organisation. Even if all WTO members acted unanimously in their capacity as Ministerial Conference, this cannot be put on the same level as their acting as states. As WTO organ, they do not possess the competence to disregard the law of the organisation, which constitutes the very foundation of their existence.[145] For legality as an act of WTO law, adherence to the law of the organisation is essential.[146] Country-specific rule-making upon accession can therefore not be legally justified as subsequent practice.[147]

5.2.2.1.3.10 Compliance as Non-WTO Agreement

The WTO does, however, not constitute an *"island"*,[148] which is totally disconnected from general international law. Rather, the "self-contained regime" is embedded into the sea of rights and obligations of the general international legal framework, so that the WTO members are still legally competent to conclude agreements as states with other WTO countries, which then consequently also impact their relationship under WTO law.[149] This conception appears particularly attractive with respect to the acceding countries, which are not yet party of the agreement that shall be modified in application. Importantly, however, the treaties concluded under international law do themselves not constitute WTO agreements or can be characterised as interpreting or even modifying the WTO agreements.[150] As such, they differ from the agreements of non-application under Article XIII:3 WTO Agreement,[151] so that in particular, the agreement of new substantive provisions, also without a substantive counterpart in WTO law, is possible.

Thus, if concluded outside the WTO and in the following regarded as treaty commitments that stand outside the WTO Agreement, country-specific accession commitments in anti-subsidy law can legally be agreed on between incumbent and acceding WTO members as sovereign subjects of international law.

---

[144]See Sect. 5.2.2.1.1.2.

[145]Pauwelyn, Conflict of Norms in Public International Law, at 45.

[146]See Sect. 5.2.1.2.1.

[147]Dissenting Qin, Wayne State University Law School Legal Studies Research Paper Series No. 2016-05 (2016), 1, at 14 et seq., and 55 *Virginia Journal of International Law* (2015), 369, at 407 et seq.

[148]Pauwelyn, Conflict of Norms in Public International Law, at 474.

[149]Pauwelyn, Conflict of Norms in Public International Law, at 474 et seq.

[150]Pauwelyn, Conflict of Norms in Public International Law, at 476.

[151]See Sect. 5.2.2.1.3.7.

5.2.2.2 Legitimacy of the Country-Specific Accession Commitments in Anti-Subsidy Law

That country-specific accession commitments are legally possible as non-WTO agreements which then gravely impact the WTO relationship of the contracting parties in particular gives rise to concerns regarding the legitimacy of these provisions.

5.2.2.2.1 Rationale of the Country-Specific Anti-Subsidy Rules in Accession Protocols

When looking for an explicitly laid down rationale of the country-specific commitments, e.g. in the documents surrounding China's WTO accession, one looks in vain.[152] But two options present themselves which could possibly have been followed in the adoption of the rules.

First, the new rules could be supporting the alignment of the candidate country's national law to WTO law. The adoption of the legal acquis of an organisation prior to accession is a well-established and -recognised procedure in international law and would *per se* constitute a proper rationale.[153]

Second, the country-specific anti-subsidy rules could address particular features of the acceding country's factual or legal environment that would prevent an equal standing amongst the other WTO members after accession. The special provisions would act *"as a mechanism for achieving substantive equality among WTO members"*.[154] In fact, a level playing field can be created in two different ways. On the one hand, the rules can try to approximate the factual or legal conditions of the candidate country to average WTO conditions. The provisions induce changes in the country that finally lead to it sharing the level of development of its fellow WTO members. On the other hand, the new country-specific legal regime can be modelled to offset structural in-country differences to other WTO members that otherwise are likely to be permanent. These supposedly permanent conditions would conflict with workability and effectiveness of WTO legal instruments, so that the additional rules are needed as an "aiding device" to counterbalance.

5.2.2.2.2 Coherence of Attributable Rationale and Adopted Country-Specific Rules

In order to coherently pursue the aim of enabling the acceding country to bring its national legislation in conformity with WTO law, the country-specific anti-subsidy

[152] See Sect. 3.2.1.3; Qin, 55 *Virginia Journal of International Law* (2015), 369, at 438 et seq.

[153] *Qin* mentions the example of EU accession where prospective members are required to bring their national law in accordance with EU law and, if necessary, enact additional EU-mandated provisions, see Qin, 55 *Virginia Journal of International Law* (2015), 369, at 436.

[154] Qin, 55 *Virginia Journal of International Law* (2015), 369, at 438.

provisions would have to actually induce changes in the candidate country's national law. The anti-subsidy rules adopted in the accession protocols, however, present themselves in a different attire. Instead of aiming at changes of the acceding country's legal framework, they grant incumbent WTO members additional rights when conducting anti-subsidy investigations. If at all, such a legal regime only very indirectly induces amendments in the national law of the candidate country—out of fear of further application of an extremely inconvenient set of rules.

To aid in levelling the playing field of incumbent and acceding WTO members, the provisions would either have to effect changes in the new member's national legislation that lead to alignment with the other WTO members' conditions or provide the new member with a means to compensate persistent structural differences.

With regard to the former, the permanent character of the special anti-subsidy regulations speaks against it. If amendments removing existing disadvantageous conditions were intended, a transitory mechanism would have been the means of choice. This view is supported by the "sibling" anti-dumping regulations. In all cases of country-specific anti-subsidy rule-making to date, a corresponding regime for anti-dumping has also been established.[155] In contrast to the anti-subsidy rules, the anti-dumping provisions include an expiry date.[156] With anti-dumping and anti-subsidy law often having been designed to counter the same structural problem—both counter market failures following undue financial incentives that lead to existing in-country prices not adequately reflecting true market conditions—why the anti-dumping rules contain an expiry clause, whereas the anti-subsidy rules do not, lacks justifiable reason and lastly disqualifies the permanent anti-subsidy accession commitments under both potential rationales.

5.2.2.2.3 Conformity with WTO Law and General International Law Principles

Besides constituting a major point of reference for the assessment of legality, e.g. in Article I:1 GATT,[157] non-discrimination amongst members also serves as fundamental principle of the WTO. As successor of the GATT, the WTO was intended to be an organisation granting equal rights and obligations to its members—to achieve the *"elimination of all discrimination in international trade relations"* (Recital 3 WTO Agreement). Unless expressly allowed, all difference in treatment amongst WTO members in WTO law contravenes the founding principle of

[155]Regarding China, for instance, Section 15(b) CAP addresses the use of alternative benchmarks in connection with anti-subsidy investigations. Section 15(a) CAP set up a corresponding regime for anti-dumping proceedings.

[156]In the example of China, the anti-dumping rules for NMES were set to expire 15 years after China's accession, while the anti-subsidy rules are permanent.

[157]See Sect. 5.2.2.1.2.

non-discrimination, notably MFN.[158] The country-specific accession commitments thus violate the principle of non-discrimination.

It could be argued that, despite being in violation of WTO law principles, in particular the principle of non-discrimination, the country-specific anti-subsidy rules advance other principles, notably the principle of reciprocity, which would offset and thus justify potential violations of other principles. This was typically the case with tariff commitments, which, albeit country-specific, were entered into by incumbent members and newly acceding members on an exchange basis.[159] The anti-subsidy rules, however, differ in design and conception. They constitute unilateral concessions of the acceding country, which are in no way counterbalanced by obligations or the granting of additional rights by the other members.[160]

As the country-specific provisions are adopted during the accession negotiations, it is doubtful whether the WTO founding principles already apply.[161] In the light of the overall conception behind the WTO, it may, however, well be asked if its particular nature in fact demands the applicability of constituent features of WTO law already during the accession proceedings. More than other international organisations, the WTO stands for and is founded on non-discrimination amongst its members in matters of international trade.[162] According to its expressed conceptual design in contrast to its predecessor, the GATT, equality in rights and obligations is the very key feature of the WTO. Uniform application of the WTO rules of conduct constitutes one of its *"most salient features"*[163] and is regarded as the *"major achievement of the Uruguay Round*".[164] All permitted deviations from this principle are explicitly provided for in the agreements, or ought to at least be inspired by the same benevolent spirit.[165] Allowing general country-specific rule-making beyond the exceptions enshrined in its legal framework, though legally permitted, like e.g. non-WTO agreements,[166] would undermine the very core of the objectives the WTO was set up for. To preserve its authority as a decision-making organ, the WTO must not only honour its principles, notably non-discrimination, with regard to its incumbent members, and in particular with regard to pre-accession matters. Otherwise, legal situations would be created that set the WTO in contradiction with its own founding principles and will lastly not maintain its status as a credible, reliable and continuous organisation for the regulation of international trade.

---

[158]Qin, 37 *Journal of World Trade* (2003), 483, at 513.

[159]Qin, 55 *Virginia Journal of International Law* (2015), 369, at 440.

[160]Qin, 55 *Virginia Journal of International Law* (2015), 369, at 440.

[161]For the like discussion on the applicability of Article I:1 GATT see Sect. 5.2.2.1.2.1.

[162]Bayefsky, 11 *Human Rights Quarterly* (1990), 1, at 5.

[163]Qin, 37 *Journal of World Trade* (2003), 483, at 514.

[164]Qin, 37 *Journal of World Trade* (2003), 483, at 515.

[165]E.g. granting temporary exceptions from the WTO acquis for transitory countries though Articles 27 and 29 ASCM have *per se* expired.

[166]See Sect. 5.2.2.1.3.10.

Furthermore, the lack of precision of the special anti-subsidy provisions themselves and the non-public negotiations prior to the enactment of an accession protocol violate the transparency principle.[167] Their permanent validity in contrast to the anti-dumping rules lastly conflicts with the proportionality principle.

The principles of general international law at least provide a minimum protection of due process during negotiations. Incoherent rule-making during the accession process is in breach of the due process principle of international law and also violates fair treatment amongst equal subjects of public international law. Country-specific rule-making does not *per se* constitute a breach of these principles. But the country-specific alternative benchmark provisions in anti-subsidy law would, for instance, not be legitimate due to their gross inconsistency.

5.2.2.3 Conclusion

The introduction of county-specific accession commitments in anti-subsidy law is not justified. Although the mere wording of Article XII WTO Agreement, the central provision regulating the accession to the WTO, does not impose on members any restriction as to the substantive content of accession commitments, the relevant context as well as rationale and historical genesis of the provision make clear that country-specific rule-making beyond the exceptions provided for in WTO law is illegal. The same is true for Article I:1 GATT. One of the most strongly advocated means of justification, subsequent practice, cannot remedy the situation as the negotiation of country-specific rules, e.g. the alternative benchmark regimes, cannot be regarded as common and coherent practice of virtually all WTO members. Furthermore, the special character of the WTO as "self-contained regime" demands adherence to its institutional framework. The classification of accession protocols as narrowly understood agreements of non-application in the sense of Article XIII:3 WTO Agreement would be legal but only include a small part of the agreed rules and moreover often be virtually inapplicable at present due to the impossibility to clearly substantively setting apart general and country-specific regimes in WTO anti-subsidy law. Only as agreements outside the WTO, which due to the uniformity of the sphere of international law would also be applicable in the context of the WTO, country-specific accession commitments can be truly legally concluded. But the introduction of county-specific rules beyond the exceptions provided for in the WTO agreements violates the WTO's founding principle of non-discrimination, which is also applicable on the pre-accession phase. The maxim of coherent rule-making derived from general international law principles also effects the illegitimacy of so grossly incoherent provisions like the current country-specific alternative benchmark regimes for NMES in anti-subsidy law.

[167] Qin, 55 *Virginia Journal of International Law* (2015), 369, at 441 et seq.

5.2.3 *Justification of the Establishment of a General Alternative Benchmark Regime for NMES in Anti-Subsidy Law*

As second recent development in the area of WTO anti-subsidy law which gives rise to doubts, the establishment of a general alternative benchmark regime for NMES in anti-subsidy law through Appellate Body jurisprudence is now subjected to further scrutiny. All alternative methodologies share one feature which could make them susceptible to illegality: unlike the methodology in cases of market conditions, i.e. calculation on the basis of figures actually yielded during the investigation procedure, the alternative methodologies all contain a varying degree of estimation to establish designated comparable values.[168] The use of surrogate prices would be in breach of WTO law if it required the employment of the actually existing values.

5.2.3.1 Legality of the Establishment of a General Alternative Benchmark Regime for NMES in Anti-Subsidy Law

From the perspective of legality, contraventions against Articles 14, 19.3 and 19.4 ASCM as well as against Article VI:3 GATT seem possible. Furthermore, one could ponder whether the introduction of NMES rules for anti-subsidy undermines and thus contravenes existing anti-dumping law. In addition, if Appellate Body reports constitute the legally suitable means of implementation is doubtful.

5.2.3.1.1 Compliance with Article 14 ASCM

Constituting the only provision in general WTO anti-subsidy law explicitly dealing with the calculation of the amount of benefit, the introduction of alternative benchmark methodologies could violate Article 14 ASCM. A violation of Article 14 ASCM depends on whether or not this provision mandatorily requires the use of existing in-country benchmarks for the calculation process or if it permits deviation and the use of alternative benchmarks.

The wording of Article 14 ASCM does not reliably qualify the values that have to be employed in the benefit calculation.[169] As no definite obligation to use existing in-country prices in the entire Article 14 ASCM could be detected, the use of alternative benchmarks is neither expressly allowed but also not expressly forbidden.

Two provisions from the context of Article 14 ASCM might elucidate on the matter: Article 1.1(b) ASCM and Item (k) of the Illustrative List of Subsidies. But as

[168]Hoyt, 136 *University of Pennsylvania Law Review* (1988), 1647, at 1666.

[169]See Sect. 2.4.2.4.1.

the interpretation by the WTO judiciary has already demonstrated,[170] both provisions do not clearly require the use of existing in-country prices—and thus do not prohibit the use of alternative benchmarks.

The objective of Article 14 ASCM (and the ASCM as a whole), as the Appellate Body states it,[171] is disciplining the use of subsidies on the one hand and granting members remedies in cases of injury to their economies on the other. This is reflected in the pairs of Articles 3 and 4, Articles 5 and 7 and Articles 8 and 9 respectively for the three different categories of subsidies of the ASCM. Using alternative benchmark methodologies enables a meaningful application of WTO anti-subsidy law in NMES and would therefore be warranted. But whether the rationale indeed necessarily requires it can again not be answered decidedly in the positive or negative.

The genesis of anti-subsidy legislation in the pre-WTO era might also give hints. Article 15 Subsidies Code expressly stipulated an alternative benchmark regime.[172] The successor agreement, the ASCM, does not comprise rules of this nature. Thus, one might conclude that this was a deliberate turn-over to make clear Article 14 ASCM does not allow for the use of alternative methodologies, but always requires to use existing prices for the benefit calculation. On the other hand, the Subsidies Code only constituted a plurilateral agreement. If a rule contained in such an agreement does not find its way into a subsequent multilateral agreement on the same subject, this might also simply reflect the minimum consensus of the negotiating parties regarding the content of the new agreement and not in any way state that the new regulation of Article 14 ASCM does not allow for an alternative benchmark regime. The indications offered by the genesis of WTO anti-subsidy law remain of limited significance.

5.2.3.1.2 Compliance with Article 19.3 ASCM

Article 19 ASCM as a whole regulates the imposition of countervailing duties. Although not directly dealing with the process of calculating the amount of subsidy, it might contain requirements that a methodology for calculation different from the one provided for in Article 14 ASCM violates.

Article 19.3 ASCM stipulates that a countervailing duty shall be collected *"in the appropriate amounts"* to the amount of subsidy. If there is no recognisable relation between subsidy amount investigated and countervailing duty imposed, this requirement is violated.

But the requirement *per se* refers only to the process of price comparison and not to the prior process of price comparability, which forms the object of this study. In no

---

[170] See Sect. 2.4.2.4.2.1 regarding the interpretation of the Appellate Body in *Canada – Aircraft* of Art. 1.1(b) ASCM and Sect. 2.4.2.4.2.2 regarding the interpretation of the Appellate Body in *Brazil – Aircraft* of item (k) of the Illustrative List of Subsidies.

[171] Appellate Body Report, *US – Softwood Lumber IV*, at para. 93, 95.

[172] For details see Sect. 3.1.1.2.

way characterising the amount of subsidy with respect to the calculation process, the way the final amount of subsidy is rendered is lastly not covered by Article 19.3 ASCM. Propriety only needs to be reflected in the amount of countervailing duty itself. Therefore, the introduction of the NMES rules for anti-subsidy does not contravene Article 19.3 ASCM.

5.2.3.1.3 Compliance with Article 19.4 ASCM

According to Article 19.4 ASCM, a countervailing duty shall not be levied *"in excess of the amount of the subsidy found to exist"*. In theory, two different lines of interpretation can be rendered, depending on where to attribute *"found to exist"* to.

On the one hand, *"found to exist"* could be attached to *"amount"*. In this reading, it would only refer to the result of the calculation process and not qualify the subsidy in any way. Like this, it would correspond to the regulatory content of Article 19.3 ASCM. But considering the rather unusual use of English grammar it would require to conclude on such a result, this option is rather *de arguendo*.

On the other hand, therefore, the wording could be attributed to the subsidy that must have been *"found to exist"*. But again, two alternative understandings are possible. On the one hand, it could be argued that the use of alternative benchmarks simply constitutes a means of detection of the subsidy—it enables that a subsidy can be *found* to exist.[173] Discarding existing prices to quantify the amount of subsidy would fully be in line with this requirement—the subsidy may also have been detected by a procedure involving estimation, e.g. the use of alternative benchmarks. According to the WTO judiciary, however, *"found to exist"* means that a countervailing duty was only to be levied if it has been demonstrated that the product benefitted from a financial contribution.[174] This implies the invariable use of actual in-country prices for the calculation—merely calculated prices would not render an amount of a subsidy found to *exist* and would therefore not be in accordance with Article 19.4 ASCM.[175] But again, it could be objected that in NMES, only alternative methodologies can effectively depicture the amount of benefit received, so that their application is warranted here as well to actually demonstrate subsidisation.

Thus, the use of the NMES regime does not contravene Article 19.4 ASCM—due to lack of normative clarity.

---

[173]Emphasis by the authoress.

[174]Appellate Body Report, *United States – Countervailing Measures Concerning Certain Products from the European Communities*, WT/DS212/AB/R, adopted 8 January 2003, DSR 2003:I, 5, at para. 139; Panel Report, *United States – Imposition of Countervailing Duties on Certain Hot-Rolled Lead and Bismuth Carbon Steel Products Originating in the United Kingdom*, WT/DS138/R and Corr.2, adopted 7 June 2000, as upheld by the Appellate Body Report, WT/DS138/AB/R, DSR 2000:VI, 2631, at para. 6.52.

[175]Emphasis by the authoress.

5.2.3.1.4 Compliance with Article VI:3 GATT

The NMES rules for subsidy calculation could also contravene Article VI:3 GATT. Although in cases of conflict, the ASCM principally prevails over the GATT,[176] developments in anti-subsidy law must accord with both legal agreements to be fully consistent with WTO law.[177]

According to Article VI:3 GATT *"no countervailing duty shall be levied [...] in excess of an amount equal to the estimated bounty or subsidy determined to have been granted"*. The wording seems to provide a straightforward answer: by differentiating between bounties, where estimation is readily recognised, and subsidies, which, to the contrary, have to be determined, Article VI:3 GATT apparently requires a subsidy to be accurately calculated using existing values. NMES rules always contain an element of estimation and would thus contravene Article VI:3 GATT.

Unfortunately, the solution is not that simple. Article VI:3 GATT has its origin in the GATT 1947. After having been transferred into the WTO legal framework through the GATT 1994 upon the conclusion of the Uruguay Round, its wording remained unchanged. Therefore, it does not take into account the definition of subsidy, which has been rendered in the new Article 1.1 ASCM. The ASCM does not distinguish between *"bounty"* and *"subsidy"*. It contains one comprehensive definition of subsidy. Arguably, Article 1.1 ASCM explicitly states that the subsidy definition is only valid for the context of the ASCM. This narrow view, however, conflicts with the premise that the two agreements jointly set the framework for the regulation of subsidies. It also does not accord with the approach of *"harmonious interpretation"* of the WTO agreements required by the Appellate Body.[178] As both agreements have to be read *"taken together"*[179] and the differentiation between bounty and subsidy in the wording of Article VI:3 GATT does not invariably mandate the employment of exact, i.e. existing values for the subsidy calculation, the textual argument does not take effect.

Moreover, Article VI:3 GATT stipulates that the countervailing duty imposed must not be levied *"in excess"* of the subsidy amount. This only permits offsetting the amount of subsidy found to exist—Article VI:3 GATT has been held to accord with Article 19.4 ASCM in this regard.[180] The investigating authority *"must ascertain the precise amount of a subsidy"*.[181] From *"ascertain"* and the determination of the *"precise amount"* follows on the one hand that the use of estimated values does not meet this requirement—the subsidy rendered must reflect the precise amount of financial contribution actually granted.

---

[176] See general Interpretative Note to Annex 1 A.

[177] Appellate Body Report, *Brazil – Desiccated Coconut*, at 14.

[178] Appellate Body Report, *US – Gasoline*, at 17.

[179] Appellate Body Report, *Brazil – Desiccated Coconut*, at 16.

[180] Appellate Body Report, *US – Countervailing Measures on Certain EC Products*, at para. 139.

[181] Appellate Body Report, *US – Countervailing Measures on Certain EC Products*, at para. 139.

The problem with this view is that Article 14 ASCM itself, the ultimate provision for the calculation of subsidies, never positively requires to establish the exact amount of subsidy. It seems to inhere an element of estimation. Thus, taking this as standard for *"exactness"*, NMES alternative methodologies cannot be deemed to fall outside this scope. They help in determining an amount of subsidy at all—an approach which has been discovered Article 14 ASCM does not explicitly prohibit. Taking again the principle of *"harmonious interpretation"* of the WTO agreements into account, in particular enshrined in Article 10 ASCM regarding the relationship between the ASCM and Article VI GATT, this leaves no room for Article VI:3 GATT requiring exactness in the sense of actually existing market values.

5.2.3.1.5 Compliance with WTO Anti-Dumping Law

Unlike general WTO anti-subsidy law in Article 14 ASCM, anti-dumping law contains explicit stipulations with regard to alternative methodologies in NMES in Article 2.2 and 2.3 ADA and Article VI:1 GATT. As anti-subsidy and anti-dumping law overlap in cases of subsidy-induced dumping,[182] new NMES rules for anti-subsidy law might undermine a concept that seems to include that price distortion phenomena in NMES are addressed more effectively or even exclusively by anti-dumping law.

No textual evidence for such a conception can, however, be found. Rather, with respect to Article 15.1 Tokyo Round Subsidies Code, explicitly setting down that a choice must be made between anti-dumping investigations and anti-subsidy investigations if both are applicable, which has no correspondent provision in any of the WTO agreements, it seems more convincing that anti-dumping and anti-subsidy proceedings are not mutually exclusive. As there apparently is no concept a NMES anti-subsidy law could undermine, it finds itself in accordance with existing WTO anti-dumping law.

5.2.3.1.6 Compliance with Articles IX:2 and X WTO Agreement and Articles 3.2 and 19.2 DSU

Apart from the discussed substantive issues, it is doubtful whether the Appellate Body acted within its competence when adopting the alternative benchmark regime for general WTO anti-subsidy law. Formally, WTO panels and the Appellate Body must observe the legal boundaries of Articles 3.2 and 19.2 DSU on the one hand and Articles IX:2 and X WTO Agreement on the other hand.[183] The WTO judiciary is entitled to interpretation, but not authoritative interpretation or even amendment. The competences of the Ministerial Conference must not be undermined. The

[182]Mueller (2016), available at SSRN: http://ssrn.com/abstract=2665960, 1, at 6.

[183]For the details see Sect. 3.1.2.4.1.

problem, obviously, is where and how to draw the line—and if by establishing the general alternative benchmark regime, the Appellate Body has crossed it.

Historically, the GATT era can provide indications how to answer this question. Early GATT anti-dumping law already dealt with alternative benchmark methodologies for NMES. In the Kennedy Round, the Anti-Dumping Code was designed to provide for a more extensive legal framework than Article VI GATT, which constituted the only provision on anti-dumping in the GATT 1947. In the first draft list of 1966, the Anti-Dumping Code comprised potential elements for inclusion into the prospective anti-dumping framework.[184] Amongst these proposals was NMES methodology for the determination of the normal value.[185] Clearly, by the degree of impact on the legal framework, the introduction of NMES rules was considered an amendment—despite the proposals not constituting altogether new ideas, but merely elaborations of already existing structures of NMES methodologies in Article VI:1 GATT.

Considering the principles which guide the Appellate Body in its reasoning, notably *in dubio mitius* and *non liquet* (Article 3.2 DSU), the legal boundaries which restrain the Appellate Body in its activities are rather strict. In particular, the dissociation from authoritative interpretation (Article IX:2 WTO Agreement) as "intermediate level" between mere judicial interpretation and amendment emphasises that.

In its reasoning establishing the general alternative benchmark regime, the Appellate Body did not give meaning to expressions that could already be found in the existing provisions. Rather, it created an altogether new set of rules from scratch by filling lacunae. Instead of clarifying what was provided for, the tribunal relied on what was missing in the legal texts. As a consequence, the reasoning substantively fitted the existing framework not because it was derived from it but because it did not explicitly contravene it.

Considering the scope of the jurisprudence that followed the Appellate Body's initial introduction of alternative benchmarks in the environment of Article 14 (d) ASCM through *US – Softwood Lumber IV*, it cannot be assumed that the tribunal merely compensated a "lapse" of the negotiating parties of the Uruguay Round. The existing anti-subsidy framework had obviously not been designed for an alternative benchmark regime, which becomes particularly obvious in the lack of structures for the integration of the new provisions.[186] Thus, the Appellate Body has acted *ultra vires* when creating the NMES anti-subsidy rules in *US – Softwood Lumber IV* and *US – Anti-Dumping and Countervailing Duties (China)*.

---

[184] Possible Elements to be Considered for Inclusion in an Anti-Dumping Code, TN.64/NTB/W/13, 9 December 1966.

[185] Possible Elements to be Considered for Inclusion in an Anti-Dumping Code, TN.64/NTB/W/13, 9 December 1966, at 4.

[186] See Sect. 5.2.2.1.1.2.

5.2.3.2 Legitimacy of the Establishment of a General Alternative Benchmark Regime for NMES in Anti-Subsidy Law

Whether a general alternative benchmark regime for NMES finds itself in accordance with WTO and general international law principles poses several questions.

5.2.3.2.1 The Rationale of NMES Rules in WTO Anti-Subsidy Law

The anti-subsidy rules for NMES can be attributed different potential rationales.

First, the NMES rules could be deemed to enable the identification of subsidies in NMES. In *US – Softwood Lumber IV*, the first case Article 14 ASCM has been interpreted to contain NMES methodology, the Appellate Body basically attributed to the NMES rules the prevention of the otherwise non-meaningful application of the ASCM in cases of government distortion.[187] It acknowledged that such situations also warranted the imposition of countervailing duties because the harm to the economy of the import state existed all the same.[188] Article 14 and the objective of the ASCM as a whole would be undermined if investigating authorities lacked the means to calculate the subsidy amount and consequently impose a countervailing duty.[189]

Second, the NMES rules could serve easing the integration of accession candidate countries that have not yet fully turned into market economies into the WTO. As in these countries, trade-distorting subsidies are still present, other WTO members will not be much inclined to speed up accession negotiations and grant such countries entry into the WTO. Enabling the application of the WTO's anti-subsidy framework could lead to the incumbent WTO members seeing themselves equipped with the necessary degree of protection and allow transitory countries to accede to the WTO without having to comprehensively adopt the WTO acquis first.

5.2.3.2.2 Coherence of Rationale and Adopted NMES Rules

The discovered rationales must have been implemented coherently.

The alternative methodologies enable the finding of subsidies in NMES, which would otherwise be impossible. Thus, they are perfectly in line with this attributable rationale.

Arguably, the integration of China and Viet Nam into the WTO with the negotiation of special anti-subsidy rules has shown the demand of incumbent WTO members for rules enabling the application of the anti-subsidy rules. As the NMES rules could be seen to establish a permanent and general anti-subsidy

---

[187] Appellate Body Report, *US – Softwood Lumber IV*, at para. 95.

[188] Appellate Body Report, *US – Softwood Lumber IV*, at para. 95.

[189] Appellate Body Report, *US – Softwood Lumber IV*, at para. 93, 95.

framework for this purpose, they coherently reflect their attributed rationale of easing the acceding countries' integration in the WTO.

5.2.3.2.3 Conformity with WTO and International Law Principles

Finally, the NMES rules must be in accordance with WTO and international law principles to be legitimate. Principally, the alternative benchmark methodologies enable the application of WTO anti-subsidy law in NMES and thus promote the principle of trade liberalisation (recitals 3 and 4 WTO Agreement).[190] But there are doubts with respect to other principles.

5.2.3.2.3.1 Violation of the Principle of Mandatory Market Economy Transition

Permanent NMES provisions could violate the principle of mandatory transition of members to market economy countries. The alternative benchmark rules ultimately accept that NMES will always be present in the WTO members' economies, which would stand against an inherent market economy conception of the WTO. Not having been recognised by the Appellate Body so far, such a WTO law principle would first have to be uncovered in its general framework.

From historical perspective, it has been stated that the GATT *"was designed by market economies and for market economies"*.[191] The question is whether this indeed so because centrally-planned economies have in fact always been a reality under the GATT. The legal framework and its development reflect that. Rules for NME countries were discussed extensively during the negotiations for the establishment of the ITO.[192] Regulations on the "Expansion of Trade by Complete State Monopolies of Import Trade" for NME countries originally should comprise three articles.[193] That the GATT finally only contained one single provision on NMES, or state trading precisely (Article XVII GATT), is due to the fact that these countries were not actively promoting their interests and taking part in the negotiations.[194] For the market economies left at the round table, there simply was no necessity to particularly consider NMES issues. It is thus rightly said that the GATT was *"designed by market economies"*.

[190]See Sect. 2.4.3.1.

[191]Polouektov, 36 *Journal of World Trade* (2002), 1, at 5.

[192]Polouektov, 36 *Journal of World Trade* (2002), 1, at 5.

[193]Detlof/Fridh, 2 *Global Trade and Customs Journal* (2007), 265, at 268.

[194]Due to the Soviet Union, which basically was the only state economy country taking part in the negotiations for the ITO, the draft ITO Charter contained a section on 'Expansion of Trade by Complete State Monopolies of Import Trade'. After it became apparent that the Soviet Union would not be joining the GATT, the respective provisions were removed from the agenda, see Detlof/ Fridh, 2 *Global Trade and Customs Journal* (2007), 265, at 268; Polouektov, 36 *Journal of World Trade* (2002), 1, at 6.

But was it also created *"for market economies"*? Since its coming into existence, the number of members of the GATT, and later the WTO, has risen constantly—new members being market and NME countries alike.[195] This leads to ask whether the new NME members were admitted only upon binding themselves to aspire to market economy or whether their accession served any other greater aims. The practice of country-specific regulations regarding the general WTO acquis in accession protocols has developed well before the accession of China. Its origin lies in the integration of Soviet countries into GATT, beginning in 1967 with the accession of Poland.[196] Besides some accession commitments, the new NME members were in no way legally obliged to conduct economic reforms. Being state economies with no perceivable intention to fundamentally change this system before or upon accession was apparently not deemed an obstacle to GATT contracting party status.[197] The existence of Article XVII GATT signifies that the world trade regime may have largely been designed for market economy countries, but it does not exclude NME countries. Rather, it has become established practice to tailor rules to smooth their integration into a conceptually opposite regime.

What has been valid for the GATT is still valid for the WTO today. Recital 1 of the preamble of the WTO Agreement states that *"large and steadily growing volume of real income and effective demand, and expanding the production of and trade in goods and services"* counts amongst the goals of the organisation. A strong market economy connotation underlies these guidelines. Real income, effective demand and the expansion of production are ideas that inhere the very conception of market economy. Although generally present in market economies, these principles are not *per se* alien to non-market economies, e.g. centrally-planned economies. Embedded in their ideological framework also lies the idea of increasing production and creating better conditions for everybody.[198] Thus, although seemingly strongly indicating the transition to market economy status, the preamble is not fully coercive. Moreover, many of the new multilateral agreements of the Uruguay Round contain rules for privatisation and transition economies, e.g. Articles 27 and 29 ASCM in anti-subsidy law, which promote but do not require a transition to market economy status. The inclusion of the GATT 1947 into the GATT 1994 also transferred Article XVII GATT into the new world trade regime and carried on the GATT heritage of NME country recognition, so that a principle of mandatory market economy transition cannot be discovered in the WTO.

5.2.3.2.3.2 Violation of the WTO Transparency Principle

Besides problems of law, NMES rules for anti-subsidy law present another very particular problem: a problem of reason. The accurate establishment of a subsidy

---

[195] Polouektov, 36 *Journal of World Trade* (2002), 1, at 5; Du, 63 *International & Comparative Law Quarterly* (2014), 409, at 427.

[196] See Sect. 5.2.2.1.1.4.

[197] Polouektov, 36 *Journal of World Trade* (2002), 1, at 5.

[198] Jain/Khanna, Economic Concepts and Methods, at 26 et seq.

always requires meaningful market conditions.[199] If a market does not exist, the determination of a subsidy in terms of difference to the market conditions is impossible. That the alternative benchmark methodologies replace the missing market values by substitute values and enable the identification of subsidies solves the applicability problem from a legal point of view but remains irreconcilably contrary to the factual circumstances of subsidisation and ignores economic realities.[200] The irrationality of the legal provisions might conflict with the WTO transparency principle, as it could be argued that because of their irrationality, the NMES rules are also non-transparent.

The problem with this contention is that the NMES rules themselves principally set down an inherently perfectly clear regime. It cannot be convincingly argued that the factual conception of anti-subsidy law always has to accord with the legal one. One truth is determined by the factual conception of subsidisation—the other by the rules applied to counter it. By creating legal rules that regulate and sometimes sanction the use of subsidies, the WTO membership agreed that subsidisation is not exclusively governed by pure economic reasoning. By creating NMES rules that are merited by the rationale of the law, the Appellate Body sticks to this line and only brings the inherent fundamental dissociation between factual and legal conception of subsidisation to light. Thus, the introduction of alternative benchmark methodologies does not contravene the transparency principle.

5.3 Chapter Summary

Perceivedly arbitrary benefit calculations in NMES do not only present themselves in EU anti-subsidy investigations against China but constitute an evolving global problem. With an increasing number of WTO members setting up general alternative benchmark regimes in their national anti-subsidy laws, the question of the use of alternative benchmark methodologies in NMES has grown to be a highly relevant issue on the stage of international trade.

Of the two major recent developments in WTO anti-subsidy law, the introduction of country-specific accession commitments in anti-subsidy law has turned out to be legal only as agreement of non-application and as non-WTO agreement. But country-specific accession commitments that go beyond the exceptions provided for by the WTO framework contravene the WTO founding principle of non-discrimination and are consequently illegitimate. To preserve the credibility of the WTO as major organisation in the regulation of international trade, members should restrain from such provisions.

[199]See Sect. 2.4.3.1.

[200]Qin, 7 *Journal of International Economic Law* (2004), 863, at 870; Feldman/Burke, 62 *American University Law Review* (2008), 787, at 805.

The establishment of a general alternative benchmark regime for NMES in anti-subsidy law by the WTO Appellate Body is illegal in its *status quo*, but legitimate. The finding of illegality is, however, only rendered because Appellate Body reports do not constitute the correct means of introduction of such rules. On the substantive side, the introduction of NMES methodologies accords with WTO law. From the conceptual point of WTO anti-subsidy law, they serve to promote the principle of trade liberalisation by enabling the applicability of the ASCM. In the light of the established practical and legal deficiencies of current general WTO anti-subsidy law, it thus merits reform. Parties investigated but also investigating authorities and ultimately the WTO itself will profit from an improved alternative benchmark regime. To which extent reform is possible, advisable and indeed actually conductible, stands to be analysed in the next chapter.

Chapter 6
Rethinking the Alternative Benchmark Regime in WTO Anti-Subsidy Law

In the light of current legality deficits and, in particular, the WTO's crumbling legitimacy, rethinking the alternative benchmark regime in WTO anti-subsidy law is essential. The study will contribute hereto in this chapter by presenting a reform proposal for WTO anti-subsidy law that addresses the most pressing substantive issues in the use of alternative benchmark methodologies in NMES (Sect. 6.1). Consequently, it deals with the question of implementation (Sect. 6.2) and concludes with a draft reform proposal for an alternative benchmark regime for NMES in general WTO anti-subsidy law (Sect. 6.3).

What consequently falls outside the scope of the reform proposal are questions that were raised in the aftermath of the Appellate Body decision in *Canada – Renewable Energy and Canada – FIT Program.* Apart from this case, the newly developed derogation clause from the ordinary alternative benchmark regime of Article 14 (d) ASCM has not yet been put to the test in further investigations. It remains to be seen whether the special alternative benchmark approach of the WTO Appellate Body with respect to government intervention on the renewable energy market actually manifests itself. Here, the study will limit itself to highlighting aspects that might eventually turn into problematic issues in the future and to pointing out areas that will reward further scrutiny. In particular, the Appellate Body's reasoning in the benefit analysis may inspire attempts of NME WTO members to interpret the derogation clause of *Canada – Renewable Energy* and *Canada – FIT Program* as a lifeline from the rising number of anti-subsidy investigations they face by their fellow WTO members.

6.1 Substantive Issues of Reform

With regard to the country-specific alternative benchmark regimes in anti-subsidy law, presently applicable on China and Viet Nam, the reform proposal is a simple one: to prevent these provisions from undermining further the authority of the WTO

S. Müller, *The Use of Alternative Benchmarks in Anti-Subsidy Law*,
European Yearbook of International Economic Law 4,
https://doi.org/10.1007/978-3-319-77613-2_6

as major organisation for the regulation of international trade,[1] they should be completely eliminated.

The addition of a general alternative benchmark regime for NMES to WTO anti-subsidy law, on the other hand, has been found illegal only in its present state—but *per se* legitimate. The following reform proposal effectively tackles the grave deficits of the current alternative benchmark regime that have been discovered in the course of the study.

6.1.1 The Problematic Issues of the Present Alternative Benchmark Approach

The above analysis of EU anti-subsidy investigations against China has unearthed that the problems in the application of the alternative methodologies can be traced back to two basic stumbling blocks in the entire process: the determination of market distortion and the actual selection of the alternative benchmark.

6.1.1.1 Problematic Issues in the Determination of Market Distortion

The substantive content of the market distortion requirement is still unclear, which leads to a varying standard of evidence and to the reasoning of the investigating authorities more often than not being rather general. *"Distorted"* market situations are principally situations *"giving a misleading or false account or impression"* or being *"pulled or twisted out of shape; contorted"*.[2] In the view of the WTO judiciary, this is the case for government predominance.[3] To what degree, however, government actions give rise to concern with respect to misrepresentation of the existing market conditions is basically undeterminable under the present regime. Market shares as formal indicator and market power as substantive indicator are employed to sufficiently provide evidence.[4] The market is thus the pivot in the entire process of assessing distortion in NMES. It constitutes the baseline, the starting point, for the assessment.

The problem at hand is that the details of the notion of market underlying WTO law have been defined nowhere in written WTO law or Appellate Body jurisprudence.[5] Market is understood in an abstract and general way—which is fatal,

[1]See Sect. 5.2.2.2.

[2]http://www.oxforddictionaries.com/definition/english/distorted (last visited 1 January 2018).

[3]Appellate Body Report, *US – Anti-Dumping and Countervailing Duties (China)*, at para. 444; emphasised by the WTO Appellate Body in Appellate Body Report, *US – Countervailing Measures (China)*, at para. 4.59.

[4]Appellate Body Report, *US – Anti-Dumping and Countervailing Duties (China)*, at para. 444 et seq.

[5]Appellate Body Report, *US – Softwood Lumber IV*, at para. 87.

because the term is *per se* multi-layered and complex. "The" market simply does not exist—either the market-as-is or the perfect market or another market model altogether forms the basis of the entire process of determining the amount of countervailing duty.

With only the perfect market allowing for the use of alternative prices, the question of how the conception of market underlying WTO anti-subsidy law could indeed have been left undecided by the WTO judiciary is not easy to perceive. Permitting deviation from existing in-country prices seems by itself to have answered this question in favour of a perfect market approach. That the notion of the underlying market is in fact still unclear roots in a particular twist of reasoning on part of the Appellate Body. In *US – Softwood Lumber IV* and *US – Anti-Dumping and Countervailing Duties (China)* the tribunal has shattered the once uniform understanding of the WTO law's underlying conception of market on the one hand and the question whether or not existing market conditions may be deviated from on the other. Instead of defining a standard for the market conception and accordingly answering the question whether or not deviation from existing market prices was permitted, in its interpretation the tribunal focused on the comparative elements of the wording of the ASCM. In Article 14(d) ASCM, the adequacy of remuneration was to be assessed *"in relation to"* prevailing market conditions. For loan subsidies, Article 14(b) ASCM stated that the benchmark loan had to be *"comparable"*. Thus, the Appellate Body was able to take a stand in favour of the permissibility of deviation without providing a definite answer to the question of the underlying market conception.

Market distortion, however, constitutes the only legal prerequisite for the use of the alternative benchmark system. In leaving the underlying market undefined, the baseline for the whole process of assessing market distortion has been omitted to set. The lack of a predefined starting point lead to investigating authorities being basically free in their choice of evidence. Whether a certain means of proof supports the finding of market distortion is never sufficiently ascertainable because the lack of a fixed baseline leaves the degree of market distortion that must necessarily be shown to fulfil the requirement of market distortion fully open. If reasonably supporting the distortion of a market, evidence can hardly be deemed insufficient. Trying to retort evidence for market distortion in defence remains a largely vain attempt of arguing against an unknown basic standard.

6.1.1.2 Problematic Issues in the Selection of the Alternative Benchmark

Investigating authorities employ various methodologies in the process of selecting the alternative benchmark price—most frequently used in anti-subsidy law today are price construction and out-of-country benchmarks. More often than not, however, the use of alternative benchmarks results in high and arbitrarily set countervailing duties.

There are various reasons for this. To begin with, some methodologies are by their economic design inherently abler to produce alternative prices that are still in an appropriate relation to existing in-country prices. From a legal point of view, the way investigating authorities exercise their large amount of discretion in the selection process turned out to be the worrisome aspect. Guidance is scarce, so that freedom of assessment is more often than not employed in favour of the national industries. The sheer unlimited number of potential methodologies for choosing surrogate prices makes it impossible for parties investigated to anticipate the final outcome. Instead of following one clear-cut way to establish an alternative price for the calculation of benefit in NMES, the authorities employ one methodology or the other, in most cases without actual reasons for doing so, e.g. the lack of essential data.

6.1.2 The Objectives of the Reform Proposal

The topic of alternative benchmark regimes in NMES, be it in anti-dumping or anti-subsidy law, has always been influenced greatly by economic debate. More often than not, arguments or reform proposals tend to address economic difficulties rather than legal ones.

So far, this approach has not yet significantly improved the situation in anti-subsidy law. With the economic model of anti-subsidy law being a constant battlefield amongst economists,[6] a solution of the feuds in this area cannot be expected in the foreseeable future. Repeating constantly conflicting economic arguments when aiming at legal improvements is of no palpable use. Legal reform cannot and should not aim to answer the question of the economically "most correct" approach.

Ability and thus objective of legal reform are of a different nature. What it can and should ensure is that, regardless of the underlying economic approach, the practical application of a legal framework does not unjustifiably disadvantage parties.[7] Legal standards should be upheld to promote non-discrimination amongst WTO members and enable more effective judicial control.

Reform must address the hole of the market conception underlying WTO anti-subsidy law that has been left by the WTO Appellate Body and endeavour to strengthen market distortion as a legal prerequisite, based on the market baseline underlying WTO anti-subsidy law.

The selection of alternative benchmarks is presently weakened through a sheer uncontrollable amount of discretion on part of the investigating authorities, firstly in the selection of the kind of alternative benchmark methodology and, secondly, in the application of the methodology itself. Legal reform has to aim at narrowing down the wide range of choices to one single clear-cut methodology, which is then constantly applicable.

---

[6]Just see Sykes, 89 *Columbia Law Review* (1989), 199; Tarullo, 100 *Harvard Law Review* (1987), 546.
[7]Consentient Firestone, 8 *Journal of Comparative Business and Capital Market Law* (1986), 75, at 87.

6.1.3 Test Criteria for Legal Reform

In order to strengthen and shape the legal prerequisites of the alternative benchmark regime for NMES in an effective and coherent manner and to carry the reform objectives through to the final proposal, legal standards that serve as guiding principles or test criteria are needed.

The principles of legal certainty and transparency will best serve this purpose. Both incorporate the ability to improve a situation of legal vagueness by prompting more detailed and coercive argumentation on part of the investigating authorities. For the country investigated, this entails the advantage of being able to effectively challenge a decision due to the altogether more open and diligent process of reasoning. In addition, the practical applicability of the reform proposals is essential. A theoretically-best solution will fail in investigation practice nevertheless, if implementation is afflicted with inherent difficulties.

6.1.4 Substantive Legal Reform Proposals

Taking into consideration legal certainty, transparency and applicability, workable and implementable proposals for legal reform of the two most problematic issues of the current alternative benchmark regime, i.e. the determination of market distortion and the process of selecting the alternative benchmark in NMES, shall now be developed.

6.1.4.1 Reforming the Determination of Market Distortion

For a new approach in the determination of market distortion it is indispensable to establish the conception of market underlying WTO anti-subsidy law as a first step. Systemic and meaningful criteria for the determination of market distortion hinge on this conception, because it is on this basis only that parameters can be discussed which ultimately add to the legal certainty and transparency that are necessary to conduct a fair investigation. Strengthening the substantive content of market distortion will also increase its justiciability as true legal prerequisite.

6.1.4.1.1 The Conception of Market Underlying WTO Anti-Subsidy Law

The provisions of WTO anti-subsidy law do by themselves not directly identify distinct features of its underlying market conception. Panels and the Appellate Body have so far only embarked on *ad hoc* reasoning and have employed the type of market that best suited their respective reasoning.[8]

[8]See Sect. 2.4.2.4.2.

Two aspects of the ASCM that have not been considered so far might, however, implicitly enlighten to a degree its underlying market conception: the systemic regulatory concept of the ASCM as a whole as well as the regulation of actionable subsidies.

6.1.4.1.1.1 Indications from the Systemic Regulatory Concept of the ASCM

The systemic regulatory concept of the ASCM as it has been designed in the Uruguay Round distinguishes three categories of subsidies: prohibited, actionable and non-actionable subsidies.[9] *Per se*, this does not seem to reveal much about the precise underlying market conception. Yet, the distinction between three different kinds of subsidies, notably non-actionable subsidies, makes two things very clear: first, the ASCM does recognise the persistent presence of subsidies in a market. Second, not all types of subsidies are considered harmful. According to the conception of the ASCM, "good" subsidies exist. This basic regulatory decision already sets the market conception of the ASCM in contrast to the market conception that underlies Ricardo's and Mill's approach in the theory of comparative advantages, which contends a pure market without any form of externalities like subsidies.[10] Although this is mostly deemed to be the WTO market model,[11] obviously, this does not conform with how the notion of market has been envisaged in the ASCM.

The fact that the rules on green light-subsidies expired on 1 January 2000 does not change the significance of the original conception of the ASCM. Rather, the expiry of Articles 8 and 9 according to Article 31 ASCM was due to the fact that the members, in particular because of the developing countries gaining a more powerful voice in the negotiations, could not agree on the terms of extension.[12] During the negotiations, the rules on "green-light-subsidies" were overly regarded as essential feature for maintaining the "*general balance of the Agreement*"[13] and an "*essential element in pursuing the goals underpinning the principles of the WTO*".[14] Their expiry constitutes collateral damage of more fundamental jarring interests amongst members and not a deliberate and wilful act of their disposal. Some members even doubted the competence of the committee to decide on the prolongation of the provisions[15] and did not attach a special importance of the expiry clause, as they

[9]See Sect. 2.3.3.1.

[10]See Sect. 2.2.1.

[11]See Sect. 2.2.1; Zheng, 19 *Minnesota Journal of International Law* (2010), 1, at 35 et seq., according to whom the WTO Appellate Body concluded on a perfect market model in the understanding of Ricardo, i.e. without externalities.

[12]E.g. Committee on Subsidies and Countervailing Measures, G/SCM/M/22, at para. 2 et seq.; Committee on Subsidies and Countervailing Measures, G/SCM/M/24, at para. 20 et seq.; Wu (2015), at 3 et seq., available at http://e15initiative.org/wp-content/uploads/2015/07/E15_Industrial-Policy_Wu_FINAL.pdf.

[13]Committee on Subsidies and Countervailing Measures, G/SCM/M/24, at para. 37.

[14]Committee on Subsidies and Countervailing Measures, G/SCM/M/24, at para. 42.

[15]See e.g. the statement of the representative of Panama, Committee on Subsidies and Countervailing Measures, G/SCM/M/22, at para. 5.

expressed the opinion that the rules on non-actionable subsidies were to be on the agenda of the next General Council meeting in 2000 in any case, where their fate would finally be decided.[16]

6.1.4.1.1.2 Indications from the Regulation of Actionable Subsidies

The regulation of actionable subsidies in the ASCM gives further valuable insight into the market conception that underlies the ASCM. Actionable subsidies are subject to the control regime of Articles 5 to 7 ASCM. Article 5 ASCM states that members must not cause *"adverse effects"* to the economies of fellow WTO members through using subsidies. *"Adverse effects"* comprise injury to the domestic economy of the other members, nullification or impairment of benefits granted under the GATT, notably Article II GATT, and lastly, serious prejudice to the interests of the other members. The notion of serious prejudice, being rather vague a term, is elaborated upon in Article 6 ASCM. The clause lists several situations that either constitute or are explicitly exempt from constituting serious prejudice. Just as with Articles 8 and 9 ASCM, the expiry of Article 6.1 ASCM in 2000 does not signify a wilful removal from the anti-subsidy framework and thus an intentional conceptional change, but roots in irreconcilable negotiating positions.[17] Article 7 ASCM then completes the picture and grants members the right to seek remedies against subsidies allegedly causing adverse effects.

In contrast to the exemptions in the form of non-actionable subsidies under Article 8 ASCM, non-adverse subsidies are not limited to promoting activities in certain areas but apply to all kinds of governmental financial support without limitation. The fact that non-adverse subsidies are accepted under the ASCM and hence not allowed to be countervailed necessarily means that a market where they are found to be present cannot be classified as distorted. Thus, the ASCM mandates strict differentiation between adverse and non-adverse subsidies.[18] It espouses as "perfect market" a market that includes subsidies not causing adverse effects as defined in Article 5 and 6 ASCM.

While the sector-specific exemptions of non-actionable subsidies could by themselves be interpreted as policy exceptions from an otherwise perfect "subsidy-free"

---

[16] See the statements of the representatives of Mexico, Pakistan and India, Committee on Subsidies and Countervailing Measures, G/SCM/M/22, at para. 4, 7 and 9.

[17] For the parallel discussion on Articles 8 and 9 ASCM, see Sect. 6.1.4.1.1.1.

[18] *Sykes* also argues for a useful anti-subsidy law having to be capable of distinguishing "undesirable from desirable subsidies", see Sykes, Stanford Law and Economics Olin Working Paper No. 380 (2009), 1, at 23. Especially in situations of economic crisis, subsidies may constitute a legitimate instrument of state regulatory policy. Furthermore, non-protectionist subsidies serve the WTO objectives by protecting market access commitments and must thus be exempt from disciplines on subsidies. As a consequence, a useful anti-subsidy law must be designed to be able to distinguish between gross and net subsidisation, see Sykes, Stanford Law and Economics Olin Working Paper No. 380 (2009), 1, at 23 et seq. According to *Sykes*, the "utility of any system of disciplines that ignores the myriad of potentially offsetting government measures is questionable", see Sykes, Stanford Law and Economics Olin Working Paper No. 380 (2009), 1, at 25.

market baseline, the explicit acceptance of non-adverse subsidies of a general nature does no longer permit such a conclusion. Rather, this implies that the market baseline, i.e. where market distortion begins, constitutes the point where non-adverse subsidies turn into adverse subsidies.

6.1.4.1.2 Suitability of the Present Indicators for the Determination of Market Distortion

The suitability of the major indicators used for the determination of market distortion, i.e. market shares and market power,[19] thus depends on three aspects.

First, the indicators must prove meaningful in the light of the rationale behind the concept of market distortion. Secondly, the indicators must accord with the objectives pursued through legal reform, i.e. conform with the test criteria of legal certainty, transparency and applicability. Thirdly, the indicators must also be competent in enabling the determination of market distortion that founds on the market baseline discovered for WTO anti-subsidy law.

6.1.4.1.2.1 The Rationale Behind the Selection of the Indicators

The WTO Appellate Body included situations of market distortion into the alternative benchmark regime for NMES because it deemed situations of government predominance substantively close to situations of government monopolies.[20] A monopoly is a particular market situation in which there is only one actor supplying a market with goods, so that price setting on this market is entirely under its control.[21] The tribunal explicitly stated that *"[i]n terms of market distortion and effect on prices, there may be little difference between situations where the government is the sole provider of certain goods and situations where the government has a predominant role in the market as a provider of those goods"*.[22] Resort to alternative benchmarks in the calculation of countervailing duties in markets under predominant government influence was therefore only granted because of the quasi-monopolistic market situation.

6.1.4.1.2.2 Assessment of the Indicator of Market Shares

Market shares *"[m]easure [. . .] the relative size of a firm in an industry or market in terms of the proportion of total output or sales or capacity it accounts for"*.[23] As

---

[19]For the Appellate Body's reasoning on Article 14(d) ASCM see Sect. 3.1.2.1, on Article 14 (b) ASCM see Sect. 3.1.2.2.

[20]Appellate Body Report, *US – Softwood Lumber IV*, at para. 100; Appellate Body Report, *US – Anti-Dumping and Countervailing Duties (China)*, at para. 442.

[21]Haber, Price Determination, at 53.

[22]Appellate Body Report, *US – Softwood Lumber IV*, at para. 100; Appellate Body Report, *US – Anti-Dumping and Countervailing Duties (China)*, at para. 442.

[23]OECD Glossary of Statistical Terms, (2008) available online at http://www.oecd-ilibrary.org/economics/oecd-glossary-of-statistical-terms_9789264055087-en, at 325.

formal indicator they reflect the amount of participation in production or presence on the market of each market actor. The higher the amount of market shares, the more dominant the market position.

Depicting the composition of a market, market shares are principally able to demonstrate a high level of government participation. They can show to what degree the situation on the market under scrutiny resembles a government monopoly and thus conform with the rationale. Market shares also offer a proficiently high degree of legal security, transparency and applicability. Market data is often publicly available, so that parties investigated have insight into the basis of the investigating authorities' reasoning and the outcome of the process of reasoning is in turn relatively predictable. Even if the percentage of market shares lies in a grey area where the result of the assessment might be unclear, then this very fact that a finding of distortion will possibly be made, is as well advantageous for a party investigated from the view of legal security. Referring to a comparatively easily obtainable economic figure, market shares also possess a high degree of applicability.

But whenever current investigation practice refers to market shares, it usually uses a certain percentage of market shares to deduce from it the amount of influence of a market actor. The higher the amount of market shares, the more market control is attributed. Thus, market shares are understood as an absolute, static indicator. The static understanding does, however, conflict with the market baseline in WTO anti-subsidy law. Its "perfect market" comprises "good" subsidies. Thus, subsidies form part of a perfectly competitive market unless they start to exercise adverse effects in the sense of Article 5 ASCM and become countervailable.

If a market actor, be it a company receiving a subsidy and trading the subsidised good on the market or the government itself providing certain goods directly, competes in the market under the influence of subsidies, this can constitute accepted market behaviour. Under no account may market participation that founds on non-adverse subsidies be taken into consideration for assessing market distortion because the ASCM declares it *de jure* non-distortive. The analysis may only rely on market actions that have been supported by adverse subsidies.

Market shares, however, always reflect the entire amount of government participation. They are unable to make a distinction of market participation based on "good" and "bad" subsidies. In their static understanding, market shares are always over-inclusive—and hence not fit to serve as indicator for the determination of market distortion.

A solution to remedy over-inclusiveness of the static single-figure concept of market shares could lie in raising the amount of market shares for a positive finding of distortion to cover for the market shares which reflect market participation based on non-adverse subsidies. But this simple amendment remains insufficient. Increasing the required market share would mean trivialising the determination process without theoretical justification—a certain amount of *de jure* non-distortive market participation based on subsidies not exercising adverse effects can simply not be estimated or assumed across-the-board.

Understood dynamically, however, market shares, or rather, the change in market shares of a market actor over a particular period of time, can indicate irregularities in accordance with the market baseline. An example of this dynamic understanding can be found in the ASCM. The ASCM contains altogether seven references to market shares, mostly in connection with the elaboration of the understanding of serious prejudice in the sense of Article 5(c) ASCM, i.e. one form of adverse effect of subsidies. Article 6.3(d), 6.4, 6.6 and Annex V para. 5 ASCM all explicitly regard a change in market shares as potential evidence for serious prejudice.[24] Article 15.4 ASCM deals with the determination of injury caused by the import of subsidised goods into the market of another WTO member and simply lists the "market share" as possible indicator for the assessment of the amount of injury. What is meant to be quantified, though, is the *"impact of the subsidized imports on the domestic industry"*—i.e. a change in market shares is actually referred to.

A change in market shares that is unaccounted for in the light of the developments of the competitors' shares certainly gives rise to the suspicion of undue means of market participation. Together with other indicators, this change in market shares can also in the context of countervailing duty calculation serve as a minor indicator to conclude on the adversity of a subsidy and thus on market distortion. But its indicative power is diminished by far in comparison to the role of static market shares in today's investigation practice.

6.1.4.1.2.3 Assessment of the Indicator of Market Power

The Appellate Body refers to market power as substantive indicator for the determination of market distortion,[25] but does not provide an exact definition of the term. In economics, *"market power"* is usually understood as *"ability of a firm (or group of firms) to raise and maintain price above the level that would prevail under competition"*[26] or, more generally, as the *"ability to control price and exclude rivals"*.[27] Attributed is a loss of economic welfare.[28] Lastly, a like understanding is expressed by the Appellate Body in *US – Anti-Dumping and Countervailing Duties (China)*, with the tribunal observing that a government could exercise market power through its own pricing strategy by putting pressure on private competitors to

[24] Article 6.3(d) ASCM refers to an "increase in the world market share of the subsidizing Member", whereas Article 6.4 ASCM mentions "a change in relative shares of the market", which is then defined as "(a) there is an increase in the market share of the subsidized product; (b) the market share of the subsidized product remains constant in circumstances in which, in the absence of the subsidy, it would have declined; (c) the market share of the subsidized product declines, but at a slower rate than would have been the case in the absence of the subsidy". The wording of Annex V para. 5 ASCM reads "changes in market shares".

[25] Appellate Body Report, US – Anti-Dumping and Countervailing Duties (China), at para. 444.

[26] OECD Glossary of Statistical Terms, (2008) available online at http://www.oecd-ilibrary.org/economics/oecd-glossary-of-statistical-terms_9789264055087-en, at 324.

[27] Greer in Peterson (ed.), 53, at 53.

[28] OECD Glossary of Statistical Terms, (2008) available online at http://www.oecd-ilibrary.org/economics/oecd-glossary-of-statistical-terms_9789264055087-en, at 324.

fall in line with the government prices.[29] The higher the degree of potential influence on prices of a market actor, the higher the degree of monopoly on a market. Market power is able to show the influence of a market actor on the market situation in general and prices in particular, so that its choice as indicator accords with the rationale behind the alternative benchmark regime for market distortion.

At present, the process of reasoning does not present itself as particularly legally certain and transparent, because the parameters used for measuring market power are not predetermined but in the discretion of the investigating authority. The final result might catch parties investigated flat-footed. On the other hand, the flexibility of procedure is designed to induce investigating authorities to provide solid arguments to justify the parameters they rely on for the measurement, which entails an increase of overall transparency. With a great range of possible parameters for measurement, a sufficient degree of security as regards constant applicability of market power to serve as indicator in the determination of market distortion exists. Overall, market power is a suitable indicator for the establishment of market distortion. A predefined pool of selectable parameters could be introduced to dispose of the deficits in legal certainty and transparency.

Generally, when assessing market power, it has to be distinguished carefully whether alignment with government prices on part of the private competitors truly roots in the pricing strategy of the government or is in fact motivated by other reasons. In addition, against the backdrop of the market baseline in WTO anti-subsidy law, not every supporting governmental contribution to the market can be declared to trigger such behaviour. The influence of non-adverse subsidies cannot be taken into account when determining the amount of influence that the government exercises upon other market participants.[30] Parameters able to distinguish "good" and "bad", i.e. adverse and non-adverse subsidies are needed to gather meaningful evidence for market power. Then, market power constitutes a meaningful indicator also in the light of WTO anti-subsidy law's market baseline.

6.1.4.1.3 Redefining the Indicator of Market Power

The inclusion of market distortion into the alternative benchmark regime founds on its proximity to monopoly situations.[31] The parameters must thus ensure that such situations are reliably identified.[32]

---

[29]Appellate Body Report, US – Anti-Dumping and Countervailing Duties (China), at para. 455.

[30]See Sect. 6.1.4.1.1.

[31]See Sect. 6.1.4.1.2.1.

[32]As made clear by the wording of Article 14(d) ASCM, government purchases may also be subject to undue exertion of government influence. In these so-called monopsonistic situations the government operates as the only buyer of goods in a market, i.e. it creates and determines the market of demand and has the power to determine the price, see Blair/Harrison, Monopsony in Law and Economics, at 53. Problematic issues with regard to market power and its determination can,

6.1.4.1.3.1 Potential New Parameters for the Determination of Market Power

Therefore, new parameters must meet three requirements. First, the parameters must prove themselves in the light of the test criteria for legal reform. Secondly, they must be able to make the necessary distinction between non-adverse and adverse subsidies, which is required by the market baseline of WTO anti-subsidy law. Only the latter category of subsidies may be taken into account for the assessment of distortion. Thirdly and lastly, the methodologies must either already accommodate the particularities of a government or a government-supported monopoly or be amendable in this regard because private entity monopolists are generally eager to exploit their predominant market positions by raising prices and maximising profits, whereas a government or a government-supported entity rather adopts the opposite strategy and lowers prices in order to steer market currents in its favour.[33]

As the concept of monopolistic power and its measurement are subject of lively debate amongst economists,[34] there is not one single universally accepted methodology for its assessment. Instead, various approaches offer guidance and help to obtain an ultimately more profound understanding of monopoly power. In consequence, none of the methodologies is economically unassailable. But as all of the following six methodologies are discussed in economics as possible varieties for the measurement of monopoly power, and the objective of legal reform is, above all, to find a legally certain, transparent and applicable methodology, the question whether the approach also constitutes the economically most convincing remains outside the scope of legal reform.

6.1.4.1.3.1.1 Number-of-Firms Criterion

The number-of-firms criterion, as indicated by its name, takes reference to the number of firms competing in a certain sector of economy to measure monopoly power.[35] The less companies are active in a market segment, the greater is their potential influence on prices and thus their monopoly power.

Referring to the number of firms in a market bases on clear and comprehensible figures. It is thus *per se* a very legally certain and transparent criterion. The number of firms in a market is also a figure that is comparatively easy to obtain, so that the approach also shows a high degree of applicability. But first-glance aptness encounters objections upon a closer look.

First, difficulties might arise with respect to the definition of the relevant market. Investigating authorities might refer to another, possibly narrower, understanding of the respective market than the parties investigated, so that the outcome of the assessment of monopoly power might indeed surprise after all because fewer

---

however, equally be found in monopolies. Thus, monopsonistic situations will not be addressed separately in the following discussion.

[33]Detlof/Fridh, 63 *Global Trade and Customs Journal* (2007), 265, at 270.

[34]Dwivedi, Microeconomics, at 346.

[35]Dwivedi, Microeconomics, at 347.

companies are taken into account for the assessment than expected. The process of determining the relevant market therefore constitutes a preliminary step in the analysis that puts the initially convincing evaluation of legal certainty and transparency into perspective.

On the other hand, the exercise of discretion on part of the investigating authorities when making the preliminary assessment of the market situation has to be supported by convincing evidence, which is supposed to make the whole process more transparent—the investigating authorities seem to be bound to duly explain their choices, so that the exercise of discretion ought to be at least justiciable. As transparency is only added to the process retrospectively by disclosure of the reasoning, the parties are indeed referred to judicial action if they consider the determinations of investigating authorities to be incorrect. Their argumentation will, however, largely defy judicial control.[36]

As regards aptness to a government or government-supported monopoly, by referring to the presence of an actor on the market, the criterion only takes into account external circumstantial factors and not internal business decisions of a market actor in the form of pricing policy. It thus conforms with this requirement.

As well, the methodology would have to comply with the market baseline in WTO anti-subsidy law. By referring to the number of companies active in the market, the methodology quintessentially uses market shares to assess the influence of an actor on the market. But static market shares are not a suitable indicator for market distortion under the market baseline that underlies WTO anti-subsidy law.[37] Therefore, the number-of-firms criterion does not accord with the ASCM's conception of market.

6.1.4.1.3.1.2 Concentration Ratio

The concentration ratio is a widely used approach for the measurement of monopoly power.[38] It is calculated by determining the percentage share of the largest group of firms in the total output of a market. The larger the share of these companies, the greater the power they exert on the market. The methodology is, however, not adopted fully uniformly as the number of firms constituting the largest group of companies depends from country to country. Whereas, for instance, the United Kingdom resorts to the three biggest competitors of a particular industry, the US take the four biggest competitors of each industry into account.

The number of companies referred to varying from country to country could prove a detriment to legal security and transparency. The number of firms used for the assessment ultimately determines the outcome because the concentration ratio of one firm depends on the number of competitors it is measured against. With the number of companies not being predetermined, parties subject to the investigation

[36]See Sect. 4.2.4 for the case study example of EU investigations against China.

[37]See Sect. 6.1.4.1.2.2.

[38]Dwivedi, Microeconomics, at 347 et seq.

might be surprised by a change of practice in this regard. But though not totally excludable, such changes are unlikely to happen. Procedures in each country are quite settled—changes are certainly possible, but there is no need and desire for investigating countries to deviate from a well-established methodology. The impairment of legal certainty and transparency is therefore only a minor one. The methodology is also well-applicable, the necessary data are comparatively easy to obtain and process.

Only referring to an abstract notion of dominance based on the amount of presence on the market rather than material decisions, the approach conforms with the notion of government monopoly.

But its suitability from the perspective of the market baseline of WTO anti-subsidy law turns out problematic. Employing the company's share in the total output of one particular economic sector, the methodology includes all market actions, also these potentially based on non-adverse subsidies. In its present form, the concentration ratio methodology does therefore not accord with the market baseline.

6.1.4.1.3.1.3 Hirschman-Herfindahl Index

The Hirschman-Herfindahl Index (HHI) constitutes another form of concentration-based measurement instrument. It is calculated as the sum of the squares of the market shares of all firms in the industry.[39] It reaches up to 10,000 in a pure monopoly and is 0 when the market is divided amongst various very small firms. It is often used as a tool in competition law to assess the effect of a merger on the market situation of the respective industry.[40]

The HHI substantively presents itself as a mixture between the number-of-firms criterion and the concentration ratio. What has been said from the perspective of legal reform for the latter two remains more or less true for the HHI. Relying on easily obtainable and processable data, the HHI presents a highly applicable methodology. As it is not in any danger of sudden parameter changes, the index agrees very well with legal certainty, transparency and applicability.

The HHI is based on market shares, which as a purely formal criterion are in accord with the notion of government or government-supported monopoly.

But because the HHI in essence relies solely on market shares for the assessment of monopoly power, its conformity with the market baseline does not differ from the one of the number-of-firms criterion and the one of concentration ratio: market shares as a single figure are not a suitable parameter for the determination of monopoly power under the ASCM—and so, the HHI does not accord with the requirements for new parameters.

---

[39] http://www.ictregulationtoolkit.org/en/toolkit/notes/PracticeNote/2880 (last visited 1 January 2018).

[40] See Hausmann/Sidak, 74 *Antitrust Law Journal* (2007), 387.

6.1.4.1.3.1.4 Excess Profitability Criterion

The excess profitability criterion by Bain relies on excess profits to measure the degree of monopoly.[41] Excess profits are calculated by deducting the firm's opportunity costs and a margin for the risk from the actual profits achieved. The greater the result, the higher the degree of monopoly. A profit rate significantly higher than all opportunity costs[42] that are reasonably required to remain competitive in or to enter a market is deemed to prove that competition in the market is not strong enough to prevent the formation of monopolistic structures.[43]

The determination of monopoly power based on excess profits uses one single value for each company which is ascertainable by basically clear-cut parameters. These are known to the parties of the investigation in advance.[44] Insecurities arise in connection with the risk factor which is to be deducted from the actual profits achieved because it depends entirely on the discretion of the investigating authority and is therefore only subject to limited judicial scrutiny. The risk factor is, however, only one component in the overall measurement and thus not likely to render the whole process obscure. Thus, excess profitability is a legally highly certain and transparent method of assessment. In principle, the necessary data are also quite easily obtainable for investigating authorities and its processing smooth, so that the methodology also proves applicable.

In contrast to the approaches scrutinised before, excess profitability does not rely on market shares for the measurement of monopoly power. Instead, it takes a closer look at the individual market actor and its business policy in pricing. But nevertheless, what is considered in the final determination of the amount of profits achieved is the revenue of all investments, irrespective of them resulting from adverse or non-adverse subsidies. The amount of profit is therefore over-inclusive if the methodology is used in its present form. But in difference to the methodologies scrutinised before, excess profitability offers the opportunity to be redesigned in a manner accommodating the requirements set by the market baseline. If the amount of profits achieved would actually be based on solely the part of profits that has been realised by the use of subsidies exercising adverse effects, the amended excess profitability criterion and the conception of market of WTO anti-subsidy law would conform.

Lastly, the excess profitability methodology would also have to accord with the notion of government monopoly. In such a situation, the aim of the monopolist is not maximising profits, but more generally, price control. Relying on the amount of profits achieved, the idea of excess profitability is indeed that the respective market actor aims at using its influence to gain as much economic advantage on the market

[41]Dwivedi, Microeconomics, at 348.

[42]Opportunity costs are defined as the value of the next best alternative in a necessary decision between two alternatives so that only one alternative can be realised, see Baumol/Blinder, Microeconomics, at 41.

[43]Van den Bergh/Camesasca, European Competition Law and Economics, at 26.

[44]Dwivedi, Microeconomics, at 348.

as possible. Realisation of the advantageous market position would come through increasing prices, resulting in a large revenue. As presently employed, the excess profitability criterion does therefore not accord with the notion of government monopoly. To be eligible for legal reform, it must examined whether the criterion can be adapted to conform with the general ideological conception of government monopoly.

6.1.4.1.3.1.5 Lerner Index

The Lerner Index of monopoly power follows a similar approach as the excess profitability criterion just discussed above. It also relies on excess profits.[45] According to Lerner, the absence of a monopoly is characterised by the equality of price or average receipts and of marginal costs.[46,47] Thus, the degree of monopoly power is the excess of price over marginal costs—which under perfect market conditions equals the reciprocal of cross-price elasticity.[48]

The index of monopoly power developed by Lerner also bases on excess profits, although it determines excess profits slightly differently than the excess profitability approach developed by Bain, the basic concept remains the same. Legal certainty, transparency and applicability of the Lerner Index are thus at an equally high level.

Resorting to a market actor's individual pricing policy, the methodology does not take into account the overall competitive structure of the market in the form of market shares. But as well as the excess profitability criterion, at present the company data used for the Lerner Index are not differentiated according to the nature of the subsidies that were used for production. Profits based on both adverse and non-adverse subsidies are considered. The Lerner Index does hence not accord with the market baseline of WTO anti-subsidy law.

Because the Lerner Index presumes that the aim of the market actor is maximising profits once the monopolistic position has been taken, just like the excess profitability criterion, the Lerner index conflicts with the notion of government monopoly. But again, adaption could prove a way out and make the methodology fit as option for legal reform.

6.1.4.1.3.1.6 Criterion of Cross-Price Elasticity by Triffin

The criterion of cross-price elasticity is the only parameter Triffin relies upon to measure monopoly power. Cross-price elasticity expresses product substitutability.[49] Low cross-price elasticity means that the product in question does not have

---

[45]Dwivedi, Microeconomics, at 348 et seq.

[46]Marginal costs are defined as extra or additional cost that arises from an extra unit of production of a certain good, see Gans/King, Principles of Economics, at 288.

[47]Haber, Price Determination, at 53.

[48]Dwivedi, Microeconomics, at 349.

[49]Dwivedi, Microeconomics, at 349.

an adequate like product. If the provider of a product with low substitutability is the sole provider, it dominates the market, because consumers cannot resort to another product. Low cross-price elasticity can therefore signify a high degree of monopoly power. In detail, cross-price elasticity of a good can be calculated as the relation between the change in demanded quantity of one good to the change in price of another good.[50]

As the determination of cross-price elasticity of a product is based on clear and easily obtainable parameters, the degree of legal security, transparency and applicability of the methodology is very high.

Cross-price elasticity refers to the demand of a product and the price change of its potential substitutes. It excludes any proposition on the circumstances under which the respective good has been produced. Not being connected in any way to the nature of the subsidy underlying the production of the product, the parameter conforms with the ASCM's market baseline.

Not referring to profit maximising aspirations of a market actor, but to the product itself, cross-price elasticity is in accord with the notion of government monopoly.

6.1.4.1.3.2 Adaption of the Potential Parameters for the Determination of Market Power

The only methodology that fulfils all the necessary requirements to be suitable for legal reform is the criterion of cross-price elasticity by Triffin. The other methodologies ail from several detriments—at least in their original conception. Maybe the parameters can be adapted to erase the deficits and to make them conform with the requirements of legal reform.

6.1.4.1.3.2.1 Centralisation of the Exercise of Discretion

One major deficit of the determination of market power roots in the ample amount of discretion granted to investigating authorities, which lessens the degrees of legal certainty and transparency because of its abusive potential. In spite of actually evaluating the same market or market sector on the basis of the same set of data, the final assessment of different national investigating authorities is very likely to differ. Parties investigated will feel treated unjustly without grounds. Furthermore, the amount of discretion is often exercised in an overly extensive way, which is then not subject to sufficient judicial control.

This problem could be circumvented by centralising the process of reasoning. If the final evaluation of the market data was made by an independent separate authority having the power to issue determinations that are legally binding on all members, the risk of inexplicable deviations would be eradicated.

---

[50] McEachern, Microeconomics, at 110.

6.1.4.1.3.2.1.1 Existing Structures for Centralised Reasoning in WTO Anti-Subsidy Law

Existing structures as role model for such an independent separate authority can already be found in WTO anti-subsidy law. Three bodies exist that might either be referred to for such a binding assessment or whose structure can at least provide further indications for legal reform.

The Permanent Group of Experts was established under Article 24.3 ASCM as a body consisting of five independent, highly qualified experts.[51] It has been assigned three functions.[52] First, a panel may call the Permanent Group of Experts to decide whether or not a subsidy belongs to the category of prohibited subsidies according to Article 4 ASCM. Article 4.5 ASCM makes such a decision binding for the panel. Secondly, according to Article 24.3 ASCM, the Permanent Group of Experts can be asked by the Subsidies and Countervailing Committee to provide an advisory opinion on existence and nature of a subsidy. Thirdly, the same question may be referred to the group by any WTO member which plans to introduce or maintain a certain subsidy (Article 24.4 ASCM). Although established already in 1996, the Permanent Group of Experts has never been called to activity until today.[53]

Another body available would be the Informal Group of Experts. Established in 1995, it examines matters not specified in Annex IV or which need further clarification for the purposes of Article 6.1(a) ASCM.[54] Thus, it serves to develop a common understanding amongst WTO members in these two matters.[55]

Expert Review Groups are established under Article 13.2 DSU in connection with Annex IV. They are set up as *ad hoc* bodies with advisory function only and remain fully under panel authority.[56] But they as well have never been referred to by a tribunal so far.

6.1.4.1.3.2.1.2 Suitability of the Existing Structures for Legal Reform

Although the bodies differ in composition and scope of competence, what they have in common is that none has ever been made use of until today. One wonders, though, if the reasons that lie behind this would hinder the instalment of such a kind of body for the determination of market power or market distortion in general.

With regard to the lack of consultation of the Permanent Group of Experts, it appears likely to be the result of the bindingness of its assessments (Article 4.5

---

[51] Kazeki, 43 *Journal of World Trade* (2009), 1031, at 1032; Mavroidis, The Regulation of International Trade, at 272.

[52] Kazeki, 43 *Journal of World Trade* (2009), 1031, at 1032 et seq.

[53] Mavroidis, The Regulation of International Trade, at 272.

[54] Appellate Body Report, *EC – Hormones*, at para. 152 et seq.; Appellate Body Report, *United States – Anti-Dumping Act of 1916*, WT/DS136/AB/R, WT/DS162/AB/R, adopted 26 September 2000, DSR 2000:X, 4793, at para. 150.

[55] Kazeki, 43 *Journal of World Trade* (2009), 1031, at 1042.

[56] Kazeki, 43 *Journal of World Trade* (2009), 1031, at 1042.

ASCM).[57] The panel, itself comprising distinguished expert members (Article 8 DSU), resents deferring authority to another body but deems itself competent enough to deal with the issue at hand. But also when the bodies only render an advisory opinion that does not bind the panel, difficulties arise. The missing procedural framework in connection with advisory opinions makes the whole process non-transparent.[58] Parties and tribunals alike wish to avoid any risks resulting from such an insecure situation. Furthermore, the advisory powers of the Permanent Group of Experts do not include actionable subsidies, so that a major area, where advice would prove useful, is left uncovered.[59] Also, the independency of the group members is an indeterminate factor.[60] "Independence" from governments is nowhere defined. Whether it is thus actually ensured, remains uncertain. But parties will not submit requests of a delicate nature if strict confidentiality is not provided for.

With regard to the Informal Group of Experts, the nature of its scope of competences rather makes it a body useful for the adaption of new policies and rule-making in general, but not for the decision of actual cases.[61]

The existing structures the ASCM presents as models for the centralisation of the exercise of discretion cannot convince by themselves but give valuable guidance with regard to the design of a new body that could be established for this purpose as part of legal reform.

6.1.4.1.3.2.1.3 The New Expert Group for the Determination of Market Distortion

The new expert group for the determination of market distortion must act independently from any government influence and thus ensure that the outcomes of its reasoning are accepted by all parties. Because the question of market distortion is raised frequently in anti-subsidy investigations, establishing a permanent body that can then perform these determinations on a routine basis makes more sense than creating the group as *ad hoc* body. Furthermore, the expert group shall have exclusive and mandatory competence for the assessment of market distortion. If the single investigating authorities of members were to decide whether or not to refer this issue to a separate entity, the purpose of eliminating the deficits in legal certainty and transparency would be made redundant. In consequence, the determinations of the expert group would also have to exercise binding effect.

6.1.4.1.3.2.2 Introduction of a Preliminary Distinction Analysis

As five out of six potential new parameters, some of which appear very suitable candidates for reform otherwise, do not conform with the market baseline that has

---

[57]Kazeki, 43 *Journal of World Trade* (2009), 1031, at 1033.
[58]Kazeki, 43 *Journal of World Trade* (2009), 1031, at 1034.
[59]Kazeki, 43 *Journal of World Trade* (2009), 1031, at 1034.
[60]Kazeki, 43 *Journal of World Trade* (2009), 1031, at 1039.
[61]Kazeki, 43 *Journal of World Trade* (2009), 1031, at 1043.

been discovered to underlie WTO anti-subsidy law, it would prove fortunate if the methodologies could be adapted accordingly.

At present, all methodologies employ market data of the entities under scrutiny without differentiating between market activities based on adverse and non-adverse subsidies. This differentiation is, however, essentially required by the market baseline of WTO anti-subsidy law.[62] Instead of adjusting the results of the market analysis retrospectively, it would be more advisable to already filter the input data. After market activities that have been based on non-adverse subsidies have been singled out, the analysis can proceed as usual but would produce the accurate result.

Thus, all the methodologies can actually be made suitable again for legal reform if a preliminary distinction analysis was introduced to ensure the use of input data in accordance with the ASCM's market baseline.

6.1.4.1.3.2.3 Introduction of the Criterion of Non-profitability

Criteria based on excess profits, i.e. the excess profitability criterion by Bain and the Lerner Index, are held in high regard by economists because they are deemed to produce very precise and meaningful results in the measurement of monopoly power.[63] Unfortunately, profit orientation is precisely what rules them out as candidates for legal reform.

Instead of being directed towards a positive amount of profit that reflects the revenue of purely private market monopolists exploiting their dominant market positions, the methodologies would have to aim at the opposite. A government or government-supported entity does not seek to maximise profits, but deliberately prices its products lower than its competitors. Profits are not maximised but minimised or negative, so to speak.

Thus, in order to make the methodologies useable again for legal reform, they would have to be adapted so that the smaller the amount of "excess profit", i.e. the result from deducting of the firm's actual profits the opportunity costs or the marginal costs, the greater its monopoly power. The amount of profit forgone indicates the amount of power on the market.

6.1.4.1.4 Conclusion

The concept of market distortion needs to be substantively redesigned to enhance it as legal prerequisite that accords with the market baseline underlying WTO anti-subsidy law. As the indicator of market shares has turned out to conflict with the market baseline in its static understanding and having far less indicative power in its dynamic understanding it ought to be eliminated from the scope of the reform proposal.

[62] See Sect. 6.1.4.1.1.

[63] Dwivedi, Microeconomics, at 348 et seq.

Market power, on the other hand, has proven a suitable indicator. In order to employ it more accurately and to fully implement the objectives of legal reform, the determination of market power needs to be based on meaningful parameters. Considering the original idea behind the extension of the alternative benchmark regime in NMES to market distortion, methodologies for the measurement of monopoly power are resorted to for the assessment of market power. All the methodologies introduced have proven suitable for this purpose, mostly upon adaption, and shall therefore be included in a comprehensive pool of potential methodologies. For most parameters, adaption means the addition of a preliminary distinction analysis to filter non-adverse subsidies, as they are *de jure* non-distortive and must hence not be reflected in any measurement of market power. Which methodologies will be used in the analysis ultimately depends on the available market data. The predefined pool of possible parameters increases legal certainty and transparency for parties investigated and prevents them from being overly surprised by the outcome of the process of reasoning.

In order to minimise the risk of abuse of discretion or other inexplicable diversity of outcomes, the process of determination shall be put into the hands of a new permanent group of experts, which mandatorily decides on market distortion with binding force for the investigating authorities of the single members.

6.1.4.2 Reforming the Selection of the Alternative Benchmark

Improving the selection of the alternative benchmark must tackle the wide and uncontrollable amount of discretion investigating authorities presently enjoy. Ideally, the range of potential methodologies can be narrowed down to one single clear-cut approach that is applicable in all cases.

6.1.4.2.1 Potential Alternative Benchmark Methodologies for Legal Reform

First of all, all potential alternative benchmark methodologies must prove themselves in the light of the test criteria for legal reform, i.e. legal certainty, transparency and applicability.

6.1.4.2.1.1 Price Construction

For a long time, price construction has been a well-established methodology amongst investigating authorities of WTO members worldwide. The construction of the alternative benchmark price bases on existing market data in the country under investigation.[64] The costs of production form the foundation of the constructed price,

[64] See Sect. 2.4.3.2.1.

which are added to by a reasonable amount of selling costs and profits. The result is the surrogate price for the calculation of benefit.

With regard to legal certainty, price construction is only partially worthy of praise. Whereas the use of actual existing market data in the country under investigation gives the parties investigated prior knowledge of components of the future alternative price and enables them to make arrangements according to that knowledge, the reasonable adjustment in selling costs and profits adds a large amount of insecurity to the process. The exact extent of such adjustments is hard to predict and may be judged very differently, even by the same investigating authority in investigations against the same country under only slightly differing circumstances. Thus, it is lastly not foreseeable for the parties to what extent adjustments of existing data will be made and what outcome the determination of a comparable in-country price will have. With respect to transparency, price construction holds major disadvantages because guidelines that would make the process of reasoning more open and comprehensible only exist very sparsely. The methodology is, however, reasonably well applicable because of the flexibility regarding the respective data that is used for the calculation. If factual data is obtainable, it is used for the determination; if it is not, estimates may be resorted to.

6.1.4.2.1.2 Out-of-Country Methodologies

There are two different out-of-country methodologies for the determination of alternative benchmarks in the process of benefit calculation in NMES.[65] One variation uses the price of the like product on a single third-country market. The other variation refers to prices on the world market.

6.1.4.2.1.2.1 Third-Country Methodology

The third-country methodology is also widely used amongst investigating authorities today. It entirely disregards existing market prices in the country under investigation.[66] Instead, it exclusively resorts to prices of a like product in a comparable market economy third-country to generate a surrogate price for the calculation of the amount of benefit in NMES. The selection of a comparable third-country is deemed to recreate the market conditions that would prevail in the NMES country if not for the distortion.

Apart from having to be *"comparable"* (Article 14(b) ASCM) or *"in relation to"* existing terms and conditions (Article 14(d) ASCM) according to the general alternative benchmark regime in WTO law, no further legal prerequisites or other guidelines exist that narrow down the numerous options these open terms offer investigating authorities for the selection of the third-country. Because the selection of the respective third-country as well as the concise handling of the determination

---

[65] See Sect. 2.4.3.2.2.2.

[66] See Sect. 2.4.3.2.2.2.

process is entirely in the discretion of the investigating authorities, the outcome of the reasoning remains totally unpredictable. Thus, the third-country methodology has deficits with respect to legal certainty. Due to the lack of criteria guiding—and also binding and thus limiting the discretion of—investigating authorities, the third-country methodology is also non-transparent. The criteria according to which a third-country is selected are not uniform but change from country to country as well as from investigation to investigation. Even if the same market is investigated a second time by the same investigating authority in close temporal connection to a prior investigation, there is no guarantee that the alternative benchmark determination will have the same result. Moreover, the lack of transparent reasoning prevents the results of the third-country methodology from being comprehensible. Regardless of the parameters referred to in the process of reasoning by investigating authorities, final results mostly appear to have been conveniently and arbitrarily set. The methodology does, however, prove highly applicable, as the loose requirements for the determination of the subsidiary third-country values will not prevent its performance.

6.1.4.2.1.2.2 World Market Price

The world market price is the less often used variation of out-of-country methodology. Instead of only one single third-country price, it relies on the world market price that forms the market benchmark against which the price of the governmental contribution is measured and the amount of benefit conferred is assessed. A concise definition of the term world market price does, however, not exist. Its determination remains entirely in the hands of the investigating authorities—so that it depends on the discretion of the respective investigating authority, how many and which countries may actually contribute to the determination of the "world" market price. The high flexibility of this approach makes it well applicable, but both legal certainty and transparency are both seriously impaired. The framework of the process of reasoning as well as the process itself are secluded from a truly objective assessment.

6.1.4.2.1.3 Adjustment of Existing Distorted In-Country Prices

Strictly speaking, the adjustment of existing distorted in-country prices does not create a genuinely "alternative" benchmark. Nevertheless, the methodology offers a possibility to create a benchmark value for the calculation of the amount of benefit in NMES. In cases where in-country prices do indeed exist but are considered to be too distorted to still serve as meaningful benchmarks for the benefit calculation, these prices are adjusted in order to reflect the market conditions that would prevail in the respective sector of economy if not for the distortive government influence. But concise parameters for conducting the adjustment or any other guidance on the exact process do not exist. Although the term *"adjustment"* implies that the final price after the completion of the adjustment procedure and the original price do not differ significantly in their respective amounts, this is not necessarily the case. From the perspective of legal certainty, the outcome of an adjustment is as unpredictable as the use of a third-country price. Without parameters or guidelines for the adjustment procedure, the outcome depends on a case-by-case basis from authority to authority. In terms of legal certainty and transparency, the parties of the investigation cannot benefit from their previous knowledge of the initial price that forms the basis of the determination of the alternative benchmark price. Due to the indeterminateness of the criteria that can be employed for the adjustment of the distorted existing domestic prices in the country under investigation, both reasoning and result remain largely incomprehensible. This impairs transparency of the determination process. Furthermore, the methodology is not always applicable. In some situations of government influence on the market, in-country prices are not available because the distortive influence prevents price building or even the formation of a market. Then, the initial value for the determination process is missing.

6.1.4.2.1.4 Artificial Pricing

By many, transferring the alternative NMES methodologies from anti-dumping to anti-subsidy law has been regarded as merely *"least-worst"* solution to enable the application of countervailing law.[67] Artificial pricing has been introduced early as independent alternative methodology that enables the application of anti-subsidy law in NMES.[68] For the determination of surrogate values, artificial pricing resorts to price construction. In contrast to the methodology of price construction introduced earlier, which preferably uses actual market figures of the country under investigation that are available as starting point for the determination, artificial pricing is exclusively based on fictitious variables.

Instead of distorted in-country prices of the country under investigation, the so-called *"minimum allowable import price"* forms the point of reference for the assessment of price comparability. Import prices that are below the minimum allowable import price are considered unfairly low and a countervailing duty is imposed accordingly to offset the price difference. Several opinions exist how to create the minimum allowable import price. Five options are constantly in discussion: the lowest average price of the most suitable in-country producer of a like product in sales to domestic purchasers, the lowest average price of all domestic producers of a like product in sales to domestic purchasers, the lowest average price of the most suitable market economy producer of a like product in sales to domestic purchasers, the lowest average price of all market economy producers of a like product in sales to in-country purchasers and the lowest average price of each market economy producer of a like product comprising a commercially significant part of the sales to domestic purchasers.[69] Artificial pricing does not distinguish between the origins of price undercutting. Whether actions of a private individual or entity or of a

[67]Firestone, 8 *Journal of Comparative Business and Capital Market Law* (1986), 75, at 84.
[68]Firestone, 8 *Journal of Comparative Business and Capital Market Law* (1986), 75, at 76.
[69]Firestone, 8 *Journal of Comparative Business and Capital Market Law* (1986), 75, at 83.

government stand in question to have caused low prices is irrelevant from the perspective of imposing remedial duties.[70]

From the perspective of legal certainty, artificial pricing is a highly suitable approach. The minimum allowable import price is known to the parties of the investigation beforehand. Critics hence consider it too predictable—the methodology makes it easy for producers that receive governmental contributions to price their goods lower than their competitors on the market of the importing country by setting their prices at or slightly above the minimum allowable import price.[71] The use of predetermined and openly accessible determinants makes the entire process of reasoning very transparent to all parties from the very beginning. Keeping the amount of discretion of investigating authorities at a minimum is a particularly appealing feature of artificial pricing. The artificial price that is used as alternative benchmark for the benefit calculation is the result of a quasi-automatic application of the procedure which at the end determines the amount of artificial price. The only flexible part of the approach remains the decision how to determine the minimum allowable import price. As well, the applicability of the methodology is never endangered because the minimum allowable import price is easily obtainable once it has been decided which method of determination to follow. Furthermore, it is applicable towards all countries across-the-board, no concessions to individual market circumstances are made.

6.1.4.2.1.5 Injury-Based Determination

The injury-based determination of the alternative price derives from the reform proposal for trade remedies developed by *Zheng*.[72] Originally, the proposal addresses anti-dumping reform. But as *Zheng* writes himself, its essential idea is equally valid for anti-subsidy law.[73] In his comparatively radical proposal for anti-dumping reform, *Zheng* contends to eliminate the determination of the dumping margin altogether. Instead, the amount of anti-dumping duty shall be based on the injury margin alone. According to *Zheng*, this ensures that all the weaknesses of anti-dumping law—economic credibility,[74] posterior negative effect on trade[75] and democratic deficit[76]—are effectively eradicated. Instead of the *"mechanical number-crunching process"*[77] that usually follows the establishment of the dumping margin, a more flexible duty determination based on party negotiation is recommended. The amount of duty is not arithmetically predetermined, but entirely

[70] Firestone, 8 *Journal of Comparative Business and Capital Market Law* (1986), 75, at 84.

[71] Firestone, 8 *Journal of Comparative Business and Capital Market Law* (1986), 75, at 83.

[72] Zheng, 34 *Michigan Journal of International Law* (2012), 151.

[73] Zheng, 34 *Michigan Journal of International Law* (2012), 151, at 240 et seq.

[74] Zheng, 34 *Michigan Journal of International Law* (2012), 151, at 160 et seq.

[75] Zheng, 34 *Michigan Journal of International Law* (2012), 151, at 163 et seq.

[76] Zheng, 34 *Michigan Journal of International Law* (2012), 151, at 176 et seq.

[77] Zheng, 34 *Michigan Journal of International Law* (2012), 151, at 178.

the result of a negotiation process. A cap of the amount of duty shall, however, be provided for by the amount of injury caused through the imports to the domestic industry of the importing country. With respect to the determination of benefit conferred to the recipient, this means that the amount of benefit is made dependent on the outcome of negotiations—capped at the top by the amount of injury. The application of the alternative benchmark regimes would be rendered dispensable. The injury-based determination of the alternative benchmark price, or rather, the amount of countervailing duty, offers the comfort of setting aside completely all the present insecurities and difficulties. But it must indeed be questioned whether the negotiation-based approach does not merely substitute current weaknesses through other weaknesses that effectively do not improve the situation of parties of an anti-subsidy investigation.

In the light of legal certainty and transparency, in principle transferring the determination of the alternative price or rather, of the entire amount of benefit, to the round table, seems highly problematic with regard to legal certainty. Restricted only by the amount of injury, the exact amount of countervailing duty depends on the bargaining power of the parties. As *Zheng* himself admits, his proposal will not have the effect of diminishing the deliberateness of the duty setting process but rather legitimise it by lessening the democratic deficit.[78] With respect to transparency, however, the injury-based approach has advantages in comparison to the current system. Now, the process of setting the alternative price is entirely in the hands of the investigating authorities. Countries investigated have the opportunity to supply respective figures by answering the questionnaires during the period of investigation but other than that, they can exercise no influence or have no insight into the process of price setting. At the negotiation table, the very process of price determination is laid open to all the parties. Although certain countries enjoy more bargaining power than others, so that a consensus given to a certain amount of remedial duty is not as voluntary as it appears, the actual process of price setting is nevertheless open and comprehensible. Without any mandatory requirements for the actual process of reasoning apart from the cap at the injury margin, the methodology is also constantly applicable.

6.1.4.2.2 Assessment

Of all the methodologies presented, none meets the test criteria in a way that would permit to employ it for the purpose of legal reform without alteration. In their present guise, all methodologies lack the legal certainty and transparency that is necessary to effectively control the amount of discretion of investigating authorities. Thus, the methodologies are only truly suitable for reform if they can be amended to provide the necessary restraint for the reasoning of investigating authorities. In principle, all

[78]Zheng, 34 *Michigan Journal of International Law* (2012), 151, at 202 et seq.

methodologies can be equipped with predefined criteria for the process of determination.

But for the three currently well-established methodologies price construction, third-country methodology and adjustment of existing distorted in-country prices the initial problem, however, will remain. The criteria that could be added to guide in the application of these methodologies, e.g. mandatory factors that have to be taken into consideration in the analysis, inheres a final subjective element on part of the investigating authority. Even if the authorities adhere to a catalogue of certain criteria in their assessment, the final decision will depend on their subjective assessment whether the criteria are met and is in danger of being deliberate. This exercise of discretion remains beyond scrutiny from third parties.

The out-of-country methodology relying on the world market price, however, can be predefined as comprehensively including all countries or all countries of a certain type, e.g. all market economy countries to effectively limit the amount of discretion of investigating authorities. The methodology would thus be endowed with the legal certainty and transparency it is currently lacking.

Of the two new methodologies that have been presented, artificial pricing offers safety from excessive use of discretion through a predetermined process of reasoning—just like the world market price methodology in its amended form.

The injury-based determination is, however, characterised by an in fact even greater amount of discretion in the determination of the alternative price than any other methodology. Negotiations *per se* offer a good opportunity to carefully consider the individual situation of a country. Duties can easily be prevented from having a negative effect on the country's economy by not going beyond the actual amount of duty that is needed to offset undue advantages. In contrast, artificial pricing or comprehensive world market prices as comparatively crude measures leave no room for taking into account such particularities. But the high degree of individuality in the process of duty determination proves as major setback in the light of legal certainty. Although the process of setting the alternative price is *per se* under full control of the parties that are present at the round table, and thus highly transparent, the lastly unequal bargaining power of the negotiating parties puts weaker parties in permanent danger of being coaxed into agreeing to high amounts of duty. As such, the procedure is highly dependent on rationality and restraint of the negotiating parties. Otherwise, protection is only offered by introducing a cap of the amount of duty at the injury margin. Duties then must not be imposed beyond what is necessary for removing the actual negative impacts on the industries in the importing country. In addition, the potential overly long duration of duty determination negotiations is another factor that counts in disfavour of the injury-based methodology.

Both artificial pricing and the comprehensive world market price offer the greatest potential for reform. The quantity of discretion that remains is limited to the choice how to establish the minimum allowable import price or the world market price—which could easily be removed by setting a default determination procedure.

6.1.4.2.3 The Default Alternative Benchmark Methodology

According to the methodology of artificial pricing, the alternative parameters that may be selected to form the minimum allowable import price are the lowest average price of the most suitable in-country producer of a like product in sales to domestic purchasers, the lowest average price of all domestic producers of a like product in sales to domestic purchasers, the lowest average price of the most suitable market economy producer of a like product in sales to domestic purchasers, the lowest average price of all market economy producers of a like product in sales to in-country purchasers and the lowest average price of each market economy producer of a like product comprising a commercially significant part of the sales to domestic purchasers. Not all are equally circumventing the trap of indeterminateness that predetermination seeks to abolish. References to *"the most suitable"* domestic or market economy producer as well as to *"a commercially significant part of the sales"* unnecessarily open the door to dubious reasoning with protectionist intention. Such points of reference can lastly not be identified—or justified—in a truly objective and comprehensible manner. Relying on average values of an entire group constitutes the sounder alternative.

The two options that remain are thus the lowest average price of all in-country producers of a like product in sales to domestic purchasers and the lowest average price of all market economy producers of a like product in sales to in-country purchasers. In the light of the underlying overall objective of the alternative benchmark regime, i.e. making the application of anti-subsidy law workable for NMES by offering methodologies to generate market economy price surrogates, resorting to the prices of in-country producers does not convince. If, apart from the subsidy-receiving in-country producers, other in-country producers exist, it cannot be ascertained to what extent the market price they provide is already influenced by competition with subsidy-receiving entities. Furthermore, it offers no solution for situations of complete non-existence of in-country prices.

The most suitable alternative is hence the lowest average price of all market economy producers of a like product in sales to in-country purchasers. The world market price must contain all countries which contribute to global price-building. In order for the global price to be meaningful and to stay in line with the basic prerequisites of the new alternative benchmark regime, prices that are distorted on the basis of the underlying market conception of WTO anti-subsidy law shall be excluded from the range. Only prices that derive from MES shall be relied on for the purpose of world price building. This reflects best the value the price in the country of investigation would have if price building was influenced by market forces.

In effect, the substantive differences between using the world market price and the proposed variety of artificial pricing cancel each other. The alternative benchmark value that most effectively controls the discretion of the investigating authorities is the world market price generated out of the in-country sales prices of the respective product in all market economy countries. In fact, the use of a predetermined minimum import price for the benefit calculation in cases of allegedly unfairly priced imports from NME countries indeed reflects the very first solution, which was discussed during the negotiations for the establishment of the ITO. The later abandoned section on "Expansion of Trade by Complete State Monopolies of Import Trade" stipulated that market and NME countries should negotiate a price at which imports from the latter must always at a minimum enter the markets of the former.[79]

6.1.4.2.4 Further Necessary Adaptions

Some further adaptions are necessary for the sake of full compliance of the new alternative benchmark methodology with the existing WTO framework.

6.1.4.2.4.1 Cap at the Injury Margin

One of the advantages of resorting to a predefined benchmark lies in the simplicity of application. But attention must be paid that the methodology does not offset comparative advantages that the country under investigation actually enjoys. The WTO Appellate Body emphasised this in *US – Softwood Lumber IV* and explicitly forbade the imposition of an amount of countervailing duty that set off real comparative advantages of a country.[80]

In its current "crude" form, the world market price benchmark value is not able to offer this guarantee. But if added a cap at the injury margin to ensure that offsetting benefits is kept limited to undue advantages and does not include comparative advantages, it would possess the necessary safeguard that prevents the imposition of excess amounts of countervailing duties. WTO anti-subsidy law already offers this possibility (Article 19.2 ASCM), and members like the EU have adopted it in their national legislation.[81] A mandatory cap of the amount of countervailing duty at the injury margin must thus be added.

6.1.4.2.4.2 Centralisation of the Process of Reasoning

Putting the process of determining market distortion in the hands of one central expert group was essential to secure a fair and independent process of reasoning.[82] With respect to the choice of the alternative benchmark, this kind of problem is circumvented by the detailed predetermination of how to obtain the world market price. Whether or not the correct way to establish the world market price has been

[79]Polouektov, 36 *Journal of World Trade* (2002), 1, at 5 et seq.; Detlof/Fridh, 2 *Global Trade and Customs Journal* (2007), 265, at 268.

[80]Appellate Body Report, *US – Softwood Lumber IV*, at para. 109.

[81]See Article 12(1)(3) BASR regarding a cap in the imposition of provisional duties and Article 15 (1)(5) BASR regarding a cap in the imposition of definitive duties.

[82]See Sect. 6.1.4.1.3.2.1.3.

adhered to, is fully subject to judicial scrutiny. Centralising the process of reasoning is therefore unnecessary.

6.1.4.2.5 Conclusion

The proposal for the determination of the alternative benchmark exclusively has a substantive dimension. To address the deficits that have been identified in the present process of selecting the alternative benchmark, the world market price generated out of the in-country sales prices of the respective product in all market economy countries shall be used as benchmark and as such substitute the distorted or otherwise unavailable in-country price of the country of investigation. Suiting best the objectives of legal reform, it shall replace the currently available range of alternative benchmark methodologies. Necessary further addition to the system is a cap at the injury margin which ensures that no real comparative advantages are offset through countervailing duties. Judicially uncontrollable elements of discretion have been eliminated entirely from the determination process, which finally removes the insecurity and potential arbitrariness of the present approach.

6.2 Implementation of the Reform Proposal at WTO Level

What remains to be answered is the question how the substantive reform proposals can be implemented at WTO level and lawfully be integrated into the current anti-subsidy framework.

With interpretation by the Appellate Body having been found *ultra vires* due to a contravention against the principles *in dubio mitius* and *non liquet*,[83] authoritative interpretation and amendment are left as promising options WTO law offers for implementing the reform proposals.

6.2.1 Necessity of Amendment as Suitable Means of Implementation

Considering that WTO law has deliberately been designed as a *"veil of ignorance"*,[84] which entails that open and ambiguous terms have been included into the framework by default,[85] one would presume that the task of integrating the alternative benchmark regime in WTO anti-subsidy law is made for authoritative

[83]On the principles in general see Sect. 3.1.2.4.1. On the discussion of legality see Sect. 5.2.3.1.6.

[84]Rawls, A Theory of Justice, at 118.

[85]Schropp, Trade Policy Flexibility and Enforcement in the WTO, at 201.

interpretation as means of implementation.[86] Surprisingly, precedence of authoritative interpretation in general is still scarce. No authoritative interpretation has ever been issued. One possible explanation for the persisting reluctance of the WTO members in this regard is the general preference of solving problematic issues by consent rather than majority voting. In contrast to GATT procedure, where voting—also on controversial issues—has been a common occurrence,[87] the WTO membership usually refrains from majority voting.

Apart from the lack of practical experience with authoritative interpretations, which makes them a rather insecure procedural means, the envisioned scope of the reform proposal for the new alternative benchmark regime requires formal amendment. It affects existing rights and obligations of the members. First, the introduction of one single compulsory alternative benchmark methodology restricts the presently unlimited array of potential methodologies. Second, the creation of a separate independent body conducting a centralised determination of market distortion, which is then legally binding for all members curtails the current right of members' investigating authorities to conduct this analysis themselves.

There are, however, multiple ways to realise the amendment. Either, with Article 14 ASCM, an existing provision could be textually altered to explicitly cover the use of alternative benchmarks in NMES. Alternatively, an entirely new agreement between WTO members on the understanding of Article 14 ASCM could be concluded. Regardless of its designation, the prerequisites of Article X WTO Agreement must be observed.[88] Although the provision expressly only covers amendments of existing multilateral agreements, i.e. the former amendment variety, the provision must *a fortiori* be applicable to amendments of the WTO Agreement itself.[89] As a separate agreement would very likely only add to the confusion that already inheres the discussion of the applicable legal alternative benchmark provisions, it seems more recommendable to textually amend Article 14 ASCM and finally create one single provision that regulates the benefit calculation in both MES and NMES.

6.2.2 Risks of an Amendment

For the success of the proposed reform, it is important that the amendment uniformly exercises legally binding force upon all members. In this respect, the process of amendment might produce an undesirable result. An amendment only obtains

[86]Convinced of the power of authoritative interpretations as solution for long-standing problems at WTO level in the light of current deadlock of the Doha Round and unreliableness of the Appellate Body Ehlermann/Ehring, 8 *Journal of International Economic Law* (2005), 803, at 812.

[87]Ehlermann/Ehring, 8 *Journal of International Economic Law* (2005), 803, at 818.

[88]Pauwelyn, Conflict of Norms in Public International Law, at 41 and 43.

[89]Pauwelyn, Conflict of Norms in Public International Law, at 43, footnote 65.

comprehensively legally binding force if it is adopted by unanimous decision of all members. In case of a lack of unanimity, according to Article X:3 WTO Agreement, all amendments to the multilateral agreements, including the ASCM, *"of a nature that would alter the rights and obligations of the Members"* can be submitted to the national parliaments for ratification if a two-third majority of the members votes in favour of it. But the amendment agreement would then only bind members which have actually ratified the proposal themselves once two-thirds of all members have completed the ratification process.

Thus, it is possible that the anti-subsidy legal regime is split and the newly enacted alternative benchmark regime would only be applicable to part of the membership. To the rest, the present regime would continue to apply. This development would be a major setback for the transparency of the system and non-discrimination amongst members, which are important objectives of the proposed reform because incomprehensible differences in the application of *per* se uniform legal rules are endemic to the present provisions. Successive amendments then run the risk of further aggravating the situation. Although a consequence of the application of WTO procedural rules, the only partially effective adoption of the necessary reform proposal would lead to perseverance of current problems and lastly prove fatal for the success of the reform in its core.

Yet, despite this risk, for a lawful integration of an alternative benchmark regime into general WTO anti-subsidy law, an amendment is without alternative.

6.2.3 Realisability of an Amendment

In the light of current reform negotiations at WTO level, however, it is doubtful whether the reform proposals will ever be carried through the entire amendment procedure and one day actually be implemented.

6.2.3.1 The Status Quo of the Current Doha Development Agenda

The current negotiations on reforming the WTO agreements, the Doha Development Agenda or Doha Round, began in November 2001.[90] At the outset, WTO members declared *"to maintain the process of reform and liberalization of trade policies, thus ensuring that the system plays its full part in promoting recovery, growth and development"*.[91] Special attention was to be devoted to the needs of developing countries.[92]

---

[90]Doha Ministerial Declaration, WT/MIN(01)/DEC/1, 20 November 2001.

[91]Doha Declaration, at para. 1.

[92]Doha Declaration, at para. 2.

But the Doha negotiations as a whole quickly came to a standstill. Developing countries were defending their interests more fiercely than before. Paired with the big industrial nations' unwillingness to part from convenient advantages of the past, this resulted in the "big round" never truly making significant progress towards conclusion.[93]

Negotiations have, however, resulted in one major partial success with the adoption of the Bali Package on 7 December 2013. It mainly contained regulations on three different aspects: an agreement on trade facilitation, agreements on various agricultural topics and provisions addressing the economic advancement of developing countries.[94] On 27 November 2014, the General Council adopted necessary subsequent decisions to further implement and realise some of the Bali commitments.[95] In the subsequent Nairobi Package of 2015, WTO members agreed on other issues of like subjects and again contributed in small scale to further developments with regard to least-developed countries or agriculture at WTO level.

6.2.3.2 The Doha Round's Reform Proposals on the Use of Alternative Benchmark Methodologies (2008)

The area of anti-subsidy law is included in the scope of the current Doha Round negotiations. The mandate expressly affirms that the negotiations are *"aimed at clarifying and improving disciplines"* of, *inter alia*, the ASCM *"while preserving the basic concepts, principles and effectiveness of these Agreements and their instruments and objectives"*.[96] Here as well, interests and needs of developing countries are to be considered particularly.[97] The provision of subsidies, especially in the fisheries sector, forms essential part of the discussions.[98]

The draft consolidated chair texts of the ADA and the ASCM date from 2008 and also comprise reform proposals for the rules on the calculation of benefit in anti-subsidy investigations.[99] In the proposals for the use of alternative benchmark methodologies in anti-subsidy investigations, much presents itself as familiar from current investigation practice and judicial decisions. The latest reform proposals of 2008 largely endorse the integration of the WTO Appellate Body's jurisprudence on alternative benchmarks into written WTO law. Both the subsidy definition in Article

[93]Coppens, WTO Disciplines on Subsidies and Countervailing Measures, at 37; on the shift from large negotiation rounds to smaller congregations in international law-making and respective reasons for this change see Pauwelyn et al., 25 *European Journal of International Law* (2014), 733.

[94]Coppens, WTO Disciplines on Subsidies and Countervailing Measures, at 35.

[95]Post-Bali Work Decision of 27 November 2014, WT/L/941, 28 November 2014.

[96]Doha Declaration, at para. 28.

[97]Doha Declaration, at para. 28.

[98]Doha Declaration, at para. 28, 31.

[99]New Draft Consolidated Chair Texts of the AD and SCM Agreements, TN/RL/W/236, 19 December 2008, at 37, 53 et seq.

1 ASCM and the methods for the calculation of benefit in Article 14 ASCM are subject to the amendment proposals.

6.2.3.2.1 The Article 1 ASCM Reform Proposals

With respect to Article 1 ASCM, a new footnote shall be added to Article 1.1 (b) ASCM clarifying the conferral of a benefit. Thereby, *"a benefit is conferred when the terms of the financial contribution are more favourable than those otherwise commercially available to the recipient in the market"*.[100] This transfers the WTO Appellate Body's ruling from *Canada – Aircraft* into the ASCM, which has long served as the yardstick for the definition of benefit in anti-subsidy practice, thus finally making it compulsory for investigating authorities of all WTO members.

6.2.3.2.2 The Article 14 Reform Proposals

In addition, Article 14 ASCM is scheduled to be subjected to major amendments. Draft Article 14 ASCM contains three paragraphs altogether.

The first change has been proposed with regard to the title of Article 14 ASCM. So far explicitly referring to the amount of subsidy *"in terms of the benefit to the recipient"*, the latter part shall be deleted. Here, opposition amongst negotiating parties has formed, largely preferring to keep the wording of the title as it stands.[101]

In connection with draft Article 14.1 ASCM, at first additions to Article 14(b) and (c) ASCM with respect to contributions of long-term loss-incurring institutions are discussed.[102] The EU, which suggested the respective introduction of a new red light category of subsidies, regards this type of government financing to be not sufficiently covered under the present framework.[103] Unity is, however, not in sight—too many dissenting opinions on to many different issues, e.g. singling out legitimate government subsidisation, the benchmark for measuring the benefit and the necessity to adopt the new category at all, presently prove too much.[104] Secondly, Article 14 (d) ASCM stands to be extended to include alternative benchmark methodologies for cases of regulated prices.[105] The amendment regulation allows for the use of either the export price in the country of provision or any market-determined

[100] Draft ASCM Chair Text, at 37.

[101] Communication from the Chairman of the Negotiating Group on Rules, TN/RL/W/254, 21 April 2011, at 42.

[102] Communication from the Chairman (2011), at 54.

[103] Communication from the Chairman (2011), at 37.

[104] Communication from the Chairman (2011), at 37 et seq.

[105] Draft ASCM Chair Text, at 54.

out-of-country price as benchmarks for the benefit calculation in cases where there is no in-country price or the existing in-country price is distorted. If an unregulated in-country price can be identified, however, this price is to be employed for the benefit calculation.

Draft Article 14.2 ASCM regulates the question whether subsidies granted to the producers of parts confer a benefit to the final product. This so-called pass-through of domestic subsidies has been vividly discussed amongst academia[106] and WTO judiciary[107] alike. The draft stipulates that principally no benefit shall be passed through unless the producer of the final product itself received the input at terms advantageous to the market.

Draft Article 14.3 ASCM stipulates methods for the attribution of benefits to particular periods of time by either allocation or expense. It lists circumstances in which either the one or the other approach shall be applied.

6.2.3.3 Substantive Overlap of the 2008 Draft Proposals and the Study's Reform Proposals

The 2008 draft proposals majorly address three aspects. They introduce a definition of the term *"benefit"* in Article 1.1(b) ASCM, add long-term loss-incurring financing as new type of subsidy and stipulate an explicit alternative benchmark regime for NMES in Article 14(d) ASCM. To what extent do the 2008 draft proposals correspond to the study's substantive reform proposals can indicate the success rate of the latter's proposals.

6.2.3.3.1 Overlap in the Definition of Benefit in Draft Article 14.1 ASCM

Reflecting the approach of the panel in *Canada – Aircraft*, the new definition of benefit has already been widely and commonly referred to by investigating authorities. Integrating the definition into the written law of the ASCM will secure this common understanding.

Regrettably, it will not change much the present way of calculating the benefit. It still remains too vague to offer any significant guidance for investigating authorities in how to concisely proceed with the calculation. The type of market benchmark is, for instance, still not defined in the necessary detail. The benefit definition will bring security but not much news for the process of benefit calculation—in both MES and NMES.

[106]See Kaplan/Francois, 21 *Tulane Journal of International and Comparative Law* (2013), 467, at 473 et seq.; Kelly, M. (2013), available at SSRN http://ssrn.com/abstract=2273938, 1, at 21 et seq.
[107]See in particular Panel Report, *US – Anti-Dumping and Countervailing Duties (China)*, at para. 12.39 et seq.

6.2.3.3.2 Overlap in the Addition of Long-Term Loss-Incurring Financing as Type of Subsidy to Draft Articles 14(b) and (c) ASCM

The proposal to add as a new type of subsidy long-term loss-incurring financing does not expressly refer to the application of this guideline in NMES. Thus, this feature of the 2008 draft proposals falls outside the scope of the study's reform proposals.

6.2.3.3.3 Overlap in the Alternative Benchmark Regime of Draft Article 14.1(d) ASCM

Just like the reform ideas suggested in the course of the study, draft Article 14.1 (d) ASCM explicitly addresses amendments of the alternative benchmark regime for NMES. Unfortunately, with both inherited liabilities and new particularities that render it unfit to meet the demands a reform proposal would have to address, draft Article 14.1(d) ASCM falls short in scope of necessary legal changes. Two issues in particular make this obvious.

First, it is not clear under which circumstances "unregulated prices" exist in NMES that hinder the resort to alternative benchmarks. Does the impossibility to find such unregulated prices include a mandatory attempt of prior price adjustment or maybe even an attempt to construct an undistorted in-country price? Other situations of price distortion are also not covered. The WTO Appellate Body explicitly held that the situations addressed in its decisions concerning Article 14 (d) ASCM so far were not exclusively permitting the use of alternative methodologies for the benefit calculation. Moreover, in *US – Anti-Dumping and Countervailing Duties (China)*, it also has interpreted Article 14(b) ASCM to include an alternative benchmark regime. Draft Article 14.1 ASCM would be unnecessarily limiting, causing problems of applicability of the alternative benchmark regime in the future—which might in turn again produce jurisprudence extending the scope of the codified alternative benchmark regime and re-establish the present situation.

Second, the range of permitted alternative benchmark methodologies surprises. Constructed prices, which have been included in the alternative benchmark methodologies of both anti-subsidy and anti-dumping law from the very beginning, are no longer listed in draft Article 14.1(d) ASCM. Of the methodologies currently used for the determination of price comparability in anti-subsidy law, price construction represents a comparatively transparent and well documentable concept.[108] Removing it from the range of alternative benchmark methodologies lacks a convincing reason. Thus bereft, the alternative benchmark regime is weakened in its ability to render comprehensible results. Making matters worse, the draft proposal expressly refers to out-of-country benchmarks, which have in their present forms so far served as an open door for arbitrary treatment in the imposition of countervailing duties.

[108] See Sect. 6.1.4.2.1.1.

With the reform proposal hardly placing any restrictions or guidelines on the application of the out-of-country methodologies, the potential for arbitrariness of the present system is likely to be preserved beyond the Doha Round amendments.

6.2.3.4 Realisability of the Study's Reform Proposals

The reform concept for benefit calculation in the 2008 report of the WTO Negotiating Group on Rules is substantially insufficient. It will probably only marginally advance the cause of a clearer and more transparent legal framework in this area.

But given the development of the current Doha Round, it may well be doubted whether even this "small scale reform" will be implemented at all. The circumstances of the Doha Round negotiations have remained difficult since having been launched in 2001. Not much progress has been made in all problematic legal areas for a long time. But the adoption of the Bali Package in 2013 has inspired hopes that a conclusion of the negotiations is indeed still possible to some extent—maybe a "Bali Package approach" is also feasible in anti-subsidy law.

The area of anti-subsidy law proves no exception to the general standstill of the Doha Round. The last significant development in the process of amending the general ASCM framework dates back to the year 2008. The 2011 Communication by the Chairman of the Negotiating Group on Rules acknowledged that since then, *"there have been no significant signs of convergence"*.[109] In addition, the *"early harvest of some low hanging fruits"*[110] in the Bali and Nairobi Rounds did not result in any further progress. The array of dissenting opinions that remains until today renders a swift, if any, conclusion of the Doha Round rules negotiations on anti-subsidy law highly unlikely.[111]

In the light of the *status quo* of the anti-subsidy rules negotiations, which substantially remain behind the study's reform proposals, the latter's successful introduction into WTO law appears hardly feasible. Too many different negotiating positions regarding the present "small-scale" proposal will also prevent unity in anti-subsidy talks in the foreseeable future.

6.2.4 *Conclusion*

With authoritative interpretation falling short when it comes to covering the envisaged substantive alterations of the members' rights and obligations, the reform proposal for the alternative benchmark regime in general WTO anti-subsidy law needs to be implemented as amendment according to Article X WTO Agreement.

---

[109]Communication from the Chairman (2011), at 1.

[110]Coppens, WTO Disciplines on Subsidies and Countervailing Measures, at 35.

[111]Consentient Coppens, WTO Disciplines on Subsidies and Countervailing Measures, at 37.

For the sake of legal clarity, it is recommendable to conduct a textual amendment of Article 14 ASCM.

The realisation of the study's reform proposals through means of amendment is, however, hardly feasible at present—if ever. The *status quo* of the Doha Round makes apparent that the problematic issues identified with regard to the calculation of benefit in anti-subsidy law will not be solved in the foreseeable future. New negotiations addressing the same issues will only be confronted with the same problems and the same inflexible negotiating positions.

6.3 Draft Reform Proposal for an Alternative Benchmark Regime for NMES in WTO Anti-Subsidy Law

The integration of the reform proposal for the alternative benchmark regime for NMES into existing WTO anti-subsidy law as it stands requires a positive amendment of Article 14, 17 and 19 ASCM. Upon reform, the three articles thus may take the following wordings:

Article 14
Calculation of the Amount of a Subsidy in Terms of the Benefit to the Recipient

14.1. For the purpose of Part V, any method used by the investigating authority to calculate the benefit to the recipient conferred pursuant to paragraph 1 of Article 1 shall be provided for in the national legislation or implementing regulations of the Member concerned and its application to each particular case shall be transparent and adequately explained.

14.2. In market economy situations, any such method shall be consistent with the following guidelines:

(a) government provision of equity capital shall not be considered as conferring a benefit, unless the investment decision can be regarded as inconsistent with the usual investment practice (including for the provision of risk capital) of private investors in the territory of that Member;
(b) a loan by a government shall not be considered as conferring a benefit, unless there is a difference between the amount that the firm receiving the loan pays on the government loan and the amount the firm would pay on a comparable commercial loan which the firm could actually obtain on the market. In this case the benefit shall be the difference between these two amounts;
(c) a loan guarantee by a government shall not be considered as conferring a benefit, unless there is a difference between the amount that the firm receiving the guarantee pays on a loan guaranteed by the government and the amount that the firm would pay on a comparable commercial loan absent the government guarantee. In this case the benefit shall be the difference between these two amounts adjusted for any differences in fees;
(d) the provision of goods or services or purchase of goods by a government shall not be considered as conferring a benefit unless the provision is made for less than adequate remuneration, or the purchase is made for more than adequate remuneration. The adequacy of remuneration shall be determined in relation to prevailing market conditions for the good or service in question in the country of provision or

purchase (including price, quality, availability, marketability, transportation and other conditions of purchase or sale).

14.3. In non-market-economy situations, the use of alternative benchmark methodologies is expressly permitted for the purpose of benefit calculation in anti-subsidy investigations. A non-market-economy situation is defined as a situation, where no market prices for a certain product exist on the in-country market at all, or where the existing in-country market price for a certain product is distorted by government influence, so that the market situation in the country under investigation resembles a monopoly (market distortion).

14.3.1 For the determination of market distortion, a market distortion analysis shall be conducted.

14.3.1.1 In the market distortion analysis, the following methodologies shall be used especially but not exclusively:

(i) the number-of-firms criterion;
(ii) the concentration ratio;
(iii) the Hirschman-Herfindahl Index;
(iv) the excess profitability criterion, under inverse orientation towards non-profit maximisation;
(v) the Lerner Index, under inverse orientation towards non-profit maximisation, and
(vi) the criterion of cross-price elasticity by Triffin.

14.3.1.2 The process of the determination of market distortion shall be conducted only under exclusion of subsidies of non-adverse effect.

14.3.1.3 The expert group on the determination of market distortion shall have exclusive authority to conduct the market distortion analysis and issue the final determination of market distortion. The decision of the expert group shall be binding on all Members.

14.3.2 The minimum allowable import price shall be used as alternative benchmark price in the benefit calculation. The minimum allowable import price is defined as the lowest average price of all market economy producers of a like product in sales to in-country purchasers.

[...]

Article 17
Provisional Measures

[...]
17.2 Provisional measures may take the form of provisional countervailing duties guaranteed by cash deposits or bonds equal to the amount of the provisionally calculated amount of injury.
[...]

Article 19
Imposition and Collection of Countervailing Duties

[...]
19.4 No countervailing duty shall be levied on any imported product in excess of the amount of the injury found to exist, calculated in terms of injury per unit of the subsidized and exported product.
[...]

6.4 Chapter Summary

The principles of legal certainty, transparency and applicability have been identified as test criteria that address adequately the current systemic deficits and ensure a sustainable and actually workable outcome of legal reform. Substantively, the reform proposals addressed the determination of market distortion and the selection of the alternative benchmark methodology.

The new approach for the determination of market distortion founds on the basis of the market baseline that underlies WTO anti-subsidy law. The reform proposal substantively strengthens the indicator of market power through applying for its assessment several parameters for the measurement of monopoly power. This also serves the original conception of the alternative benchmark regime for NMES. Putting the determination process entirely into the hands of one single new expert group at WTO level effects procedural enhancement and ensures that parties are provided with a fair process of reasoning.

Improving the selection of the alternative benchmark price has been found to centre around the world market price generated out of the in-country sales prices of the respective product in all market economy countries as best benchmark value to tackle potential misuse of discretion. It introduces a quasi-automatic determination process that eliminates the risk of judicially uncontrollable decisions.

Altogether, the proposal for legal reform offers the opportunity to introduce a fairer and more transparent system that will benefit investigating authorities, parties investigated and the WTO itself alike. But because the substantive scope of the reform proposal mandatorily requires an amendment according to Article X WTO Agreement, WTO members need to overcome their differences on the round table that impede the current Doha Round in order to successfully implement the proposal.

Chapter 7
Summary

The use of alternative benchmarks in NMES in anti-subsidy law is a vast field which has so far only been subject to legal research to a moderate extent. Examining the use of alternative benchmarks in NMES between the poles of the WTO, the EU and China has uncovered several problematic aspects of different natures.

7.1 Major Findings of the Study

The present study has focused on four major issues. China's applicable WTO anti-subsidy law, WTO law compatibility as such and as applied of current EU anti-subsidy law and practice as well as legality and legitimacy of the introduction of country-specific accession commitments into the WTO legal anti-subsidy framework and the introduction of an alternative benchmark regime for NMES in general WTO anti-subsidy law by means of Appellate Body reports have been closely examined and, to the extent possible, feasible legal solutions have been developed. In addition, the thesis has identified areas that reward further research in the future.

7.1.1 China's Applicable WTO Anti-Subsidy Law

The clear line between the application of the general WTO regime of Article 14 ASCM in MES on the one hand and the application of the China-specific regime of Section 15(b) CAP in NMES on the other, that has been established upon the adoption of the CAP in 2001, has been blurred irreversibly by subsequent Appellate Body jurisprudence. With the exact systemic relationship between WTO agreements and CAP still in the dark, the question of the applicable legal alternative

S. Müller, *The Use of Alternative Benchmarks in Anti-Subsidy Law*,
European Yearbook of International Economic Law 4,
https://doi.org/10.1007/978-3-319-77613-2_7

benchmark regime can to date only be attempted to be solved by feazing the interaction of the two provisions on a microcosmic level.

But even so, it is not ascertainable beyond doubt which regime to apply in NMES. The respective legal prerequisites are both ambiguous and vague and have not yet received any of the direly necessary elaboration. Given the undefined terms, it cannot even be stated to what extent the two basic regimes actually differ.

The study has developed applicability models that reflect the potential relationships between the NMES regimes of Article 14 ASCM and Section 15(b) CAP for China. For now, the models contribute to scientific discussion by providing an overview of the theoretically possible outcomes. Once the prerequisites have become increasingly defined, they will eventually aid in tracing the finally applicable framework.

But on the long term, an ultimate and truly sustaining solution of the question of China's applicable alternative benchmark regime in WTO anti-subsidy law can only be reached once the overall relationship between WTO agreements and the CAP has been satisfactorily cleared. Here as well, future research for a timely conclusion of this open issue is direly needed.

7.1.2 WTO Law Compatibility As Such and As Applied of Current EU Anti-Subsidy Law and Practice

At WTO level, Article 14 ASCM stipulates an open legal framework for the benefit calculation that endows the investigating authorities of WTO members with a large amount of discretion. The EU has always made ample use of this discretion. Both the EU legal framework and the Commission's investigation practice to date heavily draw from the undefined WTO prerequisites.

In spite of the indeterminateness of the legal provisions, which would *per se* let assume a topsy-turvy case handling that is largely influenced by the particularities of each case, EU investigation practice has quickly become predictable. As the study of EU cases against China has unearthed, once a line of reasoning alleging the non-conformity of a certain kind of subsidy has been employed successfully in one investigation, it is usually re-used in the subsequent case in a slightly adapted way, to fit the particularities. This is possible because the government of China itself mostly keeps reapplying particular subsidy schemes to the different sectors of economy. In consequence, the EU Commission is able to conduct anti-subsidy investigations with less effort as precedent grows.

Although considerable leeway is provided for by the WTO legal framework, both EU anti-subsidy legislation and investigation practice are not fully in accordance with its prerequisites. With regard to the legal framework, Article 6(d)(ii) BASR does not adequately reflect the priority of adjustment of existing in-country prices in the process of benefit calculation that is required by WTO Appellate Body jurisprudence. Although in fact not contrary to written WTO law of Article 14 ASCM, the

BASR provision would very likely be held to contravene WTO law as it is opposed to the Appellate Body's reasoning in *US – Softwood Lumber IV* and *US – Anti-Dumping and Countervailing Duties (China)*. The EU Commission's reasoning regarding the permissibility of deviation from existing in-country prices as too heavily distorted for further meaningful use in the benefit calculation as well as the subsequent selection of an alternative benchmark does not in all particulars find itself fully in accordance with WTO law prerequisites. This may well give rise to successful challenges of EU case handling in front of the WTO judiciary in the future. Especially with regard to China and the potential shift in the case practice from anti-dumping to countervailing proceedings in cases of subsidy-induced dumping, which constitutes the greater share of dumping investigations against China, in consequence of the expiry of Section 15(a)(ii) CAP granting permission to resort to alternative benchmarks in NMES in anti-dumping proceedings only until December 2016, the prospects of judicial challenge rise.

7.1.3 Legality and Legitimacy of the Introduction of Country-Specific Accession Commitments in Anti-Subsidy Law

After the "GATT à la carte" experience, which signifies that the GATT acquis was not uniformly applicable amongst signatories, one of the founding principles of the WTO as successor of the GATT was the principle of non-discrimination. Whereas market access commitments of acceding countries naturally differed depending on the state of their economic development, the general WTO rules of conduct have always been the same for all members, incumbent and acceding, alike. The country-specific rules, which have been adopted in the CAP, were the first of this severity in the history of the WTO and casted severe doubts with regard to legality and legitimacy in the light of the conception of the WTO. This study has unveiled that genuine WTO law itself prohibits the creation of new substantive country-specific accession commitments in anti-subsidy law. Other than often acclaimed, country-specific rule-making upon accession violates Article XII:1 WTO Agreement. WTO law does not offer any justification for this breach of law. The context of Article XII WTO Agreement as well as the rationale of accession protocols and the historical dimension of country-specific rule-making in the GATT era make apparent that WTO law as it stands inherently rejects differentiation in the applicable legal framework amongst its members. In particular, more modern approaches like subsequent agreement or subsequent practice cannot overcome the strict legal boundaries that exist for treaty amendment in WTO law. Only if classified as non-WTO agreements between WTO members as sovereign states, which then also determine their relationship inside the WTO, country-specific rule-making would indeed be permitted. But when it comes to the legitimacy of this approach, the principle of non-discrimination, which has been found applicable already to the prospective member during the process of accession, renders the adoption of country-specific accession commitments exceeding the exceptions provided for in the WTO legal framework illegitimate. Country-specific rulemaking on accession thus leads to an erosion of the WTO's authority as major institution for the regulation of global trade. By adhering to this policy, the WTO would ultimately undermine itself its very conception, gradually deteriorating in standing and losing the justification for its existence.

7.1.4 Legality and Legitimacy of the Introduction of an Alternative Benchmark Regime for NMES in General WTO Anti-Subsidy Law by Means of Appellate Body Reports

For the first time, an alternative benchmark regime for NMES in anti-subsidy law has been introduced in Section 15(b) CAP in 2001. With the Appellate Body adopting a NMES regime for general WTO law within the framework of Article 14 ASCM, the practical permissibility of resorting to alternative benchmarks for the benefit calculation in cases where no market benchmarks exist at all or the existing in-country benchmarks are so heavily distorted by government influence that their employment in the calculation process does not render meaningful results, has manifested itself. Based on the respective Appellate Body decisions in *US – Softwood Lumber IV* and *US – Anti-Dumping and Countervailing Duties (China)*, the study has examined legality and legitimacy of this approach. Substantively, WTO law hardly places any restrictions. Neither Article 14, 19.3 or 19.4 ASCM or Article VI:3 GATT explicitly require the application of existing in-country market data. Their open and undetermined wordings do also not prohibit the use of alternative benchmarks. Procedurally, however, Appellate Body reports do not constitute the correct legal means of introducing an alternative benchmark regime into WTO anti-subsidy law. By its legal quality, the introduction of such a regime no longer constitutes interpretation of an existing legal framework but a treaty amendment. The power for treaty amendments is, however, beyond the power of the Appellate Body, which is determined by the principles *in dubio mitius* and *non liquet*. But as the adoption of NMES rules has been uncovered to constitute an altogether legitimate undertaking that promotes trade liberalisation by enabling the application of anti-subsidy law also in NMES, reform was indicated to provide WTO anti-subsidy law with an alternative benchmark regime devoid of present defects.

7.2 A Reform Proposal Concerning the Alternative Benchmark Regime for NMES in Anti-Subsidy Law

To substantively renew the present approach, it is necessary to redefine the indicators for market distortion and improve the process of selecting the alternative benchmark.

Of the two indicators presently used in accordance with Appellate Body jurisprudence to determine market distortion through government action, market shares and market power, only the latter has been discovered to be in conformity with the market conception underlying WTO anti-subsidy law. As the prerequisite of market distortion has originally been understood by the Appellate Body to signify monopoly-like market situations, the indicator of market power has been redesigned by closely adhering to this original understanding. Several methodologies for the assessment of market power in the sense of monopoly power have been evaluated with regard to their suitability in the light of legal certainty, transparency and applicability. Conclusively, all of the methodologies under scrutiny, some after having been adapted, are apt to be used for the assessment of the degree of market power. In order to limit the problems of incomprehensibly differing determinations of market distortion by different investigating authorities in spite of the same or almost the same factual circumstances, the process of reasoning is to be put into the hands of one single expert group at WTO level that bindingly performs these determinations.

As alternative benchmark, using the world market price out of the in-country sales prices of the respective product in all market economy countries has been found most suitable in the light of legal certainty, transparency and applicability. It leaves no room for discretion on part of the investigating authorities that could be misused, and thus tackles a major problem that persists in the investigating authorities' process of reasoning to date.

Procedurally, the only possible means of implementation of the reform proposal constitutes an amendment according to Article X WTO Agreement. For the sake of legal clarity, it is highly advisable to extend Article 14 ASCM to cover a written framework for the use of alternative benchmarks in NMES that provides both investigating authorities and investigated WTO members with the necessary knowledge of the legal requirements that are to be observed in the process of reasoning. Despite the minor risk that such an amendment will in fact not be uniformly applicable to all WTO member alike, it offers a promising legally binding solution. The current state of impasse of the anti-subsidy law reform in the Doha Round does, however, not give rise to high hopes that the proposed reforms will actually one day be implemented.

7.3 Future Prospects and Developments

The area of anti-subsidy law, on WTO and EU level alike, will continue to face serious challenges in the coming years. To maintain its present position as important legal means in trade defence, convincing solutions for the current problems with respect to benefit calculation have to be found timely. From the question of how to best regulate the calculation process in NMES to the question of how to integrate the new generation of accession protocols into the existing WTO legal framework, answers are direly needed. With China having become majorly involved in international trade relations and increasingly pursuing its rights and alleged violations of these rights in front of the WTO judiciary, the prospective regulation of the use of alternative benchmarks in NMES constitutes a highly sensitive issue. In finding answers for a balanced and sustaining future legal environment for world trade, it is important to keep in mind that the foremost objective of law is the development of a legally sound solution. In the long-term interest of the international community, economic and other considerations must never overshadow this process.

Table of Treaties and Legal Instruments (as of 1 January 2018)

Short Title	Full Title and Citation
ADA	Agreement on the Implementation of Article VI of the General Agreement on Tariffs and Trade 1994 (Anti-dumping Agreement), LT/UR/A-1A/3, 15 April 1994, 1868 UNTS 201.
ASCM	Agreement on Subsidies and Countervailing Measures, LT/UR/A-1A/9, 15 April 1994, 1869 UNTS 14.
Bali Declaration	Bali Ministerial Declaration. WT/MIN(13)/DEC, 11 December 2013.
BASR	Regulation (EU) 2016/1037 of the European Parliament and of the Council of 8 June 2016 on protection against subsidised imports from countries not members of the European Union (Basic Anti-Subsidy Regulation), OJ 2016 L 176/55, 30.6.2016.
CAP	Protocol on the Accession of the People's Republic of China, WT/L/432, 23 November 2001.
COM(2013) 192 final	Proposal for a Regulation of the European Parliament and of the Council amending Council Regulation (EC) No. 1225/2009 on protection against dumped import from countries not members of the European Community and Council Regulation (EC) No. 597/2009 on protection against subsidised imports from countries not members of the European Community, COM(2013) 192 final, 10 April 2014.
Communication from the Chairman (2011)	Communication from the Chairman of the Negotiating Group on Rules, TN/RL/W/254, 21 April 2011.

(continued)

S. Müller, *The Use of Alternative Benchmarks in Anti-Subsidy Law*,
European Yearbook of International Economic Law 4,
https://doi.org/10.1007/978-3-319-77613-2

Short Title	Full Title and Citation
Council Regulation (EC) No. 1225/2009	Council Regulation (EC) No. 1225/2009 of 30 November 2009 on protection against dumped imports from countries not members of the European Community (Basic Anti-Dumping Regulation), OJ 2009 L 343/51, 22.12.2009.
Council Regulation (EC) No. 2026/97	Council Regulation (EC) No. 2026/97 of 6 October 1997 on protection against subsidized imports from countries not members of the European Community, OJ 1997 L 288/1, 21.10.1997.
Council Regulation (EC) No. 597/2009	Council Regulation (EC) No. 597/2009 of 11 June 2009 on protection against subsidised imports from countries not members of the European Community (Basic Anti-Subsidy Regulation), OJ 2009 L 188/93, 18.7.2009.
Customs Act 1901	An Act relating to the Customs (Customs Act 1901), C1901A00006 No. 6, 3 October 1901, last amended on 5 May 2016.
Customs Tariff Act	An Act relating to certain Special Duties of Customs (Customs Tariff (Anti-Dumping) Act 1975), C2004A00298 No. 76, 20 June 1975, last amended on 23 March 2016.
Customs Tariff Regulation	Customs Tariff (Anti-Dumping) Regulation 2013, F2013L00891 SLI 2013 No. 91, 30 May 2013,
Doha Declaration	Doha Ministerial Declaration, WT/MIN(01)/DEC/1, 20 November 2001.
Draft ASCM Chair Text	New Draft Consolidated Chair Texts of the AD and SCM Agreements, TN/RL/W/236, 19 December 2008.
DSU	Understanding on Rules and Procedures governing the Settlement of Disputes, LT/UR/A-2/DS/U/1, 15 April 1994, 1869 UNTS 401.
Final Act	Final Act Embodying the Results of the Uruguay Round of Multilateral Trade Negotiations, LT/UR/A/1, 15 April 1994, 1867 UNTS 14.
GATT 1947	General Agreement on Tariffs and Trade, LT/UR/A-1A/1/GATT/2, 30 October 1947, 55 UNTS 194.
GATT 1994	General Agreement on Tariffs and Trade, LT/UR/A-1A/1/GATT/1, 15 April 1994, 1867 UNTS 187.
Guidelines	Guidelines for the Calculation of the Amount of Subsidy in Countervailing Duty Investigations, 98/C 394/04, OJ 1998 C 394/6, 17.12.1998.
ILC Statute	Statute of the International Law Commission, UN GA Resolution 174 (II), 21 November 1947.
Nairobi Declaration	Nairobi Ministerial Declaration, WT/MIN(15)/DEC, 21 December 2015.
Other EU appellant submission	Other appellant submission by the European Union, *Canada – FIT Program*, AB-2013-1 / DS426, 11 February 2013.

(continued)

Short Title	Full Title and Citation
Possible Elements to be Considered for Inclusion in an Anti-Dumping Code.	Possible Elements to be Considered for Inclusion in an Anti-Dumping Code, TN.64/NTB/W/13, 9 December 1966.
Post-Bali Work Decision	Post-Bali Work Decision of 27 November 2014, WT/L/941, 28 November 2014.
Proposals by the Czechoslovak Delegation	Proposals by the Czechoslovak Delegation, W.9/86, 9 December 1954.
Protocol of Accession of Viet Nam	Protocol on the Accession of the Socialist Republic of Viet Nam, WT/L/662, 15 November 2006.
Regulation (EC) No. 2026/97	Council Regulation (EC) No. 2026/97 of 6 October 1997 on protection against subsidized imports from countries not members of the European Community, OJ 1997 L 288/1, 21.10.1997.
Regulation (EU) 2015/476	Regulation (EU) 2015/476 of the European Parliament and of the Council of 11 March 2015 on the measures that the Union may take following a report adopted by the WTO Dispute Settlement Body concerning anti-dumping and anti-subsidy matters, OJ 2015 L 83/6, 27.3.2015.
Report by the Chairman of the Negotiating Group on Rules	Report by the Chairman of the Negotiating Group on Rules, TN/RL/W/255, 25 March 2014.
SIMA	Special Import Measures Act, RSC 1985, chapter S-15, 1 December 1984, last amended on 1 November 2014.
Singapore Declaration	Singapore Ministerial Declaration, WT/MIN(96)/DEC, 18 December 1996.
Subsidies Code	Agreement on Interpretation and Application of Articles VI, XVI and XXIII of the General Agreement on Tariffs and Trade, MTN/NTM/W/236, 12 April 1979, 1186 UNTS 204.
Tariff Act of 1930	Tariff Act of 1930, Pub. L. 71-361, 46 Stat. 59019, 17 June 1930, 19 USC 4 (§§ 1202-1683g), last amended 15 July 2015.
UN General Assembly Resolution 2758	United Nations General Assembly Resolution 2758, A/RES/2758(XXVI), 25 October 1971.
VCLT	Vienna Convention on the Law of Treaties, 23 May 1969, 1155 UNTS 331.
Working Party Report of China	Report of the Working Party on the Accession of China, WT/ACC/CHN/49, 1 October 2001.
Working Party Report of Tajikistan	Report of the Working Party on the Accession of the Republic of Tajikistan, WT/ACC/TJK/30, 6 November 2012.
Working Party Report of Viet Nam	Report of the Working Party on the Accession of Viet Nam, WT/ACC/VNM/48, 27 October 2006.
WTO Agreement	Marrakech Agreement Establishing the World Trade Organization, LT/UR/A/2, 15 April 1994, 1867 UNTS 154.

Tables of Cases (as of 1 January 2018)

WTO Cases

Short Title	Full Case Title and Citation
Brazil – Aircraft	Appellate Body Report, *Brazil – Export Financing Programme for Aircraft*, WT/DS46/AB/R, adopted 20 August 1999, DSR 1999:III, 1161.
Brazil – Aircraft	Panel Report, *Brazil – Export Financing Programme for Aircraft*, WT/DS46/R, adopted 20 August 1999, as modified by Appellate Body Report, WT/DS46/AB/R, DSR 1999:III, 1221.
Brazil – Desiccated Coconut	Appellate Body Report, *Brazil – Measures Affecting Desiccated Coconut*, WT/DS22/AB/R, adopted 20 March 1997, DSR 1997:I, 167.
Canada – Aircraft	Appellate Body Report, *Canada – Measures Affecting the Export of Civilian Aircraft*, WT/DS70/AB/R, adopted 20 August 1999, DSR 1999:III, 1377.
Canada – Aircraft	Panel Report, *Canada – Measures Affecting the Export of Civilian Aircraft*, WT/DS70/R, adopted 20 August 1999, upheld by Appellate Body Report WT/DS70/AB/R, DSR 1999:IV, 1443.
Canada – Renewable Energy and Canada – FIT Program	Appellate Body Reports, *Canada – Certain Measures Affecting the Renewable Energy Generation Sector / Canada – Measures Relating to the Feed-in Tariff Program*, WT/DS412/AB/R / WT/DS426/AB/R, adopted 24 May 2013, DSR 2013:I, 7.
Canada – Renewable Energy and Canada – FIT Program	Panel Reports, *Canada – Certain Measures Affecting the Renewable Energy Generation Sector / Canada – Measures Relating to the Feed-in Tariff Program*, WT/DS412/R and Add.1 / WT/DS426/R and Add.1, adopted 24 May 2013, as modified by Appellate Body Reports WT/DS412/AB/R / WT/DS426/AB/R, DSR 2013:II, 471.

(continued)

S. Müller, *The Use of Alternative Benchmarks in Anti-Subsidy Law*,
European Yearbook of International Economic Law 4,
https://doi.org/10.1007/978-3-319-77613-2

Short Title	Full Case Title and Citation
China – Publications and Audiovisual Products	Panel Report, *China – Measures Affecting Trading Rights and Distribution Services for Certain Publications and Audiovisual Entertainment Products*, WT/DS363/R and Corr.1, adopted 19 January 2010, as modified by Appellate Body Report WT/DS363/AB/R, DSR 2010:II, 261.
China - Rare Earths	Appellate Body Reports, *China – Measures Related to the Exportation of Rare Earths, Tungsten, and Molybdenum*, WT/DS431/AB/R / WT/DS432/AB/R / WT/DS433/AB/R, adopted 29 August 2014, DSR 2014:III, 805.
China – Raw Materials	Panel Reports, *China – Measures Related to the Exportation of Various Raw Materials*, WT/DS394/R, Add.1 and Corr.1 / WT/DS395/R, Add.1 and Corr.1 / WT/DS398/R, Add.1 and Corr.1, adopted 22 February 2012, as modified by Appellate Body Reports WT/DS394/AB/R / WT/DS395/AB/R / WT/DS398/AB/R, DSR 2012:VII, 3501.
EC – Bananas III	Appellate Body Report, *European Communities – Regime for the Importation, Sale and Distribution of Bananas*, WT/DS27/AB/RW2/ECU, DSR 2001:VIII, 591.
EC – Chicken Cuts	Appellate Body Report, *European Communities – Customs Classification of Frozen Boneless Chicken Cuts*, WT/DS269/AB/R, WT/DS286/AB/R, adopted 27 September 2005, and Corr.1, DSR 2005:XIX, 9157.
EC – Fasteners	Appellate Body Report, *European Communities – Definitive Anti-Dumping Measures on Certain Iron or Steel Fasteners from China*, WT/DS397/AB/R, adopted 28 July 2011, DSR 2011:VII, 3995.
EC – Hormones	Appellate Body Report, *EC Measures Concerning Meat and Meat Products (Hormones)*, WT/DS26/AB/R, WT/DS48/AB/R, adopted 13 February 1998, DSR 1998:I, 135.
EC – Seal Products	Appellate Body Reports, *European Communities – Measures Prohibiting the Importation and Marketing of Seal Products*, WT/DS400/AB/R / WT/DS401/AB/R, adopted 18 June 2014, DSR 2014:1, 7.
EC and certain Member States – Large Civil Aircraft	Appellate Body Report, *European Communities and Certain Member States – Measures Affecting Trade in Large Civil Aircraft*, WT/DS316/AB/R, adopted 1 June 2011, DSR 2011:I, 7.
EC and certain Member States – Large Civil Aircraft	Panel Report, *European Communities and Certain Member States – Measures Affecting Trade in Large Civil Aircraft*, WT/DS316/R, adopted 1 June 2011, as modified by Appellate Body Report, WT/DS316/AB/R, DSR 2011:II, 685.
India – Patents (US)	Appellate Body Report, *India – Patent Protection for Pharmaceutical and Agricultural Chemical Products*, WT/DS50/AB/R, adopted 16 January 1998, DSR 1998:I, 9.

(continued)

Short Title	Full Case Title and Citation
Japan – Alcoholic Beverages II	Appellate Body Report, *Japan – Taxes on Alcoholic Beverages*, WT/DS8/AB/R, WT/DS10/AB/R, WT/DS11/AB/R, adopted 1 November 1996, DSR 1996:I, 97.
Japan – DRAMs (Korea)	Appellate Body Report, *Japan – Countervailing Duties on Dynamic Random Access Memories from Korea*, WT/DS336/AB/R and Corr.1, adopted 17 December 2007, DSR 2007:VII, 2703.
Korea – Dairy	Appellate Body Report, *Korea – Definitive Safeguard Measure on Imports of Certain Dairy Products*, WT/DS98/AB/R, adopted 12 January 2000, DSR 2000:I, 3.
Mexico – Anti-Dumping Measures on Rice	Appellate Body Report, *Mexico – Definitive Anti-Dumping Measures on Beef and Rice*, Complaint with Respect to Rice, WT/DS295/AB/R, adopted 20 December 2005, DSR 2005:XXII, 10853.
Mexico – Olive Oil	Panel Report, *Mexico – Definitive Countervailing Measures on Olive Oil from the European Communities*, WT/DS341/R, adopted 21 October 2008, DSR 2008:IX, 3179.
US – 1916 Act	Appellate Body Report, *United States – Anti-Dumping Act of 1916*, WT/DS136/AB/R, WT/DS162/AB/R, adopted 26 September 2000, DSR 2000:X, 4793.
US – Anti-Dumping and Countervailing Duties (China)	Appellate Body Report, *United States – Definitive Anti-Dumping and Countervailing Duties on Certain Products from China*, WT/DS379/AB/R, adopted 25 March 2011, DSR 2011:V, 2869.
US – Anti-Dumping and Countervailing Duties (China)	Panel Report, *United States – Definitive Anti-Dumping and Countervailing Duties on Certain Products from China*, WT/DS379/R, adopted 25 March 2011, as modified by Appellate Body Report WT/DS379/AB/R, DSR 2011:VI, 3143.
US – Carbon Steel (India)	Appellate Body Report, *United States – Countervailing Measures on Certain Hot- Rolled Carbon Steel Flat Products from India*, WT/DS436/AB/R, adopted 19 December 2014, DSR 2014:V, 1727.
US – Clove Cigarettes	Appellate Body Report, *United States – Measures Affecting the Production and Sale of Clove Cigarettes*, WT/DS406/AB/R, adopted 24 April 2012, DSR 2012:XI, 5751.
US – Countervailing Measures (China)	Appellate Body Report, United States – *Countervailing Duty Measures on Certain Products from China*, WT/DS437/AB/R, adopted 16 January 2015.
US – Countervailing Measures (China)	Panel Report, *United States – Countervailing Duty Measures on Certain Products from China*, WT/DS437/R and Add.1, adopted 16 January 2015, as modified by Appellate Body Report WT/DS437/AB/R.
US – Countervailing Measures on Certain EC Products	Appellate Body Report, *United States – Countervailing Measures Concerning Certain Products from the European Communities*, WT/DS212/AB/R, adopted 8 January 2003, DSR 2003:I, 5.

(continued)

Short Title	Full Case Title and Citation
US – FSC	Appellate Body Report, *United States – Tax Treatment for "Foreign Sales Corporations"*, WT/DS108/AB/R, adopted 20 March 2000, DSR 2002:VI, 2517.
US – Gambling	Appellate Body Report, *United States – Measures Affecting the Cross-Border Supply of Gambling and Betting Services*, WT/DS285/AB/R, adopted 20 April 2005, DSR 2005:XII, 5663 (and Corr.1, DSR 2006: XII, 5475).
US – Gasoline	Appellate Body Report, *United States – Standards for Reformulated and Conventional Gasoline*, WT/DS2/AB/R, adopted 20 May 1996, DSR 1996:I, 3.
US – Gasoline	Panel Report, *United States – Standards for Reformulated and Conventional Gasoline*, WT/DS2/R, adopted 20 May 1996, as modified by Appellate Body Report WT/DS2/AB/R, DSR 1996:I, 29.
US – Hot-rolled steel	Appellate Body Report, *United States – Anti-Dumping Measures on Certain Hot-Rolled Steel Products from Japan*, WT/DS184/AB/R, adopted 23 August 2001, DSR 2001:X, 4697.
US – Lead and Bismuth II	Panel Report, *United States – Imposition of Countervailing Duties on Certain Hot-Rolled Lead and Bismuth Carbon Steel Products Originating in the United Kingdom*, WT/DS138/R and Corr.2, adopted 7 June 2000, as upheld by the Appellate Body Report, WT/DS138/AB/R, DSR 2000:VI, 2631.
US – Line Pipe	Appellate Body Report, *United States – Definitive Safeguard Measures on Imports of Circular Welded Carbon Quality Line Pipe from Korea*, WT/DS202/AB/R, adopted 8 March 2002, DSR 2002:IV, 1403.
US – Shrimp	Appellate Body Report, *United States – Import Prohibition of Certain Shrimp and Shrimp Products*, WT/DS58/AB/R, adopted 6 November 1998, DSR 1998:VII, 2755.
US – Softwood Lumber III	Panel Report, *United States – Preliminary Determinations with Respect to Certain Softwood Lumber from Canada*, WT/DS236/R, adopted 1 November 2002, DSR 2002: IX, 3597.
US – Softwood Lumber IV	Appellate Body Report, *United States – Final Countervailing Duty Determination with Respect to Certain Softwood Lumber from Canada*, WT/DS257/AB/R, adopted 17 February 2004, DSR 2004:II, 571.
US – Softwood Lumber IV	Panel Report, *United States – Final Countervailing Duty Determination with Respect to Certain Softwood Lumber from Canada*, WT/DS257/R and Corr.1, adopted 17 February 2004, as modified by Appellate Body Report WT/DS257/AB/R, DSR 2004:II, 641.
US – Upland Cotton	Appellate Body Report, *United States – Subsidies on Upland Cotton*, WT/DS267/AB/R, adopted 21 March 2005, DSR 2005:I, 3.

EU Cases

Short Title	Full Case Title and Citation
Gold East Paper and Gold Huasheng Paper v Council	Case T-444/11, Judgment of the General Court (Third Chamber) of 11 September 2014, Gold East Paper (Jiangsu) Co. Ltd and Gold Huasheng Paper (Suzhou Industrial Park) Co. Ltd v Council of the European Union, ECLI:EU: T:2014:773.

ICJ Cases

Short Title	Full Case Title and Citation
Namibia	Legal Consequences for States of the Continued Presence of South Africa in Namibia (South West Africa) notwithstanding Security Council Resolution 276 (1970), Advisory Opinion, ICJ Reports 1971, 16.
Wall	Legal Consequences of the Construction of a Wall in the Occupied Palestinian Territory, Advisory Opinion, ICJ Reports 2004, 136.

US Cases

Short Title	Full Case Title and Citation
Georgetown Steel Corp. v. United States	*Georgetown Steel Corp. v. United States*, US Court of Appeals, Judgment of 18 September 1986, 801 F.2d 1308.

EU Cases

Short Title	Full Case Title and Citation
[illegible]	Case T-[illegible], Judgment of the General Court ... of 11 September 2014 ... Hundsbong Paper ... [illegible]

[illegible] Cases

[illegible]

[illegible] Cases

[illegible]

Tables of Investigations (as of 1 January 2018)

EU Investigations

Short Title	Full Title and Citation
Bicycles (China)	Commission Decision 2013/227/EU of 22 May 2013 terminating the anti-subsidy proceeding concerning imports of bicycles originating in the People's Republic of China, OJ 2013 L 136/15, 23.5.2013.
Bicycles (electric) (China)	Notice of initiation of an anti-subsidy proceeding concerning imports of electric bicycles originating in the People's Republic of China, OJ 2017 C 440/22, 21.12.2017
Certain Filament Glass Fibre Products (China)	Commission Implementing Regulation (EU) No 1379/2014 of 16 December 2014 imposing a definitive countervailing duty on imports of certain filament glass fibre products originating in the People's Republic of China and amending Council Implementing Regulation (EU) No 248/2011 imposing a definitive anti-dumping duty on imports of certain continuous filament glass fibre products originating in the People's Republic of China, OJ 2014 L 367/22, 23.12.2014.
Certain Hot-rolled Flat Products of Iron, Non-alloy or Other Alloy Steel (China)	Commission Implementing Regulation (EU) 2017/969 of 8 June 2017 imposing definitive countervailing duties on imports of certain hot-rolled flat products of iron, non-alloy or other alloy steel originating in the People's Republic of China and amending Commission Implementing Regulation (EU) 2017/649 imposing a definitive anti-dumping duty on imports of certain hot-rolled flat products of iron, non-alloy or other alloy steel originating in the People's Republic of China, OJ 2017 L 146/17, 9.6.2017.

(continued)

S. Müller, *The Use of Alternative Benchmarks in Anti-Subsidy Law*,
European Yearbook of International Economic Law 4,
https://doi.org/10.1007/978-3-319-77613-2

Short Title	Full Title and Citation
Certain Organic Coated Steel Products (China)	Council Implementing Regulation (EU) No 215/2013 of 11 March 2013 imposing a countervailing duty on imports of certain organic coated steel products originating in the People's Republic of China, OJ 2013 L 73/16, 15.3.2013.
Coated Fine Paper (China)	Council Implementing Regulation (EU) No 452/2011 of 6 May 2011 imposing a definitive anti-subsidy duty on imports of coated fine paper originating in the People's Republic of China, OJ 2011 L 128/18, 14.5.2011.
Polyester Staple Fibres (China)	Commission Implementing Decision 2014/918/EU of 16 December 2014 terminating the anti-subsidy proceeding concerning the imports of polyester staple fibres originating in the People's Republic of China, India and Vietnam, OJ 2014 L 360/65, 17.12.2014.
Solar Glass (China)	Commission Implementing Regulation (EU) No 470/2014 of 13 May 2014 imposing a definitive anti-dumping duty and collecting definitively the provisional duty imposed on imports of solar glass originating in the People's Republic of China, OJ 2014 L 142/23, 14.5.2014.
Solar Panels (China)	Council Implementing Regulation (EU) No 1239/2013 of 2 December 2013 imposing a definitive countervailing duty on imports of crystalline silicon photovoltaic modules and key components (i.e. cells) originating in or consigned from the People's Republic of China, OJ 2013 L 325/66, 5.12.2013.
Stainless Steel Cold-rolled Flat Products (China)	Commission Implementing Regulation (EU) 2015/1206 of 23 July 2015 terminating the anti-subsidy proceeding concerning imports of stainless steel cold-rolled flat products originating in the People's Republic of China and repealing Implementing Regulation (EU) No 1331/2014 making imports of stainless steel cold-rolled flat products originating in the People's Republic of China and Taiwan subject to registration, OJ 2015 L 196/4, 24.7.2015.
Tyres for buses or lorries (new and retreaded) (China)	Notice of initiation of an anti-subsidy proceeding concerning imports of new and retreaded tyres for buses or lorries originating in the People's Republic of China, OJ 2017 C 346/9, 14.10.2017.
Wireless Wide Area Networking (WWAN) Modems (China)	Commission Regulation (EU) No. 209/2011 of 2 March 2011 terminating the anti-dumping and anti-subsidy proceedings concerning imports of wireless wide area networking (WWAN) modems originating in the People's Republic of China and terminating the registration of such imports imposed by Regulations (EU) No. 570/2010 and (EU) No. 811/2010, OJ 2011 L 58/36, 3.3.2011.

US Investigations

Short Title	Full Case Title and Citation
Circular Welded Carbon Quality Steel Pipe (China)	*Circular Welded Carbon Quality Steel Pipe from the People's Republic of China*, Case C-570-911, Final Affirmative Countervailing Duty and Final Affirmative Determination of Critical Circumstances, 73 Fed. Reg. 31966, 5 June 2008.
Coated Free Sheet Paper (China)	*Coated Free Sheet Paper from the People's Republic of China*, Case C-570-907, Notice of Initiation of Countervailing Duty Investigations, 71 Fed. Reg. 68546, 27 November 2006.
Coated Free Sheet Paper (China)	*Coated Free Sheet Paper from the People's Republic of China,* Case C-570-907, Amended Preliminary Affirmative Countervailing Duty Determination, 72 Fed. Reg. 17484, 9 April 2007.
Coated Paper Suitable for High-Quality Print Graphics Using Sheet-Fed Presses (China)	*Coated Paper Suitable for High-Quality Print Graphics Using Sheet-Fed Presses*, Cases C-570-959 and A-570-958, Initiation of Countervailing Duty Investigation and Initiation of Antidumping Duty Investigations, 74 Fed. Reg. 53703 and 53710, 20 October 2009.

Bibliography

Adamantopoulos, K., 'Article 1 SCMA', in Rüdiger Wolfrum, Peter-Tobias Stoll and Michael Koebele (eds.), *WTO: Trade Remedies* (Heidelberg: Max Planck Institute for Comparative Public Law and International Law, 2008), 423-52.

Adamantopoulos, K., 'Article VI GATT', in Rüdiger Wolfrum, Peter-Tobias Stoll and Michael Koebele (eds.), *WTO: Trade Remedies* (Heidelberg: Max Planck Institute for Comparative Public Law and International Law, 2008), 759-779.

Adamantopoulos, Konstantinos and Pereyra-Friedrichsen, María J., *EU Anti-Subsidy Law and Practice*, 2nd ed. (London: Sweet & Maxwell, 2007).

Ahn, Dukgeun and Lee, Jieun, 'Countervailing Duty against China: Opening a Pandora's Box in the WTO System?', 14 (2) *Journal of International Economic Law* (2011), 329-68.

Arato, Julian, 'Subsequent Practice and Evolutive Interpretation. Techniques of Treaty Interpretation over Time and Their Diverse Consequences', 9 (3) *The Law & Practice of International Courts and Tribunals* (2010), 443-494.

Arato, Julian, 'Treaty Interpretation and Constitutional Transformation: Informational Change in International Organizations', 38 (2) *Yale Journal of International Law* (2013), 289-351.

Armingeon, Klaus; Milewicz, Karolina; Peter, Simone and Peters, Anne, 'The constitutionalisation of international trade law', in Thomas Cottier and Panagiotis Delimatsis (eds.), *The Prospects of International Trade Regulation. From fragmentation to coherence* (Cambridge: Cambridge University Press, 2011), 69-102.

Avgustidi, Vassiliki; Ballschmiede, Sven, 'Comparative Overview of EU and US Subsidies Regulation', in Rüdiger Wolfrum, Peter-Tobias Stoll and Michael Koebele (eds.), *WTO: Trade Remedies* (Heidelberg: Max Planck Institute for Comparative Public Law and International Law, 2008), 856–940.

Bagwell, Kyle and Staiger, Robert W., 'Will International Rules on Subsidies Disrupt the World Trading System?', 96 (3) *American Economic Review* (2006), 877-895.

Bagwell, Kyle and Staiger, Robert W., 'An Economic Theory of GATT', 89 (1) *American Economic Review* (1999), 215-248.

Bagwell, Kyle; Staiger, Robert W. and Sykes, Alan O., 'Border Instruments', in Henrik Horn and Petros C. Mavroidis (eds.), *Legal and Economic Principles of World Trade Law* (New York: Cambridge University Press, 2013), 68-204.

Unless otherwise indicated, all internet sources have last been accessed on 1 January 2018.

S. Müller, *The Use of Alternative Benchmarks in Anti-Subsidy Law*,
European Yearbook of International Economic Law 4,
https://doi.org/10.1007/978-3-319-77613-2

Baldwin, Richard, '4.3 The Systemic Impact', in World Economic Forum (ed.), *Mega-regional Trade Agreements. Game-Changers or Costly Distractions for the World Trading System?* (2014), 8, 26-27, available at http://www3.weforum.org/docs/GAC/2014/WEF_GAC_TradeFDI_MegaRegionalTradeAgreements_Report_2014.pdf.

Barani, Luca, 'Hard and Soft Law in the European Union: The Case of Social Policy and the Open Method of Coordination', Constitutionalism Web-Papers, ConWEB No. 2/2006, 1-31, available at https://www.researchgate.net/publication/5014867_Hard_and_Soft_Law_in_the_European_Union_The_case_of_Social_policy_and_the_Open_Method_of_Coordination.

Barfield, Claude and Groombridge, Mark, 'Avoiding Deadlock', in Sylvia Ostry, Alan S. Alexandroff and Rafael Gomez (eds.), *China and the Long March to Global Trade: The Accession of China to the World Trade Organization* (London and New York: Routledge, 2002), 30-43.

Barry, Michael, 'China Reaches a WTO Agreement with the United States', International Economic Review (February/March 2000), USITC Publication 3276, 7-10.

Barton, John H.; Goldstein, Judith L.; Josling, Timothy E. and Steinberg, Richard H., *The evolution of the trade regime. Politics law and economics of the GATT and the WTO*, 4th ed. (Princeton: Princeton University Press, 2008).

Bansal, N. S., *The World Trade Organisation. From Singapore to Hong Kong (2 Parts). Part 1* (New Delhi: Mittal Publications, 2007).

Baumol, William J. and Blinder, Alan S., *Microeconomics. Principles and policy*, 11th ed. (Mason, OH: South-Western/Cengage Learning, 2009).

Bayefsky, Ann F., 'The principle of Equality or Non-discrimination in International Law', 11 (1/2) *Human Rights Quarterly* (1990), 1-34.

Baylis, Katherine, 'Unfair Subsidies and Countervailing Duties', in William A. Kerr and James D. Gaisford (eds.), *Handbook on International Trade Policy* (Cheltenham: Edward Elgar, 2007), 347-360.

Bentley, Philip and Silberston, Aubrey, *Anti-Dumping and Countervailing Action. Limits imposed by Economic and Legal Theory* (Cheltenham: Edward Elgar, 2007).

Bhagwati, Jagdish, 'Gains from trade, the WTO and the recent trends towards mega-regionals' (2014) available at http://www.notenstein-laroche.ch/sites/nlr_ch/files/attachments/white_paper_series_jagdish_bhagwati.pdf.

Bishop, Bernard, *European Union Law for International Business: An Introduction* (Melbourne: Cambridge University Press, 2009).

Blackhurst, Richard, 'The Capacity of the WTO to Fulfill Its Mandate', in Anne O. Krueger (ed.), *The WTO as an International Organization* (Chicago and London: University of Chicago Press, 1998), 31-58.

Blair, Roger D. and Harrison, Jeffrey L., *Monopsony in Law and Economics* (Cambridge: Cambridge University Press, 2010).

Blumental, David M., 'Applying GATT to marketizing economies: the dilemma of WTO accession and reform of China's state-owned enterprises (SOEs)', 2 (1) *Journal of International Economic Law* (1999), 113-153.

Bodansky, Daniel, 'The Concept of Legitimacy in International Law', UGA Legal Studies Research Paper No. 07-013 (2007), 1-9, available at SSRN: http://ssrn.com/abstract=1033542.

Bogdany, Armin von/ Wagner, Markus, 'Article XIII WTO Agreement', in Rüdiger Wolfrum, Peter-Tobias Stoll and Karen Kaiser (eds.), *WTO: Institutions* and *Dispute Settlement* (Heidelberg: Max Planck Institute for Comparative Public Law and International Law, 2006), 153-158.

Bronckers, Marco C. E. J., 'Better rules for a new millennium: a warning against undemocratic developments in the WTO', 2 (4) *Journal of International Economic Law* (1999), 547–566.

Carmody, Chi, 'Softwood Lumber Dispute (2001-2006)', 100 (3) *The American Journal of International Law* (2006), 664-674.

Cattaneo, Olivier and Primo Braga, Carlos A., 'Everything You Always Wanted To Know About WTO Accession (But Were Afraid To Ask)', Policy Research Working Paper No. 5116 (2009), 1-34, available at http://www19.iadb.org/intal/intalcdi/PE/2009/04400.pdf.

Charnovitz, Steve, 'Mapping the Law of WTO Accession', GWU Law School Public Law Research Paper No. 237 (2013), 1-83, available at http://scholarship.law.gwu.edu/cgi/viewcontent.cgi?article=1430&context=faculty_publications.

Charnovitz, Steve, *The Path of World Trade Law in the 21st Century* (Singapore: World Scientific, 2014).

Charnovitz, Steve and Fischer, Carolyn, 'Canada – renewable energy: implications for WTO law on green and not-so-green subsidies', FEEM Working Paper No. 94 (2014), 1-55, available at http://ssrn.com/abstract=2523814.

Chichilniski, Graciela, 'International payments for ecosystem services: Principles and practices', in Thomas Koellner (ed.), *Ecosystem Services and Global Trade of Natural Resources: Ecology, Economics and Policies* (London, New York: Routledge, 2011), 204-224.

Cini, Michelle, 'The soft law approach: Commission rule-making in the EU's state aid regime',8 (2) *Journal of European Public Policy* (2011), 192–207.

Conway, Gerard, *EU Law* (London and New York: Routledge, 2015).

Coppens, Dominic, *WTO Disciplines on Subsidies and Countervailing Measures. Balancing Policy Space and Legal Constraints* (Cambridge: Cambridge University Press, 2014).

Cornelis, Joris, 'Applying Countervailing Duty Law to Non-market Economies - Will the EC Follow the US Example?', 2 (11/12) *Global Trade and Customs Journal* (2007), 421-424.

Cornelis, Joris, 'China's Quest for Market Economy Status and its Impact on the Use China's Quest for Market Economy Status and its Impact on the Use of Trade Remedies by the European Communities and the United States', 2 (2) *Global Trade and Customs Journal* (2007), 105–115.

Dawidowicz, Martin, 'The Effect of the Passage of Time on the Interpretation of Treaties. Some Reflections on Costa Rica v. Nicaragua', 24 (1) *Leiden Journal of International Law* (2011), 201-222.

Detlof, Helena and Fridh, Hilda, 'The EU Treatment of Non-Market-Economy Countries in Anti-dumping Proceedings', 2 (7/8) *Global Trade and Customs Journal* (2007), 265–281.

De Witte, Bruno, 'Treaty Revision Procedures after Lisbon', in Andrea Biondi, Piet Eeckhout and Stefanie Ripley (eds.), *EU Law after Lisbon* (Oxford: Oxford University Press, 2012), 107-127.

Du, Ming, 'China's state capitalism and world trade law', 63 (2) *International & Comparative Law Quarterly* (2014), 409-448.

Durling, James P., 'Article 14 SCMA', in Rüdiger Wolfrum, Peter-Tobias Stoll and Michael Koebele (eds.), *WTO: Trade Remedies* (Heidelberg: Max Planck Institute for Comparative Public Law and International Law, 2008), 591-597.

Dwivedi, D. N., *Microeconomics. Theory and Applications*, 2nd ed. (Delhi: Dorling Kindersley, 2008).

Elsig, Manfred, 'The World Trade Organization's legitimacy crisis: What does the beast look like?', 41 (1) *Journal of World Trade* (2007), 75-98.

Ehlermann, Claus-Dieter and Ehring, Lothar, 'Decision-Making in the World Trade Organization: Is the Consensus Practice of the World Trade Organization Adequate for Making, Revising and Implementing Rules on International Trade?', 8 (1) *Journal of International Economic Law* (2005), 51-75.

Ehlermann, Claus-Dieter and Ehring, Lothar, 'The Authoritative Interpretation Under Article IX. 2 of the Agreement Establishing the World Trade Organization: Current Law, Practice and Possible Improvements', 8 (4) *Journal of International Economic Law* (2005), 803-824.

Feldman, Elliot J. and Burke, John J., 'Testing the Limits of Trade Law Rationality: The GPX Case and Subsidies in Non-Market Economies', 62 (4) *American University Law Review* (2013), 787-826.

Ferejohn, John, 'Judicializing Politics, Politicizing Law', 65 (3) *Law and Contemporary Problems* (2002), 41–68.

Firestone, Robert F., 'Artificial Pricing as an Alternative to Countervailing Duties Against Imports From Nonmarket Economies', 8 (1) *Journal of Comparative Business and Capital Market Law* (1986), 75–100.

Fortunato, Susanna, 'Article 49 [Accession to the Union]', in Hermann-Josef Blanke and Stelio Mangiameli (eds.), *The Treaty on European Union (TEU): A Commentary* (Berlin, Heidelberg: Springer, 2013), 1357-1384.

Francois, Joseph, 'After Bali: Multilateralism and Mega-Regionals', 15 (4) *CESifo Forum* (2014), 14-19.

Gaisford, James D. and Hester, Annette, 'Why are there trade agreements?', in William A. Kerr and James D. Gaisford (eds.), *Handbook on International Trade Policy* (Cheltenham: Edward Elgar, 2007), 57-70.

Gans, Joshua; King, Stephen; Stonecash, Robin and Mankiw, N. Gregory, *Principles of Economics*, 5th ed. (Melbourne: Cengage Learning, 2012).

Gantz, David A., 'Polyethylene Retail Carrier Bags: Non-Market Economy Status and U.S. Unfair Trade Actions against Vietnam', 36 (1) *North Carolina Journal of International Law and Commercial Regulation* (2010), 85–135.

Gao, Henry, 'China's ascent in global trade governance: from rule taker to rule shaker and maybe rule maker?', in Carolyn Deere-Birkbeck (ed.), *Making global trade governance work for development: perspectives and priorities from developing countries* (Cambridge: Cambridge University Press, 2011), 153-180.

Gatta, Brian, 'Between 'Automatic Market Economy Status' and 'Status Quo': A Commentary on 'Interpreting Paragraph 15 of China's Protocol of Accession', 9 (4) *Global Trade and Customs Journal* (2014), 165–172.

Genest, Alexandre, 'The Canada—FIT Case and the WTO Subsidies Agreement: Failed Fact-Finding, Needless Complexity, and Missed Judicial Economy', 10 (2) *International Journal of Sustainable Development Law and Policy* (2014), 239-258.

Gertler, Jeffrey L., 'What China's WTO Accession Is All About', in Deepak Bhattasali, Shantong Li and William J. Martin (eds.), *China and the WTO: Accession, Policy Reform, and Poverty Reduction Strategies* (Washington D.C.: The World Bank, 2004), 21-28.

Giannakopoulos, Themistoklis K., *A Concise Guide to the EU Anti-dumping/Anti-subsidies Procedures* (Alphen an Rijn: Kluwer Law International, 2006).

Greer, Douglas F., 'The Concentration of Economic Power', in Wallace C. Peterson (ed.): *Market Power and the Economy. Industrial, Corporate, Governmental, and Political Aspects* (Dordrecht: Springer Science & Business Media, 2012), 53-81.

Grossmann, Gene M. and Horn, Henrik, 'Why the WTO? An Introduction to the Economics of Trade Agreements', in Henrik Horn and Petros C. Mavroidis (eds.), *Legal and Economic Principles of World Trade Law* (New York: Cambridge University Press, 2013), 9-67.

Grynberg, Roman; Ognivtsev, Victor and Razzaque, Mohammad A., *Paying the Price Paying the Price for Joining the WTO: A Comparative Assessment of Services Sector Commitments by WTO Members and Acceding Countries* (London: Commonwealth Secretariat, 2002).

Haber, Fred, *Price Determination in Theory and Reality: Lessons for Liberalization and Globalization Policy* (New Delhi: Atlantic Publishers and Distributors, 2000).

Haley, Usha C.V. and Haley, George T., *Subsidies to Chinese Industry: State Capitalism, Business Strategy, and Trade Policy* (New York: Oxford University Press, 2013).

Hausmann, Jerry A. and Sidak, J. Gregory, 'Evaluating Market Power using Competitive Benchmark Prices instead of the Herfindahl Hirschman Index', 74 (2) *Antitrust Law Journal* (2007), 387-407.

He, Juan, *The WTO and Infant Industry Promotion in Developing Countries. Perspectives on the Chinese Large Civil Aircraft Industry* (London and New York: Routledge, 2015).

He, Lingling and Sappideen, Razeen, 'Reflections on China's WTO Accession Commitments and Their Observance', 43 (4) *Journal of World Trade* (2009), 847–871.

Hilf, Meinhard, 'Power, rules and principles - which orientation for WTO/GATT law?', 4 (1) *Journal of International Economic Law* (2001), 111-130.

Hoekman, Bernard M., *Supply Chains, Mega-Regionals and Multilateralism: A Road Map for the WTO* (London: CEPR Press, 2014).

Hoekman, Bernard M. and Kostecki, Michel M., *The Political Economy of the World Trading System. The WTO and Beyond*, 3rd ed. (Oxford: Oxford University Press, 2013).

Hoekman, Bernard M. and Mavroidis, Petros C., 'WTO 'à la carte' or 'menu du jour'? Assessing the Case for More Plurilateral Agreements', 26 (2) *European Journal of International Law* (2015), 319-343.

Hoogmartens, Jan, *EC Trade Law Following China's Accession to the WTO* (The Hague: Kluwer Law International, 2004).

Howse, Robert, 'The legitimacy of the World Trade Organization', in Jean-Marc Coicaud and Veijo Heiskanen (eds.), *The Legitimacy of International Organizations* (Tokyo: United Nations University Press, 2001), 355-407.

Hoyt, Robert F., 'Implementation and Policy: Problems in the Application of Countervailing Duty Laws to Nonmarket Economy Countries', 136 (6) *University of Pennsylvania Law Review* (1988), 1647–1675.

Hu, Jiaxiang, 'A Small Difference in Wording, but a Big Difference in Rule-Making: A Retrospective and Prospective View on the Development of China's Economic Zones', in Jiaxiang Hu, Matthias Vanhullebusch and Andrew Harding (eds.), *Finance, rule of law and development in Asia: perspectives from Singapore, Hong Kong and mainland China* (Leiden and Boston: Brill Nijhoff, 2016), 137-167.

Hughes, Valerie, 'WTO rule-making: WTO Accession Protocols and jurisprudence', in Uri Dadush and Chiedu Osakwe (eds.), WTO Accessions and Trade Multilateralism: Case Studies and Lessons from the WTO at Twenty (Cambridge: Cambridge University Press, 2015), 309-347.

Inagaki, Osamu, 'Evolutionary Interpretation of Treaties Re-examined: The Two-Stage Reasoning', 22 (2/3) *Journal of International Cooperation Studies* (2015), 127–149.

Jackson, John H., 'Global economics and international economic law', 1 (1) *Journal of International Economic Law* (1998), 1–24.

Jackson, John H., 'International Law Status of WTO Dispute Settlement Reports: Obligation to Comply or Option to "Buy Out"?', 98 (1) *The American Journal of International Law* (2004), 109-125.

Jackson, John H., *The World Trading System. Law and Policy of International Economic Relations*, 2nd ed. (Cambridge, MA/London: MIT Press, 1997).

Jain, T.R. and Khanna, O.P., *Economic Concepts and Methods* (V.K. Publications: New Delhi, 2007).

Kaplan, Seth T. and Francois, Joseph F., 'The Pass-Through of Countervailable Subsidies to the Export Price', 21 (2) *Tulane Journal of International and Comparative Law* (2013), 467–484.

Kazeki, Jun, 'Permanent Group of Experts under the SCM Agreement', 43 (5) *Journal of World Trade* (2009), 1031-45.

Kelly, Matthew R., 'Resolving the Double Remedy Dispute. A Critique of the WTO Appellate Body's Decision in United States - Definitive Anti-Dumping and Countervailing Duties on Certain Products from China', 1-27, available at SSRN http://ssrn.com/abstract=2273938.

Kleimann, David, 'The vulnerability of EU anti-dumping measures against China after December 11, 2016', EUI Working Paper RSCAS No. 37 (2016), 1, available at http://cadmus.eui.eu/handle/1814/42546.

Kreinin, Mordechai E. and Plummer, Michael G., 'Economic Principles of International Trade', in Patrick F. J. Macrory, Arthur E. Appleton and Michael G. Plummer (eds.), *The World Trade Organization. Legal, Economic and Political Analysis* (New York: Springer Science + Business Media, 2005), 1602-1621.

Kock, Karin, *International Trade Policy and the GATT, 1947-1967* (Stockholm: Almqvist & Wiksell, 1969).

Kong, Qingjiang, *China and the World Trade Organization: A Legal Perspective* (Singapore: World Scientific, 2002).

Kongolo, Tshimanga, *Unsettled International Intellectual Property Issues* (Alphen aan den Rijn: Kluwer Law International, 2008).

Koul, Autar Krishen, *Guide to the WTO & GATT. Economics, Law and Politics*, 5th ed. (New Delhi: Satyam Law International, 2015).

Lamont, Owen A. and Thaler, Richard H., 'Anomalies: The Law of One Price in Financial Markets', 17 (4) *Journal of Economic Perspectives* (2003), 191-202.

Lester, Simon, 'The Problem of Subsidies as a Means of Protectionism: Lessons from the WTO EC - Aircraft Case', 12 (2) *Melbourne Journal of International Law* (2011), 1–28.

Lincicome, Scott, 'Countervailing Calamity. How to Stop the Global Subsidies Race', Policy Analysis No. 710 (9 October 2012), available at http://object.cato.org/sites/cato.org/files/pubs/pdf/PA710.pdf.

Luo, Yan, *Anti-dumping in the WTO, the EU, and China: The Rise of Legalization in the Trade Regime and Its Consequences* (Alphen aan den Rijn: Kluwer Law International, 2010).

Lynam, Garrett E., 'Using WTO Countervailing Duty Law to Combat Illegally Subsidized Chinese Enterprises Operating in a Non-Market Economy: Deciphering the Writing on the Wall', 42 (3) *Case Western Reserve Journal of International Law* (2010), 739–773.

Lysons, Sarah E., 'Resolving the Softwood Lumber Dispute', 32 (2) *Seattle University Law Review* (2008), 407-441.

MacLean, Robert M., 'Adored and Despised in Equal Measure: An Assessment of the EU's Principle of Market Economy Treatment in Anti-Dumping Investigations Against China', in Christoph Herrmann, Jörg Philipp Terhechte (eds.), *European Yearbook of International Economic Law 2012*, Volume 3 (Berlin, Heidelberg: Springer, 2012), 189–239.

Matsushita, Mitsuo; Schoenbaum, Thomas J.; Mavroidis, Petros C. and Hahn, Michael, *The World Trade Organization: Law, Practice, and Policy*, 3rd ed. (Oxford: Oxford University Press, 2015).

Mavroidis, Petros C., 'The Genesis of the GATT Summary', in Henrik Horn and Petros C. Mavroidis (eds.), *Legal and Economic Principles of World Trade Law* (New York: Cambridge University Press, 2013), 1-8.

Mavroidis, Petros C., *The Regulation of International Trade. The WTO Agreements on Trade in Goods*, Volume 2 (Cambridge, MA/London: MIT Press, 2016).

McEachern, William A., *Microeconomics. A contemporary introduction*, 10th ed. (Mason, Ohio, Andover: South-Western Cengage Learning, 2013).

McNelis, Natalie, 'What Obligations Are Created by World Trade Organization Dispute Settlement Reports?', 37 (3) *Journal of World Trade* (2003), 647–672.

Meléndez-Ortiz, Ricardo, '2.1 Mega-regionals: What Is Going on?' in World Economic Forum (ed.), *Mega-regional Trade Agreements. Game-Changers or Costly Distractions for the World Trading System?* (2014), 6, 13-14, available at http://www3.weforum.org/docs/GAC/2014/WEF_GAC_TradeFDI_MegaRegionalTradeAgreements_Report_2014.pdf.

Meunier, Sophie, 'Is the WTO still relevant? Memo prepared for the workshop "Global Trade Ethics and the Politics of WTO Reform" at Princeton University, 19 February 2009' (2009), 1-6, available at https://www.princeton.edu/~pcglobal/conferences/wtoreform/Meunier_memo.pdf, 1.

Michalopoulos, Constantine, 'WTO Accession', in Bernard M. Hoekman, Aaditya Mattoo and Philip English (eds.), *Development, Trade, and the WTO: A Handbook*, Volume 1 (Washington, DC: World Bank Publications, 2002), 61-70.

Miranda, Jorge, 'Interpreting Paragraph 15 of China's Protocol of Accession', 9 (3) *Global Trade and Customs Journal* (2014), 94–103.

Moloo, Rahim, 'When Actions Speak Louder Than Words: The Relevance of Subsequent Party Conduct to Treaty Interpretation', 31 (1) *Berkeley Journal of International Law* (2009), 39-87.

Mueller, Sophia, 'Chinas Beitrittsprotokoll zur WTO – eine Zwischenbilanz', 27 (8) *Europäische Zeitschrift für Wirtschaftsrecht* (2016), 291-296.

Mueller, Sophia, 'Mapping the Aftermath of Accession – Which Is China's Applicable World Trade Organization Anti-Subsidy Law for the Use of Alternative Benchmarks?', 50 (5) *Journal of World Trade* (2016), 867-884.

Mueller, Sophia, "One Country, Two Systems'? The Prospects of EU Trade Defence Against Chinese Imports after 2016' (2016), 1-23, available at SSRN: http://ssrn.com/abstract=2665960.

Murphy, Sean D., 'The Relevance of Subsequent Agreement and Subsequent Practice for the Interpretation of Treaties', in Georg Nolte (ed.), *Treaties and Subsequent Practice* (Oxford: Oxford University Press, 2013), 82-94.

Nedumpara, James J., 'Renewable Energy and the WTO: The Limits of Government Intervention', 9 *Indian Journal of Law & Technology* (2013), 1-19.

Nguyen, Nham, 'WTO Accession At Any Cost? Examining the Use of WTO-Plus and WTO-Minus Obligations for Least-Developed Country Applicants', 22 (1) *Temple International & Comparative Law Journal* (2008), 243-277.

O'Connor, Bernard, 'Market economy status for China is not automatic' (2011), 1-2, available at http://www.voxeu.org/article/chinamarketeconomy.

Orakhelashvili, Alexander, *The Interpretation of Acts and Rules in Public International Law* (Oxford and New York: Oxford University Press, 2008).

Organisation for Economic Co-operation and Development, 'OECD Glossary of Statistical Terms', (2008), available at http://www.oecd-ilibrary.org/economics/oecd-glossary-of-statistical-terms_9789264055087-en.

Palmeter, David and Mavroidis, Petros C., 'The WTO Legal System. Sources of Law', 92 (3) *The American Journal of International Law* (1998), 398-413.

Pauwelyn, Joost, *Conflict of Norms in Public International Law: How WTO Law Relates to other Rules of International Law* (Cambridge: Cambridge University Press, 2003).

Pauwelyn, Joost, 'Treaty Interpretation or Activism? Comment on the AB Report on United States – ADs and CVDs on Certain Products from China', 12 (2) *World Trade Review* (2013), 235–241.

Pauwelyn, Joost; Wessel, Ramses A and Wouters, Jan, 'When Structures Become Shackles: Stagnation and Dynamics in International Lawmaking', 25 (3) *European Journal of International Law* (2014), 733–763.

Polouektov, Alexander, 'Non-Market Economy Issues in the WTO Anti-Dumping Law and Accession Negotiations: Revival of a Two-tier Membership?', 36 (1) *Journal of World Trade* (2002), 1–37.

Qian, Wenjie, 'The Dilemma of China as Respondent to Anti-Subsidy Proceedings – A Study of the First EU Anti-Subsidy Investigation against China', 46 (4) *Journal of World Trade* (2012), 961–978.

Qin, Julia Ya, 'China, India, and the Law of the World Trade Organization', Wayne State University Law School Legal Studies Research Paper Series No. 07-31 (2008), 1-40, available at SSRN: http://ssrn.com/abstract=1016208.

Qin, Julia Ya, 'Judicial Authority in WTO Law: A Commentary on the Appellate Body's Decision in China-Rare Earths', Wayne State University Law School Legal Studies Research Paper Series No. 2014-11 (2014), 1-14.

Qin, Julia Ya, 'Mind the Gap. Navigating between the WTO Agreement and Its Accession Protocols', Wayne State University Law School Legal Studies Research Paper Series No. 2016-05 (2016), 1-41, available at SSRN: http://ssrn.com/abstract=2727031.

Qin, Julia Ya, 'The Challenge of Interpreting 'WTO-Plus' Provisions', Wayne State University Law School Legal Studies Research Paper Series No. 09-18 (2009), 1-51, available at SSRN: http://ssrn.com/abstract=1428976.

Qin, Julia Ya, 'The Conundrum of WTO Accession Protocols: In Search of Legality and Legitimacy', 55 (1) *Virginia Journal of International Law* (2015), 369–450.

Qin, Julia Ya, '"WTO-Plus" Obligations and Their Implications for the World Trade Organization Legal System', 37 (3) *Journal of World Trade* (2003), 483–522.

Qin, Julia Ya, 'WTO Regulation of Subsidies to State-Owned Enterprises (SOEs) - A Critical Appraisal of the China Accession Protocol', 7 (4) *Journal of International Economic Law* (2004), 863–919.

Rawls, John, *A Theory of Justice*, 6th ed. (Cambridge, MA: Harvard University Press, 2003).

Reich, Utz-Peter, *National Accounts and Economic Value: A Study in Concepts* (Basingstoke: Palgrave Macmillan, 2001).

Rhodes, Sylvia A. and Jackson, John H., 'United States law and China's WTO accession process', 2 (3) *Journal of International Economic Law* (1999), 497–510.

RIS, *World Trade and Development Report. Mega Regionals, WTO and New Issues* (2015), available at http://ris.org.in/pdf/FINAL_PRINT%20_WTDR.pdf.

Rubini, Luca, *The Definition of Subsidy and State Aid: WTO and EC Law in Comparative Perspective* (Oxford: Oxford University Press, 2010).

Rubini, Luca, 'What does the recent WTO litigation on renewable energy subsidies tell us about methodology in legal analysis? The good, the bad, and the ugly', EUI Working Paper RSCAS No. 5 (2014), 1, available at http://cadmus.eui.eu/handle/1814/29518.

Samuelson, Paul A. and Nordhaus, William D., *Economics*, 18th ed. (Boston: McGraw-Hill, 2005).

Schropp, Simon A. B., *Trade Policy Flexibility and Enforcement in the WTO: A Law and Economics Analysis* (Cambridge: Cambridge University Press, 2009).

Schwartz, Warren F. and Harper, Eugene W., 'The Regulation of Subsidies Affecting International Trade', 70 (5) *Michigan Law Review* (1972), 831–858.

Shell, G. Richard, 'Trade Legalism and International Relations Theory An Analysis of the World Trade', 44 (5) *Duke Law Journal* (1995), 829–927.

Smith, Adam, *The Glasgow Edition of the Works and Correspondence of Adam Smith. Volume I and II. An Inquiry into the Nature and Causes of the Wealth of Nations*, edited by W. B. Todd (Oxford: Clarendon, 1976).

Smith, Jane M., 'U.S. Trade Remedy Laws and Nonmarket Economies: A Legal Overview', Congressional Research Service 7-5700 (2013), 1-35, available at https://www.fas.org/sgp/crs/misc/RL33976.pdf.

Stanbrook, Clive and Bentley, Philip, *Dumping and Subsidies. Law and Procedures Governing the Imposition of Anti-Dumping and Countervailing Duties in the European Community*, 3rd ed. (London/The Hague/Boston: Kluwer Law International, 1996).

Steinberg, Richard H., 'Judicial Lawmaking at the WTO: Discursive, Constitutional, and Political Constraints', 98 (2) *The American Journal of International Law* (2004), 247-275.

Stoler, Andrew L., 'Will the WTO have Functional Value in the Mega-regional World of FTAs?', E15Initiative (Geneva: International Centre for Trade and Sustainable Development (ICTSD) and World Economic Forum, 2014), available at http://e15initiative.org/wp-content/uploads/2015/09/E15-Regional-Trade-Agreements-Stoler-FINAL.pdf.

Strand, Jon, 'Introduction', in Jon Strand (ed.): *The Economics and Political Economy of Energy Subsidies* (Cambridge, MA/London: MIT Press, 2016).

Stuart, Henry W., 'Subjective and Exchange Value', 4 (2) *Journal of Political Economy* (1896), 208-239.

Suranovic, Steve, *International Trade: Theory and Policy* (Washington D.C.: Flat World Knowledge, 2010).

Sykes, Alan O., 'Comparative advantage and the normative economics of international trade policy', 1 (1) *Journal of International Economic Law* (1998), 49-82.

Sykes, Alan O., 'Countervailing Duty Law: An Economic Perspective', 89 (2) *Columbia Law Review* (1989), 199-263.

Sykes, Alan O., 'Countervailing Duty Law: An Economic Perspective', Stanford Law and Economics Olin Working Paper No. 380 (2009), 1-41, available at SSRN: http://ssrn.com/abstract=1444605.

Sykes, Alan O., 'The Economics of WTO Rules on Subsidies and Countervailing Measures', University of Chicago Law & Economics Olin Working Paper No. 186 (2003), 1-36, available at SSRN: http://ssrn.com/abstract=415780.

Szamosszegi, Andrew and Kyle, Cole, 'An Analysis of State-owned Enterprises and State Capitalism in China', (2011), 1-116, available at http://www.uscc.gov/sites/default/files/Research/10_26_11_CapitalTradeSOEStudy.pdf.

Tarullo, Daniel K., 'Beyond Normalcy in the Regulation of International Trade', 100 (3) *Harvard Law Review* (1987), 546–628.

Tatham, Allan F., *Enlargement of the European Union* (Alphen aan den Rijn: Kluwer Law International, 2009).

Thorstensen, Vera; Ramos, Daniel; Muller Carolina and Bertolaccini, Fernanda, 'WTO – market and non-market economies: the hybrid case of China', 1 (2) *Latin American Journal of International Trade Law* (2013), 765–798.

Tietje, Christian and Nowrot, Karsten, 'Myth or Reality? China's Market Economy Status under WTO Anti-Dumping Law after 2016', Policy Papers on Transnational Economic Law No. 34 (2011), 2-12.

Torp Helmersen, Sondre, 'Evolutive Treaty Interpretation: Legality, Semantics and Distinctions', 6 (1) *European Journal of Legal Studies* (2013), 127–148.

Trebilcock, Michael J.; Howse, Robert and Eliason, Antonia, *The Regulation of International Trade*, 4th ed. (Abingdon/New York: Routledge, 2013).

Tyagi, Mitali, 'Flesh on a Legal Fiction: Early Practice in the WTO on Accession Protocols', 15 (2) *Journal of International Economic Law* (2012), 391–441.

Van Alstine, Michael P., 'Dynamic Treaty Interpretation', 146 (3) *University of Pennsylvania Law Review* (1998), 687-793.

Van Bael, Ivo and Bellis, Jean-François, *EU Anti-Dumping and Other Trade Defence Instruments*, 5th ed. (Alphen aan den Rijn: Kluwer Law International, 2011).

Van Damme, Isabelle, Treaty Interpretation by the WTO Appellate Body (Oxford, New York: Oxford University Press, 2009).

Van Damme, Isabelle, 'Treaty Interpretation by the WTO Appellate Body', 21 (3) European Journal of International Law (2010), 605–648.

Van den Bergh, Roger, Camesasca, Peter D., *European Competition Law and Economics: A Comparative Perspective* (Cambridge: Intersentia, 2001).

Van den Bossche, Peter and Zdouc, Werner, *The Law and Policy of the World Trade Organization* (Cambridge: Cambridge University Press, 2013).

Vermulst, Edwin and Gatta, Brian, 'Concurrent Trade Defence Investigation in the EU, the EU's New Anti-Subsidy Practice against China, and the Future of Both', 11 (3) *World Trade Review* (2012), 527–553.

Viner, Jacob, *Dumping: A Problem in International Trade* (New York: Kelley, 1966).

Watson, K. William, 'It's Time to Dump Nonmarket Economy Treatment', Free Trade Bulletin No. 65 (9 March 2016), available at http://object.cato.org/sites/cato.org/files/pubs/pdf/ftb65.pdf.

Winham, Gilbert A., 'An Interpretative History on the Uruguay Negotiation', in Patrick F. J. Macrory, Arthur E. Appleton and Michael G. Plummer (eds.), *The World Trade Organization. Legal, Economic and Political Analysis* (New York: Springer Science + Business Media, 2005), 3-26.

Winham, Gilbert A., 'The Evolution of the World Trading System – The Economic and Policy Context', in Bethlehem, Daniel; McRae, Donald; Neufeld, Rodney and van Damme, Isabelle (eds.), *The Oxford Handbook of international trade law* (Oxford: Oxford University Press, 2009), 5-29.

Wu, Chien-Huei, 'Key Issues Regarding the EU's Concurrent Imposition of Anti-Dumping and Countervailing Duties against Chinese Coated Fine Papers: Analogue Country, Market Economy Treatment, Individual Treatment, and Double Remedy' (2015), 1-23, available at http://papers.ssrn.com/sol3/papers.cfm?abstract_id=2306345.

Wu, Mark, 'Re-examining "Green Light" Subsidies in the Wake of New Green Industrial Policies', E15Initiative (Geneva: International Centre for Trade and Sustainable Development (ICTSD) and World Economic Forum, 2015), available at http://e15initiative.org/wp-content/uploads/2015/07/E15_Industrial-Policy_Wu_FINAL.pdf.

Wu, Xiaohui, 'Rethinking China's Membership in the WTO', 10 (2) *Chinese Journal of International Law* (2011), 227-270.

Yu, Yanning, 'Rethinking China's Market Economy Status in Trade Remedy Disputes after 2016: Concerns and Challenges', 8 (1) *Asian Journal of WTO and International Health Law* (2013), 77–113.

Zang, Michelle Q., 'EC – Fasteners: Opening the Pandora's Box of Non-Market Economy Treatment', 14 (4) *Journal of International Economic Law* (2012), 869–892.

Zhang, Daowei, *The Softwood Lumber War: "Politics, Economics, and the Long U.S.-Canadian Trade Dispute"* (Washington, DC: Resources for the Future, 2007).

Zhao, Longyue and Wang, Yan, 'Trade Remedies And Non-Market Economies. Economic Implications Of The First US Countervailing Duty Case On China', Policy Research Working Paper No. 4560 (2008), 1-48, available at https://openknowledge.worldbank.org/bitstream/handle/10986/6319/wps4560.pdf?sequence=1&isAllowed=y.

Zheng, Wentong, 'Reforming Trade Remedies', 34 (1) *Michigan Journal of International Law* (2012), 151-207.

Zheng, Wentong, 'The Pitfalls of the (Perfect) Market Benchmark: the Case of Countervailing Duty Law', 19 (1) *Minnesota Journal of International Law* (2010), 1–54.

Zhou, Weihuan, 'Australia's Anti-dumping and Countervailing Law and Practice: An Analysis of Current Issues Incompatible with Free Trade with China', 49 (6) *Journal of World Trade* (2015), 975–1010.

Index

S. Müller, *The Use of Alternative Benchmarks in Anti-Subsidy Law*,
European Yearbook of International Economic Law 4,
https://doi.org/10.1007/978-3-319-77613-2

MIX
Papier aus verantwortungsvollen Quellen
Paper from responsible sources
FSC® C105338

If you have any concerns about our products,
you can contact us on
ProductSafety@springernature.com

In case Publisher is established outside the EU,
the EU authorized representative is:
Springer Nature Customer Service Center GmbH
Europaplatz 3, 69115 Heidelberg, Germany

Printed by Libri Plureos GmbH
in Hamburg, Germany